a special gift

presented to:

_____

from:

_____

date:

_____

Therefore, God's chosen ones, holy and loved,
put on heartfelt compassion, kindness, humility, gentleness,
and patience, accepting one another and forgiving one another if anyone
has a complaint against another. Just as the Lord has forgiven you, so you
must also forgive. Above all, put on love—the perfect bond of unity.

—Col. 3:12-14, HCSB

Altogether Lovely

EDITORS

Ardis
Dick
Stenbakken

with **Carolyn**
Rathbun
Sutton

REVIEW AND HERALD® PUBLISHING ASSOCIATION
Since 1861 | www.reviewandherald.com

Published by Review and Herald® Publishing Association, Hagerstown, MD 21741-1119

Review and Herald® titles may be purchased in bulk for educational, business, fund-raising, or sales promotional use. For information, e-mail SpecialMarkets@ reviewandherald.com.

The Review and Herald® Publishing Association publishes biblically based materials for spiritual, physical, and mental growth and Christian discipleship.

This book was
Edited by Carolyn Sutton
Copyedited by Judy Blodgett
Cover designed by Paricia Wegh / Review and Herald® Design Center
Cover photos by © Shutterstock and © Thinkstock.com
Typeset: Minion Pro 10.5/13.5

PRINTED IN U.S.A.

18 17 16 15 14   5 4 3 2 1

Library of Congress Control Number: 2014942275

ISBN 978-0-8280-2808-0

Scholarshipping Our Sisters
Women Helping Women

There is an aspect of this book that is unique . . .

None of these contributors has been paid—each has shared freely so that all profits go to scholarships for women. As this book goes to press, approximately 2,200 scholarships have been given to women in 127 countries.

For more current information, or to contribute to these scholarships, please go to http://adventistwomensministries.org/index.php?id=52. In this way you too can help fulfill the dream of some woman—or even yourself—to attend college or university.

General Conference Women's Ministries Scholarship Fund

The General Conference Women's Ministries scholarship program supports higher education for Adventist women globally. Recipients are talented women of vision who are committed to serving the mission of the Seventh-day Adventist Church.

Among Friends, published in 1992, was the first annual women's devotional book. Since then, proceeds from 22 of these devotional books have funded scholarships for Adventist women seeking to obtain higher education. However, as tuition costs have risen and more women have applied for assistance, funding has not kept pace with the need. Many dedicated women who apply must be turned down.

Recognizing the importance of educating women—to build stronger families, stronger communities, and a stronger church—each of us can help. Together we can change lives!

There are many ways to support our sisters, such as . . .

- Praying for women worldwide who are struggling to get an education.
- Telling others about the Women's Ministries scholarship program. (Materials are available to share.)
- Writing for the women's devotional book. (Guidelines are available.)
- Your gift or pledge to support women's education.

To make a gift or receive materials, send us a postcard with the following information. (Our address is on page 8.)

Name _____

Street _____

City _____ State/Province _____

Postal Code _____ Country _____

E-mail _____

About the Editors

Ardis Dick Stenbakken has had a zeal for women and women's ministries for many years. She loves to encourage women to use their God-given gifts and to learn how God led the women of the Bible. In 2004 Ardis retired as director of the General Conference Women's Ministry Department and now lives in Colorado.

Carolyn Rathbun Sutton finds great joy in "being there" for other women, especially those struggling to find renewed purpose after a major life setback. She particularly enjoys helping women share with others their own personal stories of God's faithfulness.

To contact us:

Women's Ministries Department
General Conference of Seventh-day Adventists
12501 Old Columbia Pike
Silver Spring, MD 20904

Phone: 301-680-6636

Fax: 301-680-6600

E-mail: womensministries@gc.adventist.org

Web site: http://adventistwomensministries.org

Scholarship application and devotional book writers' guidelines are available at our Web site.

Happy New Year

So will I sing praise unto thy name for ever,
that I may daily perform my vows. Ps. 61:8.

Happy New Year! For many of us, those words are synonymous with making New Year's resolutions in hopes that the upcoming year will be better than the previous one. However, keeping resolutions is a daily endeavor and not a once-a-year commitment.

During one of my recent personal devotion times I thumbed through the Bible to find texts that would be good personal resolutions for me to make in order to have a closer walk with God and represent Him better. Keeping these resolutions would also make my life more exemplary. I commend these resolutions to you as well.

Resolved, that I will this day endeavor, with God's help, to—

"Let all bitterness, and wrath, and anger, and clamour, and evil speaking, be put away from [me]" (Eph. 4:31).

"Let [me] cleanse [myself] from all filthiness of the flesh and spirit, perfecting holiness in the fear of God" (2 Cor. 7:1).

"Let integrity and uprightness preserve me" (Ps. 25:21).

"Let [my] conversation be without covetousness; and be content with such things as [I] have" (Heb. 13:5).

"Let not [my] heart be troubled: [I] believe in God" (John 14:1).

"Let [me] not love in word, neither in tongue; but in deed and in truth" (1 John 3:18).

"Let [my] light so shine before men, that they may see [my] good works, and glorify [my] Father which is in heaven" (Matt. 5:16).

"Let the words of my mouth, and the meditation of my heart, be acceptable in thy sight, O Lord, my strength, and my redeemer" (Ps. 19:14).

"Let [me] trust in the name of the Lord, and stay upon [my] God" (Isa. 50:10).

"Let [me] not sleep, as do others; but let [me] watch and be sober" (1 Thess. 5:6).

Instead of New Year's resolutions, let us each make a new commitment every morning to be His daughter for that day. Let us sing praises to God who provides for us 24 hours a day, seven days a week, and 365 days every year.

Edith Fitch

No Gift Can Compare

*To the one who is victorious, . . . I will also give
that person a white stone with a new name written on it,
known only to the one who receives it. Rev. 2:17, NIV.*

New beginnings. A fresh start. Clean slate. How many of you could use one? How many of you long for one? Does it sound scary, or does it sound rejuvenating? Sometimes it's just what we need but what we are most afraid of.

My mind often contemplates heaven, but on one particular day God brought something to my attention that I had bypassed many times, but the Holy Spirit finally reeled me in and helped me focus on Revelation 2:17.

I have to say I love how the verse starts: to the one who is victorious. Do you know how good it feels to become victorious over something? Can you even imagine? Imagine how we will feel facing Jesus, knowing that because of Him we have overcome sin.

We have not even entered the pearly gates yet, but Jesus has something that He cannot wait to give us! He has been waiting our whole life to give this to us, and now the time has come. Can you feel His anticipation? Can you feel the intimacy of this moment?

Then He hands you the gift: a white stone that has a new name, chosen by Jesus, just for you and Him to know. You may wonder, *So what does the white stone mean, and why is He giving it to me before I enter the gates of heaven?* It is a symbol of your new start, it is a symbol that you are free of condemnation; it is your token to allow you into heaven; it means that you are accepted; it represents righteousness. Now, before you start getting too puffed up, remember, it is a gift. This is your fresh start; this name reflects to you what Jesus thinks of you. That is amazing.

Now tell me that Jesus does not love you! We may never overcome all the things we want to in this world. I know there are things in my life that I have prayed for years to be free of and have not yet overcome, but you know what? Jesus has something even better for us! When you are discouraged and longing for a fresh start, remember, Jesus has something waiting for you. Something more than you can imagine. Take this hope and give it to all of those around you, because they need it too!

Robyn Williams

Rubble Hill

His great love is new every morning.
Lord, how faithful you are! Lam. 3:23, NIrV.

Just southwest of the town of Stuttgart, Germany, is the Birkenkopf, a hill that stands 1,677 feet (511 meters) tall—a fact that is not particularly remarkable until you learn that this is a human-made monument composed of all the rubble left after Stuttgart was bombed in World War II. I have many times had the privilege of climbing Rubble Hill, as we Americans called it.

My favorite adventure was late at night December 31, 1975. Penny, my best friend from high school, had come over to spend the holidays with my family, and we hiked up Rubble Hill with blankets, thermoses of hot cocoa, and all the optimism that comes with ringing in the new year. As midnight struck, we looked down on all the fireworks that were going off all around us. It was a beautiful sight.

Much later, December 31, 2007, found me sitting with my husband as we encountered our first "empty nest" New Year's celebration—it was a quiet, unceremonious, and somewhat lonely welcome to 2008, and that New Year's gathering so long ago came to mind. I realized that I was metaphorically doing the same thing this year: looking back over the "rubble" of 2007. I realized that there were events I wanted to forget, people I should apologize to, celebrations I wanted to revisit, and prayers I needed to pray.

How good it is that we practice new beginnings each year. How much greater it is that we can do this each day. In Lamentations 3:22, 23 we are told that God's mercies are new every morning, with each day offering us a clean slate to start anew. Each day God's redemptive power can change us and make us better people.

We are now a few days into a new year; as you look at this year, thank God that He offers us a clean slate through forgiveness and mercies to last our lifetime and for eternity. Psalm 103 is a good psalm to look at just now. David says, "For his unfailing love toward those who fear him is as great as the height of the heavens above the earth. He has removed our sins as far from us as the east is from the west" (Ps. 103:11, 12, NLT). Then it is up to us to celebrate each new day with Him. He will take the "rubble" of your life and make it into a beautiful monument to His glory and your redemption.

Candace DeVore

I Had No Doubt

*I will be your God throughout your lifetime—until your hair
is white with age. I made you, and I will care for you.
I will carry you along and save you. Isa. 46:4, NLT.*

Having spent so much time on the road by myself, I have developed a system that works for me. It is important to place the music and CDs that I want to listen to, the box of tissue, the GPS, and bottle of water all close at hand. I prepare as best I can. But there are always surprises! Like the heavy snowstorm I drove into on a lonely stretch of highway in eastern Colorado.

I knew there was a snowstorm developing, but the weather stations reported that it was not going to snow heavily and that the storm path was supposed to be far north in Wyoming. What a surprise when the snow began hitting my windshield in what seemed like heavy clumps. Soon my windshield wipers were unable to even move. They were frozen!

Stopping on the side of the road, I did my best to clear the snow from the wipers and windshield. Cautiously I continued slowly along the snow-packed highway looking for a place to stop for the night. Eastern Colorado along Interstate 76 is pretty desolate, and there are not many exits and towns along the way.

I stopped twice when I saw an inn right off the interstate; they had no room at the inn. I began to feel a little like Mary and Joseph. Knowing it would be dangerous just to pull off the road or an exit and park, I slowly inched along. I had no idea how long this storm would last, and I knew I couldn't just park and let my car run all night.

The only place I could turn was to Jesus; I prayed for a place to stop. It wasn't long before I realized it was not snowing as fast or as heavily as it had been a short time before. I began to murmur one of my favorite verses, today's text.

Finally, there ahead on the road, I could see a light! It was an inn! I was not surprised. I knew when I claimed the promise that He would carry me along and save me—that He would. Oh, yes; they had a room! I had no doubt! And I thanked God for protecting me. How thankful I was to climb into a warm bed for the night.

Now, I still travel lots and I always prepare the same way; except I also murmur His promises to me and expect Him to be there with me.

Candy Zook

Hope

Be still, and know that I am God. Ps. 46:10, NIV.

Many years ago I was diagnosed with ankylosing spondilytis. It is an inflammation of the soft tissues in the body that cause the tissues to become hard and fuse to the bone. Nothing can prevent the loss of mobility and movement that occurs because of that fusion. Several years ago I went through a major flare-up in which I spent two thirds of every day paralyzed with pain and stiffness. The only thing that moved was my right arm.

Thankfully, I have been anointed, as recommended in James 5:14, 15: "Is anyone among you sick? Let them call the elders of the church to pray over them and anoint them with oil in the name of the Lord. And the prayer offered in faith will make the sick person well; the Lord will raise them up" (NIV). And the inflammation has burnt itself out. Even though I have a degree of pain and stiffness, as long as I follow a daily program of exercises and pace myself, I can live a normal life.

However, when the inflammation was rampant, I hated the nights. I longed to lie down, as my body was racked with pain, yet dreaded getting into bed. I knew that once I lay flat, the pain would intensify, and I would become as rigid as an ironing board. The pain and stiffness were so severe that I was unable to turn my body. And then my jaw would stiffen, and I would be unable to open my mouth to speak.

It was during those times of utter helplessness that I really got to know God. In the stillness of the night, when all was quiet, apart from the sounds of my family sleeping, I would talk with God. I shared with Him the fear I felt about the lack of control I had over my illness and my worries about not being there for my family. I know God listened, as in exchange He gave me the expectation of something good—He gave me hope.

I also began to see God differently. I began to experience on a deeper level all those things that I knew about God. The more I meditated on His character, the more hope I seemed to have. And if I think about it long enough, I can still feel that sense of quietness, that calm assurance and hope that comes just from being with God. With God, our struggles can indeed become a lot easier to handle—if we take time to be still with Him.

Mary Barrett

If Tamar Had Known

The Lord works righteousness
and justice for all the oppressed. Ps. 103:6, NIV.

If Tamar, David's daughter, had known Jesus, God's only Son, things would have turned out differently for her. Such a sad story. The "beautiful sister" of Absalom unknowingly drew the lustful attentions of Prince Amnon. How ironic that innocent sweetness can provoke the vilest lust, but it can. And it did. The sex-obsessed Amnon sought the advice of his conniving cousin Jonadab. "Pretend to be sick," Jonadab hissed, "then request of your father that Tamar be your nurse." Amnon did just that, and soon Tamar came to his bedside. There in the dark sickroom he sent the servants away and beckoned her near. Well-trained to submit, Tamar crept closer. In an instant thick male hands wrapped around her thin wrists. Defenseless against his male strength, she cried, "No! Don't force me! Ask the king, and we can marry!" In that culture a nonvirgin had few marriage prospects. Marrying a rapist beat the ostracism she'd suffer.

Tragically, outrageously, egregiously, "he raped her" (2 Sam. 13:14, NIV).

Resembling the shift from stifling heat to torrential rain, the sociopathic "Amnon . . . hated her more than he had loved her." "Get up and get out!" he screamed. He forced her again, this time away from him instead of to him (verse 15).

"No!" she protested, pleading for him to make right the wrong by marrying her (Deut. 22:28, 29). But Amnon prevailed. Standing in the hall outside the barred door, the disgraced princess tore her virgin garments and smeared ashes on her head, wailing all the way to the house of her brother Absalom. The Bible says that she stayed with Absalom, "a desolate woman" (verse 20). We hear nothing more of her; just desolation, or in Hebrew, *shamem*.

Shame 'em, that's what rapists like Amnon do. *Shamem* can mean "astonished" or even "stupefied." It seems Tamar lost her mind. Absalom named his own daughter Tamar (2 Sam. 14:27) as a kind of memorial to his sister Tamar. Ultimately, Absalom murdered Amnon.

What if Absalom, instead of bitter, murderous revenge, had cherished godly justice? What if he had gently ministered to Tamar's psychological wounds by teaching her of a God who would never force her, who valued her soul? Then Tamar would have known healing instead of desolation. Peace instead of insanity. She would have known Jesus.

Jennifer Jill Schwirzer

The Old Almond Tree

But thanks be to God, which giveth us the victory
through our Lord Jesus Christ. 1 Cor. 15:57.

We will have to cut this tree down, because the space is needed to expand the new parking area. Furthermore, I do not want to be charged for damages sustained to any vehicles parked beneath it from falling dried branches." These words from the gardener reverberated like a final sentence from a frustrated judge.

As I stood there reminiscing, I imagined the tree in its better days. The almond tree must have stood in that place for many years, a stately, strong trunk, dressed in fluffy green leaves, and laden with luscious fruits. Now it was a bother to the gardener and patrons who used it as shade for their cars. With each puff of wind the dried branches snapped, littering the ground and the cars parked beneath it.

On the morning of the cutting, though I tried desperately to maintain reason, I was overcome with sad emotions; it seemed to me like an impending radical surgery. I anticipated the robust trunk being severed close to its roots. Instead each branch was removed, leaving the bare trunk. The remains looked like a person whose head, neck, shoulders, and arms were removed, leaving a stripped torso. The poor remains were left standing, left to die!

I questioned, *What should we do with it now? Why not just cut it to a stump and set some potted plants on the trunk*? Various ideas were recommended, but the trunk was left standing.

A few months passed. Then, much to my surprise, tiny buds were seen appearing all over the once-naked trunk. What resilience! It was as if the tree were saying, "I will not die."

This experience mirrors the pain with which I have watched many of my loved ones, friends, and acquaintances being ravished by the effects of sin. Diseases, divorce, imprisonment, apostasy, and broken dreams have stripped them to near nothingness, some even considered of no value. I am, however, comforted that just as that bare tree trunk budded again, soon and very soon the Lord will restore all to a state of newness. He has promised, and He cannot fail.

Have you lost a loved one, friend, or acquaintance? Or do you feel like that trunk? There is a blessed hope, a day of renewal coming. So take hope in the fact that "weeping may endure for a night, but joy comes in the morning" (Ps. 30:5, NKJV).

Gloria Gregory

Looking Toward the Goal

Forgetting what is behind and straining toward what is ahead,
I press on toward the goal to win the prize for which God has called
me heavenward in Christ Jesus. Phil. 3:13, 14, NIV.

When we were children, we liked to trace lines in the snow with sticks. Sometimes we competed to see who could trace the straightest line. Two boys decided to trace a line toward a certain tree, their goal. Both of them set off and soon reached the goal. After looking back at the lines, one of the boys wondered why his friend's line was so much straighter than his. The answer: "I kept looking at the tree as my goal and didn't look away." The other boy had looked back from time to time and lost sight of the goal.

The apostle Paul wrote something similar to that in today's verses from Philippians: "Straining toward what is ahead, I press on toward the goal." He had a goal to reach, his heavenly calling, eternal life that God gives through Jesus Christ.

Verse 12 of this same chapter says that Paul was not perfect, but Jesus has taken hold of him in His love and had forgiven him. That is why he always wanted to look to Jesus, stay in His will, and follow Him faithfully. If we want to reach our goal with God we must look forward. Looking back is not good; neither is stopping. Jesus walks before us on our life's path; He forms the path with His footprints, and all we need to do is to follow Him.

However, in our spiritual walk it is good to stop from time to time and to look back in order to consider what God has done and how He has blessed us. We truly do have nothing to fear for our future as we review and remember how God Himself has led us in our walk with Him. As we do that we should forget all that hinders our progress toward our goal.

Isaiah reflected this same idea when he wrote, "I will lead the blind by ways they have not known, along unfamiliar paths I will guide them; I will turn the darkness into light before them and make the rough places smooth. These are the things I will do; I will not forsake them" (Isa. 42:16, NIV). Truly, it is only God who can lead to the worthwhile goal.

Our goals vary according to our age. But it is always good to strive to reach our elevated goals. The highest goal of a Christian should be the wish to be united with God our Father one day in heaven. That is a goal worth living and pressing on to.

Kathi Heise

The Basket of Fruit

A branch can't produce fruit when severed from the vine.
Nor can you be fruitful apart from me. John 15:4, TLB.

When I was a young girl, we lived in a New York City apartment building. My father's sister, Aunt Frances, and her family lived in the same apartment building. After school I often asked my mother for permission to go visit Aunt Frances. She was easy to talk to and always gave me milk and cookies to eat while I watched her work. I think I liked going there because I didn't have to share her with my siblings. She was all mine for as long as I stayed there.

Aunt Frances had a basket of plastic fruit that sat on her table. They looked so real that it was impossible to tell they were fake by looking at them. My aunt would wipe the dust off the fruit while we talked about my day at school. I could ask her about anything and she always had an answer. I thought she was the smartest woman ever.

One day as I was on my way to see Aunt Frances I met my friend Mercedes in the stairwell and she asked where I was going. When I told her I was on my way to Aunt Frances' place, she asked to come along. I decided I could share Aunt Frances that one time. I introduced her to my aunt, and she invited us both in and offered us cookies and milk.

We sat at the kitchen table and waited for our treat. Suddenly Mercedes reached out and grabbed a beautiful, shiny red apple from the basket as she asked Aunt Frances if it was OK for her to eat one. Before waiting for an answer, she tried to take a bite out of the apple! We all laughed, then enjoyed our cookies and milk while we visited with Aunt Frances. From her vast store of wisdom she pulled out an object lesson for us.

She compared the fake fruit that looked so real to people who say they are Christians, and look like they are, but all along they are fakes, imitations. They have no real connection with God. She stressed to us the importance of being genuine and engaged us in a discussion of how to be a real Christian. As John the apostle says in 1 John 5:2: "This is how we know that we love the children of God: by loving God and carrying out his commands" (NIV). In other words, being like Jesus. I decided that day that I wanted to live my life being a genuine Christian. Have you made that decision for your life? It's the best life ever!

Celia Mejia Cruz

How Cold?

*Because of the increase of wickedness, the love of most will grow cold,
but the one who stands firm to the end will be saved. And this gospel
of the kingdom will be preached in the whole world as a testimony
to all nations, and then the end will come. Matt. 24:12-14, NIV.*

The thermometer registered 37 degrees below zero one January morning in northwestern Minnesota. Not only was the temperature very cold, but a strong wind blew, making the wind chill factor even colder. Too cold, you might think, for anyone to be outdoors and survive.

Surely, one might think, the animals and birds would perish in such extreme temperatures. However, the Lord has provided wildlife with an inner sense of how to protect themselves during such extreme temperatures.

The birds seek a sheltered area and fluff out their feathers, providing themselves with a nice down coat to warm them. Animals also seek shelter and depend upon their extra growth of hair to keep them warm. When wildlife has been adequately fed, they are able to live through extremely cold temperatures. Snow that falls thickly may even cover some of the small animals and they stay snug within this blanket until the weather changes. Then they shake off the snow and emerge hungry and ready to resume their normal routines.

Humans have warm homes, and if they are careful to remain in a safe area they too survive winter weather very well. Even our cars are serviced with the right oil and antifreeze in the radiators so they will operate in the cold. If you have ever seen a car go by with an electrical plug hanging out of the grill you know that car is from a cold climate. Cars equipped with heaters that warm the engine and make them easier to start is a standard fixture in the North.

As humans, we don't have electric heaters to warm our hearts and keep our love aglow. Instead, if we choose, we are blessed with the inner glow of the love of our Savior. When we have His love, we are privileged to go out and share it with the world.

We are not all preachers who can give eloquent sermons to convince and convict souls, but everyone can share His love with others. Our very countenances will show that we have Jesus within our hearts and minds. His love will be demonstrated through our actions and our words of kindness and love. His love can shine through us to warm the hearts of others.

Evelyn Glass

Final Boarding Call

Prepare to meet thy God. Amos 4:12.

Travelers know there is preparation to be made before leaving. We booked tickets in October for January. Immediately I analyzed what needed doing, and got at it: bookkeeping—done; sewing—done. As time shortened, the list lengthened. I collected items on my packing list, but the last night before departure I had to stay up all night getting everything packed and ready.

At the airport, tickets are printed, baggage is checked, security is gone through, and finally at the gate, there is a wait to board the plane. At boarding time the passengers are called by rows, and then comes the "final boarding call." When the staff is satisfied that everyone is on the plane, they close the doors, and there is usually no way a latecomer can persuade them to open the door to still get on.

One day soon the "final boarding call" to leave Planet Earth will be made. Am I, are you, ready? Have we packed our characters with things God wants in His kingdom? God's checklist starts in Galatians 5:22: love, joy, peace, patience, gentleness, goodness, faith, meekness, temperance. Are we asking God daily for experiences that create and strengthen these virtues within us? He tells us in Philippians 4:8 to think on things that are true, honest, just, pure, lovely, and of good report. How do we change our thoughts to the kind He wants us to have? It starts by spending quality time with Him each morning, listening to His voice coming from the pages of our Bible, and talking to Him through prayer, then doing things with Him all day long.

In some places women can't read or don't have Bibles, but we can all pray, asking God to lead us—and them—in His path. Where I live, we have Bibles throughout our houses; but we don't have time to read because we are being pushed by society to work more, to have more. As time flies, I realize more and more that having stuff is not nearly as important as having the virtues that God requires. You can find the rest of God's packing list in Ephesians 5:9; 1 Timothy 6:11; 2 Timothy 3:10; 2 Peter 1:5-7; Romans 5:4, 5; Colossians 3:1-17; and 1 Corinthians 13.

Are we packing? Do we realize how quickly time is running out? I like the chorus of the song "I Want to Be Ready" when Jesus comes. "Earth's pleasures grow dim, while I'm waiting for Him," and I have found that to be so true. Heaven must be our goal; don't miss the "final boarding call."

Elizabeth Versteegh Odiyar

The God Who Grieves

When Jesus saw her weeping, and the Jews who had come
along with her also weeping, he was deeply moved in spirit and troubled.
"Where have you laid him?" he asked. "Come and see, Lord,"
they replied. Jesus wept. John 11:33-35, NIV.

I was leaving a retreat in Sydney, Australia, when a young woman touched my shoulder asking to talk. I looked at her beautiful face and invited her to share her story. Immediately and with much emotion, she poured out her pain of the past year. The loss of her parents, her brother, her husband. And, because of the fire in some parts of Australia that year, she'd lost her house. All in one year. When I asked how she'd been coping, she opened a small Bible and showed me a handwritten message from her father before he died of cancer: "Keep your faith in Jesus despite what life brings to you." Through tears she said, "Now you know why and how I am still alive."

When we lose someone or something that is very important to us, it can take time for us to adjust and learn to live our life again despite the new vacancy. In order for grief to lead to healing and spiritual growth, our losses need to be identified and acknowledged. We need to pay attention to the losses we have experienced. And we need someone other than ourselves to pay attention to them as well.

Looking at my new Australian friend, I said, "Tell me what has helped you in your healing process." I pray that what she shared with me will help you if you're grieving a loss.

"First," she said, "I invited God to grieve with me." The Bible teaches that God does not minimize or deny the reality of our losses. He grieves with us. We are not alone. "Second," continued my new friend, "I'm taking the time I need to get back into my life—no big decisions right now until I can think clearly." There's no specific time limit to grief when we need "to move on" or "get over it," as some might tell us to do. There isn't a set time limit on grief, so try not to put pressure on yourself or others to "move on" or "get over it." "Finally," she concluded, "I let others help me." How important to explain our feelings and let others know what they can do to help—whether that be emotional support, helping plan meals, or looking after our children.

She added, "Someone I don't know paid for me to come to this retreat. I now have hope and healing." Remind someone today that God both grieves with them—and offers them new hope.

Raquel Queiroz da Costa Arrais

The Older I Get

Whoever believes in him may have eternal life. John 3:15, RSV.

The older I get"; funny how those words have come more naturally since my last birthday. Yet as I study and relate the Bible to my own life, I realize it took this long for God to get me to where He wants me. I can be a stubborn and pushy woman—and hardheaded to boot.

When I was 30, doing public relations for the church and busy with a career at the largest hospital in my state, I was bold and courageous. I told everyone I knew I loved God and had accepted Jesus as my Savior. But there were times that, to get important things done, I was strong in my demands. My boss said that if she wanted something done, she would sic me on that department. And I insisted on having my way, because it was important; I would not ask if it were not necessary.

Then during one telephone call to maintenance regarding something very important they needed to get done, I heard the secretary's voice crack. "Are you OK?" She answered she had a cold; but I knew that sound. She was afraid of me. And I thought I—who was bold and courageous and pushy—was the woman who would do anything for a family member or friend in need.

So with a nudge from the Lord I walked swiftly to the office where this woman was working. She greeted me with a forced smile, red eyes, and tale-telling tissue pushed aside. The Holy Spirit softened my heart by first breaking it. This woman was my sister, and I had chosen to treat her with disrespect. With apologies and a better understanding of how rude and abrupt I had been, I asked for forgiveness and made a new friend. My life changed that day in the maintenance office in the presence of a woman I'd abused.

While reading Matthew 17, I read that the disciples could not heal a demon-ridden son. Jesus turned from that man's son to the men with whom He lived and said to them that He had been with them such a long time, and they were still disbelievers.

Now that I'm older and have experienced that same abuse on the other side, my compassion has grown. Always praying my spirit will be more in tune with God's Spirit in me, I ask Jesus to stay closer to me than a second skin, with hopes that in the near future I will live with Him forever.

Sally J. Aken-Linke

Adventure in Italy

A man's heart plans his way, but the Lord directs his steps. Prov. 16:9, NKJV.

Several years ago I studied French at Campus Adventiste du Salève in Collonges, France. Five of us students wanted to visit Italy during our first school vacation, so we planned an itinerary.

On the day of our trip we arrived in plenty of time at the nearby train station in Geneva, Switzerland. One member of our group, Maurice, decided he wanted to get breakfast. The train hadn't arrived, so he figured he had plenty of time. We weren't familiar with the European train system, so we had no idea that inbound trains stay in the station for only a few minutes before departing again. When the train pulled in, we got on board and saved Maurice a seat. Imagine our alarm when after only three minutes the train took off with no Maurice! None of us had cell phones, and Maurice did not know where our accommodations were in Rome. We figured he would just go back to the school. Two days later we were enjoying a pizza at the famous Trevi Fountain, and who appeared but Maurice! He'd caught the next train to Rome and had been looking for us. We were very happy to be reunited.

Venice was next on our itinerary. We'd booked train reservations, but since Maurice hadn't been with us, he didn't have a reservation, and our train was full. Thankfully, he was able to take another Venice-bound train within a few minutes of ours. When we got to Venice, we discovered there were two main train stations, and his train had gone to the other one. Happily, we found Maurice within the hour!

We managed to stay together through Venice and then Florence. But when we got back to Geneva, Maurice insisted on catching a different bus back to France. We told him that that bus was headed to the wrong city, and to wait a few minutes and catch the bus to Collonges with us. He got on the wrong bus anyway, and arrived back to school several hours after we did.

How many times are we like Maurice? Do we wander off, not bothering to ask God for His guidance? Or are we seemingly connected with God, but insist on our own way? Thankfully God is always there for us and is waiting for us to submit our lives to Him. He will always lead us on the right path. Won't you ask Him to direct your steps today?

Amanda N. Gaspard

A Future and a Hope—
Even in Tough Times

"For I know the plans I have for you," declares the Lord, "plans to prosper you and not to harm you, plans to give you hope and a future." Jer. 29:11, NIV.

It's a promise we claim. God has plans. A future for us. A future filled with hope and good things. We believe it, but sometimes we begin to wonder. Doubt that His plans are good. Sometimes our lives are hard. Cancer. Financial problems. Divorce. A child who wanders from God. A husband who no longer loves us or is emotionally engaged. A job that leaves us overworked and undervalued. Where, then, are the hope and good plans God promises?

We forget that the promise of Jeremiah 29:11 was written to the Israelites when they were in captivity in Babylon. A captivity that God had caused (verse 4). They were slaves. Life was tough. They were far from where they wanted to be. This wasn't the life they wanted. So God sent a letter through Jeremiah, promising them a future and a hope. But the future and the hope weren't for that moment. They were for the future. Seventy years in the future. A long time to wait! In the meantime, God told them to live where they were. Not just endure. Live. "Build houses and dwell in them; plant gardens and eat their fruit" (verse 5, NKJV). They were to enjoy their children and their grandchildren—all while in captivity. They were to "seek the peace of the city" where they were captive. Live in that peace. Pray for it without listening to the lies or believing their own daydreams of a better life (verse 8). Live, without complaint in these tough times, as if this is where they're supposed to be . . . and trust God had something better coming.

Too often I don't like living in captivity—whether it's a tough job, failed relationship, or times of disappointed expectations. I really don't want to plant a garden. Or build a house as if I'm going to stay stuck in this spot for long. I want life to be easy and good. And I want it now.

Yet when I trust Him—when I pray for a peaceful heart when life isn't peaceful—He answers. Reveals His love. Whispers words of hope. Courage. Sends a friend with a cup of tea, a listening ear, an encouraging word. A friend who says, "You're not crazy. Keep going. You've got this." I sense His love. Again I seek the One who promises we'll find Him (verse 14). Even when we feel . . . captivity. And eventually He delivers us from these tough moments—or years. But for now, we know He hasn't forgotten or abandoned. We can live here because He's here.

Tamyra Horst

I Had an Evil Spirit Cast Out

*A woman was there who had been crippled
by a spirit for eighteen years. She was bent over and could not
straighten up at all. . . . Jesus . . . said to her, "Woman, you are set free." . . .
Immediately she straightened up and praised God. Luke 13:11-13, NIV.*

Someone in my Bible study class asked the question "What is the spirit of a man? When Jesus cast out an evil spirit, what did He set people free from?"

"I think it's their attitude," I explained. "I have had one mind-set all my life, and suddenly Jesus touches that way of thinking and I am healed. I feel set free of that evil spirit that was pressing me down!"

Later I thought of an example. While very young I began to subconsciously think that it was my responsibility to hold the universe together—keep us all in control. When I was 4 months old, my daddy was drafted into the Army, so I was left to "take care of" my mother. When my twin sisters were born, my mother needed lots of help. When my parents joined the church, there were more standards to meet. Starting school added more people I felt responsible to keep in line. Two brothers joined the family when I was a teenager, so I took them on too. The stress level went higher as they all grew and became harder to control. Sometimes I felt angry from their lack of cooperation; always I was afraid. This seemed to be my life assignment, and I was failing. All these people resented all I tried to do for them, but I just tried harder.

Then I married someone who needed lots of "taking care of" since he was "so irresponsible" spiritually. When our two daughters came, for a while I seemed to be successful with them, but then they became teenagers and I realized I was failing miserably. I didn't know why, because I was trying hard, praying hard, and studying hard.

Finally a crisis situation forced us into counseling. At first I saw it as a new way to get things under control, but finally learned the truth—I could control only me, and that was all God was asking. What a relief! I learned to say the prayer "God, grant me the serenity to accept the things I cannot change and the courage to change the things I can [me]."

The woman bent over double in the Bible: was it shame or guilt with which an evil spirit weighed her down? My doctor said at my last exam that my back was straighter.

Lana Fletcher

My Love for Food

We can rejoice, too, when we run into problems and trials,
for we know that they help us develop endurance. Rom. 5:3, NLT.

When I was 17 years old, I decided, over a holiday brunch with friends, that I was going vegan. Something about the omelets and glasses of milk atop the table that morning stopped making sense to me. It wasn't until my early 20s, though, that I began to know I had food intolerances. For one thing, my skin never seemed to fully clear up. I knew it was no longer hormonal, so it had to be something else.

Food allergies and intolerances were not that widely known yet, but my mom discovered an article about wheat allergies. The thought of giving up wheat (my favorite food group—especially in bakeries) was out of the question! It would be devastating! But my quest for a clear complexion eventually took control as I began a six-week detox program that involved battling my cravings and enduring the withdrawals. At the end of the detox my skin was glowing. In the years to follow I learned that I had minor peanut, honey, and chocolate intolerances—and a severe mango allergy—to add to the list. My eating options were slimming (in more ways than one!), and I reluctantly learned the art of self-control.

Cooking and baking tasty foods still present the greatest challenges for me. I've had more misses than hits. Luckily, my husband has learned to smile through each bite. And my options are expanding as more people discover similar problems—and share workable solutions. My dietary restrictions seem to never stop. I must eat mostly gluten-free and enjoy my fruit apart from other food groups. And when I'm traveling or on a concert tour, what a challenge!

Yet I've come to discover that we all have challenges. No one gets away problem-free. We all end up with *something* with which we have to deal, either directly or indirectly, at some point in our lives. That's just how it is living here on earth in an environment permeated by sin. Somehow that knowledge helps me to put things into perspective. I can't feel sorry for myself, because there are others who have it much worse. Nor can I feel proud, for I know my reality.

Besides, my challenges make me more considerate of others, more grateful for my blessings, and more eager to live—and eat—in heaven. What do your challenges do for you?

Naomi Striemer

Something Beautiful

He has made everything beautiful. Eccl. 3:11, NIV.

To give them beauty for ashes. Isa. 61:3, NKJV.

I was rummaging through things at a garage sale when something unique caught my eye. It was a garden table that was made up of various pieces of broken glass. It wasn't for sale, but I fell in love with how the colors caught the sunlight. They glistened and gleamed like nothing I'd ever seen before. As I examined the table I realized that all the pieces of glass shared a strong similarity and had to have come from the same piece or set. I approached the owner, and he told me the story of this table.

Austin's grandmother had a very large beautiful vase that she had found on a visit to Europe. She had loved this vase for many years, and she often filled it with large bouquets. One day when Austin was young he accidentally knocked the vase over and broke it. It made her sad to lose this beautiful piece that she treasured so much. Unwilling to throw these pieces away, the grandfather gathered them in hopes of gluing them back together. Unfortunately, he couldn't. Then he had a brilliant idea. He took the pieces out into the backyard and started hammering the larger pieces into smaller ones. He fetched a table that had been sitting around for years and began gluing the pieces of the vase to the tabletop. He transformed both the broken vase and the all-but-discarded table into this one-of-a-kind thing of beauty. Austin said he'd kept the table all these years to remind him that when things seem broken beyond repair or worn beyond use, that they can still be transformed into something beautiful.

I have been thinking about the broken parts of my life, the crushed hopes and botched opportunities all apparently lost and beyond repair. But I know the Master Artist who works with things that seem beyond redemption to create exquisite things of beauty. His advertisement slogan is "Beauty for Ashes." His promise is to repair, restore, or transform while you wait. His work is impeccable, and His promise is backed by a guarantee beyond compare. What have you got to gain but something beautiful in return?

"Master Artist, I praise You for seeing everything in my life, not just for what it is, but what it could be."

Twinkle Guimaraes

How God Led Me Close to Him

"For I know the plans I have for you," declares the Lord, "plans to prosper you and not to harm you, plans to give you hope and a future." Jer. 29:11, NIV.

Until I was 14 years old I lived in three Bulgarian orphanages. The Lord drew me close before I knew Him. In 1996 I moved to a children's home with 100 kids, near Lukovit, a mountain town near Romania. A boy who was crippled and could get around only by crawling, was adored by the caregivers and children because he was so loving and always smiling.

When he was 8 and I was 11, he was taken to the hospital, but soon died. All I knew about death was from TV. The boy was the first person I knew who died. I felt very sad and had unanswered questions. At the small funeral for him, some of my friends giggled. I felt miserable, but I laughed too. "Rosalina, don't laugh; this is serious!" the caregiver reprimanded.

I thought I had done a terrible thing to the boy and wanted to make up for it. I didn't know where he was, but I couldn't sleep, so I started to talk to him in my head. I told him I was sorry. Each night I told him what had happened that day, and sometimes sang in Bulgarian.

I talked to him until Easter, when I saw a movie on TV about Jesus. It told how He came to save us and that He would come back. I didn't understand a lot of it, but I remembered His friends prayed to Him after He went back to heaven. So I tried talking to the Lord and asked Him to take care of my friend—and me, too.

Sometimes a family would come to adopt children, so I prayed someone would come for me and teach me about God. Two years later an American couple came to meet me! We spent a great week together, and when they left, they told me they would come back for me. I didn't know if they would, but I received a picture of their house with a key taped to it. When my friends saw it, they said, "Now you have a home and a family," and I did!

The Lord answered my prayers, and He kept His promise "to give me hope and a future." I found out my little friend was sleeping, and just like I used to talk to him, I could pray or sing to my Father. And sometimes I think that the Lord might appreciate a little song, so I sing one to Him. My heart was filled with love for God, so in 2006 I was baptized. I thank God for teaching me His truth and for blessing me.

Rosalina Matheson

Remembering Names

And those who know Your name will put their trust in You, for You, O Lord, have not forsaken those who seek You. Ps. 9:10, NASB.

One day while shopping, before it was my turn to be served, I glanced at the name tag of the girl working the register. When I got to the front of the line, I began an enthusiastic conversation, using her name as if I really knew her! Bewildered and stunned, she stood there trying desperately to figure out how we might know each other! When I told her that really, she *didn't* know me, she was quite relieved! But honestly, there are times I have felt that sense of bewilderment myself when I should have known someone's name! I'm always amazed at those people who may not have seen me for years, yet warmly greet me using my name when they see me! I cringe inwardly, trying to remember their name! To my dismay, I do not have the gift of remembering names well. At times I wish I had a little pin to wear that says, "Please remind me of your name and how I know you!"

There is someone who never forgets my name. It is my enemy. Oh, he knows my name, studies my faults, sees my sins, and he doesn't forget. He talks to God about me. The Bible says he is my accuser. I imagine he says something like this: "You see DeeAnn? You know what a failure she is to You! She says she serves You, but look at this and this and *this*!" Then he proceeds to accuse me before my God with all of the ways that I have indeed failed! I hang my head, ashamed and condemned. He's right, after all, and there's no doubt about it—he didn't mistake me for someone else. He remembered my name.

But he's stopped by an outstretched hand. On that hand is *my name!* "I know DeeAnn very well," says my friend. "See this? I have her name engraved on my hand! She's my darling daughter, the treasure of my heart, my forgiven princess. And you might as well leave, Satan, because I have no idea what you're talking about!" Yes! He *remembers* my name! But wonder of wonders, He *forgets* the sins I have asked Him to forgive! He says, "I wipe away your sins because of who I am. And so, I will forget the wrongs you have done" (Isa. 43:25, CEV).

I do wish I was better at remembering names. Yet the only name I need to remember is that of Jesus, my Redeemer, Savior, and Friend. How about you? Jesus knows *your* name.

DeeAnn Bragaw

The Beauty of Jesus

But covet earnestly the best gifts. 1 Cor. 12:31.

My favorite childhood chorus was "Let the Beauty of Jesus Be Seen in Me." I frequently sing this song as an adult, but now I sing with more understanding and meaning. In fact, the song has become my prayer because I sense the beauty of Jesus to be a wonderful thing—something worth aspiring for. Oh, how I yearn to be like Jesus and radiate His beauty. I have tried to be like Jesus, but I have not been consistent. I seem to be like Him when things are going well, but when I get crushed, unlike the rose that perfumes the air when crushed, I am nothing like Jesus! But what is the beauty of Jesus? How can I obtain it, and how can this beauty be seen in me?

Jesus is altogether lovely; in Him there is no darkness at all, for He is the light of the world. When I consider other attributes of my Savior, they reveal that He is indeed lovely: Jesus is full of compassion, mercy, forgiveness, kindness, love, meekness, Wonderful Counselor, Prince of Peace, Faithful One, Eternal Life, Lover of my soul, Lamb of God, Redeemer, the Good Shepherd, the Bread of Life, Living Water, the Bright and Morning Star, Lily of the Valley, the Rose of Sharon, the Friend of Sinners, the Savior of the World, and so much more!

The Bible is replete with references to beauty in holiness. Beauty is holiness, and holiness is beauty. There is no true beauty outside of Jesus, who is the epitome of holiness. It seems to me, therefore, that the two are inseparable. Here are some Bible references: 1 Chronicles 16:29: "Give unto the Lord the glory due unto his name: bring an offering, and come before him: worship the Lord in the beauty of holiness." Psalm 96:9: "O worship the Lord in the beauty of holiness: fear before him, all the earth." Psalm 110:3: "Thy people shall be willing in the day of thy power, in the beauties of holiness from the womb of the morning: thou hast the dew of thy youth."

Jesus is the holy and righteous one. This means that He knows no sin, He is the perfect one. Sin is dark, evil, and ugly; it is the direct opposite of Jesus. But everyone can be like Jesus. It begins with a desire and is followed by a request. Jesus has promised to hear us when we call, and so to be like Jesus is only a prayer away. And when we possess the beauty of Jesus, those who live, work, and interact with us will know by the words we speak and by our actions.

Jacqueline Hope HoShing-Clarke

It Could Happen to Me

Take therefore no thought for the morrow: for the morrow shall take thought for the things of itself. Sufficient unto the day is the evil thereof. Matt. 6:34.

The earthquake and tsunami that struck Japan in 2011 and the resulting devastation have brought very forcefully to my mind the reality that life is indeed fragile. Thousands of people in and around Sendai were going about their normal activities. No one expected an earthquake of 9.0 magnitude, not a tsunami that would careen inland up to six miles. But that is exactly what happened. People and property were swept away in an instant. And as if that were not enough trouble, there followed the radiation leak from the damaged nuclear plant.

As I reflect on these recent events, I am led to ponder my own life and the fact that my life can change drastically as suddenly as it did for people who survived earthquakes in China, Chile, New Zealand, Haiti, and other places. The reality is that if I survive a natural disaster of the greatest magnitude, I could find myself homeless. But why should I worry about this? In Matthew 6:34 we are reminded to deal with today's issues, not tomorrow's.

If God cares for the birds, the plants, the animals, He will take care of us in His own way. And what if disaster should come my way and I lose all my material possessions and even my life? As long as I am in God's hand, I am safe. The story of Job is a real inspiration for people who lose everything. Not only was Job deprived of his material wealth, but his body was tormented with pain; and his children, the pride and joy of his heart, had been swept away in an instant. He was indeed alone, except for his wife, who was no comfort to him in his hour of need.

The Bible does not say that Job lost his earthly home, but when one loses everything he has, he might feel homeless. All that he values and all that means security vanishes. Yet in spite of his losses, Job did not lose faith. He trusted God because he knew that God knew what was best for him. That is why he could say, "Though he slay me, yet will I trust in him" (Job 13:15).

So what if I become homeless down here! God is preparing a home for you and for me. In John 14:2, 3 Jesus assures us, "In My Father's house are many mansions; if it were not so, I would have told you. I go to prepare a place for you. And if I go and prepare a place for you, I will come again and receive you to Myself; that where I am, there you may be also" (NKJV).

Carol Joy Fider

The Wrong Way

There is a way that appears to be right,
but in the end it leads to death. Prov. 16:25, NIV.

For about two years there have been expansion deviations and detours on the busy thruway we travel out of and back into our neighborhood. My husband has kept a close watch on every development, every twist and turn of new road structure. He prides himself on reading the indicators, figuring out what the finished product will look like, and he is remarkably accurate.

For this reason I was astonished when he reported that although the scores of warning barrels were still in place, he had, in broad daylight, unsuspectingly veered off the designated path onto a lane of the roadway that was under construction and not ready for auto traffic. Surely this man who had studied the realignments and knew the road so well could not have done this. Yet he was not alone. He shared that he had been the last driver in a line of five who had made the foolishly impulsive decision to follow the car just ahead of it onto a dangerous path.

Although the drivers soon realized their error, getting back onto the proper path was not as easy as turning off. To find a turnabout, the little caravan had to traverse a lengthy span of rough, bumpy, unpaved roadway laden with construction obstacles, equipment, and vehicles in order to return to the approved road. Imagine the shock and dismay of the civil engineers and construction workers at the approach of the errant automobiles. What could be casually classified as insignificant clearly reveals, under closer scrutiny, potential major consequences to the drivers and life-threatening encounters to others.

This little story has several correlations to our spiritual journey. The two most obvious are (1) the perils of blindly following others, and (2) the tragedy of leading others astray. We know the waymarks for Christian living and the journey from this world to heaven and the new earth. Yet too often we are drawn off course at a moment's consideration of the direction we're taking by following the fads and fashions of society. Perhaps worse, there are far too many times in our lives that we lead others astray. I cringed when my husband reported that the driver that led others off course was a woman. How often do we, my sisters, allow ourselves to be drawn away from God's plans for our lives and in doing so draw others after us into harm's way? Let us by God's grace remain vigilant at all times, bidding others to follow us as we follow Jesus.

Ella Louise Smith Simmons

Bring Your Tithe Into the Storehouse

In all your ways acknowledge Him,
and He shall direct your paths. Prov. 3:6, NKJV.

Bring my tithe into the storehouse—that really is what I intended to do; I mean, pay my tithe. But did you ever have one of those days when nothing you did was right and you had to do everything over at least twice? That's how my day was going—a week of those days to be truthful.

I had recently moved to New Mexico from Chehalis, Washington, to be of some help to my sister. Having gone to the local church a couple times I picked up a supply of tithe envelopes. I was paying tithe at my Chehalis church at the time and realized I did not have a current Washington area church envelope to use. So, being frugal, I used the New Mexico tithe envelope I recently picked up and made the check out to the Washington area church headquarters. I set it aside while paying my other monthly obligations so that I could put a note along with the envelope requesting an envelope supply be sent to me.

As it so often happens, I was distracted, and when I got back to my desk it was time for the mail, so I put everything out just in time for the mailman. To my surprise, when I looked for the tithe envelope, it was gone. Evidently I had put it in the mail with the other items. It is very convenient that the tithe envelopes have the address on them of the local church headquarters.

First I called the local post office for my route to see if the mailman had found the envelope. But no, they could not track it as everything is sent to the main station for sorting. Then I called the New Mexico church secretary of the treasurer to alert them to watch for the small envelope; she suggested I cancel the check and send another. I did. She also said she would mail it to Chehalis if it did show up.

A week and much prayer later the dear woman called and said she had received the envelope and mailed it to the other church. We were all amazed that such a small item would go through the mail system in such a large city, and no one had opened it.

We have such a marvelous God who is so interested in our busy daily lives that He watches out for us, and I don't doubt that He most likely laughs with us in the silly things that happen—just to watch us smile.

Georgia Lee Anderson

Patience

Be still, and know that I am God: I will be exalted among the heathen, I will be exalted in the earth. Ps. 46:10.

My husband and I were on our way home from his homeland of Jamaica. We arrived in Miami at 10:30 a.m. and went to check in for our connecting flights. The attendant informed us that she could check us in and secure our boarding passes, but she could not tag our luggage as it was too early. Our flight was at 3:45 so we would have to come back at 12:30. We were planning to visit with my aunt and cousins, so it would have been a hassle to have to lug our bags with us. Since it was already 11:00 I asked if she could just complete the process as we were already at the counter. The attendant said, "No, there is a rule."

I was frustrated, but remained calm. Three boarding passes printed, but the last one didn't print, because the printer was out of cards. The attendant apologized and went to the back to retrieve more cards. She inserted them into the printer, but the boarding pass still did not print. Puzzled, she went to the computer and tried to get things going, but to no avail. My husband and I patiently watched the process. When nothing seemed to work, the attendant called for a colleague to assist her. I was tired and hungry, but did not say a word, because I knew that God was working out His plan.

While the two attendants fidgeted with the computer and the printer, I again asked the woman if our bags could be checked. I knew that my cousin was on her way to pick us up. The plan was to go to south Miami for a meal and a quick visit. Still the answer was no. By this time an hour had elapsed, and it was now 11:30 a.m. Finally they got the system working, and the boarding pass was printed. We were checked in and good to go. But what about the bags? The other attendant said that it was OK, we could check them. He informed his colleague that it was fine, and they took the bags. I quietly praised God. I did not dare tell them that He jammed the system just long enough for us to get the bags checked.

How often, when things go wrong, we become upset and angry about the situation. How much better to pray and be still long enough for God to work things out. I am thankful that in my tiredness I did not make a scene. He said, "Be still and know that I am God."

Sharon (Brown) Long

Amazing Grace

But grow in grace. 2 Peter 3:18.

Have you ever had a problem with knowing what you wanted to say but it came out all wrong? Most of us have at one time or another. Around the time that recycling became mandatory in our area we had a guest over; we just sat around talking, sipping on a soft drink. When we had finished, my guest picked up her can, went into the kitchen, then turned back and asked, "Do you guys litter?" Now, we all know she didn't really think we littered, but that's what came out. Thoroughly embarrassed, she managed to find the recycling bin and toss her can.

My sister always liked to tell the story of being in the sixth grade and stuck in study hall because she didn't have the money to go to the ball game that was taking place in the gym at that very moment. But what bothered Bonnie more than missing the ball game was her thirst. She needed a drink. She thought, *I must have a drink of water.* At that time her classes were being held in an older section of the building and the water fountains were not working, so she needed permission to enter the newer area that went directly past the gym. Mustering up her courage, she walked to the front of the room, almost tasting the cool drinking-fountain offering, and said desperately, "Miss Grace, could I go to the ball game?" Again, we know that was not what was supposed to come out, but our minds play tricks on us.

Our heavenly Father knows what we need before we even ask. In fact, He shapes the words for us so that they have the correct meaning. I meant to say, "Thy will be done" but it came out, "Please don't let her die." I meant to say, "Change me so that I might know how to deal with my alcoholic father," but it came out, "Why can't he just go away?" I meant to say, "Thank You for my job," but it came out, "I don't want to go to work today!" I really meant to say, "Come into my heart, Lord Jesus," but it came out, "Another day."

My sister really needed that drink of water and somehow Miss Grace knew that. She answered, "No, Bonnie, you didn't pay to go to the ball game." Then she smiled and with twinkling eyes said, "But you can go get a drink of water."

That's the kind of grace I want and need in my life. *Turn my words and thoughts around, Lord. Make them meaningful to You.*

Carol Wiggins Gigante

Open Arms

Love one another as I have loved you. John 15:12, NKJV.

After eight months of staying away from home, often without our knowing where and with whom she was staying, my 20-year-old daughter returned home unexpectedly in the early hours of a morning. The first I knew she was back was when she stood at the side of my bed trying to wake me up. She had been trying to get into the house for a while, but unlike the father of the prodigal son, who was watching for him to return, I wasn't awake to greet her. And she couldn't make me hear her knocking at the front door, or tapping on the window, and had to resort to reaching in through the cat flap and turning the key in the back door.

Of course, I was thankful she was finally home, but then came the next question: was it all right for her and the new man in her life, who was already in the house, to stay the night? I was happy to see her and would have agreed to anything on that first night. But as one night turned into a few nights I was sorry that the house was no longer my own, and began to take a stronger line and ask them to smoke further away from the house.

It's interesting, isn't it? We pray for our children to come home, but we want it on our terms. As I was trying to come to terms with the changes, I actually began to bemoan the situation to friends. It was then that I was reminded of a story that our preacher once told me: A somewhat elderly church warden was cleaning up the church after a youth service. Other members of the church were complaining about the presence of beer cans under the pews. He responded, "I am happy to clean up beer cans if it means that the young people are coming to church!"

Maybe it should be equally so with my daughter, and I wondered if the father of the prodigal son worried about the disruptions and adjustments—which surely there were—when he welcomed his son home with open arms. And what about our heavenly Father who doesn't sleep and who always welcomes us. Scripture records, "'For this my son was dead and is alive again; he was lost and is found.' And they began to be merry." "'It was right that we should make merry and be glad, for your brother [or daughter] was dead and is alive again, and was lost and is found'" (Luke 15:24 and 32, NKJV). I am so thankful for a Father like that!

Laura A. Canning

Is God High-Tech? You Bet He Is!

Before they call I will answer;
while they are still speaking I will hear. Isa. 65:24, NIV.

Wendy Guptill was a missionary working in the outback of the Philippines, totally devoted to her work as a nurse among the villagers. She wrote me: "This computer I'm typing on is another miracle that just happened when I started this letter. I was having problems with it for months before I went on furlough. It would crash every time I turned it on . . . and then I got it fixed while I was in the United States, and it was working great until I turned it on the other day to start this letter. It crashed immediately and again as soon as I restarted it.

"I did not want to get discouraged as I knew that there would be little hope of getting it fixed again any time soon, and I really wanted to write this letter and also work on a big project that I was starting for the clinic. So I stopped and prayed as I always do, knowing that He could heal a computer just as easily as a person.

"Even after I jiggled some parts, it just refused to boot up. Then I stopped my frantic efforts and simply knelt down and said a prayer. In faith I turned the computer on again. The screen flickered, and voilà! I wrote the whole letter without it crashing and have used it every day since in the clinic! What can I say: we have a mighty God who would heal even a computer!"

A similar story comes from the outskirts of Siem Reap, a busy tourist town in Cambodia where the ruins of the Angkor Wat are found. Here is a special training center, school, and orphanage (for HIV/AIDS children) named "Wat Preah Yesu" (or Jesus' Pagoda) run by Tim and Wendy Maddocks, an Australian couple who felt impressed by the Holy Spirit to set this up solely on faith and prayer in 1996. Tim told me how the Lord provided their every need.

However, during the printing of some needed training materials for the Cambodian gospel workers, the printer ink ran out. They were completely out of funds. Tim did the most natural thing—knelt and prayed. After the prayer Tim replaced the empty print cartridge, clicked the mouse button, and sent the document to print again. The printer responded, and carried on printing four more reams of paper! God had come through again for His faithful workers!

Is God high-tech? You bet He is. Truly nothing is impossible for a God who looks down on earth and hears the faintest prayer and rewards the tiniest iota of faith.

Sally Lam-Phoon

New Identity in Jesus

Therefore if any man be in Christ, he is a new creature:
old things are passed away; behold, all things are become new. 2 Cor. 5:17.

Today's verse talks about being given a new identity when one receives Jesus Christ as his or her personal Savior. I remember when I went to secondary school Form One in 1978; l was nicknamed "Lady Melody" simply because I was a great singer and dancer. Coming from a strict Methodist home and finding myself for the first time out of parental control, I thought I could be my better self. Although I was an astute chorister and Bible reader in church, I did not know Jesus as my personal Savior. Then I met this wonderful man Jesus through a musical concert organized by Joyful Way Incorporated. He changed my identity and gave me a new name, Osofomaame. Even my parents still call me by this name. Everything about me changed, including the caliber of friends I kept, the type of music I listened to and danced with, and even the type of food I ate. Initially, it wasn't easy losing childhood friends, being teased and given funny names, but through it all Jesus has been a faithful companion.

Being given a new identity is not by might or power but by the Spirit of God (Zech. 4:6). All that you need to do is accept that you are a sinner and believe in Jesus, for to them that believe in Him, He gave power to become the daughters of God, "even to those who believe in His name" (John 1:12, NKJV). It doesn't matter what name the world has given you if you realize that you are a sinner, because all have sinned and fallen short of the glory of God (Rom. 3:23). You can ask for forgiveness and turn away from your sins and repent; He will surely forgive you and give you a new identity.

Regardless of your past or what the world calls you, never give up, because if Jacob's name could be changed from being a "deceiver" to "Israel" meaning "God wrestler," Benoni to Benjamin, and Saul to Paul, then He can give you a new identity, because Jesus "is able to do exceeding abundantly above all that we ask or think, according to the power that worketh in us" (Eph. 3:20).

Jesus shed His precious blood on Calvary so that I can be saved from the clutches of sin. Today I once again thank Him for giving me a new identity.

Adelaide Ferguson

Carried in His Arms

And my God will fully satisfy every need of yours according to his riches in glory in Christ Jesus. Phil. 4:19, NRSV.

My mother was killed in a tragic auto accident. Two days later when we opened our devotional book, we were really amazed. There were quotations from a 50-year-old brochure that met our need that very day. One quotation said that no matter the situation you may be in, there is a promise in God's Book that fits, and it brings you the needed help. Another asked if it seems to you that your life is empty and has no sense. Is the devil suggesting to you that death is the end of everything? Now is the time for you to hear the most beautiful promise of God: "For God so loved the world that he gave his only Son, so that everyone who believes in him may not perish but may have eternal life" (John 3:16, NRSV).

I didn't understand why this accident was allowed, but Jesus assured us that He made it possible for us to meet my mother again when He comes for a second time, very soon. Until then, His promises continued to encourage us: "And surely I am with you always, to the very end of the age" (Matt. 28:20, NIV). I believe that Jesus is talking directly to us, as if we could hear His very kind voice. It is our privilege to put our own name in the text.

The booklet noted that if we are facing a difficult situation, "My grace is sufficient for you" (2 Cor. 12:9, NKJV). Are you at a turning point and are discouraged and do not know what direction to go? "I will instruct thee and teach thee on the way which thou shalt go: I will guide thee with mine eye" (Ps. 32:8).

My boyfriend Michael had been the one driving the car that accidentally hit my mother. Our dating relationship was at the very beginning when the accident happened, and the devil tried to destroy it, but the Lord carried and guided us, helping us to know each other better through this trial. The following year we married. I thank God with all my heart for the beautiful years He is giving us, to be a blessing for His people. He also took care of my father, giving him a second wife with whom he can continue to serve the Lord.

The encouraging words and the promises written those many years ago were a blessing today. May God be glorified in everything!

Teodora Goran

Forgotten Funds!

Bring all the tithes into the storehouse,
that there may be food in My house, and prove Me now in this,
says the Lord of hosts, If I will not open for you the windows
of heaven and pour out for you such a blessing that there will not
be room enough to receive it. Mal. 3:10, NKJV.

My automobile had served me well for seven years. Just imagine! I'd never had a car that long! It was time for a new one. Being retired for more than a year and living on a more limited—fixed—budget than when I was gainfully employed, such a major purchase required careful thought and planning.

Naturally the "old" car had some value and could be used as a trade-in or be sold outright. I had already been shopping for another vehicle, and a visit to one dealer was productive. I saw the new car that I wanted to purchase and subsequently made a small down payment to hold it when it arrived. The agency called several days before the time expected to say that the automobile was in the showroom and that I should complete the purchase because the price quoted was good only until the month's end.

At that, I decided to pay a visit to the bank to explore the possibilities for financing this major purchase. After discussing the alternatives and making a decision to act on one of them, the bank official reminded me of an account I had completely forgotten about! Hallelujah! I could complete the required transaction to obtain a new vehicle without experiencing any financial straits. Our God, Creator, Redeemer, Sustainer, Guide, Friend, is faithful.

Over the years it has been my practice to return tithes and offerings faithfully to the Lord and to participate actively in the Sabbath school mission investment program. I have discovered that even on a reduced income the return of faithful tithes and offerings and mission investment monies have resulted in continued blessings that have included travel abroad and locally to explore all the new resorts the country now has to offer—all this in the company of my 10-year-old granddaughter.

Truly I consider myself greatly blessed, and I encourage us all to "prove the Lord," for He will "open for you the windows of heaven and pour out for you such a blessing that there will not be room enough to receive it."

Marion V. Clarke Martin

Playing It Safe

Truly I tell you, whatever you did not do for one of the least of these,
you did not do for me. Matt. 25:45, NIV.

Ma'am, could you please help me buy some food?" I was shopping in my local co-op health food store and had wandered away from my grocery cart to look for a plastic bag. Instead, I walked right into the path of a man who appeared to be homeless. Plus, his demeanor reminded me of the special education students I used to teach—eager to please, but not quite sure how.

A host of thoughts rushed through my mind: *I don't have much cash. But I could go through the store with him and pay for his food when I write a check for my groceries. No. I'm alone. What if he follows me out to my car? What if he tries to get in? What if he tries to . . . ?* These considerations plus others reeled through my mind.

"What was that you said?" I asked him, stalling for more time to come up with a reply.

"Could you help me buy some food?"

After what felt like forever, I simply said, "No. I'm sorry."

"Thank you anyway," he replied with a smile.

Immediately I was smitten with remorse. And to make matters worse, everywhere I went after that, there he was ahead of me—a thorn in my flesh. His purchases were meager, but wise—two peaches, a box of granola, toothpaste, an Amy's frozen dinner, a deli sandwich. . . .

I also noticed that just before he chose an item, he'd ask a store clerk to help him. *Oh, no! He hasn't been asking for money.* When he first saw me, I was walking toward him without my cart. *He thought I worked in the store and was literally asking me for help with his shopping!*

Remorse stung my heart as I checked out, left the store, and drove home. I could hear God saying to me personally, "Is this not the fast I have chosen: . . . to share your bread with the hungry. . . ?" (Isa. 58:6, 7, NKJV). Then Christ whispered, "Truly I tell you, whatever you did not do for one of the least of these, you did not do for me" (Matt. 25:45, NIV).

"You thought it was best to play it safe," my husband responded when I shared with him what had happened. "So stop second-guessing yourself."

But I've been asking myself ever since, *Since when did Christ ever play it safe?*

Lyndelle Brower Chiomenti

What Is Your Talent?

And we know that all things work together
for good to them that love God. Rom. 8:28.

Our church is small—only about 80 members. We had an organ and a piano, but the piano was old, really old, and not in good shape. The organ had been donated by the woman who played it each Sabbath; however, when she got married and moved away, she naturally took the organ with her.

When a new minister and his wife came to our church, she played the piano. It didn't take her long to ask the board for a new piano! The purchase was approved, and they went to find a new one. She picked out a very nice, small black ebony one. She played each week, and it sounded wonderful. After a while that minister was transferred, and we had a new pastor coming, but his wife didn't play the piano; besides, she had small children to watch. Therefore, no one played the piano; but when we had a visitor, we asked if they played the piano. If they did, we would have piano music that day.

Now, this piano was unique, as it had to be watered. This struck me as funny. I had never heard of a piano that had to be watered. I have trouble remembering to water my flowers—let alone a piano.

One day a gentleman by the name of Virgil came to visit, and we found out that he could play the piano. How happy and grateful we all were! Virgil has stayed with us and played for a long time now. He plays all the hymns we sing and often does special music for church. I am an assistant Sabbath school superintendent, and he has been so good to play special music for us.

God has given Virgil a talent, and he is using it for the Lord. What about you? Are you using your talents for what God wants *you* to do? You may say, "I don't have any talents." But God has given each of us at least one and you may have even more. Don't waste them: use them to bless others. We are told not to hide our light under a bushel (Matt. 5:15) and to "Let your light so shine before men, that they may see your good works, and glorify your Father which is in heaven" (verse 16).

Are you using all your God-given talents? Jesus told a parable about talents and said we need to use them. Read about it in Matthew 25:15-29. Are you shining for Jesus?

Anne Elaine Nelson

Stubborn

No man cometh unto the Father, but by me. John 14:6.

Years ago while working as a resident physician I heard a one-sided phone call that stunned me. I was hanging out at the nursing station when the call came through. The nurse who took the call had a small hint of fear in her voice, which caught my attention, so I went over to figure out why. She was typing the message from the patient, and I read the message with trepidation. The patient wanted an appointment to see his physician because he was very short of breath. The nurse tried to convince him to see another doctor, as his physician was not in. He was informed that there were many other physicians working that day, all with several available appointments. The patient stated, "My doc knows me. If he is not in today, I will just stay at home and die." A few days later, while going through the newspaper, one of the nurses shrieked. She saw his name listed in the obituaries. He had been found dead at home by a relative.

This patient had confidence in his physician. He thought that for him to get better he needed to see *his* physician. Now, there are several possible lessons that can be learned from this story: the first is that in order for us to be saved we need to go to the Great Physician, for *only* He can save us. Putting our hopes and prayers in pastors, elders, friends, and family just won't do.

Second, at times when we ask God's help with a problem, we may see only one solution—our logical solution. But our eyes are sinful and cannot see what's best for us. We have to trust Him, as He loves us and knows the right path for us to take. Alternatives may come that may not look attractive or may seem just to take too long. But we have to keep our eyes open and pray that God will reveal His plan to us.

Jonah was a great example of this. He thought God's way was the wrong way and tried to run away from this plan. It took a "being in the belly of a fish" experience before he was willing to do what God wanted him to do all along.

So I don't know what lesson is meant to be yours today. I am praying that it might be revealed as you read it, as you spend time in God's Word and presence. Regardless, the take-home lesson is to trust God and Him only. Pray and allow God's will to be revealed to you today.

Sharon Michael Palmer

I Had to Lose My Hearing in Order to Hear

If anyone has ears to hear, let him hear. Mark 4:23, ESV.

Not long ago I had the opportunity to visit the excavations of the seven churches of Revelation 1-3. John wrote seven letters to seven churches after God told him through a vision to do so. In these three chapters I can find seven times in which the text is today's verse. It was quite an experience to see the seven churches and to experience them. The word in the Scripture receives a completely new meaning.

When I arrived home from the trip, I got sick. A harmless winter flu put me to bed. Just when I started to feel better, I felt terrible pain in my ears, and I had to go to the hospital to the emergency room. The next day my eardrum burst. Suddenly I heard only very, very much noise in my head. They called it tinnitus, and my hearing was gone completely. The specialist gave me a very bad prognosis. The hearing loss was a catastrophe, and I would in the future be able to hear only with strong electronic help. *Why this? What does God want to tell me?*

My husband took me for walks day by day. He took me into the snow, to a farm, to the lake, into the forest, to the llamas—every day something new. My other senses were stimulated: sight, feel, smell, touch, taste. It all helped a lot. I concentrated less on my hearing. It was somehow relaxing and did me good.

During this time something happened for which I will be thankful all my life. With strong hearing aids I could drown out the noise in my head, and I heard my first sermon after my sudden deafness. The pastor said that we are always surrounded by God, wherever we are, like a fish by water. Suddenly I remembered the many incidents during which I felt guided by God.

Could it be that only now, as I have lost my hearing, that I could finally hear? I started, deaf as I was, to listen, to hear, to understand, and to trust that He would carry me through. I knew suddenly that as my past was not coincidence, what happens now is not coincidence either. Suddenly I was looking forward to finding out what my hearing loss was good for and what God wanted to tell me. I could suddenly trust again, and I started to quote again and again, "May I never forget the good things he does for me" (Ps. 103:2, NLT).

This was a drastic experience: I had to lose my hearing to be able to hear.

Denise Hochstrasser

"Chance" Encounter

Before they call I will answer;
while they are still speaking I will hear. Isa. 65:24, NIV.

My husband and I had gone to California to welcome our new grandson in Tehachapi. As our daughter and her baby were still resting in the hospital over the Sabbath, we decided to drive to Loma Linda to meet our younger daughter and go to church there. We left early Sabbath morning and started our two-and-a-half-hour drive across the desert.

About midway we stopped in a small town to use the restroom. We felt completely out of place dressed in our church clothes while everyone else was in jeans or shorts, ready for a day at the beach or mountains. Just as we were leaving the truck stop, we passed a young woman who was also wearing a dress and high-heeled shoes. Thinking she was probably just headed to a business meeting, we continued walking. Suddenly she hurried back to us and asked quite bluntly where we were going.

We said simply that we were on our way to Loma Linda. Her face brightened; "What do you plan to do there?" We told her we were going to meet our daughter and go to church. Her face broke into a big smile and she asked, "Are you Seventh-day Adventists?" We told her we were, and she quickly added, "I am, too!" She then told us how she had a speaking appointment that morning and needed to get to Loma Linda to meet her sister, but her car was nearly out of gas. She didn't feel right buying gas on Sabbath (see Ex. 20:8-11), so she had been praying that God would somehow work things out so she could get to Loma Linda without buying gas. Excitedly she asked, "May I ride with you?" Well, of course, we were more than happy to give her a ride.

There we were in a very remote area. We had left early from Tehachapi; she had left even earlier from the San Joaquin Valley. But we met at the exact same time in the very same place. She had chosen to honor the Sabbath and God honored her and supplied her need.

God has so many ways to provide for us—ways that we know nothing about. Once again, "We know that in all things God works for the good of those who love him" (Rom. 8:28, NIV). And as our text for today says, before we even ask God already has the answer. If only we could learn to trust His promises completely!

Sharon Oster

Freely Give

Heal the sick. . . . Freely you have received, freely give. Matt. 10:8, NKJV.

I had been going through something for months. I was withdrawing more and more from friends and family. I felt as though God had abandoned me. I was fighting severe depression. I was giving up. *Where are You, God? Why is this happening? I thought I had overcome this weakness. Why am I experiencing it again? Am I a fake Christian?*

As I was preparing to attend church one morning, I prayed, *O, Lord, I need to feel Your presence. Without You I will die. How can I be of any good service to anyone when I feel dead? Lord,* I pleaded, *please help me!*

I entered church and sat in one of my favorite pews. A longtime friend, Sandra Bowman, entered church and sat in the pew directly in front of me. Sandra has been fighting severe physical ailments for a very long time, but never have I seen her lose her faith or hope. I wished her a happy Sabbath, and she returned the kindness.

It was praise time in the worship service, so I stood up to sing with the congregation. Sandra was unable to stand, and I felt compelled to touch her left shoulder with my left hand. I was unable to remove my hand from her shoulder until the last of the praise songs was completed. That was out of character for me, and I was clueless as to why I had done it.

I went up to receive special prayer, and upon my return, Sandra asked me to bend down so she could converse with me. I knelt down. Tears were in her eyes. She said that few people touched her anymore, and that it meant so much to her that I did. Then she told me the most amazing and profound testimony of what the touch had done for her. The left side of her back was in great pain that morning. She asked the Lord to take the pain away so she could enjoy the church service. Then she said that when I touched her, she felt her pain dissipating, and the longer I held the touch the more the pain went away. By the time I removed my hand the pain had completed gone away.

I shared in her tears. I shared with her what I was going through that morning, and that it was obvious that God heard both our prayers. After church service we both sat together and gave honor and praise to our compassionate God who heals the sick and the brokenhearted.

Evelyn Greenwade Boltwood

Bubble Gum Ice Cream

Let not your heart be troubled; you believe in God, believe also in Me.
In My Father's house are many mansions; if it were not so, I would have
told you. I go to prepare a place for you. . . . I will come again and receive
you to Myself; that where I am, there you may be also. John 14:1-3, NKJV.

As a child there was one place I always loved to go: The Ice Creamery. Every so often my parents would take my sister and me to downtown Oakland to ride bikes. My favorite part was when we fed the ducks. Downtown Oakland was the central location for festivals, musicals, and all sorts of exciting activities.

My sister and I attended a small school in the Bay Area in the Oakland Hills called Golden Gate Academy. My first-grade class put on a program, "God's Trombone," for Black History Month. Our teacher had promised the class ice cream after the program if we did a good job. My role in the play was Ida B. Wells. She used her pen to write about the injustice of her time. She, along with James Weldon Johnson and Phillis Wheatley, inspired me to write. Johnson was a poet, educator, activist, author, and diplomat who wrote a poem, "God's Trombone"; and Wheatley was the first African American poet, and first African American woman, to publish a book. As a slave in the 1700s, she was reading Greek and Latin classics and difficult passages from the Bible. The play was the beginning of my appreciation for the African American culture. It was good to know about African Americans who fought for a cause they believed in.

After the program we were escorted by our parents to The Ice Creamery. I ordered my all-time favorite, bubble gum ice cream. As I child I thought there was nothing as good as bubble gum ice cream because you got two treats in one. I ate the ice cream and saved the bubble gum to eat later.

The ice cream was a small reward for a great performance. In life there are rewards for our deeds, some are small and some are great. Bubble gum ice cream was one of my rewards. Jesus reminds us of the great reward in heaven that He has prepared for those who love and obey Him. If we are faithful we will receive our double reward, eternal life and a mansion in the sky. Let us be faithful until He comes again.

Kristen Hudson

God's Instruction

I will instruct you and teach you in the way you should go;
I will guide you with My eye. Ps. 32:8, NKJV.

Where do you turn at crisis points in your life when you don't have the obvious resources or the answers for resolving desperate situations?

I strongly believe that Jochebed, the mother of Moses, asked herself this question when she found herself responsible for her 3-month-old baby boy, despite the Egyptian king's orders that male Hebrew babies be slain. Trying to save her child was breaking the law of the land. Yet saving her son was in obedience to the law of God.

I can imagine the many sleepless nights Jochebed spent praying. I'm sure she hadn't much of an appetite during that time. Worry and agony nearly paralyzed her.

Then suddenly, out of nowhere, a noble plan formed in her mind. She would make a floatable ark, a small boat of bulrushes waterproofed with tar and pitch. She probably lined the basket with soft cloth before placing her precious cargo inside. How gently she must have set the basket upon the waters of the Nile River. Not knowing the basket's final destination, she left her baby's future in God's hands. Yet where did this ingenious plan come from? How could she be certain of the baby's safety? I believe it came from God.

An inspired author elaborates: "The mother's earnest prayers had committed her child to the care of God; and angels, unseen, hovered above his lowly resting place. Angels directed Pharaoh's daughter thither" (Ellen G. White, *Patriarchs and Prophets*, p. 243). As the Bible reveals, the pagan king's daughter herself rescued the apparently doomed baby and raised him as her son—with the help of his very own birth mother! What an amazing God who, from Moses' earliest months of life, preserved the life of Israel's future and first great leader. Truly, as the promise of Psalm 32:8 states, God does instruct, teach, and guide those who are doing their best to honor Him.

Dear friends, we serve the same faithful God today. In all life circumstances He has promised to instruct us and show us the way we should to go. As we carefully seek His face with humility and full assurance in His promises, we will find heaven-made solutions to our problems.

Omobonike Adeola Sessou

47

His Loving Care Is O'er Us

But deliverance is of the Lord. Prov. 21:31, NKJV.

One sunny Sunday afternoon my husband, Ashton, and a ministerial colleague and I were heading to the mining town of Linden some 67 miles (108 kilometers) from the city. We were going there to support another colleague whose dad had passed away. The funeral service was scheduled to begin at 3:00 that afternoon. Both pastors were to officiate in the service.

"What is the time?" my spouse asked. It was then 2:50 p.m. "We'll get there in time," he said. As he continued to speed down the Soesdyke/Linden highway, we noticed a red car descending the hill facing us. The very next thing we knew, our car had crossed over the curb, we were dusted with sand, and our pastor friend was crouched in the trunk of our vehicle. A double blow on the driver's side of our car had caused it to roll over three times.

The driver of the other car pulled over, and someone asked how many persons were in our car. I responded, "Three." They were ensuring that everyone was accounted for. The occupants of the red car had also been to Linden to support our colleague but were returning home even before the funeral service began, since they had a long way to go.

We decided that I would return to Georgetown to solicit help. Ashton proceeded to the funeral service by way of a passenger car, while our friend Philip stayed by to keep watch over the badly damaged vehicle. On that lonely stretch of road God provided him with some company. Around 6:00 that evening two coal miners on their way home provided him with bananas for supper as night was approaching. They remained with him until Ashton returned.

Our motor mechanic and I got Philip's car and returned to the crash site. The area church president, two other pastors, and a Bible worker came by to support us. Since it was night it was impossible to get the help we needed to make the car drivable. Three persons from the group proceeded to Linden to repair the wheels. Just after midnight we were heading to Georgetown. With much difficulty we finally got there about dawn.

Escaping with minor scratches, we knew God had a plan for our lives. We spoke to Him before embarking on the journey and knew that because of Him we were alive. Let us daily commit ourselves to Him and depend on His grace to keep us.

Ruby H. Enniss-Alleyne

Metaphor of the Apron

For God so loved the world. . . . John 3:16, NIV.

Guess what?" Melissa said as she burst through the door. "Today we sang 'His Banner Over Us Is Love,' and Teacher said we could just as well sing 'His apron over us is love.' Jeremy's dad wears an apron when he bakes bread, and Sue's mom uses one when she rolls out piecrust." Her bright little face tilted upward expectantly. "Do you have an apron?"

I shook my head. "No, but my grandmother had a wonderful apron," I said, and instantly was back in memory amid the delectable odors and mouthwatering flavors of split-pea soup, corn bread, and rice pudding. "She used that apron for ever so many things."

Melissa removed her backpack and sprawled on the carpet, obviously waiting for more.

"Grandma used her apron as a basket to carry eggs, apples, peas, radishes, asparagus, and lettuce in from the garden and empty pea pods back out. It swished dust from the piano and dining table when an unexpected visitor drove into the yard. Wound around her hands it offered protection as she took hot potatoes from the oven. It was always available to wipe perspiration from her forehead."

I paused, remembering.

"Sometimes she waved hello and goodbye with her apron or wrapped it around her arms as she stood on the back porch in cool weather. When I was sad or embarrassed, I could bury my face in its well-worn softness and feel comforted. Her apron helped stop the bleeding when one of my little cousins skinned a knee; it allowed a shy little neighbor girl to hide under its folds. It's as if it had its own brand of Grandma magic," I said, smiling.

Melissa and I googled *aprons* on the Internet, laughing at some, rolling our eyes at others, and ooing and awing over a few.

"I know," cried Melissa, "let's make aprons! Teacher was right. God's apron over us is love¾'cept His love does absolutely everything. We can wear them at Thanksgiving and tell apron stories." So that's exactly what we did.

We still have them, though Melissa's is now too small for her and she's moving toward using mine. And every so often we reminisce about the metaphor of the apron.

Arlene R. Taylor

You Are Special

So God created man in His own image; in the image of God
He created him; male and female He created them. Gen. 1:27, NKJV.

I was 24 years old when our first daughter was conceived. Unlike many of my friends, I enjoyed my pregnancy. Yes, it didn't come without the discomforts; oh, I had many! I even had morning sickness up to the ninth month! I can still remember the cramps I had almost every morning. But still, I enjoyed my pregnancy because of my excited feeling of expectancy, the excitement of opening and beholding the gift that the Lord had specially made for me and my husband. I don't know about you, but when someone gives me a gift, I cannot wait to open the gift. Sometimes I find myself opening the gift while driving or walking home. Sounds odd, but I am excited by things that I know were chosen just for me.

It was February 9, at dawn on a Wednesday, when I started feeling the pain. I woke Danny and told him, "I think this is the day!" Danny had to cancel a trip scheduled for that day because, like me, he was also excited to see the gift. However, God made it even more exciting: we had to wait until Friday, February 11, before we were able to open and see the most beautiful gift we could ever ask for: a baby girl.

The hardship of the three-day labor was all forgotten; only the feeling of being so loved by God, to be given the opportunity to bear His child, was felt.

Do you realize that you are a special gift to someone? Each of us is a special gift from God to our parents, whether they recognize it or not. Take a few moments to imagine your mother and father; can you imagine the joy they had when they first opened the special package that's you that the Lord gave them? Imagine the loving looks from your mother as she first held you in her arms and your father's gentle first touch of your little feet. Doesn't it make you feel special? And even if for some reason you didn't have that kind of parent, you can know that you are still special to God. He made you special! It doesn't matter, my sisters, whether we are young or old—the thing is, we are all special because we are a gift from the Lord.

Today is the perfect time to thank God for making each of us special. We can thank Him for loving us so much and making us His special daughters.

Jemima Dollosa Orillosa

God Is Inside My Invisible Blanket

To God belong wisdom and power;
counsel and understanding are his. Job 12:13, NIV.

Exactly three weeks ago my mother died. Actually, her death happened almost at the exact time as I started writing this meditation. The emotions that I have experienced throughout these brief 21 days have been very profound. During this time I have prayed, but I've hardly opened the Bible, although I am not mad at God. On the contrary, I have experienced an incredible feeling that God is here with me—and that is enough. I have had no need to search for comforting words in the Bible, because He is enough company for me now.

During these three weeks I have cried a lot, I have been melancholy a lot, I have gone into seclusion a lot, and I have been angry a lot! I find that I get angry when I am being forced by the outside world to solve problems, to go on living and dealing with day-to-day issues as if nothing else mattered. And for the majority of the people around me, that is what they have—the worry about their day-to-day problems! From my perspective, all these problems now seem so insignificant! In fact, so many things seem insignificant for me at this moment.

Observing this feeling from this perspective, I can see that others have felt and reacted in much the same way. Let's take, for example, C. S. Lewis, a famous Christian writer, when he describes the grieving that he experienced when his wife died: "There is a sort of invisible blanket between the world and me. I find it hard to take in what anyone says. Or, perhaps, hard to want to take it in . . . if only they would talk to one another and not to me."

Then my thoughts go to Job. Is this how he felt when so many loved ones around him died? He lost so much! And yet he didn't lose his faith in God; he just acquired a different perspective of God. Like C. S. Lewis when he says, "He seems so present when, to put it quite frankly, we don't ask for Him."

This is a time I know my faith is real. God is here for me, God is present here with me, even though I am not asking for Him to be here, even though I am in this "invisible blanket" that is separating me from the world, but in this invisible blanket God found a way to creep inside and join me. He is my comfort; He counsels me; He understands me. He is giving me what I need to go through this grieving period.

Joelcira F. Müller-Cavedon

Russian Odyssey

[Abraham] was looking forward to the city with foundations, whose architect and builder is God. Heb. 11:10, NIV.

*M*oscow—Everywhere I look, it is different from home. So different. In this frozen land weather is both central and utterly incidental to daily life. While people must constantly fortify themselves against the brutal cold, they seem totally oblivious to it, maybe resigned to that which they cannot change. Open-air markets dot the streets. Vendors, swathed in furs, scarves, mitts, and boots, pushcarts loaded with everything from matryoshka dolls to vodka—and ice cream. It's—15°F. I nearly freeze before I get to the head of the line for *my* cone!

During the day we conduct a communication workshop for our church's relief agency employees working in that part of the world. The first couple days we use a translator, but soon language really doesn't matter. We discover that we understand each other perfectly—lots of hollering and gesturing and laughing require no translation.

In the evenings we walk in Red Square, only a couple blocks from our hotel. St. Basil's Cathedral, Lenin's tomb, the Kremlin wall with its magnificent clock tower and great wooden doors that open wide every morning to admit the president's limo. Everything is so beautiful in the falling snow!

Moscow, a city of contrasts. Its museums overflow with incredible riches and beautiful objects that go back more than 600 years, yet many of its nearly 12 million people struggle to survive in a cold and inhospitable world.

So different from that *other* home. True, it too overflows with incredible riches and beautiful objects. But they're not in museums. Walls of jasper rest on foundations decorated with every kind of precious stone, beautiful objects that go back through all eternity. The 12 gates, each made of a single pearl, open wide to welcome all—you and me—if we choose to enter. And when we do, there He'll stand. The beautiful Jesus, arms outstretched!

No more cold. No more hunger. No more loneliness. No more pain of any kind. Everything is so beautiful in the light of eternal day!

"Come in!" He says, in a language that needs no translation.

Jeannette Busby Johnson

Valentine's Day Rose

I call on the Lord in my distress, and he answers me. Ps. 120:1, NIV.

I was distressed. Valentine's Day was approaching, and I was definitely unimpressed. I was 28 and single—again. Every time I went to the shopping mall I saw red love hearts stuck to the windows. I saw love heart-shaped chocolate boxes. I would see couples walking hand in hand. I heard heartwarming, romantic songs playing on the radio. I was getting to the point where all I wanted to do was run away and hide under a rock. Just disappear for the 24 hours.

A few days before the "dreaded day," I was reading my devotional, which reminded me that when I was feeling down, the best person to go to was God. I sometimes find it easier to write my prayers to God in my journal, so that's what I decided to do. The night before *that day* I reminded God (just in case He had forgotten) that I was 28 years old and getting to a stage in my life where I would like to find someone special to love, and for him to love me in return. I revealed to Him that my deepest desire was to get married and have children. I reflected that I was fully aware that the most important love relationship I should have in my life was between God and me, as God sent His Son to die for me, insignificant little me. *But God,* my heart cried out as tears rolled down my cheeks, *I need something tangible. Please!*

I woke up the next morning, and can you believe what God did for me? He gave me a single red rose on my rosebush. This rosebush sits in the front garden, sorely neglected because I dislike gardening and don't have a green thumb. Also, this rosebush had been barren for the past week or so prior to Valentine's Day. My heart was so overcome with emotion that I cried, *God, You answered my prayer. You gave me something tangible to remind me that I am special to You. That You love me and haven't forgotten me. You have definitely made my Valentine's Day special. Thank You so much!*

This rose stayed alive for four weeks before it dried up, and I keep it in a special place as a reminder of what God did for me that day. It's been months since this happened, and every time I see a red rose on the bush I am reminded that God loves me. My rosebush has become a symbol of hope. I don't need to despair, because God knows my heart, my desires, and all I need to do is trust in Him, because His timing is always perfect.

Jenny Rivera

Change Him, Please!

Surely the arm of the Lord is not too short to save, nor his ear too dull to hear. Isa 59:1, NIV.

This year I stopped attending a Christian school and started going to a public school. I was nervous, but excited, too. On the first day I saw children from my old school and a few from Miss Hester's gifted class. That helped to relax; but then I met Devin. He was the meanest and bossiest kid I had ever met! I couldn't believe it when he sat down right next to me!

Every day was the same. He would pick on me and make me unhappy. I don't think anyone liked him—not even our teachers. We had four different teachers, and each one said the same things: "Devin, be good!" "Devin, sit down!" "Stop making funny faces." "Devin, be quiet!" "Devin, sit correctly in your chair." "Devin, behave!"

One day Devin made me really angry. I was so angry that I went home and told my mom about him. Mom listened, and after a while she helped me calm down. That night during worship Mom told me about Saul. She said that Saul was an evil man who wanted to kill everyone who believed in Jesus. She said that Saul made it his mission to hurt and kill everyone he could. I don't know if it made him feel better about himself, but I know Saul was really good at his job—just like Devin. Guess what? One day God changed Saul into Paul. Paul did many good things for God.

Mom said that just like Saul, God could change Devin. I couldn't believe it. I told Mom that God couldn't change Devin, because Devin was horrible. I said it would take a miracle! Mom said, "Isn't God in the miracle business?"

I just shook my head, but when I said my prayers, I prayed for Devin. I asked God to change him. Mom prayed and asked God to change Devin, but if not, to change *how I felt about him.*

Time passed, and Devin got worse. We kept praying. One day he got suspended. When he came back, he was placed in a different class. But you know what? He actually became a good boy. God changed Devin. I learned that God can do anything, and He is still in the miracle business! I learned to trust God because sometimes things may not be the way I want them to be, but God always works in the way He knows it needs to be.

Cassandra Marquez de Smith

Meeting My Father

For God so loved the world,
that he gave his only begotten Son, that whosoever
believeth in him should not perish, but have everlasting life. John 3:16.

I grew up in a female-dominated home with no father around except for an elderly gentleman who was like a grandfather to me. He was affectionately known as "Speedy" because he walked fast. My uncle was away at college, and I looked forward to seeing him occasionally and getting horsey rides on his back, going for walks, or just enjoying listening to him talk.

My dad moved to Canada when I was an infant, and I never met him until I was 16 years old. My only picture of him was a photo my mother showed me. But he sent me letters, cards, and gifts on special occasions, such as my birthday and Christmas, so I looked forward to meeting him in person. Then I got the news that he was coming home to see me. I was excited.

Thoughts of our meeting raced through my head. I'd been told several times that I looked like him. I wondered what he would say to me. *Will he love me? Has he been longing to see me as much as I've been to meet him? Will he have a gift for me? What will we do? Where will we go?* So many questions haunted my mind.

The day arrived; I was nervous, but my fears soon melted in joy when I saw the expression on his face. He hugged me, and it felt so good. We were finally face to face! What a relief to hear him say he'd like to get to know me. Plans were made for the entire weekend around things I liked to do, which made me feel very special. I also met one of my brothers who came with him. It was fun. I was on cloud 99. The connection had been made; now I had a baseline to refer to when I thought about him; I looked forward to seeing him again.

As I grew older, I thought of my heavenly Father whom I have not seen, but I've been anticipating our meeting. He has written many love letters to me through the Bible. He says that He's coming back to take me to where He is so we can be together and there'll be no more parting. I know He wants to see me and be with me throughout eternity. Every day He shows me glimpses of Himself, and before He comes back, I am going to look like Him. I look forward to meeting Him face to face. What an absolutely wonderful experience that will be, unlike any other! Let's be there for that out-of-this-world spectacular reunion!

Maple Smith

The Tree

He shall be like a tree planted by the rivers of water,
that brings forth its fruit in its season, whose leaf also shall not wither;
and whatever he does shall prosper. Ps. 1:3, NKJV.

The townhouse where I live is located in a group of homes in a fenced community. All around the community, both within and without the fence, are beautiful, tall trees. From my bedroom, which is on the second floor of our home, I can look through the large sliding doors across from my bed and see these trees. Especially in the spring and summer I like to have my morning worship on the bed, with the blinds open, so my eyes can feast on the trees and the azure sky, helping me feel closer to God.

But in the winter and fall it's different. Those same beautiful trees lose all their leaves and stand stark and bare—almost lonely in their stance against the sky. One winter day as I was driving into our compound I spied a tree that looked lush and green. Strange for that time of year. I stopped my car and stepped out to take a closer look at this tree. Approaching, I realized it was an evergreen tree. Evergreens, as their name implies, are always green. They stay the same in all the seasons and keep their beautiful vibrant green color no matter how frigid the weather.

As I walked back to my car I remembered the text from Psalm 1:1. "[He/She] shall be like a tree planted by the rivers of water." The thought came to mind that God is calling me, calling us, to be like that evergreen tree. In all circumstances, whether good times or bad, I can always be beautiful, lush, growing, and bearing fruit.

Why? Because I am planted by the "rivers of water"—Jesus, my Savior.

I read a little about why an evergreen tree always remains green. My research revealed that evergreens are specially adapted to live in harsh climates.

Ah, something clicked. This world's climate is unrelentingly harsh, yet God still calls us to be "evergreen" Christians. A challenge, to be sure, but not an impossibility. Our Savior calls us to spend daily time with Him, drinking deeply from the water of life He gives us so freely. You see, that's the secret for evergreen-Christian beauty, growth, and spiritual productivity.

What lies ahead for you during this untried day? Only God knows. But He can help us live in harsh times when we spend time with Him each day. So drink, my friend. Drink deeply.

Heather-Dawn Small

Hard to Forget

Anyone who is among the living has hope. . . .
the living know that they will die, but the dead know nothing. . . .
Moreover, no one knows when their hour will come. Eccl. 9:4-12, NIV.

She is an exemplary woman. She is quiet but amiable and supportive of God's work, of her husband, family, and friends. In the things we have done together, and the places where we have been together, she was also supportive—especially for a good cause. After I presented the Mission Spotlight, a DVD about mission work, one Sabbath morning, she whispered to me, "That is where my husband and I want to give." She brought a good donation. She also did not mind carrying a heavy bag of gifts for everybody anytime she came back from a trip.

One morning I received news from a friend, "Mrs. M died just a few hours ago." I could not believe what I heard. Her image kept on flashing in my mind. For a moment my whole body froze. I could not get up from where I was sitting. This was really a shock to me.

Well, she is gone. There is nothing else we can do. But rather than thinking those thoughts, I realized there are things we can do. We can listen and be silent, or we may say to the family and friends, "I am here; I am with you."

We can mourn with those who mourn. Let people grieve—it is healthy. It speeds up the grieving process. Ecclesiastes 3:1 tells us: "There is a time for everything and a season for every activity under the heavens" (NIV). Verse 4 of this chapter says there is "a time to weep and a time to laugh, a time to mourn and a time to dance" (NIV).

We can also ask, "Is there anything you need? Is there anything you want me to do? Do you want me to answer your phone?" It can be something very simple—you just need to ask or look around for an opportunity to show your love. We can be creative with any appropriate words and actions that are comforting. Again, it does not have to be something profound.

Most important, we need to allow the Holy Spirit to guide the comforting party and the grieving family and friends. We may be more aware as the Holy Spirit whispers directions of what to do when there is death. After the apostle Paul assured us that Jesus is coming again, he offered us this reassurance: "Therefore encourage one another with these words" (1 Thess. 4:18, NIV).

Esperanza Aquino Mopera

Fragrance

*As for the perfume which thou shalt make,
ye shall not make to yourselves according to the composition thereof:
it shall be unto thee holy for the Lord. Ex. 30:37.*

Most people like perfume, I'm sure. I like it too, but I seldom wear it because I'm in too much of a hurry to get dressed and out of the house and on my way. Only on a special occasion do I look for my perfume. A busy mother, as usual.

Even God loved to smell the perfume that arose from the altar of incense before the veil in the tabernacle. The perfume represented the prayers of the saints going up to heaven. How lovely to know that God loves to hear our prayers like a sweet, precious perfume!

This same God had also created beautiful flowers that emit different perfumes to add to the fresh air around them. Isn't it a wonderful, relaxing experience to visit a flower garden and smell their perfume in the air?

Perfume seems to go along with beautiful things like beautiful flowers. So man has captured perfume from flowers for beautiful women to wear. If the perfume at the sanctuary was holy unto the Lord, perhaps the Lord has something to teach us. As I said, the incense represented the prayers of God's people. Not all prayers are acceptable. So we need to look into our hearts to make our prayers acceptable. The beauty of the heart is important. I consider the Bible woman Abigail to be a woman with such beauty. Of her it is said, "The piety of Abigail, like the fragrance of a flower, breathed out all unconsciously in face and word and action. The Spirit of the Son of God was abiding in her soul. Her speech, seasoned with grace, and full of kindness and peace, shed a heavenly influence" (Ellen G. White, *Patriarchs and Prophets,* p. 667).

Hannah's prayer was also like the sweet-smelling perfume that God accepted, and He blessed her with a beautiful son.

My favorite author, Ellen G. White, has written, "If our lives are filled with holy fragrance, if we honor God by having good thoughts toward others, and doing good deeds to bless others, it matters not whether we live in a cottage or a palace" (*Testimonies for the Church*, vol. 5, p. 488). God is interested not only in our outward beauty but what's in our heart. Let us go out to be perfume, a sweet fragrance, in our family and community this day.

Birdie Poddar

Caught by the Law

But where sin increased, grace increased all the more. Rom. 5:20, NIV.

The flashing lights in my rearview mirror startled me. I had finished preaching in a nearby small town and was on my way to meet my husband for a picnic lunch close to home. I had no idea why I was being stopped, since my mind was on other things.

The officer questioned me, "Lady, do you know how fast you were going?"

"No, sir, I have to admit I really hadn't noticed," I frankly responded.

"You were going 40 in a 20-mile zone." So, of course, I apologized to him. I told him that I wasn't paying attention because I was on my way to meet my husband for lunch. I explained that I knew I was running late, but I did not realize I was going that fast! I told him that I was really sorry, and I knew he was right to stop me. I apologized several more times. Then he said, "I'll tell you what, lady, I won't give you a ticket this time, but don't do it again!"

I promised I wouldn't and thanked him again.

When I got to the park, my husband was waiting and wondering what had taken me so long. The first thing I said to him were these words: "Law and grace have new meaning for me!"

He laughed as he replied, "You got stopped by the police!" He could not believe the officer didn't give me a ticket when I was going double the speed limit.

"Honey," smiled my husband. "That's not just grace—that's *amazing* grace!"

Yes, I was guilty as stated. I had not planned to speed. Nevertheless, I was speeding down that hill. I just wasn't paying attention. But that was not an excuse. The truth is I had no excuse. It's true that I was sorry for speeding. I try to obey the law. I know what can happen when drivers don't pay attention to their driving. But the fact is I had no excuse for breaking the law. The officer was more than kind to me that day. He gave me grace in every sense of the word. Perhaps he sensed that my apologies were heartfelt. I was not just saying the words I knew he wanted to hear. I was truly sorry.

That day I gained just a tiny glimpse of how God treats me when I am guilty without excuse.

Grace!

Ginny Allen

My God Is Real

*Have I not commanded you? Be strong and of good courage;
do not be afraid, nor be dismayed, for the Lord your
God is with you wherever you go. Joshua 1:9, NKJV.*

It was a serene morning as I petitioned my Savior again and again regarding my granddaughter's desire to be accepted into the hospital residency program. In fact, I was sure that my God had reserved a place for her in a church-sponsored hospital in another state. They had paid for her and her preacher husband to come and look over the place and meet with the staff. It was a very promising lead. All of us were sure this was the one, even though it was in another state from where they were stationed. Today was supposed to be "Victory Day." I prayed and waited, anxious to hear the good news. In less than an hour the telephone rang. It was my granddaughter on the line, but her voice sounded disappointed.

"Grandmother, I was not accepted for placement in that hospital."

When I asked what she would do now, she replied, "I'll just have to send out more applications and wait another year."

"God," I implored when I put down the phone, "how could You have allowed that to happen?" Then in the quietness of my bedroom, I distinctly heard a voice saying: "I am the leader; she is the follower. Let her follow Me."

I live alone, so I was surprised at the sound of another voice in my house. I checked to see if anyone had entered my room. No one was there. I quickly realized that it was the voice of my Lord. I simply answered, "Yes, Lord, I heard Your voice." I was literally shaking.

The next day the telephone rang again, *Who is this now?* I wondered. It was my granddaughter on the line. She was all excited. "Grandmother, I just received placement in a hospital 10 minutes from where we live!" That was more than a dream come true. With penitent hearts we cried, prayed, and asked forgiveness for trying to let humanity override divinity.

Now my granddaughter is safely installed in the hospital 10 minutes from their home. Our mighty God had chosen that placement just for her!

Is your God real? Mine is real! He speaks to me. He leads; will we follow?

Gloria Joyce Crarey McCalla

Dogs and Cats

Jesus said to him, "You shall love the Lord your God with all your heart, with all your soul, and with all your mind." Matt. 22:37, NKJV.

For anyone who has or has had a pet, you know it's quite amusing to observe their behavior. Dogs are my favorite, though my husband and I have had only one dog and multiple cats. Our dog Leesha taught us much about love. Her obedience, willingness to please, gentleness, and loving nature made her a joy to be around. She was always eager to greet us and bestow her affection. She was loving and kind to people, as well as to other creatures. The only time she didn't like someone was when that person intended some type of harm; she had very good discernment of character. She was very loyal and protective of me. We were truly a family.

Cats, on the other hand, tend to be less sociable or sociable only on their own terms. They will greet you when and if they feel like getting up from their cozy place of repose. They are generally not loyal to any one person, but tend to seek affection from anyone willing to bestow such upon them. As far as obedience goes, well, that is definitely something they do only when they feel like it. They can be loving and affectionate on their terms and for brief periods of time.

As I was thinking about how determined our cat Alaska was to disobey my request for her to move out from under my feet so I wouldn't trip and hurt us both, it occurred to me that dogs and cats can teach us much about spiritual things.

It has often been noted that we can see God's unconditional love through a dog's companionship. I do believe that a dog can be an object lesson from God to show us His great unconditional love for us, no matter who we are or what we do. My husband and I have experienced that with Leesha.

To me, cats serve as a reminder of sin as they reveal to us our sinful human nature—our I'll-do-it-myself attitude, which leads us to act independently of God. Rather than obey when asked, cats—like humans—tend to obey when they feel like it, on their own terms.

I don't know about you, but I want to be obedient to God. I want to reflect His character of love to others. I want to be eager to be in His presence and show my love for Him. In essence, I want to be more like a dog. What about you?

Samantha Nelson

Miracles Still Happen

Before they call I will answer;
while they are still speaking I will hear. Isa. 65:24, NIV.

I came home after a tiresome shift at the children's hospital emergency room where I worked. I took a good shower, rested a little, and went to the college. When I returned, I went walking with a friend. We had already walked quite a ways, and we were coming back home when I suddenly twisted my foot. At the moment, I did not feel much pain, only discomfort. I thought that the pain would pass soon, but it was about to get worse.

When I got home, I realized that my foot was swollen and starting to hurt. Soon the pain intensified and became so intense that I could not put my foot on the floor. My husband was working in another city, and we met only on the weekends, so I was home alone. I went to bed and tried to sleep, but I couldn't—the pain was too strong. The telephone in my bedroom was broken, and I could not walk to the other telephone in the living room to call my sister to go with me to the hospital so I could get an X-ray. I tried to put my foot on the pillow and stay still, but it did not help. The pain was unbearable. I had already asked God for help, but I had such little faith at that moment that nothing happened. I got out of bed and tried to hop on one foot to the living room to reach the telephone, but when I put the foot down, the pain I felt was so extreme that I could not stifle a scream of pain. It was then that I cried out with all the strength in my soul: *Lord, have mercy on me. Help me. I am here alone. I just have You. Touch my foot and take this pain. Please, Father, help me!* At that moment I felt like someone was there beside me. A peace flooded my heart, and the unbearable pain was alleviated. I returned to bed and finally fell asleep. The following day I realized that my prayer for help had been answered, for the pain had completely subsided and my foot was not swollen anymore.

What a wonderful God we have! The same God who has done so many miracles in the past still continues to act in the lives of those who seek Him. He is always ready to help us in times when we see no way out.

So today my prayer is to help heal the pain of people who are agonizing in this world of pain and suffering with the same urgency with which I cried out to God. He healed me. May I help others find that same healing.

Ana Maria Nogueira Nascimento Brandão

God Opens Prison Doors

*The spirit of the Lord God is upon me; because the Lord
hath anointed me to preach good tidings unto the meek;
he hath sent me to bind up the brokenhearted, to proclaim liberty to the
captives, and the opening of the prison to them that are bound. Isa. 61:1.*

One unusually beautiful Sabbath afternoon in February, our music ministry group drove more than two hours to get to a prison. Upon our arrival we were informed we'd not be able to give the concert or even enter the prison. Several employees had called in sick, and prison authorities couldn't guarantee adequate security for an event such as this. Despite our pleas, they insisted that we leave, saying they could make no exceptions to prison policy.

Convinced it was God's will that we give this concert, we formed a circle, joined hands, and prayerfully put the matter in His hands. Minutes later one of the guards came back and said, "I can't believe this, but the supervisor changed his mind. You can come on in."

The warden in charge said our concert had been moved from a small east wing room (accommodating 40) to the large courtyard that serviced four wings—but only one at a time. Until today. Guards escorted us as we set up our sound equipment and then watched approximately 400 men from *two* wings file into the courtyard. A few guards were shaking their heads in amazement at this turn of events.

As I stood up to sing before 50 curious onlookers, I felt an evil presence, a choking sensation around my throat, and a sense that our efforts would be in vain. *Lord,* I prayed, *I can't do this without You.* In faith I stepped forward and began to sing. My initially weak voice gained strength with each note. I felt a tremendous sense of peace. In just moments the other 350 inmates, standing on opposite sides of the enclosure, began to move in our direction. After the music someone shared about God's love and forgiveness. By the close of the meeting we'd handed out literature and enrolled more than 100 inmates in our correspondence Bible study school!

That day we experienced many miraculous events. Lives were changed because we believed in God's power to intervene. I want to encourage and challenge you, my friend, when you think circumstances of life are holding you prisoner. Step aside and, in faith, let God open your prison doors and set you free! Will you let Him do that for you right now?

Vonda Beerman

Illness

To everything there is a season,
a time for every purpose under heaven. Eccl. 3:1, NKJV.

It could be worse. It could be a heart-wrenching birth defect, childhood leukemia, paralysis, or any other unimaginable tragedy. It isn't terminal, but the shadows will linger every day for the rest of my life. There is nowhere to hide. Nothing will be the same again. This isn't a bad dream. College is supposed to be the time of one's life, not this. I may need intervention if an illness does not dissipate within days, but normally, illness is a short-lived setback. Chronic diseases defy this normal course of events, and are both a blessing and a nightmare, facilitating deepened perspective and empathy, while resolidifying and strengthening heavenly connections. The nightmare aspect is self-explanatory, especially for those suffering much worse than I.

In the end one must learn to balance the sentiments of perceived injustice with life's blessings and living life to the fullest. I am learning to accept uncertainty, ambiguity, and having to be on top of homework and studying; there may or may not be the physical strength or well-being to complete tasks tomorrow—or even five hours from now. There is adaptation, transition, reassessment, reflection, and forgiving: challenges when feeling trapped in another dimension, isolated, disoriented, unsure of the future, hungry for answers that may or may not exist. It's hard to place everything in God's hands, but that is all one can do, especially when the cold, stoic, impersonal, white-coated health-care model fails.

Chronic disease is about taking life one-day-at-a-time and remembering that pure, genuine faith the size of a mustard seed really can move mountains. Yet my journey isn't over. Things are light-years better, not thanks to the medical institution, but rather, lifestyle, reassessment of life's priorities, and faith. I truly believe illness was a wake-up call that the former status quo wasn't part of the plan for my life, and the necessary lifestyle changes and reflection ultimately brought me closer to His image. With the adjustments made, I could not be happier. I have found my passions, possibly even what my mission and role is on this earth. Along the way I have encountered some amazing people, not only as individuals, but in the image of the Lord. No matter what happens now, there is a plan and a purpose for my life; there is a reason for everything under the heavens, and He will be there every step of the way.

Erin Parfet

Everlasting Oil Well

I shall give [her] . . . a fountain . . . springing up
into everlasting life. John 4:14, NKJV.

My dear late cousin, Cheryl Roth Smith, fading in a Denver, Colorado, hospice facility a few years back, weakly yet confidently shared with those of us gathered about her bed one of the reasons she was at peace with God's will for her cancer-ridden body. Some of us had never heard the story that she weakly shared with us, radiance glowing on her face:

"In my little Bazine, Kansas, church," she began, "where my mother faithfully took us each week, I learned about the power of prayer. By my eighth-grade year I longed to have true Christian friends. One of my older cousins who attended a Christian high school told me, 'It's so great to study in a school where all the kids believe in Jesus!'

"'How much does it cost to go to that school?' I asked. My heart sank at her response. My struggling family scraped a living off the land—mostly wheat and maize farming, income heavily dependent on the whims of weather. Since my dad didn't attend church much, I hesitated even to bring up this fervent desire of my heart. Yet one evening during supper this burden was so heavy on my mind that I just blurted out, 'I'd sure like to go to a Christian school next year!'

"'Too expensive!' retorted Dad. His stern look silenced me. Almost jokingly, he added, 'Tell you what, though. They're drilling for oil on our property. If they strike oil, you can go to the Christian school.' He chuckled and shook his head before inhaling his supper. After finishing the dishes, I slipped into my tiny bedroom and dropped to my knees in prayer.

"*Dear Jesus,* I wept, *if You want me to go to the Christian high school,* please *let them find oil on our property. But only if it's* Your *will.* A few weeks later Dad drove into the barnyard, looking dazed. In response to Mother's questioning look, he murmured, 'They found it . . . oil! I guess Cheryl's going to Christian high school after all.' I called it *my* oil well because it didn't stop producing for my Christian education—until just after I graduated."

My cousin's peaceful smile wordlessly affirmed that God's oil well was still producing on her behalf. This time, the sacred oil of grace to anoint her current needs, along with rich memories of God's provision in the past—thereby bringing strength and comfort for her present ordeal. So, in retrospect, Cheryl's oil well never did run dry. Neither, my friend, will yours.

Carolyn Sutton

A Dog's Love

Dear friends, let us love one another, for love comes from God. Everyone who loves has been born of God and knows God. 1 John 4:7, NIV.

Years ago a friend told me God sends angels to help us. "Arfangels," he said. "They are all over the place."

"Arfangels? You must mean archangels," I responded.

"No," he insisted, "Arfangels; you hear them sayin, 'Arf, arf.'"

I thought of that story recently when I read about Jasmine, an "arfangel" living in Warwickshire, England. The story came online from 2003. It was accompanied by photos and a confirmation of its truth from Snopes.com. A local policeman opened a garden shed and found a frightened and abandoned dog locked inside. He took the dirty and skinny female greyhound to a sanctuary, a place for abused, abandoned, or otherwise needy animals.

It took weeks, but the owner, Geoff Grewcock, and his staff won her trust and restored the dog to full health. They named her Jasmine. Now a beautiful dog, they began to look for an adoptive home. But Jasmine liked the sanctuary, and began welcoming all arrivals.

Geoff tells of an early incident. "We had two puppies that had been abandoned. They were tiny, and when they arrived, Jasmine grabbed one by the scruff of the neck in her mouth and put him on the settee. Then she fetched the other one and sat down to cuddle them.

"But she is like that with all our animals, even rabbits. She takes the stress out of them, and it helps them not only feel close to her, but to settle into their new surroundings. Jasmine, the timid, abused, deserted waif, became the sanctuary's resident surrogate mother." The list of youngsters she has cared for comprises five fox cubs, four badger cubs, fifteen chicks, eight guinea pigs, two stray puppies, fifteen rabbits, and one deer fawn; tiny Bramble, 11 weeks old, was found semiconscious in a field. At the sanctuary, Jasmine cuddled up to her to keep her warm and went into the full foster-mom role. "They are inseparable," said Geoff.

There are times God uses His creatures not only to minister to other animals but to humans as well. Nature calls out "God is love," in every creature. Dogs are especially apt at caregiving. Remember to love the "arfangel" in your life.

Ella M. Rydzewski

The Home Invaders

There shall no evil befall thee, neither shall
any plague come nigh thy dwelling. Ps. 91:10.

My husband held out a long box cutter. "This isn't ours, is it?" he asked. "I found it in the dried-up daisies by the front door." We looked at each other, and said at the same time, "The home invaders!" Strangely enough, I had felt no fear the night the home invaders came to our home. The sight of that wicked cutter reminded us once again what we had been saved from that fateful night.

We had returned from a meeting, tired, and Don went straight to bed. I had a strong impression to stay awake, so I remained in my clothes and went into our study (located on the back of the second floor). This was the first miracle of the night.

It was 1:45 a.m. when I heard a soft knock on the front door, downstairs. One of the dogs came into the study and cocked his head, looking at me intently. "You heard it too, didn't you?" I whispered to him. We walked to the top of the steps, and looked silently at the front door. Someone was trying to open it. By knocking, they were checking to see if anyone was awake.

I aroused Don, and told him someone was attempting to enter. He went to an upstairs window and looked out. Three husky young men were at our doorstep. Before I could call 9-1-1, a police car with flashing lights pulled up in front of the house. This was the second miracle.

The young policeman wisely called for backup, and before long the street was filled with flashing lights. The doorbell rang, and a policeman identified himself. When I opened the door, both he and the young men, now in custody, stared in surprise at a fully clothed woman.

One of the men was immediately handcuffed and sat on the cold curb; he was wanted in another town. The two younger teens, we later found out, were being initiated into a gang, and a home invasion was an important test to see how "tough" they were.

The police quickly found a stun gun that had been tossed under our car, and other items intended for use in the assault, as well as a number of stolen items in the men's pickup. "You are very lucky," an older policeman told me. "These guys had terrible plans for you!"

"God was protecting us," I told him. "He told me to stay awake tonight." The policeman nodded his head, agreeing that he had just witnessed a miracle rescue by the Lord.

Teresa Sales

A Special Visitation

When You said, "Seek My face," my heart said to You,
"Your face, Lord, I will seek." Ps. 27:8, NKJV.

When Christmas approaches, my husband and I start our annual road trip to visit loved ones. Our schedule is strenuous—3,000 miles, four hotels, in nine to 10 days. Together we visit his family in Texas. I drive on alone to New Mexico to see my sister, Sunny. In 2012 a ministry trip cut short our holiday trek. I couldn't visit my sister. The following year she repeatedly expressed her anticipation of my arrival. Although we were wearied from 23 hours of travel in two days, my eagerness for our reunion was mounting. As I pulled into town, my sister phoned me. "What do you mean you're already here? You're several hours early," she said in an irritated tone. "I'm not ready! I still have cleaning to do, and I haven't gone grocery shopping yet!"

I volunteered to run her errands and promised not to arrive before the appointed hour. Finally I knocked on her door. Her greeting was jarring: "Don't hug me, I'm sweaty. Just go lie on the bed while I put these groceries away." When she joined me, she plopped onto the bed and promptly fell asleep, exhausted by her last-minute preparations. At 10:00 p.m. I returned to my lonely hotel room. Busy, she requested I not arrive until noon the next day—she slept through most that visit too, when she wasn't distracted by the TV. Conversation was sparse. I was frustrated that we had only one more day together. Feeling ignored and underappreciated, I shared with her on our final day my disappointment over lack of conversation and fellowship.

"What do you mean?" She sounded genuinely surprised. "We talk on the phone every day, don't we? And I see you on 3ABN TV all the time." Suddenly a thought struck me: *Is this how God feels when the Sabbath rolls in and we don't embrace Him with a warm welcome?* How often do we wear ourselves out in Sabbath preparation, only to greet the special visitation of our Lord with a lukewarm welcome on Friday evening? Do we spend our day of rest sleepily ignoring intimate conversation and fellowship with Him since we talk with Him daily in prayer? Do we take His divine presence for granted on His special day?

O Lord, forgive us for the times we ignore and underappreciate You. Help us truly seek Your face—especially on Your holy day!

Shelley Quinn

Atlas Lesson

Do nothing from selfishness or empty conceit,
but with humility of mind. Phil. 2:3, NASB.

The man whose story I was writing had grown up in Germany and also spent years in Russia, the United States, England, South Africa, Burundi, and Canada. He reached for an atlas to show me the location of a town in England. Before he opened the book, he glanced at the cover. "This one's published in Britain," he said, more to himself than to his wife or me. He opened the atlas to the first pages.

I puzzled for an instant before the impact hit me. "England is first in this atlas, isn't it?" I asked.

"Yes," he answered. He noted the recognition on my face and confirmed my conclusion. "Yes. Wherever an atlas is published, that's usually the first part of the world shown."

My friend pointed out on the map where Lincolnshire was located, but days later I still pondered atlases. I had been born and raised in North America, and so it had never crossed my mind that someplace other than North America would be first in any atlas. It wasn't wrong to have North America first. But for me not even to consider that some other location could be first suddenly seemed a bit arrogant—at the least, uninformed.

I began thinking of people from other countries and continents and realizing that they probably love their nation just as I love mine. Their village or countryside provided treasured memories as does the Northwest U.S.A. farm of my childhood. The way things are done in their household likely seem as right to them as the way I do things in mine.

That's when Paul's words in Philippians 2:3 began to mean more to me. "Do nothing from selfishness or empty conceit, but with humility of mind." In other words, don't look at everyone else by focusing on yourself first and thinking your way is right. Look first to understand a person's heart from right where they are. Whether a next-door neighbor comes from a different culture, or I travel to a different continent, or my spouse handles a situation differently than I, peace comes when I remember the lesson of the atlas, when I look outside my own backdrop and love "with humility of mind."

Helen Heavirland

Encourage One Another

Therefore encourage one another and build each other up,
just as in fact you are doing. 1 Thess. 5:11, NIV.

For many years Dorothy and I were good friends at church, even though probably many of the other members didn't even know who Dorothy was. She would always come just for the sermon hour, sit beside me, and leave soon after. We lived in a rural area, and her home was about 10 miles west of the church, and I lived about 10 miles northeast, so I never went to her house and she never came to mine. None of her family were members of our church, so I never met them in person, either.

The one thing that made me feel uncomfortable at times about this arrangement was that Dorothy was always very talkative. But it wasn't just idle chitchat. Her burden was her family, and often she would share with me a problem one of her seven grown children was having, or sometimes it was a grandchild. She would ask me to join her in prayer for them, which I was always glad to do, and she assured me that she was praying for my quadriplegic son. One time she was especially happy because one of her six sons had joined a church, even though it wasn't her church.

Then my son and his wife decided to join a smaller church in our area, and since I usually rode to church with them, I didn't get to attend my church very often. For several years I saw Dorothy infrequently and wondered if she had found another friend at church. I didn't realize she had any serious health problems until one day I saw her obituary in our local newspaper. It was quite a shock to me as I realized I wouldn't see her in church again. I asked our pastor about her, and he told me that her family had asked him to conduct her graveside service. There they all expressed their appreciation of her Christian witness and the effect it had on their lives.

Although it was now too late, I wished I had shared with her more, been more open and encouraging. She had become a Christian as an adult, and I now realized she talked to me so much because there was no one in her family who would understand.

This can be an opportunity for you and me to ask God to help us be more encouraging when the opportunity presents itself, and to think more of others and build them up.

Betty J. Adams

The Bankrupt Golden Boy

Bless the Lord, O my soul, and forget not all his benefits,
who forgives all your iniquity, . . . who redeems your life from the Pit,
who crowns you with steadfast love and mercy, who satisfies you with
good . . . so that your youth is renewed like the eagle's. Ps. 103:2-5, RSV.

It's been said that France makes money from exporting its wine. Mongolia can't, though, because the men drink it all before it can be exported. And the nomad AltanKhuu (meaning "golden boy") was a drinker! A true-blue Mongolian from Bulgan aimag (an administrative subdivision), living out on the steppe lands of Mongolia as a nomad, he had 700 animals and a large inheritance from his parents. Pretty well-to-do for a nomad. Over time, however, his drinking and the parties he held for his drinking friends resulted in bankruptcy.

By the leading of God, AltanKhuu met a pastor, Sodbyamba, on an occasion when the "golden boy" was filled with remorse over his drinking and the subsequent, frequent abuse of his wife. Pastor Sodbyamba was very direct with him. "The only way you can overcome this bad drinking habit is to come to my church," he told him.

Since AltanKhuu was broke and had nothing better to do, he turned up at church one Sabbath, to the surprise of Pastor Sodbyamba. During the service the nomad was touched by the Holy Spirit and decided to begin Bible studies with the pastor. He was eventually baptized.

I met AltanKhuu and his wife at a family ministries retreat in Mongolia in 2012. Dressed in traditional Mongolian garb, the man attentively listened to the presentations. At the end of the retreat he was too shy to stand up and speak. So, through a friend, he said, "I am glad that I came here and was impressed by the grace of God. I have learned a lot of things during these few days. I am glad that I have put aside my work to come because I have found what is important in the life of a Christian. Spending time with God is vital—I know now what to do. I have also decided to take time to listen to my children and spend more time with my family. I am forgiven and redeemed by God's mercy and grace. I am now His child."

No longer bankrupt, this transformed nomad is experiencing God's blessings. He now has more animals than he did before, and his family loves the husband and father He has become.

Have you, like the "golden boy," given God permission to completely transform your life?

Sally Lam-Phoon

In God We Trust

Trust God from the bottom of your heart; don't try to figure out everything on your own. Listen for God's voice in everything you do, everywhere you go; he's the one who will keep you on track. Don't assume that you know it all. Run to God! Prov. 3:5-7, Message.

Brisk wind, patchy sky, warm hearts overwhelming the bone-chilling temperature. After an extended lunch the three old friends walked back to the car for the ride home. There on the snowy ground by the door was a bright quarter.

"Ah!" I reached down and retrieved the gift, voicing my thankfulness as I do every time I find a coin on the ground. The words "In God We Trust" on the coin, coupled with the unexpected finding, are a pointed reminder that no matter what is happening in life, God is trustworthy. Pennies do the "remember" job nicely, but a quarter! "This must be a *big* blessing!"

And so it was. I had been in a holding pattern for four years after losing my business, enduring bankruptcy, and then resting quietly, awaiting God's leading. A time to be treasured, a time of healing and growing. A person of action, I had learned to be still and know, to long for—but with open fingers. I had a roof and warm meals, a job to do; and waiting; waiting multiplied.

Finally, the knowledge that I needed to sell the house: the listing, the showings, and a buyer! They looked like such a strong prospect. But in the end they decided not to go the distance. We went back to more showings.

Saving for the transition had not been easy. Contemplating the cost of moving 1,100 miles to be closer to family was sobering. I kept handing the situation back to God, but again and again it found its way into my thoughts. *I think God was grinning as He dropped that quarter.*

It was a busy day, so I stopped home only to take a quick look at my computer and pick up what was needed for the next meeting. The e-mail grabbed my attention. I had no idea that the earnest money the first buyers had forfeited would come to me! No wonder God had used a quarter! The check was the exact amount I had told God we needed for the moving truck! In the next week or so two more unexpected gifts swelled the moving fund. I told the story to anyone who would listen; and I marveled at the tender care of my Provider, who not only takes care of my physical needs but gently nourishes my spirit, encouraging more and more trust.

Ardie Gallant

Lost Luggage

And my God shall supply all your need according
to His riches in glory by Christ Jesus. Phil. 4:19, NKJV.

My schedule was tight, but there would be just enough time to get into Manila late that night and then on to the conference site for my first presentation the next morning. All arrangements had been made well in advance, and just the right clothes for the steamy tropical climate had been packed for each of several meetings, including the Sabbath sermon.

The trouble began with the first leg of the journey with a delay. We would not make our connection in Chicago and on to Tokyo. My fears became reality, and we were rerouted through Hong Kong. It seemed that the miracles were falling our way, however, and we finally arrived in Manila just after midnight—three hours late and an hour's drive yet to our destination.

We made the trek through immigration and customs in near record time and went to claim our luggage. There were no familiar suitcases among the dozens that passed before us. *No,* I thought, *this can't be happening—not now.* We approached an airport official; after two hours we had to admit the luggage had not arrived with us.

With promises of a soon delivery of the luggage, we departed. I made the decision to stay up the remaining hours of the morning because my first presentation was the first address of the conference. There would be participants from all over the world, including representatives from the World Bank and United Nations. There was a lot at stake here, and my first presentation would be made in what I considered "grimy," inappropriate airplane attire.

My upbringing made me particular about appearance as well as substance. This is particularly true for how I dress. I was taught to wear the right clothes for every occasion. My perspective on proper attire for a professional Christian woman has not been lost. Now I would stand before this august assembly, and I had no suitable clothes.

As I attempted to shrink into oblivion the Lord magnified the message, and all went well with the speech. It seems that listeners did not even notice my clothes. So it was with each of the presentations that followed. While I shrank behind someone else's clothes—since my luggage never arrived—God blessed the presentations. We serve a faithful God who has promised to supply all our need. We must learn the difference between our needs and our wants.

Ella Louise Smith Simmons

All Fall Down

For a just man falleth seven times, and riseth up again:
but the wicked shall fall into mischief. Prov. 24:16.

A childhood game I had played for many years began to resound in my head as I nursed yet one more fall. The way I learned it was "Ring-a-ring o' roses, a pocket full of posies, A-tishoo! A-tishoo! We all stand up. A-tishoo, a-tishoo, we all fall down." Granted that the words of the game may vary from place to place, but as I arose from the fall the solo laughter that resonated from my apartment could probably concern my neighbors.

It was less than a month since I had sustained some fractured bones and a shifted ankle while playing an organized basketball game at my university. Since nothing remotely close had ever happened to me, I had a new set of experiences. One night I fell while trying to close a window. That fall resulted in my cast being moved down. Another day I missed a fall while trying to get down some stairs. Falls, though smaller ones, had now become a new part of my daily experience. Little imbalances on my left leg and crutches proved to be the absolute recipe for a braced fall, a real fall, or a missed fall.

One evening as I tried to stabilize my left foot to stand, I somehow miscalculated and found myself falling right back on the bed. I realized that since that one major fall a month before, these series of little falls had become easier. I once walked uprightly without the fear of falling, but now it had become part of my life.

That is when I realized how dangerous one fall can be in our spiritual walk. One fall, one mistake, can open the door to a series of small falls or mistakes. Physical falls may not always cause fractures or shifted bones, but they may affect other parts of the body. In the spiritual walk any series of falls can lead us to fall repeatedly. I realized how easy it is for us to ignore smaller falls that seem to come with least evidence or consequences. Today I thank God that He allowed me to fall so I could recognize that I need not accept small falls in my walk with Him. Today I thank God that despite the months in a cast, I learned that falling, no matter how small, can have damaging long-term effects whether physically or spiritually. I praise Him for the assurance of His Word in today's text, that though we fall, we can rise again.

Nadine A. Joseph

The Bible on Autopilot

Thy word is a lamp to my feet and a light to my path. Ps. 119:105, RSV.

I've been a Christian since childhood, and have worn out several Bibles in my 70-plus years. When someone starts to quote a Scripture verse, chances are I can finish it before they do. However, it took me many years to make friends with the Bible. Even as a Christian I found it hard to understand. I grumbled because the New Testament was so repetitious and thought it could profit by a good editor—until someone pointed out that the Gospels provide four different viewpoints of Jesus' life. Even now I often shake my head over a verse and mutter, *What did they mean by that?* But as I've prayerfully continued to read—and learn about—the Bible, I increasingly appreciate and enjoy it.

Recently the Holy Spirit woke me up to the fact that I often put the Bible on autopilot. Autopilot means doing something without really thinking. I was reading a book on Christian growth. The author began each chapter with a Scripture reference at the top of the page. I had glanced at it, ignored it, and went on into the chapter. *It's a New Testament text—probably one I've read many times before,* I reasoned. *I can get the author's point without looking it up.*

About three chapters later the Holy Spirit whispered, "Hypocrite!" Only days earlier I'd counseled someone about the importance of letting God's Word settle into our hearts! How can that happen if we avoid it? Even when we read a scripture for the umpteenth time, pausing to reread and ponder the words often brings the spiritual nurture of fresh insight.

I realized I'd gotten into a habit of ignoring Scripture references in my reading material, assuming that whatever the verse or passage said would truly support the author's point (which isn't always the case). More important, I had overlooked the value of exposure to God's Word. "All scripture is given by inspiration of God, and is profitable for doctrine, for reproof, for correction, for instruction in righteousness" (2 Tim. 3:16).

I'm thankful the Holy Spirit whispered to me that time. Now I'm working on a new habit: whenever I come across a Scripture reference, I look it up, no matter how familiar I think it may be. It may take a little longer to get through a book, but I've already found God's Word shedding welcome light on my path.

Dolores Klinsky Walker

God's Plan

"For I know the plans I have for you," declares the Lord, "plans to prosper you and not to harm you, plans to give you hope and a future." Jer. 29:11, NIV.

While growing up, I lived in the inner-city township of Wellston in St. Louis, Missouri. My mom was a teacher, and my dad was an alcoholic. When Dad drank, he became violent and took the money my mother had reserved to pay bills to buy alcohol.

During those days life wasn't easy for my sister, brother, and me, but the winter months were the hardest for our family. Often we had no electricity or gas, and had to use flashlights to do our homework. When I was 8 years old, my younger brother and I came home to a burned and boarded-up house. Dad had fallen asleep while smoking cigarettes, and our house caught on fire and burned down.

Because of all the chaos at home, I was not what teachers would call an A student. Most days I daydreamed through lesson presentations, pretending I lived in a perfect world with a nice house and a car, and that I wore new clothes, not hand-me-downs from my older sister.

When I was in seventh grade, my teacher, Mr. Medford Lloyd Brown, who was also the school's principal, introduced a lesson unit on multiplication and division of decimals to the class. Since I was the only student who understood how to solve the problems, Mr. Brown asked me to "work them out on the board" for my classmates. The confidence my teacher showed in me not only built my self-confidence but awakened my desire to teach. I have been an educator for almost 30 years, and I am currently the principal of the largest high school in the state of Missouri. Each time a student makes an appointment to speak with me, it is usually because they are experiencing some type of crisis; without fail, the problem is an issue that I experienced during my childhood.

As a result of my struggles, God has given me the opportunity to encourage thousands of young people who are trying to make sense out of life as they determine their personal "calling." I am so glad to have learned that God is not limited by our circumstances or by our past, and that He continues to turn curses into blessings for His children. "The Lord is a refuge for the oppressed, a stronghold in times of trouble" (Ps. 9:9, NIV).

Cheryol Mitchell

My Daily Bread

Give us this day our daily bread. Matt. 6:11.

I'm sure there are daily routines that all of us perform in our lives, such as eating, exercising, studying the Bible, and going to work or school. For me, it involves walking the dog at 6:30 a.m., and then I have quiet time with God. Afterward I proceed with the normal activities for the day. In the early morning when I have my "daily bread," or time spent with God, my day seems to run so much better. I have shared my devotional books with family and close friends, so when they read something they can relate to, I will get a phone call asking, "How did you like to-day's devotional?" And that will start a discussion.

Sometimes I will read devotional passages to my husband, who is legally blind. We attend meetings once a month for the visually impaired. He shared with the group about my writing ability. The group volunteered me for secretary and asked me to bring some of my readings to share with the group. I did, and they enjoyed it and agreed that I should read one at every meeting. However, after reading something at several of the meetings, there seemed to always be a reason I couldn't read at later meetings, although the group really wanted me to. I knew God was in control, and He had a plan. A few months later I was asked to read again. I wasn't sure which articles I had already read, so I asked the group which one they wanted to hear of two different suggestions. They answered, "Read both!" I explained to them that I was told to read only one, so they picked one for me to read. At this particular meeting the supervisor asked me to read the other one as well, because she wanted to know about the bus ride. Again I explained that I was told to read only one, so when she got up to start the meeting, she said, "OK, that means we can hear it next time." I agreed to bring it back.

When I was asked to read my devotions, it was a blessing and an honor. It didn't take long to realize that this was my mission field, and the medium was a devotional book of personal experiences showing God's love, and the field was the heart of a small group of people who are visually impaired, but were willing to hear of God's Word through the daily experiences of others.

We each have something we can share with someone close to us or someone we meet in our daily lives. Let's look for opportunities to share God's love.

Elaine J. Johnson

Assumptions

Do not judge by appearances, but judge with right judgment. John 7:24, ESV.

As I sorted through some files, I found a copy of an old story. I'm sure I had read it before on e-mail, and you may have too. It was about a woman waiting for a plane; she had bought some cookies to eat while waiting for her flight. As she munched some of the cookies, she became very irritated when the businessman next to her kept reaching down and eating her cookies. Finally the businessman's flight was called, and the cookie package was empty. She was really upset! But then as she approached her own gate and opened her purse for her boarding pass, there was her package of cookies! She had actually been eating his cookies!

The morning after rereading this story, I read John 7. Here was another story in which people had made assumptions but were so very wrong. Some people said Jesus could not possibly be the Messiah, because "we know where this man comes from, and when the Christ appears, no one will know where he comes from" (verse 27, ESV). Later in the chapter others said, "Is the Christ to come from Galilee? Has not the Scripture said that the Christ comes from the offspring of David, and comes from Bethlehem, the village where David was?" (verses 41, 42, ESV). They were so certain about something that they really didn't know, causing them to miss their opportunity for knowing and following the Messiah—a mistake of eternal consequences.

I think of how often I have made assumptions about someone or something only to eventually find out that I was wrong. I remember when our children were young and there was a fuss between the two, I often assumed I knew who was at fault, but if I was wise enough to investigate and to listen, I would sometimes find I had made a wrong assumption.

I am afraid that in our churches and communities we often assume that people are aware of programs, benefits, or other happenings, but they are not. And we assume that people know enough about Jesus to make a decision to follow Him.

I assume you have a personal experience with Jesus Christ and that you have the assurance that He can and will save you. If this is not true, today is the day to make it happen. We cannot assume that we will have another day or another opportunity to make that lifesaving decision. Today is the day to "judge with right judgment."

Ardis Dick Stenbakken

House Hunting

I saw the Holy City, the new Jerusalem, coming down out of heaven from God, prepared as a bride beautifully dressed for her husband. Rev. 21:2, NIV.

As the real-estate agent fumbled with the lock, Jim peeked through the window in the door. "You're gonna love this one," my husband said, giving me a wink. Floor plans, paint colors, wallpaper all swirled through my head after a long, tiring day of house hunting. Stepping into the entry, I gasped at first glimpse of the hanging chandelier and curved stairway. It was excitement around every corner. Obviously a teenager lived in the house, as an upstairs bedroom had clothes strewn all over the floor. I understood that, however, as I had teenagers of my own.

We bought the house and faced moving day with anticipation. Opening the door with our own key this time, I gasped in dismay as I saw three wires hanging down in the dining room where a beautiful chandelier had hung a short time before. I heard my husband holler from the garage, "The riding lawn mower we paid for isn't here!" Upstairs in the teen bedroom I discovered the previous strategically placed clothes had purposely covered holes in the carpet.

Anticipation and reality often don't match. But I like to think of heaven. I'm guessing that anticipation and reality won't match there, either! Sharing his Spirit-revealed excitement, Paul wrote, "No eye has seen, . . . no ear has heard, . . . no human mind has conceived—the things God has prepared for those who love him" (1 Cor. 2:9, NIV). I can hardly wait!

I like to visualize the Holy City in my imagination. The Bible actually describes it with a good bit of detail as the apostle John saw it in vision when imprisoned on Patmos. My curiosity has taken me to the commentary and the computer. I have collected pictures of the gorgeous foundation stones: red, orange, yellow, green, blue, and purple—you know, the rainbow colors. Some of the stones have mixed colors, but all are iridescent and glorious! Twelve spectacular foundation colors. And can you imagine a gate that's made of a single pearl? The city has 12 of them. John describes the streets of gold as looking like transparent glass. No street lights there or even sunshine, because the glory of God is the light. Wow!

In Revelation 21 John is like the real estate agent handing us the stat sheet of our prospective home. I can hardly wait to step over the threshold!

Roxy Hoehn

Three Rockers

That my joy might remain in you, and that your joy might be full. John 15:11.

My husband and I purchased a cozy little three-bedroom, two-bath house in a choice, pristine community. The dwelling was so convenient and commodious; we felt that when the time came, that would be an ideal place for us to retire.

All my needs were satisfied, with one exception: a recliner for the master bedroom. So I made a formal request for one rocking chair. To my surprise, I was given three rocking chairs.

The chairs were very comfortable, so I placed them in strategic areas in different rooms, and they enhanced the homey ambience of the house.

We used the chairs constantly and enjoyed the comfort and relaxation they provided. I was to discover, however, that such commodious furniture could inflict real pain. I kicked the chair—unintentionally, of course—as I hurried about the room one afternoon. Tiny, needlelike splinters pierced the big toe of my right foot as it connected with the pointed end of the rocker. *Ouch! That hurts!* The pain was severe and subsided to some degree only after I was rushed to the hospital and had the splinters removed.

The blame was mine, of course. I must admit that the chair made no move toward me. The chair was innocent. *You asked for it,* I reminded myself. Furthermore, I had requested only one but had been blessed with three chairs.

Often we inflict ourselves with behaviors that rob us of peace and diminish the joy that comes with the overflowing of the Spirit of God. Sometimes, as we react to circumstances in our lives, we upset our relationship with God; but when our relationship to Jesus Christ is right, we experience joy, real joy.

The three rockers symbolize, to me, the bounteous gifts of God. He gives abundantly more than we are able to ask or think. How do we respond to the opportunities to improve our situation in life? How do we use or misuse the blessings we receive?

The splinters are reminiscent of the thorns that come with the rose, of the imperfections that naturally accompany the seemingly perfect models we observe in life. Thank God for the perfect Model, Jesus our Savior, who supplies peace and everlasting joy.

Quilvie G. Mills

Growing Old Gracefully

Cast me not off in the time of old age;
forsake me not when my strength faileth. Ps. 71:9.

When I first became a Christian, a dear old woman came to me, patted me on the back, and said, "You are excited about Jesus now, but eventually you will be like the rest of us." *What?* She meant I would grow old spiritually and fall into the pitfalls of old-woman religion.

I never wanted old-woman religion. The old woman who lived next to me was mean, went to church every week, hated all kids, and swore like a sailor. If she was Christian, I never wanted to be one! Neither of these women understood the choke factors of being long in the church, but the psalmist certainly did. He isn't talking just about old age; he's talking about how to maintain the vigor of spirituality day after day surrounded by nursing home religious people.

One of the pitfalls of old age is confusion. We begin to think we know more than we know and make what we do know so complicated that we forget how simple it really is. Psalm 71:1 says, "Let me never be put to shame" (NKJV). It's a prayer that God will help us keep our head screwed on straight, to keep our focus on things that really matter and not get sidetracked by insignificant nonessentials.

The wicked one is constantly trying to confuse our thinking, to get us twisted and gnarled in our relationship with God and others. He uses cruelty to produce cruelty, abuse to spawn abuse, neglect to generate neglect. Soon we are not living by the golden rule; our strength and resolve fail us.

Old spiritual age can be cruel; it can make us mean. We begin to think we are God's gestapo; we are here to dissect and micromanage the young punks. We used to have a saying, "Who died and made you God?" Our spiritual years have not earned us any condemnatory privileges. We are just on a journey like the rest; we just have more dust on our shoes.

The thing we need to remember is what the psalmist says in verse 5 of Psalm 71: "You are my trust from my youth" (NKJV). The secret to growing old gracefully is to keep that fresh connection with God, keeping it about *Him*, not about what we have learned or gone through. He is our trust, yesterday, today, forever! Grow old gracefully, not just in body and mind, but in your spiritual life especially.

Angie Joseph

The Gift of Sages

The older women . . . that they be . . . teachers of good things. Titus 2:3.

We know them as the elders, wise ones, grandparents, matriarchs and patriarchs. Those who have lived their lives, raised their children, paid their dues. I first heard the word "sage" when planning an honors program with other South African sisters here in Jo'burg. The word "sage" connotes someone with wisdom. A caretaker of our past. A midwife for our future. Sages share gems such as "Baby, I can show you better than I can tell you!" I go out of my way to be in their presence. Two, in particular, have taught me many good things.

Helen Sampson, a woman of virtue, wise and powerful in word and deed, would be the last person to see Mommy alive. "Gail," my mother said to Ma Helen, "is going to need a mommy. Helen. Please . . ."

"Yes, of course, I'll be there for your children, Joyce," Helen assured her. Ma Sampson tightly held my hands as we stood beside the coffin viewing my mother's remains. Through her own tears, she whispered in my ear, "It's going to be all right, child. It's going to be all right." In many ways throughout the years, she stayed by my side. At 85 years of age, eyes bright and head held high, this quick-witted sage made the 27-hour (plus) flight with her husband and six adult children to Africa to help build a church. We loved hosting them on their layover.

Another sage, Mom Russell, appeared the day after my son Jonathan was born. Hospital chaplain at Nashville's Madison Hospital, this sweet, kindhearted woman was there for me during the postpartum emotional and physical decline I suffered. With each of my subsequent surgeries and hospital stays, Mom Russell showed up with homemade gifts, food, hugs, smiles, and well-wishes. As with Ma Sampson, Mom Russell adopted me and my family—even after my medical emergencies were resolved. She was thrilled when I revealed she was the inspiration for my eventually becoming a chaplain as well.

These two sages, long-term earth angels, allowed me room, space, and places to grow. Both were raised in the 1920s American South. Ma Sampson is Black; Mom Russell is White. Both lived their wisdom well, leading and teaching by example. Observing them, I learned, received, and followed in new footsteps. For both invited me never to be the same again.

Gail Masondo

Assurance of God's Presence

I will never leave you nor forsake you. Joshua 1:5, NIV.

I have lived most of my life in Texas, a large and geographically diverse state with mountains, vast prairies, rolling hills, piney woods, and hundreds of miles of tropical coastline. One thing Texas is missing is beautiful picture-postcard autumns. Leaves on trees in most parts of Texas simply turn from green to a disappointing brown and fall off.

Since 2005 I have lived in Maryland, where we are blessed with beautiful autumns. Each fall I thank God for allowing me to live in a place where there is an abundance of autumn glory several months each year.

Outside my patio door is a large maple tree that is ablaze with shades of red, orange, and gold each autumn. No matter how busy I am, I take time to look at it each morning before I leave for work to savor its brilliance.

Last fall its fiery colors reminded me of the pillar of fire that protected the children of Israel by night on their journey through the wilderness. It, and the pillar of cloud by day, were visible manifestations of the presence of God with the children of Israel during their 40-year journey to the Promised Land. Jesus Himself was in the pillar, guiding and protecting His people.

In our text Jesus is assuring Joshua, the leader of Israel after Moses' death, that it was time to cross the Jordan into the Promised Land, and that He would still be with them even though the pillars of cloud and fire would not be seen. What a precious promise to Joshua—and to us. He is always with us, even at times when we can't discern Him.

This same promise is repeated in the New Testament (Heb. 13:5, NIV) in a different context: "Keep your lives free from the love of money and be content with what you have, because God has said, 'Never will I leave you; never will I forsake you.'" We are not to worry about money and material possessions, because God is our provider. The next verse makes that clear: "So we say with confidence, 'The Lord is my helper; I will not be afraid.'" When we experience times in the "wilderness," whether in our spiritual lives, our relationships, our finances, or with our health or emotions, we have the assurance that God is with us constantly to comfort and guide us. Best of all, He will *never* leave us or forsake us. What a precious promise!

Carla Baker

Precious Stones

Fashion a breastpiece for making decisions—
the work of skilled hands. Ex. 28:15, NIV.

I am not a lover of jewelry. I've never bought gemstone jewelry for myself, and I've never received it as a gift—which is fine with me. For me, a well-chosen gift is a good book or CD.

Revelation 21 describes the New Jerusalem, the Christian's final home, as a city of gold and jewels. Being the type of woman that I am, I have a hard time becoming enthusiastic about these descriptions. I love the parts of Revelation 21 that talk about God dwelling in the midst of His people, but gold and jewels don't impress me.

It wasn't until a recent read-through of Exodus that I began to be excited about the gold and precious stones in Revelation 21. Although I typically yawn my way through the Old Testament passages itemizing every detail of the tabernacle, on this particular reading my attention was caught by the high priest's breastplate in Exodus 28. Verses 15-29 describe it. Listed were 12 precious stones, and on each stone was engraved the name of a tribe of Israel.

Exodus 28:29 hints toward the meaning of the gemstones on the high priest's breastplate. "So Aaron shall bear the names of the sons of Israel on the breastplate of judgment over his heart" (NKJV). As shown by the names of the 12 tribes engraved on them, the precious stones symbolized the people of Israel, and the stones were worn on the priest's breastplate to show that the high priest must always carry God's people next to his heart.

In light of Exodus 28 I began to see a new beauty in Revelation 21. In Exodus 28 the precious stones of the 12 tribes of Israel were to be put into settings of gold. In the New Jerusalem the precious stones are also set into gold. First Peter 1:7 speaks about "the genuineness of your faith, being much more precious than gold" (NKJV).

Though I may not personally be delighted by gold and gems, to many they are most valuable. God used them as a picture of how precious His people and their faith are to Him.

I'm excited about my future home because I can hardly wait to live in the presence of God. He is my treasure. That shouldn't be surprising. What is astonishing is what Exodus 28 and Revelation 21 tell us about the way God sees His people. We are His treasures, His precious stones, and He wants us as close to Him as we can be. He carries us always over His heart.

Connie Cook

Faith of a Little Girl

*I assure you that whoever does not receive the Kingdom of God
like a child will never enter it. Mark 10:15, TEV.*

It was on a Sunday afternoon. My friend and her 7-year-old daughter were in my house. While the little girl busied herself watching Bible character DVDs in the living room, the two of us had our heads buried in our books preparing for examinations that were only two days away. No sooner had we begun serious studying than a phone rang. "Aunt G," a terrified voice shouted, "they are on their way to kill me. Come and pick me up."

I knew the caller. He was a boy in his early teens who lived about 30 minutes' driving time from my place. He was very sick and having hallucinations. His father had died about a year before, and his mother was also very sick. They were members of our church. The church offered some financial assistance, and I volunteered to buy groceries and medication for the family on a weekly basis.

My friend looked at me, her face full of question marks. "Is something wrong?" she asked as she closed her book. I told her what he had said, and she too knew the issue. We looked at the pile of books on the table, looked at each other, and quickly stood up, called her 7-year-old daughter, prayed, and were in my car on our way to pick the boy up.

After driving for about 20 minutes, I noticed that my fuel gauge was on empty. *What?*

"What is it, Aunt G?" the 7-year-old asked.

"I forgot to buy fuel on Friday. The gas tank is empty." We were only 10 minutes from the boy's house, and the only gas station I knew was back beyond my house.

"Let's just continue," the little girl said. "Remember, we prayed. Jesus will see us through." Her mother and I looked at each other and continued to drive, but I was very nervous.

We drove, reached the house, picked the boy up, and drove back to our house. As we were about to arrive at the house, the little girl cleared her throat and said, "Did I not tell you that Jesus would take care of the car?"

No wonder Jesus said that we need to have the faith of a little child. And you know what? We passed our examinations.

Gertrude Mfune

God Also Cries

But when he saw the multitudes, he was moved
with compassion on them. Matt. 9:36.

Thick, humid tears fell down my cheeks. I could not contain myself. Why did my father have to have cancer? Why was his life ending so suddenly? Why was this terrible fungal infection eating him alive? I wiped my eyes and tried to keep cooking. I was making a big pot meal for the church's potluck the next day, but the tears kept coming down. I was deeply hurt. I suppose I was even mad at God for allowing this to happen. My father had always been a faithful Christian, and it seemed so unjust that he needed to suffer so much.

Slowly stirring with the wooden spoon and sobbing helplessly (even out loud), I heard the small still voice of the Holy Spirit: "I love him too, you know." It was then that I understood. God loved my father even more than I did, because He loves with an eternal love that no human can have, and He was sad too for my father's sufferings. I was moved. I wasn't alone. He was there with me, crying too.

I suddenly realized God must cry like this every day and every minute of every day as He sees His most loved creatures hurt in the midst of the problems and tribulations of this sinful planet. But what about us? Sure, just like me, when someone close to us is hurt or facing difficulties, we cry and feel deep sorrow; but how much do we feel empathy when we don't really know the person? We may be sympathetic to the situation, try to help, and even feel moved at times, but does it really touch our hearts for more than a moment? Are our feelings really affected as are those of our heavenly Father? Could this be an indication of how Satan has desensitized our hearts, bringing almost imperceptibly cold indifference toward our brethren and humanity at large?

I learned that day that it is time to weep for our fellow humans. It is time to weep for our neighbors, our societies. It is time to be emotionally involved with the sorrows of others just as Jesus did and does, because only then will we be able to care for one another in the same unity as the early Christians and the apostles did. Ellen White once said, "A revival of true godliness among us is the greatest and most urgent of all our needs. To seek this should be our first work" (*Review and Herald*, Mar. 22, 1887).

Ana Giovanella

The Changing Flower

Jesus Christ the same yesterday, and to day, and for ever. Heb. 13:8.

M an's character" is the name of a special plant given to me by a friend some time ago. My friend explained that the plant bears a beautiful flower, and she encouraged me to watch the flower carefully when it bloomed because, according to her, "You will enjoy it." So I tended to the plant, watering it daily and pulling the weeds that grew around it. Then I waited, and waited. When would I see this wonderful flower? What color would it be? Would it resemble a lily, a hibiscus, or a rose?

Finally, one morning a few months later, when I looked through the window, there to greet me was a lovely flower on my special plant. Large and white, it resembled a rose. By about 11:00, as the day grew warmer, the white color had changed to a pale pink, and later in the day to a darker pink. In the cool evening my flower was no longer white or pink, but a deep red. Each time I looked at the changing flower, it appeared more beautiful than the last time. I finally understood why my friend had suggested that I would enjoy the flower.

As I looked at my flower, I began to think of all the wonderful blessings I have received from God in the changing scenes of my own life. I thought of where God had brought me from, and all He has led me through. Just like my flower, I have experienced so many changes. It is "man's character" to change and to experience change, isn't it? Yet our God, the great "I Am," is still there watching over us, directing us, and taking care of us. Like a loving gardener, He cares for us through our changes, and promises never to leave us alone.

Truly our God never changes. He remains the same yesterday, today, and forever, as our text reassures us. What a comfort to know that no matter our situation, His love abides. No matter our unworthiness, He cares for us. James sums this situation up: "Every good and perfect gift is from above, coming down from the Father of the heavenly lights, who does not change like shifting shadows" (James 1:17, NIV).

Sisters, my prayer for you today is that we too never stray from our devotion to Him, that we constantly love and serve Him, no matter the changing circumstances, until we make it to heaven at last.

Eileen M. Joseph

Surprised by Joy

*He who began a good work in you will carry it on
to completion until the day of Christ Jesus. Phil 1:6, NIV.*

If you are anything like me, you have at some point in your life doubted yourself, felt worthless, helpless—or all of the above. And as humans, we are also quick to judge others and to see the negative in people; it's just in our nature. As such, we are never satisfied with the condition of ourselves, this world, or of those who inhabit it. We tend to be indifferent to others and their lot in life, especially those that we don't know and love. But we are not only humans; we are God's children, first and foremost. A good friend of mine once sighed, "Oh, that we could just see ourselves [and others] as Jesus sees us." We are, each and every one of us, beloved children of Christ Jesus, each granted the wonderful and perfect gift of eternal life with Him, if we only accept it. We are all heirs of His kingdom, blessed with His unfailing love. "While we were still sinners, Christ died for us" (Rom. 5:8, NIV), all of us.

In God's eyes we are all unique, valued, loved creations of His very own; some know Him, and too many don't. God adores the old man at the newspaper kiosk and the mysterious teen who hangs out in the pub just as much as He loves you and me. He yearns for their companionship in heaven just as much as He wants us there. The salvation I was so blessed to discover and understand and accept for myself is meant for the person down the street just as much as it is for me. It is for me, it is for you, it is for them. If we remember this every time we look in the mirror, it will greatly enrich our relationships with others. It will open our eyes to a bigger picture, to our purpose here on earth. God does not want anyone to miss out on paradise with Him in His kingdom—we shouldn't either. He created each of us with the intent to take us home again with Him, forgiven and justified in Him. Our purpose should be to share with as many as possible what God has done in our lives: who He is, and how they can come to know that same God and the wonderful hope He offers.

When we doubt ourselves or feel worthless, we must remember that we are not worthless in God's eyes—far from it! Let's open ourselves up for His work and plan in our lives and see what happens. I have a feeling we'll be surprised by joy.

Taylor Bajic

Hope

Be joyful in hope, patient in affliction, faithful in prayer. Rom. 12:12, NIV.

He sat alone, interacting with other students only when necessary. His face was down and hidden most of the time. When the rest of the classroom rocked with laughter, not even a smile traced his face. What was the problem?

I was in Cuba teaching family-life classes to third-year theology students at a seminary located near Havana. Most students enjoyed my classes on marriage, dating, and parenting. But something prevented a breakthrough with this man.

When I learned that one student had lost his wife recently, I guessed it to be he. This would explain his failure to interact while I was teaching the marriage material. His pain was too fresh. Several days into the course he asked to speak to me privately. My schedule was tight, but I agreed to talk with him over lunch when a translator was available.

Through the translator I learned he had pastored for 15 years. His marriage had been a good one. He was grieving deeply. I explained the stages of grief and that he needed to pass through the stages and grieve his loss. After discussing this through the translator, he asked if there was any hope that he would find another woman around his age. (He was 50.) I told him there were many 50-year-old women who would be interested in a relationship with a fine pastor who knew how to be a good husband. (We had just covered this subject in class.) He admitted with a twinkle in his eye that some ladies in his church were already inviting him over for a meal. Once again I urged him to take time to grieve the passing of his wife. And when the time came to begin dating again, to date women his own age rather than women 20 years younger.

Our lunch was over. He stood and shook my hand. And for the first time he smiled. I told him that this was the first time I had seen him smile. The next day he was a totally different person. He had a bright-blue shirt on. But the brightest thing he wore was his smile. A load had been lifted from his shoulders. He entered into class with enthusiasm and got a great laugh when he volunteered to participate in a class skit.

The change in attitude came when he had hope for the future. He was alone now; he grieved. But beyond the grief, he had hope.

Nancy L. Van Pelt

Olga, My Sweet Singer

"My thoughts are nothing like your thoughts," says the Lord. "And my ways are far beyond anything you could imagine. For just as the heavens are higher than the earth, so my ways are higher than your ways and my thoughts higher than your thoughts." Isa. 55:8, 9, NLT.

A melodious voice resounded behind me. I'd never heard it before in this care facility where my husband and I have a weekly musical program. *Who is this woman?* I pondered as I continued playing with my back to her.

Each week as months fled past Olga ministered to us with her enthusiasm and warmth. One Wednesday morning one of the caregivers pulled us aside after our program. She informed us that when Olga arrived at this facility, she wanted to die, but our music programs each week gave her the will to live. How humbled we felt that God could use us, seniors ourselves, to extend Olga's life and also bless the other residents in this facility.

Fast-forward two years. My husband and I took almost a month's vacation. When we returned, our sweet singer was missing. We were told by one caregiver that she was "over the hill." I hoped what I thought she meant was not true. To verify my hunch, I asked another caregiver, and she confirmed my worst assumptions: Olga was dying.

At the close of our program I went to her bedside, but there was absolutely no response. My heart was heavy. The next week I checked the door plate outside her room. Yes, Olga was still there. Again, after we finished I went to Olga's bedside. This time she was alert. I told her how much we missed her and asked if I could pray with her. She readily agreed. Since my mind was fixed on her departure from this world, I prayed that we would be able to go on making music together in the new earth where there would be no illness, pain, or sorrow.

Joy beyond measure flooded my soul the next week when I heard Olga's melodious voice behind me once more. At the close of our program I rushed to hug her. The words she spoke shook me to the core. "It was your prayer that healed me."

How could that be? I pondered. Even though my faith was small, God's thoughts were far above my thoughts. Now, years later, with Olga still making music behind me, all I can do is praise the awesome God we serve.

Donna Lee Sharp

In Praise of Martha

"Martha, Martha," the Lord answered, "you are worried
and upset about many things, but few things are needed—or indeed
only one. Mary has chosen what is better." Luke 10:41, 42, NIV.

Jesus loved Martha and her sister and Lazarus. John 11:5, NIV.
Poor Martha usually seems to be portrayed in a negative light; but that is hardly fair. While we should acknowledge Martha's weaknesses, I think we should also acknowledge her strengths, and I'm not referring merely to her catering skills. It is apparent that in her anxiety to prepare a meal worthy of Jesus and His friends, Martha lost her perspective. She let her anxiety spill over into frustration and annoyance with her sister and earned a gentle reproof from Jesus. But when Martha's experience is used as an illustration, that is the point at which the lesson usually ends. After this brief glimpse of Martha, we are not told her reaction. However, later events suggest that Martha responded positively to Jesus' loving rebuke.

Now, I doubt there was any radical change in Martha's personality; she probably would always be more a woman of action than of contemplation, but I'm sure her priorities changed. Martha wasn't lacking in appreciation for spiritual things, and she must have learned, as Mary, to spend time sitting at Jesus' feet. How do I know that? When we next see Martha, as John takes up the story (in John 11), she is mourning the death of her beloved brother, Lazarus. Yet in the midst of her grief and disappointment, and though bewildered by Jesus' failure to come in time to save Lazarus from dying, Martha is able to make a declaration of faith to rival Peter's.

You will recall that when Jesus asked His disciples, "Who do people say I am?" Peter, with heaven-sent insight, made the assertion, "You are the Messiah, the Son of the living God" (Matt. 16:13-17, NIV). Now, as Jesus comforts Martha, He shares with her one of the great "I am" statements recorded by John: "I am the resurrection and the life. The one who believes in me will live, even though they die. . . . Do you believe this?" Jesus asks her. Although her cheeks are stained with tears, Martha doesn't hesitate; "Yes, Lord, . . . I believe that you are the Messiah, the Son of God, who is to come into the world" (John 11:25-27, NIV). Praise God for Martha's example of tenacious faith! And praise God for a loving Savior with a special place in His heart for Martha—and for you—and for me.

Jennifer M. Baldwin

Sin's Addiction

*Don't you realize that you become the slave of whatever
you choose to obey? You can be a slave to sin, which leads to death, or you
can choose to obey God, which leads to righteous living. Rom. 6:16, NLT.*

January 2013 I underwent my fourth, and hopefully last, knee-replacement surgery. It was my third surgery on my right knee. It was very hard to accept that I would have to undergo another knee replacement and then go through the nightmare of recovery and physical therapy once more. I was still struggling to get over the pain of the third surgery just a year before, and now here I was again—facing another surgery on the same knee.

As a result of surgery number two on the right knee, I had been on very strong pain meds for a year and was just about to wean my body completely off them. Another surgery meant that the dosage of those pain meds would rise again and my journey to release my body from the medications would begin again. I think that concerned me more than the surgery.

After that fourth surgery I found myself on increased dosages of the same pain meds with a couple more added. It was my worst nightmare. I knew I could not face the pain without medication, yet having to take them caused me great concern. And so the journey began—to wean my body off the pain medications . . . again. By September 2013 I stopped taking my last pain tablet, and then the struggle began. Withdrawal. I had read about withdrawal symptoms, but this was my first time experiencing them. My body was craving those medications whether I needed them or not. I realized that my struggle was truly one of the flesh. I turned to Father in heaven for strength during the many nights I walked our hallway, unable to sleep because of cold sweats, headaches, or irritability.

As Christians, we struggle with the flesh. Paul says we become slaves to sin. Sin can be an addiction that is hard to break, The withdrawals from that sin can result in sleepless nights as we struggle to deal with the desire for the sin. Paul tells us that the grace of God sets us free from sin's addiction (Rom. 6:15). And that's why we need to die to self each day and choose to live in Christ Jesus (verses 6, 7), for only in Jesus can we be free. And it *can* be done. Sin doesn't have to control our lives. I've found with Jesus at my side—and in my heart—I can truly do all things.

Heather-Dawn Small

Witnessing Regardless

And He said to them, "Go into all the world and
preach the gospel to every creature." Mark 16:15, NKJV.

As a fifth-generation Adventist Christian, I always knew that I was commissioned to share the news of Jesus Christ's salvation and soon return, as today's text reminds us. Now well past middle age, I told myself that I had a challenge that precluded me from complying. I have MS (multiple sclerosis), and my legs are virtually nonfunctional. Yet I knew other mobility-challenged people have still answered the call. Why hadn't I?

A cogent one-liner sprang to mind in the midst of my wonderment: "To spread news, just tell three people, and they'll tell others." Now I had a simple way to implement that mandate: minister to the three aides who assist me each morning.

The very next morning I started my plan. After helping me dress, Lee,* the attendant of the day, accompanied me to the living room where Mom and I had our daily devotions. I simply invited her to join us. Soon that became a treasured ritual for us all. After the second day, Lee mused fondly, "I haven't had 'morning prayers' since I lived with my grandfather."

Tara* seemed virtually unmoved by our morning activity. But one morning when she and I were in our rose garden, she asked, "Can we sing 'I Come to the Garden Alone' for worship today? It's my favorite. My mom used to sing it when I was little."

The next month Melissa* read aloud the day's text from a contemporary version of the Bible. I actually saw the Holy Spirit at work in that moment. "Wow," she said, wiping away a single tear. "God must be nudging my side. He needed me to see this."

We may never know who planted the gospel seed or watered the shoot until we get to heaven. We may not even know what the seed was: a smile, a gentle word, a listening heart. Nor will we always be sure of what the watering was. But there is a quote floating in cyberspace that suggests we often turn to God for help when our foundations are shaking, and then we learn that it is God who was shaking them.

Thank You, God, for the shaking—the infirmities that You used to bring me closer to You. In Your own powerful way, You've shown me that I can witness regardless.

Glenda-mae Greene

---

*not her real name

Three Are Better Than Two

Let your light so shine. Matt. 5:16.

Recently two of our grandchildren, Baraka and Malala, came for a visit from New York City. We are always excited to have them come. Our nine days together passed quickly and soon it was time for their return to the "Big Apple." On the day they left they reported that, by accident, one of three lightbulbs in the ceiling fan in one of the bedrooms had been broken by a "flying object" they had been tossing. I didn't think it would be difficult to replace. The day after they left, I went to the breaker box and turned off the power to that room, then got the ladder and went up to replace the bulb.

I soon found that the bulb was broken off in the light socket. In my effort to remove it with pliers, I destroyed the socket. What would I do now? Either call the electrician and pay a costly sum or replace it myself for much less. All the while my husband cautioned me not to bother with it right away since the two remaining bulbs were working and providing sufficient light to the room. However, I feared an electrical fire. Knowing my determination, he left me to my work, reminding me to be sure the power was off, as he left for a meeting.

The next thing I did was go online and find instructions for replacing a ceiling fan light socket. It looked simple enough, and after a quick trip to Home Depot I had what I needed for the job. Even though it took a little longer than anticipated, I completed the task, and all three lights were burning again. I was proud of myself as I stood back and looked at my work.

Then I thought: sometimes light is all around us, not altogether sufficient, but accepted as such. And sometimes we are content to exist in someone else's light, rehearsing their stories as though we have none. Our testimonies can be "points of light" and encouragement for those they are shared with. God does wonderful things for all of us, but the light of another's testimony is not sufficient for my life. I must bring light to my own story.

It is not enough to tell someone else's story. We must share our own and let God use it to shine light for still others so that they, too, will be encouraged to recognize and share their own witness with the world. Just as with our bedroom lights, three are better than two, and then it is necessary to walk in your light, *the* Light.

Gloria J. Stella Felder

Lessons From the Garbage Truck

*While it is said, To day if ye will hear his voice,
harden not your hearts. Heb. 3:15.*

A s I was reading my devotional book one morning, I was reminded of the above text. The trash had not been placed in front of our home as usual because my husband was not at home, so I knew I would have to do it.

From a far distance I could hear the garbage truck coming; I caught all the sounds that I'm accustomed to hearing and the screeching of the truck as it stopped at each house. But I kept saying to myself, *I still have time to get the trash out. They will not get here before I can get the trash outside.* Furthermore, I still had some trash cans in the house to empty.

This decision reminds me of trash that may be in my life: trash of procrastination, complacency, distractions, excuses, and time for proper study of God's Word. I hear the sounds of His coming: wars and rumors of wars, pestilences, secularism and materialism, catastrophes in divers places, spiritual decline, and a falling away from the Word of God. But am I taking action?

The Lord says in His Word: "For yet a little while, and he that shall come will come, and will not tarry" (Heb. 10:37). He is sending these warning sounds each and every day to help us prepare to meet Him. He will not delay too much longer. He wants to save us.

As I pondered these thoughts, I made a decided effort to get up and get the trash outside before the garbage truck arrived at our home. I also decided, by the grace of God, to submit to Him every day, adhering to these warning sounds, preparing for His soon coming. His Word in Revelation 22:14 says, "Blessed are they that do His commandments, that they may have right to the tree of life, and may enter in through the gates into the city." You see, my sister, there is some action that must happen, not only hearing the sounds but making a concerted effort to act.

Jesus warned, "Now learn this lesson from the [garbage truck]: As soon as its [sounds are heard] . . . you know that [the truck] is near. Even so, when you see all these things, you know that it is near, right at the door . . . this generation will certainly not pass away until all these things have happened" (Matt. 24:32-34, NIV). Won't you join me in heeding the warning sounds of His coming, preparing to meet Him in that great day? What a day that will be!

Vivian Brown

The Old Man

And he said, "Please bring them to me,
and I will bless them." Gen. 48:9, NKJV.

The old man had come again. He was one of those I thought of as a "worthy" beggar. Many missionaries know the dilemma of deciding whom to help among the many who ask for a handout. This old man truly needed my help. Widowed, elderly and ailing, without any children of his own to care for him, he lived on the charity of his sister. She was willing to feed him if he supplied the cash to pay for grinding the grain. With no way of earning the money, he came to the mission in the hope of finding someone to give him the few coins needed to grind a month's worth of grain. And so it became a regular monthly ritual. I would be told, "The old man has come again."

Taking a little money, I would go out and greet him. He was a gracious Christian man, and as I handed him the coins he would say, "Thank you, thank you, how can I thank you?"

"Just pray for us," I would repeatedly beg, for the burdens of missionary life are many.

"I am praying for you! I am praying for your family" was his invariable response. I would thank him for his prayers, and he would go his way.

The old man had come again, but this time he changed the ritual. After offering his thanks, he did not leave. Instead he asked, "Where is your husband? Bring him here. I want to pray for your family." I told him my husband was teaching a class but would be home soon. "I will wait," he said. When my husband arrived, we went out to see the old man. "Kneel down," the old man requested. "I want to pray for you."

We knelt—the missionaries and the beggar—and heaven's doors seemed to open as the old man began to pray. He prayed a beautiful blessing, a truly patriarchal blessing, on us as parents, on our children, our work, and our personal lives.

That was the last time I ever saw the old man. A few weeks later the report came that he had passed away. Through the years since that prayer we have witnessed God's abundant blessings on our family. And so I wonder which beggar's needs were met best—the old man's or mine?

Upon whom can you pray a blessing today?

Cheryl Doss

Expectations

Peace I leave with you; my peace I give you.
I do not give to you as the world gives. Do not let your hearts
be troubled and do not be afraid. John 14:27, NIV.

In my town the spring came quietly at the end of March. Leaves appeared on the branches, and the first flowers bloomed. The nights were still fresh, but the days were pleasent and warm. My baby, a little angel, turned 8 months old; she was never demanding and always in the mood to play. My husband and I worked at the Belgrade Theological Seminar in Serbia.

Our campus was located on a hill, near a forest, overlooking the river and New Belgrade City. The forest behind our campus has been a home for many small animals that visited us. We especially enjoyed the scent of acacia when it bloomed in April.

War suddenly changed everything. The students were sent home. Sirens awakened us in the middle of the night, and the first bombs dropped. After that I spent nights in the basment of the building. Our campus turned into a survival camp. We often didn't have electricity or water, so we found new ways to warm water, cook , and wash our clothes.

One night, in the basement with only a candle on the shelf, I heard air defense guns, and then a terrible explosion that shook the building as never before. Then there was another exposion, and another—a whole series. Through a window on first floor I saw fire on the other side of the river, a mile from campus, where there were huge stores of oil. Fire illuminated the sky, and again there was the sound of sirens. The roar of aircraft was lost in the night.

I went back to the room in the basement. I looked at my baby; she was still sleeping, an innocent and gentle smile on her face. I started to shake from fear. I tried to stop thinking negative thoughts. I looked my baby again and I said, "God, give me peace. Give me the trust and security that this child has."

Suddenly my thoughts stopped racing, my breathing evened out, and my thoughts turned to today's text. My baby stretched and continued to sleep peacefully. From that moment, like my baby, I was peaceful and safe because of God, who is the only one who can give us peace that overcomes all our expectations. His peace is not the worldly kind of peace, because *He* is peace. The candle created shadows on the walls, but I was no longer afraid. I chose to walk in peace. The scent of the spring came through the open window, and I quietly slept.

Aleksandra Tanurdzic

Trust and Obey

Wait on the Lord, and keep his way, and he shall exalt thee to inherit the land: when the wicked are cut off, thou shalt see it. Ps. 37:34.

Sometimes it is hard to see how God is working in our lives. Sometimes it is hard to let go and be still and watch how the Lord transforms and gives us things that we could never achieve on our own.

When I met my husband, I knew right then that he was the person God intended for me, because years before, I had prayed to God, asking Him to lead me to someone who loved Him more than He would me; by default he would love and treat me the way that God intended. And He came through; we got engaged and started planning our wedding. It so happens that when God's children depend completely on Him and trust Him blindly, the devil tries to mess things up. We had planned our wedding, a very simple ceremony with family only. We talked and made a budget for our expenses as newly marrieds, and made sure that we did things the way God wants. Then some months before the wedding, both of us lost our jobs at almost the same time. We thought that everything was over, and we would have to postpone all our plans and just wait to see if we would get jobs again to restart the planning.

But in a very nice way, God had other plans. Somehow our wedding managed to plan itself and ended up being better than we expected. We received our honeymoon as a gift, so that expense was covered. Most important, we found a place to live, a place that God provided.

We feel so blessed because we had the opportunity to spend our first month as a married couple at home in peace, and our needs were supplied in very interesting ways. After a month and a half, my husband got a job in a place that he enjoys working. Whenever we need extra money to cover something, God supplies the way to get it. God is so good to us.

I look back at these months and thank God, because I can't imagine that all this could have happened without Him. He gave me a life partner who is God-fearing and loving, but also shows me every day that what I have and what I am is only because He has done the good work in my life and in me. And I have the assurance that when God wants me to work outside of the house, He will supply the job I need. Some days it is not easy, but in God nothing is impossible.

Yvita Antonette Villalona Bacchus

Wretched or Wonderful?

A cheerful heart is good medicine. Prov. 17:22, NIV.

A big sigh alerted me to the fact that I was no longer alone in the family room. Melissa stood in the doorway, her entire body registering dejection. "I've had a completely *wretched* afternoon," she said. (Wretched was a new word for her.) "Janeva said my hair looked funny, and that hurt my feelings. How could she be so *insensitive*?"

"Did your hair look funny?" I asked.

Melissa looked at the floor and then replied, "Well, a big orange leaf was stuck in my hair. Janeva said it made me look like a giant butterfly."

"So I take it you chose to put a negative spin on Janeva's comment, take it personally, and allow your feelings to be hurt," I commented.

"What would you have done?" asked Melissa.

"Probably chuckled," I said. "If you had laughed when it happened, your afternoon likely would have been less *wretched*. It might even have been *wonderful.*"

"And if I had laughed," said Melissa, "I could have pumped some of that good stuff into my brain. The chemical stew stuff you're always talking about. Sir . . . sir . . . ."

"Serotonin," I offered.

"Yeah," said Melissa. "Serotonin, from my brain's own pharmacy!"

"The female brain has less serotonin than the male brain," I said. "So we females need to laugh every chance we get. In any situation you can choose to look for the humor and laugh about it. Even if you choose not to laugh, you can choose to perceive any comment in the best possible light. If it has nothing to do with you, let it go."

"Blew that one to *smithereens,* didn't I?" said Melissa. "I bet I did look like a giant butterfly. The leaf was really big!"

"Did Janeva get a laugh out of it?" I asked.

"Yes," said Melissa, hanging her head, "but I didn't—till now." *Obviously.* "I'm going to call Janeva and tell her I finally decided to laugh and give my brain a shot of serotonin."

Good idea, I thought. *Laughter is such good medicine.*

Arlene R. Taylor

April 2

One Hundred Years From Now!*

So we fix our eyes not on what is seen, but on what is unseen, since what is seen is temporary, but what is unseen is eternal. 2 Cor. 4:18, NIV.

When my husband and I moved into our new home, we went through the house room by room, hanging window shades, arranging furniture, and unpacking what seemed like an endless trail of boxes. We promised each other that before we'd move again, we'd have a huge yard sale!

We managed to settle the house quite nicely before Christmas arrived. None of our holiday guests were aware of unpacked boxes hidden in the basement. One day we got up the courage to start sorting. I noticed that not a few boxes had remained sealed for more than one move. In previous moves a box might have been marked "family room." But now the word "basement" was written like a judgment decree across that same box. That one word said it all! The once-precious contents had been relegated to the basement—the last stop before the garage sale or, worse yet, a trip to the dumpster.

Soon a dumpster-destined pile began to mount. But before tossing out a cloth tote from a church convention two years earlier, I ran my hand inside each tote pocket. Then from one I pulled a manila folder with the word "rush" written on its cover in bold red letters. *Horrors!* I thought, almost afraid to open the folder to see what crisis I had neglected. Inside I found three letters that had once seemed important. Now, standing in the middle of the basement, I realized that the world had kept turning even though the contents of this folder had been out of sight and out of mind for more than two years.

Ceremoniously I dropped the folder into the trash pile.

That simple incident prompted me to do a little mental exam as I folded the empty boxes and stacked them under the stairwell. "Rose, why do you usually begin your days by making lists for yourself that are next to impossible to complete? Why do you set yourself up for unwanted stress by creating too many 'rush' folders?" While I was growing up, my mother would often say to me, "Honey, a hundred years from now this isn't going to make a bit of difference!"

Lord, today may I focus on things that will make a difference a hundred years from now.

Rose Otis

*From *The Listening Heart* (Review and Herald Pub. Assn., 1993), pp. 32, 33.

Thorns

Then Pilate took Jesus and had him flogged. The soldiers
twisted together a crown of thorns and put it on his head.
They clothed him in a purple robe and went up to him
again and again, saying, "Hail, king of the Jews!"
And they slapped him in the face. John 19:1-3, NIV.

We have some fruit trees in our garden, and among them are pomegranate, loquats, a grapevine, and two lemon trees. Unfortunately, one lemon tree had to be chopped down because of "bad guys" entering our premises.

The pomegranate tree grows very high, and the fruit seems to develop on the high branches where the sun warms the fruit and it ripens. This makes it hard to get, so I have to stand on the top rung of the ladder to try to get the fruit off. My friend calls it "holy fruit." The pomegranate tree has thorns, but not as long and sharp as the lemon tree.

I wanted to pick a lemon that was ripening, but it was in an awkward position. I wondered how I would get to it without getting pricked. I tried this way and that to get to that lemon, even using a broom to hold the branches back, but it didn't help. The branches came forward, and the thorns made an ugly scratch across my hand. I was glad I finally managed to get the lemon off, but my hand needed some first aid.

That set me thinking: *If a thorn could hurt my hand so much, how much more had a crown of thorns hurt my Savior's head?* Can you imagine a soldier putting the twisted crown of thorns on the Savior's head? No, not at all. Pushed down so hard the Savior's flesh was torn and bleeding! Imagine the thorns of the day, the Savior experiencing all that mocking, sneering, and the sun beating down upon Him. He was tired and hungry, beaten and scourged, going through all that agony.

How could He endure all this? The insults, the mockery, being spat upon in His face. Can you imagine the blood streaming down His temples from the pressing of the thorns on His brow?

Friends, Jesus went through all this humiliation for you and me because He loves us. He wants our love in return. As we contemplate the sufferings of Jesus and that crown of thorns He had to wear, isn't that the most wonderful, indescribable love? Give Him your heart today. Tomorrow may be too late.

Priscilla A. Adonis

Whom Are You Seeking?

Jesus therefore, knowing all things that would come upon Him, went forward and said to them, "Whom are you seeking?" John 18:4, NKJV.

Jesus steps forward. "Whom are you looking for?" He asks the delegation marching toward Him. "Jesus of Nazareth," they respond. Jesus makes Himself available (He always does when people look for Him), yet we are uncertain about the true desire of the seekers.

Suddenly the crowd of determined onlookers, armed men, and religious leaders fall at His feet. This we did not expect. Usually people fall at His feet when they acknowledge His greatness, when they understand He is not simply another man from Nazareth in Galilee. Do these people acknowledge Him as Messiah by falling at His feet?

Even now, if they confess He is the Son of God (the centurion will do so tomorrow), Jesus will reveal Himself as their Savior. Jesus always requires us to make a decision about Him. No ambiguity is allowed. Every encounter is a life or death matter. He unhesitatingly asks what their purpose is, and He will soon clearly state that He is "the Son of the Blessed," revealing His divinity (Mark 14:61, NKJV).

While heads are still bowed, Jesus asks again, "Whom are you seeking?" He cross-examines, gives a second chance. He wants us to be certain of our answers and to believe what we say. His questions always prod the heart to examine its motives and to consciously and wisely make life-altering choices. "Who touched Me?" "Who do you say that I am?" "Who do others say that I am?" "What do you want Me to do?"

Why has the delegation come? Others seek Him to see where He lives, to be taught, to be healed, to be fed, to be comforted, to be blessed, to see miracles, to be assured they keep the law, to prove He doesn't keep the law, to trap Him with His own speech, to bring someone else trapped by their own actions, to stone Him, to anoint Him.

Why do I look for Jesus? Do I seek the King riding into Jerusalem to His coronation? Do I seek the High Priest cleansing His Temple? Do I seek the Prophet warning the religious leaders of their impending spiritual doom, or warning His followers of Jerusalem's fall and the Temple's collapse? Do I earnestly desire the one offering Himself as my Savior? Do I respond in worship by anointing His feet at Bethany?

Rebecca Timon

Friend, Why Have You Come?

But Jesus said to him, "Friend, why have you come?" Matt. 26:50, NKJV.

Judas emerges from the shadow and moves around the group fallen at the feet of Jesus. We hear him whisper, "Whomever I kiss, He is the One" (Matt. 26:48, NKJV). Drowsy confusion lulls us into thinking our own colleague brings a friendly delegation.

"Seize Him," Judas abruptly barks as he embraces the Master. Instantly alert, we smell danger, but Jesus unexpectedly regards this as an ambiguous act. "Friend, why have you come?" A question allows the heart to examine motives. Jesus will even now accept the kiss as a desire for reconciliation if Judas suddenly regrets facilitating His arrest. Ponder the possibility.

Can you hear Jesus gently responding as Joseph did with his brothers? "Come, close to me. . . . I am your brother . . . , the one you sold into [the hands of the chief priests and Pharisees]! And now, do not be distressed and do not be angry with [yourself] for selling me here, because it was to save lives that God sent me ahead of you" (see Gen. 45:4-8, NIV).

Can you hear Jesus repeating what He earlier stated in the Temple courtyard? "No one takes [my life] from me, but I lay it down of my own accord" (John 10:18, NIV).

The armed guard advances. Peter unsheathes his sword, striking against the Judas group and slashing it at the first unprotected head he can reach. Always the Restorer, Jesus halts the carnage and restores the man's ear. Always the Savior, Jesus commands, "Peter! Put away your sword," and saves Peter from committing more life-threatening, reckless acts.

Jesus is taken into custody, and Peter and John follow the crowd. John slips into the high priest's household, but a change comes over Peter. He begins to detach himself from Jesus just as he detached the ear from the servant. Separated from his Lord, Peter is open to assault from the enemy. Soon he finds himself thrashing his verbal sword against the attack of those who recognize him as Jesus' disciple. Just before the cock crows again, Jesus turns and looks at Peter with eyes silently probing, "Friend, why have you come?"

The question echoes across the centuries. Have I also detached myself from my Lord by coming to Jesus with the wrong purpose? Have I claimed in my own strength, "Even if I have to die with You, I will not deny You!" (Matt. 26:35, NKJV)?

Rebecca Timon

Time Out!

Beloved, I pray that you may . . . be in health,
just as your soul prospers. 3 John 2, NKJV.

The unspoken mantra in my birth family was: "The harder you work, the higher your worth as an individual." Following in the high-achieving footprints of my parents, I strove to emulate their examples. I referred to my overdoing as "passing on the inheritance of my parents' strong work ethic." Yet in retrospect I don't remember their taking much time for things that fed their souls. Their lifestyles proclaimed, "Work honestly. Work long hours. Work hard—even at the expense of health." Sometimes I wondered if my own inherited "drivenness" for racing from one professional or church responsibility to the next was related somehow to the atrial fibrillation (irregular heartbeat) I'd also "inherited" from my parents.

Only God knows what a backslidden workaholic I am! And since I need to backslide a whole lot more, I believe He allows "time-out" reminders into my life. The other evening, following weeks of intermittent travel, writing deadlines, and local church duties, I noticed that my chest felt tight. I located my neglected blood pressure (BP) cuff, slipped it onto my arm, and took a reading. It was sky-high—for me, anyway.

Shaken, I left my desk and wandered about my office before finding myself face-to-neck with the dusty guitar hanging on the wall. I reached for it, sank onto a nearby stool, and began finger-picking a simple hymn. Ten minutes later I took a second blood pressure reading. The systolic (top) number had dropped 10 points! Incredulous, I continued my unpolished playing of restful music. The next BP reading, only 15 minutes later, revealed a further drop of 10 points!

Although I cherish the memory of my parents and am unspeakably proud of what they accomplished in their lifetimes, I also remember sadly how work with no play weakened their health. The apostle John wished all believers to have physical health as vibrant as their soul's health. Jesus Himself modeled the importance of taking time out in order to relax, regroup, revive, and refocus (see Mark 6:31). He knew that what prospers the body also prospers the health of the soul. Since that evening's BP readings, I've unloaded some responsibilities and am getting back on my exercise plan. I've scheduled lunch with two girlfriends on two different days and am playing a bit more guitar. What do *your* time-outs look like?

Carolyn Sutton

God Cares for Churches Big and Small

Casting all your care upon Him, for He cares for you. 1 Peter 5:7, NKJV.

Sabbath afternoon, as we arrived at the little church, the children, with a certain twinkle in their eyes, wanted us to sit down. With big smiles they marched to the platform and for the first time gave the welcome, read a Bible verse, and sang two songs. This was special since all the children were under 10 years old, and they did this all by themselves. I thought to myself, *Such leadership ability, and potential—above and beyond anything I would have imagined.* Later when I was playing the accordion as we sang more hymns, one of the little girls tried to help me play, pressing on the keys.

After that my husband studied the Bible lesson with the two adults, and I took the eight children to another room; we colored a picture of a nest of birds being fed by the mother bird with today's text. We talked about how God knows all about us, and cares for us, and of the gifts He gives us. I asked the children if they had watched their father plant a seed of corn. They raised their hands, and one of them piped up, "Two seeds!" Then we talked of how a seed grows a stalk of corn that usually has two ears, and one ear of corn can have 800 kernels on it, so that as many as 1,600 seeds of corn may come from that one seed (or two!). The other day I counted the rows (16) and the kernels on a row (about 50) and did the math—and was quite impressed.

In contrast, in the morning we were in the church on the Montemorelos University campus. This church has room for 2,500 and at least 17 beautiful children's and youth's Sabbath school rooms. We have the four-manual organ and the nine-foot grand piano, and many wonderful musicians, choirs, and orchestra, and I always come home very happy from that Sabbath school and church service. But it is interesting to me that we come home even happier from the humble little place at the foot of the mountains, down a dirt road, where two or three were gathered together. I marvel we can find peace and joy, and nourishment of spirit, both in a great big church, and a tiny, humble church. To me it is evidence that it is the Holy Spirit that gives us spiritual gifts, no matter the size of the place of worship. As we watched the beautiful sunset on the drive home, we commented on this joy and peace we felt in our hearts, and praised God for the blessings we find as we worship together in churches big and small.

Ruth Ann Hagen Wade

April 8

Unsought Blessings

*And the Lord shall guide thee continually, and satisfy
thy soul in drought, and make fat thy bones: and thou shalt be like a
watered garden, and like a spring of water, whose waters fail not. Isa. 58:11.*

But as it is written, Eye hath not seen, nor ear heard, neither have entered into the heart of man, the things which God hath prepared for them that love him. 1 Cor. 2:9.

If we took enough time, we would soon realize that we are saturated daily with unsought blessings, evidences of God's provisionary agenda for His children. The fact is that these blessings come so often that we sometimes take them for granted while waiting for some dramatic scenes/presentations that we define as blessings according to our own perception and experiences.

I have been a frequent recipient of God's unsought blessings. For as long as I can remember—since my recent college days and to this day—I frequently find money at my home that many times I just do not remember putting away. I am young with a great memory—no amnesia here. Sometimes I find money in the pocket of a suit I wore earlier; other times it is in an envelope, and yet other times it seems like my spending money has more money than I knew about—I spend money but still have money left. *How did the money get there?* It seems like I experience these blessings most when I have a financial challenge. God always knows the right timing.

If I am guessing right, you also have some unsought blessings in your life that you can begin to count. Think of these things that may have happened to you: a call from an old friend, the ability to breathe fresh, unpolluted country air in the early morning, a smile from a stranger, the ability to use your five senses, the blessings of good health, the ability to enjoy nature, the ability to offer forgiveness in spite of the circumstances, a discount on an item in the store, and most important, the ability to receive salvation. Have you ever received any of these lately? I think you have.

Treasure your unsought blessings as pearls of great price. You don't have to look for them—they will find you.

Althea Y. Boxx

Moving Forward and *Not* Looking Back

There is no fear in love; but perfect love casts out fear,
because fear involves punishment, and the one who fears
is not perfected in love. 1 John 4:18, NASB.

I had a conversation recently with someone about Lot's wife and her desire to look back. We are often told that it was the loss of her possessions that caused her to look back. I have found myself feeling so sorry for her. How could she put any *thing* before God? Her family was with her, and God was with her, so how could she turn around and want to go back to what was before? Is any thing that important?

So it is time for some self-assessment. Looking around, I ask myself, *Is there anything that I could not live without? If God asked me to let it all go, would I hesitate?* The hardest and longest look was when I came to my children. What if? *What if?* The thoughts scream at me. I have to be willing to put God above it *all*. An inner fear sets in. I do not completely understand. I know what God is asking, and I believe that He is a God of love and mercy. Believing in these promises should give me peace, but there is still this nagging stress on my heart. I look at my children and I realize that they are not mine. I have two Samuels in front of me. Could I be like Hannah? These children are mine, but they are God's first. Could I open this tight grip and release to God what is already His?

With so many questions, I search the Word and find this promise: "I have learned the secret of being content in any and every situation, whether well fed or hungry, whether living in plenty or in want. I can do all this through him who gives me strength" (Phil. 4:12, 13, NIV).

God will take care of my family and of me. I can slowly loosen the grip and give it all to Him. *They are safer in His hands anyway. Let go of the fear.*

"Don't worry about anything; instead, pray about everything. Tell God what you need, and thank him for all he has done. Then you will experience God's peace, which exceeds anything we can understand. His peace will guard your hearts and minds as you live in Christ Jesus" (Phil 4:6, 7, NLT).

I am in awe that I serve a God who will give me the reins if I desire to take them. However, I really don't want them. If I search deep in my heart, I know that I need God to lead.

Joey Norwood Tolbert

In the Master's Waiting Room

Wash me thoroughly from mine iniquity, and cleanse me from my sin. Ps. 51:2.

It's the beginning of a new _____ (year, month, week, semester, season—you fill in the blank), and I'm sitting in the Doctor's waiting room. I'm here for a general checkup: physically and spiritually. I'm somewhat nervous, yet expectant. I know the symptoms. I can predict the diagnosis. I'm in a bad way, but this Doctor has never lost a patient who came in for help.

I'm in good company. On the wall (by permission), is a list of patients successfully treated by this Doctor. Featured are Adam and Abraham, who listened to beloved wives and deliberately made wrong choices. There are also both Jacob and his wife Rachel—tricksters and deceivers of their individual parents; Mary Magdalene, possessed by and finally freed of seven devils, stands in bold relief; Rahab the harlot and Ruth the Moabitess from a proscribed tribe, but both rehabilitated and saved, are named. Miriam, who mysteriously contracts and is cured from fearful leprosy is there. And finally listed is a thief dying on a cross, diagnosed with kleptomania, and saved at the last minute by the Doctor.

Yes. As I wait I take stock emotionally. I realize I need a cure. I am impatient, intolerant, and unforgiving. Physically my feet are slow to move in God's service, and my voice and speech do not always convey words of hope and love. I definitely want the cure. I need patience both with children and spouse.

Spiritually, I'm in even worse shape. My heart has proved "desperately wicked" (Jer. 17:9). In fact, I need a heart transplant! I've been told this Physician is able to "create in me a clean heart . . . and renew a right spirit within me" (Ps. 51:10).

I am expectant. I am hopeful. I am almost excited. I can hardly wait. I just know I'm in good hands. My Doctor's credentials are the best: "Who forgives all your iniquities, who heals all your diseases, who redeems your life from destruction, who crowns you with lovingkindness and tender mercies, who satisfies your mouth with good things, so that your youth is renewed like the eagle's" (Ps. 103:3-5, NKJV).

I am a woman in need of help if I am to guide my family on a successful course to heaven. My name has just been called. I am about to see the Great Physician. Pray for me!

Pamela C. Stanford-Odle

Pressed but Not Crushed: Finding Joy in Pain

In all this you greatly rejoice, though now for a little while you may have had to suffer grief in all kinds of trials. These have come so that the proven genuineness of your faith—of greater worth than gold, which perishes even though refined by fire—may result in praise, glory and honor when Jesus Christ is revealed. 1 Peter 1:6, 7, NIV.

While gathering pepper leaves for our soup, my sister and I noticed that the plants were bent low, loaded with fruit from top to bottom! We were surprised. The plants never gave us this much fruit last summer, and now this, when the weather had started to turn cold, and winter was at the door. What had happened?

"This is a common occurrence in plants. They try to propagate when they are threatened," my sister explained. An example, she said, was their jackfruit tree. One of its roots was cut, and this tree that had been so-so in its fruit production in the past began to bear more fruit that was sweeter and juicier than its previous fruit.

This was new to me, and it amazes me that plants and people are not so different. As soon as we realize that our mortality and our lives will end soon, we shape up. We evaluate our values, change our priorities. We do a course correction, usually toward a more meaningful life.

At least, that's what happened to me when I got the scary cancer diagnosis. I asked myself, *If I should die today, will someone miss me after six months? Will remembering me bring a happy thought to somebody?* Sadly, I admitted that my life had been mostly thinking and caring for myself—far different from the person I thought and hoped I was.

So multiple myeloma did me good. As one cancer survivor said, life after cancer is like "The Wizard of Oz" scene after Dorothy and her dog, Toto, landed in Munchkinland: the scene turned into full color. What had been a drifting, so-so life in black and white has turned full color since my diagnosis. Every ray of sun seems to bring smiles. Rain is a melody only those who are really listening can hear. Snow, gorgeous in itself, is magic. A breeze is a kiss from God. Spring is magnificent, autumn is love! Words from hymns cut deeper. God became closer.

Now I try to see and listen with my heart, and not just with my eyes and ears. I am not there yet, but with God I hope to bear more fruit that will be, hopefully, sweeter.

Ana Teorima Faigao

And Now I'm Old

I have been young, and now am old; yet have I not seen the righteous forsaken, nor his seed begging bread. Ps. 37:25.

It's amazing to reflect on the wonderful things that happen when we share our heart's blessings and God's love with others. I know the Holy Spirit has done much for me, and I see it more clearly as I look back on my life. Sometime after I retired, I met up with one of my former coworkers. We chatted, sharing what had happened to each of us in the interim and praising God for His goodness. In the course of our conversation I mentioned that my TV was broken.

Imagine my surprise when the very next day she and her 41-year-old son Donnie came to see me. They brought several bags of food, a DVD player, and a 26-inch flat screen television. I was beside myself with gratitude. God's child needed not beg for bread! My friend told me that her generosity was partially based on the thankfulness she felt for my training her for the job that she really wanted. She said that the patience I showed her made her fall in love with my beautiful, long-suffering personality.

The next day she told me that she and Donnie had put me on their cable television account. They also gave me tips on updating my health insurance. Another young man helped me set up the television and do other technological things that seemed beyond the understanding of my old brain. I cannot help praising God for blessing me with such wonderful friends.

God allowed me to see His power as I was sitting in church during prayer meeting one day. A beloved sister whom we'd been praying for walked through the front doors. Cancer had stolen her vibrant spirit, but it could not hide her sweetness. I'd not expected to see her again this side of heaven, yet God showed me the powerful workings of prayer and the efforts of so many saints interceding on her behalf. My heart was jubilant; I'd seen this miracle with my own eyes.

The Holy Spirit often speaks to me as I talk to the dilapidated old car He gave me. I hear Him as I travel across town, picking up an old woman who lives a great distance from our church. I know God is listening as I ask Him to make me His instrument, bringing peace, love, and joy to others.

We truly do have a God who does not forsake us. And we need not beg for food!

Geneva G. Taylor

Kindergarten Refreshments

May the Lord show mercy to the household of Onesiphorus, because he often refreshed me and was not ashamed of my chains. 2 Tim. 1:16, NIV.

Unbeknownst to me, I had integrated the kindergarten class in Wellsville, New York. Decades before "integration" became a worldwide political focus, I was the only "chocolate child" among the 4- and 5-year-olds clinging to their mothers' dresses. Well, I glued myself to an adult sister, Mae. She had been concerned that I was "way too shy" when outside the family nest. I had been surprised—and happy—when Mae had not returned to Rochester on Sunday, because Mae always taught me new songs. But Mae had another motive for staying on.

Thus on Monday morning, there I was at Wellsville Elementary. And then Mae wasn't. She had diverted my attention and slipped away. My little body shook tears down my cheeks as I silently raced down the hall in search of Mae. Right under the EXIT sign gentle hands behind me caressed and then held my shoulders. As my tears were being dried with a handkerchief that smelled of lilacs, I made out the smiling face of a woman with gray eyes and acorn-colored hair. She tweaked my chin and said, "I'm Miss Jones." Holding my hand, she drew a girl toward me. "This is Molly," she said. "What is your name?"

"Faith Johnson. F-a-i-t-h J-o-h-n-s-o-n." As I spelled my name, I focused on Molly's flaming red hair. Then I noticed her red nose.

"You two little ladies can help each other enjoy this wonderful adventure," Miss Jones said, smiling so sweetly that we believed her. Yet, we quickly learned that everybody was not kind. Unlike me, some didn't enjoy the sunlight on Molly's red hair. Unlike Molly, some hated chocolate. So Molly and I cheered one another on, holding hands in the lunch line and elsewhere. In the decades that followed that year of trial and triumph, I have applied the lessons learned that ended with Molly and me wearing little white mortarboard hats and graduation gowns. I have met many people like Molly and Miss Jones—and F-a-i-t-h J-o-h-n-s-o-n. Sometimes—as student or teacher, wife or mother, coworker, neighbor, or passing acquaintance—I have been the refreshing that moved a fearful person toward a graduation of some sort. And I too have received the blessing showered on the household of Onesiphorus. And Miss Jones. And Molly.

Faith Johnson Crumbly

God Touched Me!

The effective, fervent prayer of a righteous man avails much. James 5:16, NKJV.

I never thought it would happen to me! But it did! I never thought that someday I would be asking for the pastors to anoint and pray over me. But I decided the time had come. My health was failing, so why shouldn't I ask God to heal me? I have always had great faith in God hearing, and I am aware that I wouldn't be alive today if it wasn't for my mother's prayer of faith.

When I was only 5 years old, God saved my life from the burning fire as my mother prayed and smothered the fire with her bare hands. The doctors told my mother it would be impossible for me to live because half my body was covered with burns. But my mother knew God personally, and she refused to believe that God couldn't do the impossible. She prayed most earnestly that God could work a miracle to save my life, and He did!

For the past year I had anemia from loss of blood as a result of two operations on the same knee. I became discouraged and wondered if I would ever get back to normal. I've always had so much energy, but now I felt so helpless and had no appetite. It seemed as though I was becoming weaker and weaker. I couldn't understand why God didn't answer my prayer for healing.

Shortly after this, as I was having my morning worship, I read James 5:13-15, which says: "Is any among you afflicted? let him pray. . . . Is any sick among you? let him call for the elders of the church; and let them pray over him, anointing him with oil in the name of the Lord: and the prayer of faith shall save the sick, and the Lord shall raise him up; and if he has committed sins, they shall be forgiven." I didn't consider myself sick, but I was afflicted!

I called our pastors. After reading a few texts and having a short discussion, Pastor Brownfield and Pastor Wyman prayed and anointed me. I didn't know whether God healed me at that time, but I did know that God was present and touched me mentally as well as spiritually. And I was satisfied. If I was healed physically or not, it was OK with me.

It was just a couple of nights after this that my caring neighbor, Phyllis, who usually comes over to check on me, exclaimed: "What's happened to you, Lillian? You were like a rung-out dishrag the other evening when I was here. You're looking and doing so much better."

How grateful I am that God still answers prayers. I have always known that God is interested in every little detail of our lives—big or small—and His promises are true.

Lillian R. Guild

There Were Three and Then One

What man of you, having an hundred sheep,
if he lose one of them, doth not leave the ninety and nine . . .
and go after that which is lost, until he find it? Luke 15:4.

Years ago when my two small daughters and I lived in Miami, Florida, we noticed a stray cat hanging around. I did not want to encourage it to stay, but my animal-loving daughter had different thoughts. With a pitiful heart she would beg me to permit her to feed the cat; I couldn't resist, so of course once she fed it, the cat kept coming back.

This stray cat became pregnant and soon delivered kittens that she kept outside in an old car tire. Then one day we had a torrential rainstorm. By nighttime my daughter was so worried about those cats that she and her sister went out in the darkness to look for them. They found the mother and three babies. My children dried and warmed them and fed the mother.

By morning they looked more alive. Mother cat went to the door and tried her best to inform us that she wanted to get out. We let her out, and after a few minutes she returned soaking wet with a tiny, scraggly-looking, water-soaked kitten dangling from her mouth. She presented it to my daughter, who rescued it by drying and warming its body. If that cat had enough instinct to know that her baby was alive, we had to hope for the best. In time we were all thrilled as we realized that of the "nine lives" a cat has, that kitten still had at least one left. After several hours that revived kitten was running around with the others.

This experience brought to mind the Bible account of the 90 and nine sheep in the fold. We find the story in Matthew 18. The shepherd, like that cat, knew that one was missing. "Will he not leave the ninety-nine on the hills and go to look for the one that wandered off?" (verse 12, NIV). We too live under a deluge of sin, discouragement, financial loss, disappointment, unfaithfulness—you just name it. Troubles always seem to come down on us like that rain. Yet, Jesus knows that one who is outside and unable to cope with it all. He goes out into the deluge and dark of night to look for one precious, almost dead/lost soul.

Are you that one wet, scraggly soul waiting to be rescued? Do you not know that Someone is looking for you? Open your heart to the power of Jesus. He is out there with you, ready to rescue you, waiting for you to say, "Here I am, Lord."

Joyce O'Garro

Tiredness Kills

Very early in the morning, while it was still dark, Jesus got up, left the house and went off to a solitary place, where he prayed. Mark 1:35, NIV.

A campaign was launched in the United Kingdom several years ago to raise awareness of accidents caused when people drive tired. The message on posters was "Tiredness Kills."

One day I was driving home in a tired state. I saw the signs about taking a break, but I really just wanted to get home. My body kept warning me to stop, but I ignored it. I turned up the music, opened the windows, and nibbled on snacks to override the exhaustion about which my body cried out. And then—I fell asleep at the wheel.

When I opened my eyes, I was inches from crashing into a metal barrier. Before I could react, a miracle occurred. I felt the car being pulled back onto the road by a supernatural force. Once again God saved me in spite of my ignoring the warning signs about driving when tired. My stubbornness was dangerous. I could have caused a serious accident that day. Tiredness really can kill!

This is also true in our spiritual lives. Sometimes juggling work, family, or church commitments leaves us feeling exhausted. We know that we are tired, but we keep on going because we want to achieve our goals.

I lived a tired life for a long time. I woke up tired every morning and collapsed tired every night. My priorities were completely wrong, because the first thing to suffer was my personal devotional time with my Lord. Morning devotion was a rushed prayer, and I would fall asleep while mumbling my prayers at night. I struggled to read even a Bible verse. All the while I "kept driving." Church, work, and home had to go on as normal.

The Lord spoke to me about this (when He could get a word in!). I was slow and unhappy, and my family was feeling the negative effects. The disconnection from God was poisoning my world and everyone I cared for. After a near emotional "collision," I asked God to forgive me. He helped me to stop driving my life in a tired state. God reminded me that spending time with Him is essential for the other parts of my life to work out.

How can we reflect God to others when we don't spend time with Him?

Xoli Belgrave

No Visa

O give thanks unto the Lord; call upon his name:
make known his deeds among the people. Sing unto him . . .
talk ye of all his wondrous works. Ps.105:1, 2.

From the Far East, Europe is considered to be on the other side of the planet, so I have always wanted to go to Europe.

In 2011 my dream came true. My church headquarters organized a tour of the Reformation sites in Europe. My husband and I submitted the necessary documents for our visas, and in two weeks our passports came back with those visas.

In Rome I stood at the Colosseum and wondered if I might have been strong enough to stand for my faith the way those Christians did. We also visited the Waldensian Valley, basilicas, cathedrals, and prisons such as Paul was in. From Italy we crossed by road into Switzerland, Germany, and France.

The night before leaving France, I tried to put together all my travel documents. I could not find my visa, although I had my residence permit and other documents. My husband is from India, but I'm from the Philippines.

We went to sleep and got up early to go to the airport. We checked in without any incident. Then I remembered that I had not been able to find my visa letter, so we checked our papers again, but no visa. We asked for our luggage back to look for the document—still no visa.

We boarded the plane for Bangalore. My husband and I discussed what we should do if I wasn't allowed into the country. I prayed all the way from Paris to Bangalore whenever I thought of my predicament. I remembered Pastor Maphosa's story, during the tour, about how God got him through inspection without proper documents, and I asked the Lord to do the same for me. I prayed, *God, please put the right words in our mouths and the needed understanding in the officer's mind.*

At immigration in Bangalore we gave my residence permit, which contained my visa number. The officer read it, stamped my passport, and waved us through. My heart swelled with so much gratitude to my God in heaven that I wanted to jump and shout for joy. This was the quickest I had ever gone through immigration. Praise the Lord—His goodness endures forever!

Rosenita Christo

How Can I Know?

Be still, and know that I am God. Ps. 46:10, NIV.

As I was growing up, at times when I saw someone perform a task that I wanted to master as well, I've asked the question "How do you do that?" The question might even have been asked about something which, now from a grown-up perspective, might seem as trivial as doing a cartwheel or baking a muffin. Part of my underlying and unformed question then was "What exactly are the steps to execute the task, and how will I measure when that task is accomplished?"

Over the years I have, as a developing Christian, often heard people say such things as "The Holy Spirit told me . . ." My reactions to such expressions varied from being dismissive and skeptical to wondering, *How exactly do they know whatever it is they are claiming that the Spirit had told them? Did they have an "Aha" moment? Was it in the form of a dream? Perhaps it was an audible, hallucinatory type of encounter?* Whatever it was, I became more curious, and frankly, at times a trifle jealous as to why I was not experiencing anything near that. Goodness knows, with all the blunders I seemed to be making in and with my life, I could do with some serious "Holy Spirit speak"!

After some time and much pondering and Scripture search, a few texts provided some answers for me. Today's text, in another version, says "Calm down, and learn that I am God!" (CEV). Another realization that I came to is that as many and varied as we people created by God are, so are the ways that He reveals Himself to us. At different points in the Christian journey, and in different contexts, God may choose a myriad of ways in which to reveal Himself, some of which I may not even be able to imagine.

This realization has given me greater assurance in knowing when He is reaching out to me. It is *always!* He promises: "I know the plans I have for you. . . . They are plans for good and not for evil, to give you a future and a hope. . . . When you pray, . . . I will listen. You will find me when you seek me, if you look for me in earnest" (Jer. 29:11-13, TLB).

Each day I hope that you and I continue to look for God in earnest and truly find Him. More than that, I hope we have the assurance of really knowing when we do.

Doreen Evans-Yorke

What Is the Difference?

My brethren, count it all joy when ye fall into divers temptations;
knowing this, that the trying of your faith worketh patience.
But let patience have her perfect work, that ye may be perfect
and entire, wanting nothing. James 1:2-4.

I was recently experiencing great difficulty that saddened me. Weeping, I felt as if all I had tried to do didn't matter, and that all my hard work was in vain. I attempted to call several people for comfort. I finally reached a dear friend. In tears I said, "I am so unhappy." I was expecting an empathetic response. Instead, she asked a question that frustrated me.

Here I was pouring out my heart to her and she asked me, "Do you have joy?" I whipped back a response countering what I considered to be her sarcastic question. Not expecting her to articulate a difference, I demanded an immediate answer to my question, What's the difference?

Calmly she responded, "Happiness or unhappiness is an emotional reaction to your circumstances; joy is the assurance of knowing God is in control of your circumstances."

I was stunned, rendered silent as the words saturated my soul. The tears dried immediately, because I began to remember all God has told us in His Word regarding joy. I remembered how good God is to give us emotions to express our disappointments but how careful we must be not to allow our emotions to overshadow His promises. I then realized that the enemy goes for our emotions, because he can't touch a joy that is rooted in faith and confidence. In essence, the enemy didn't give it to us, so he cannot take it away. Joy comes from the Lord, and the only way we can lose it is if we forget the power of joy in the Lord.

We must forever remember, "The joy of the Lord is [my] strength" (Neh. 8:10, NIV). When all around us is dismal, we can still have joy and the ultimate strength available. There is much to weary us, but Psalm 126:5 promises that "they that sow in tears shall reap in joy"! Yes, weeping may endure for a night but joy truly comes in the morning (see Ps. 30:5). I am sure many of us have soaked a pillow at night weeping for a child, a spouse, or a situation. Praise God for emotions that help release our pain. Yet we have to find our way back to the hope of one day seeing our Savior face to face. And to the present joy that comes from an assurance that knows that God is in control of our circumstances.

Deborah M. Harris

Come, Lord Jesus!

I saw Heaven and earth new-created. Gone the first Heaven,
gone the first earth, gone the sea. I saw Holy Jerusalem, new-created,
descending resplendent out of Heaven, as ready for God as a bride for her
husband. I heard a voice thunder from the Throne: "Look! Look!
God has moved into the neighborhood, making his home with men
and women! They're his people, he's their God. He'll wipe every tear from
their eyes. Death is gone for good—tears gone, crying gone, pain gone—
all the first order of things gone." The Enthroned continued,
"Look! I'm making everything new." Rev. 21:1-5, Message.

I've lost two sisters recently. Losing someone is heartbreaking, even when you have the certitude that you'll see them again at Jesus' second coming. I guess when you get older the chances are you'll lose more friends and family through death. It doesn't get any easier though, does it?

One of my favorite Bible texts is Revelation 21, and in particular the verses above. When my dad died in 1955, my mom's last message to him before he died was "We'll be together again at Jesus' coming, and He'll reunite us with our little daughter." They had lost their first child at the age of 4. Mom and Dad had the firm belief that Jesus was coming again, and when He would come, all of us would be reunited. That faith helped my mom when the sister I never knew died, and when Dad died as well. Mom died in 2000, holding on to her faith.

Having parents that trust God is important, but it's the personal trust that's really needed by each of us. I was baptized at the age of 13 when an itinerant pastor came to my island and told me I was of age and it was time to be baptized! I never received Bible studies except the weekly Sabbath school Bible lessons everyone had. As you can guess, I really did not understand what it was all about. However, during my high school and college years, I regularly stood up during weeks of prayer to confirm my decision to follow Jesus, but it wasn't until I was 23, married with two children, that I was really converted. My husband gave me the book *The Desire of Ages,* and I read it through with a thirst that I hadn't realized I had. After finishing the book, I accepted Jesus and His salvation fully.

I am so thankful that I can say with confidence that I'll see my sisters and my parents again! No more tears, no more death! Yes, come, Lord Jesus!

Erna Johnson

Breastplate

Put on the full armor of God. . . . Stand firm then, . . .
with the breastplate of righteousness in place. Eph. 6:11, 14, NIV.

I told you the TLSO would be tight," stated my son, looking at my torso splint as I fastened it for the first time. "You shouldn't call it a thoracic lumbar sacral orthotic," he observed. "It should be your breastplate."

"My breastplate of righteousness," I exclaimed, and we smiled at each other. Smiles had been scarce in the six days since my husband and I were in an accident that totaled our car. He had strained muscles, I had broken six bones, and our son and daughter-in-law, whom we were visiting, needed to juggle their already-full schedules to help us. However, when I equated my TLSO with the armor of God mentioned in today's text, the whole family smiled.

Dikaiosuné—the word translated "righteousness"—was one I could relate to. It can mean "uprightness," a quality I needed. After the accident I had remained supine. I needed a 15-minute rest after brushing my teeth at the sink. Walking upstairs to join the family for supper was too much to contemplate. But once I cinched the four velcro straps of the TLSO tightly, I could sit on the couch for a short time and walk without the aid of walking sticks. The word can also mean "to perform completely." My husband and I hoped to fly home two weeks after the accident, but I feared that when we changed planes halfway through the 12-hour trip, I would be in too much pain to continue. So I set about to practice the art of wearing my breastplate for many hours. I discovered how to shift my weight slightly, relax, and fight claustrophobia when I couldn't breathe deeply. On the day we drove to the airport, I realized that, thanks to my breastplate of righteousness, my pain medication, and a lot of prayer, I could complete the journey home.

*Dikaiosun*é is righteousness that manifests itself in beneficence. When we arrived home, we received enough food for three weeks: neighbors, colleagues, and church members brought us roasts, chili, borscht, and blueberry pie. We told the meal coordinator that when we felt better, we wanted to be part of this ministry. Our injuries inspired righteousness in others that manifested itself in generosity that inspired us. My breastplate of righteousness will go into the grandchildren's dress-up trunk—with hopes its lessons will stay with me for the rest of my life.

Denise Dick Herr

Cross-country Run

For I long to see you, that I may impart to you some spiritual gift,
so that you may be established—that is, that I may be encouraged together
with you by the mutual faith both of you and me. Rom. 1:11, 12, NKJV.

I do not want Papa, Granny, my mommy or daddy to come. I don't want anyone to see me run." This was the wish my 7-year-old daughter expressed the morning of her school cross-country race. As she spoke this sentiment aloud, I said to myself, *I heard you last night when you said you didn't want Papa to come.* A few minutes later, my dad happened to walk past our kitchen window. I whispered out to him, "Dad, Guielle doesn't want you to come, but remember—the race starts at 1:50." He smiled back and said, "OK."

After I got to my school, I realized my prep for the day was from 1:30 to 2:30. At lunch I planned to try to make it to the cross-country race. I reached Guielle's school right at 1:50. The Primary Three's (second graders) race started late, but I was there to watch Guielle run.

Before the race began, I took a picture of her class. She was so surprised to see me. And guess who else was there to see her run? Yes, her Granny and Papa with camera in tow. As Guielle ran we called her by her nickname and her real name, cheering her on. I also cheered for her classmates and the others I knew as well. At the beginning of the race I was close enough for her to hear me and for me to see a smile spread across her face. Race completed, I left to hurry back to work.

On the drive, I smiled. *What was my daughter thinking? Did she really think that no one would show up just because she didn't want us to? Would she really have wanted no one there to cheer her on?* And that's when the spiritual lesson hit! We too are in a race—a spiritual one. "Therefore we also, since we are surrounded by so great a cloud of witnesses, let us lay aside every weight, and the sin which so easily ensnares us, and let us run with endurance the race that is set before us" (Heb. 12:1, NKJV). Today I want you to focus on the people who are cheering you on. Why are they here? As I hear my Father's voice calling my name, a smile spreads across my face. I run faster, knowing that when I cross the finish line a beautiful snapshot will be taken. And not just of me but one with my friends who have run this race with me.

Dana M. Bean

Witnessing in College

Whoever fears the Lord has a secure fortress,
and for their children it will be a refuge. Prov. 14:26, NIV.

I was in my last semester of college, about to prepare my thesis. I had to participate in an event that would be very important to me, because it would be a demonstration of what we had done during the semester. Everybody was supposed to take part in this, because the faculty would be evaluating us. If a student did not take part in this event, it showed that the student was not interested in demonstrating what he or she had learned. I started worrying once I knew the day I would be presenting. After preparing myself for some time, I came across a problem. The presentation of the last exhibit would be on a Saturday. They were still deciding the time it would take place: morning, afternoon, or night. After this news I began asking God to intervene, because I didn't want to do this on my Sabbath, but of course I wanted to be able to present my thesis.

I trusted in the Lord, and during that time He was with me. He always made a way for me to share His name in that institution. I prayed so that they would change the time of the presentation. I wanted them to change it to Saturday night, but the time chosen was Saturday afternoon. *Why, Lord? Why?*

The day arrived, and I was sad because I would not be able to participate and I would not get the grade I desired. I thought of going after Sabbath ended, immediately after the youth program, but I couldn't. When I called my friend, she told me that I did not need to go, because everything had already finished, and everyone had left.

I was sad, but I accepted it and knew that I would still graduate even though I didn't participate in the event on Saturday. A week later, I received a phone call from my college giving me the final grades. To my surprise, I had received the highest grade possible, even though I had not presented my thesis.

God had prepared a surprise for me. The teacher based my grades on other work I had done. I am a daughter of a God who can do anything! It was not necessary to change the day or the time. He proved that He is the God of impossible things. It was important to have been a good student in the eyes of the teacher, but above all to be a Christian in the eyes of God.

Jane Rose Alves Medeiros

Pulling Weeds

Finally, brethren, whatsoever things are true,
whatsoever things are honest, whatsoever things are just . . .
whatsoever things are of good report . . . think on these things. Phil. 4:8.

I have enjoyed gardening each spring—selecting carnations for the pots on the deck, pruning the hazel hydrangea and peach rosebush. But recently I have developed a new passion—weeding. It began with the lawn, which should have been a green blanket of waving grass. Instead it was an embarrassing mixture of struggling grass, dandelions, and assorted eager weeds. To save the lawn, I gave myself the challenge of pulling weeds for about an hour each afternoon. I now realize that putting one's face in close communication with assorted greenery is healthy, thought provoking, and spiritually enriching. Here is some wisdom from my weeding:

First, weeds grow at an alarming rate. Each weed in my garden is twice the size of the grass. If not removed, they would soon spread, replacing the grass we desired. This I call the hostile takeover syndrome. The weeds of our own experience are just as eager. Weeds of abuse, envy, jealousy, malice, and pride are there, the seeds ready to spring up in a second. On the other hand, real love grows slowly; joy is often a shadow, but how fast the weeds of gossip spread! We must pull them out daily, giving them no opportunity to take root.

Second, unwanted weeds camouflage the desired greenery. In my tall plants, weeds grow tall. In the grass, however, they remain short, spreading out in a dangerous pattern, hoping to be mistaken for the real thing. What weeds in your garden are pretending to be something else? What pernicious jealousy and backbiting mask your Christian virtues? Keep an eye on those weeds that pretend to be what they are not. God desires you to be His beautiful garden.

Third, weeds grow seeds. Don't let the innocence of the weedy flower deceive you. It is laden with tiny seeds that could spread and destroy. Malice is not pretty, though it may look so for a moment. Gossip is not attractive, no matter how innocuous the "joke" is. Once overlooked, it will go to seed, spreading and destroying as it grows.

The take-home lesson is this: Pull those weeds out. Daily. Spend that devotional hour ridding your life of weeds. Yes, *your* life. You alone can recognize the weeds in your life. Attack them daily with God's help. Then cultivate the green pastures of virtuous living. A fragrant garden awaits you.

Annette Walwyn Michael

He Has a Plan

Thou wilt keep him in perfect peace, whose mind
is stayed on thee: because he trusteth in thee. Isa. 26:3.

It was 6:15 in the morning, and I was returning from the airport. As I drove along the parkway, I noticed the reflection of the sun's rays peeking through the still-barren trees. This year's winter season had been quite different from previous ones I had experienced; it seemed to have been all four seasons wrapped up in one. The trees seemed just as perplexed as we were, with the frequent variations in temperature. It was late April, and many trees were just beginning to bud.

My vision was soothed with the intermingling muted colors of the awakening morning. The hues of sunrise were clearly visible through the almost-bare branches of the trees. Twice I pulled over onto the shoulder of the road, took out my camera, rolled down my window, and snapped some photographs of the unfolding vista. I even captured the ball of fire as it became visible above the distant horizon.

My reverie was interrupted by thoughts of my plans for the day. How I wished I could have remained longer! Sometimes I get bogged down and overwhelmed just thinking about the vast number of things I must complete by the end of a day; it seems impossible for me to finish them all. Just as suddenly as the worrying thoughts intruded, my mind jumped to the Scripture passage in Jeremiah 29:11, where our heavenly Father assured us that He has a plan for us.

What a reassuring thought: regardless of how impossible it may seem to bring to fruition all the plans we have made for one day, our Father is not constrained by the exigencies of our daily activities nor by the limits of the sunrise-to-sunset day, but can deliver the already planned-out lives He envisions for us. If only we would search for Him, with all our hearts, we would find Him and enjoy a peaceful journey here as well as an expected end: an eternity of praise and worship and never-ending fellowship.

I am thankful to God for His planning for me from the foundation of the world and for the peace promised should I keep my mind on Him. May we diligently seek Him today and every remaining day of our lives.

Florence E. Callender

The Wilted Garden

Casting all your care upon Him, for He cares for you. 1 Peter 5:7, NKJV.

The newsletter said volunteers were needed for the Community Garden. Apparently the garden is wilted. Uncertain of where the garden is, I ignore the invitation. A week later, a post card arrives. "Community Garden Needs Volunteers." So I decide to volunteer.

As it turns out, the garden is close to my home. The rusty garden gate squeaks as I push it open. In the midmorning the Community Garden is tended to by an elderly woman, hunched over, straw hat, with a bucket holding gardening tools. "They will paint the gate as soon as this garden is back to its old, beautiful self," she says. I look around. The garden is truly wilted. "I am planting tomatoes," she says. "Do you like tomatoes?"

I smile. "Yes, I do."

She hands me a packet of tomato seeds. "Well, there you go. Come and help me."

In the next hour I learn her name is Susan. A retired nurse, she has lived in this neighborhood for 10 years. "I always wanted a garden, but I was too busy working. I would spend all day here if my doctors would let me."

Doctors? I stop raking the soil. Susan's blue eyes meet mine. She has a brain tumor. It is inoperable, and she has opted not to have chemotherapy treatment at her age. Susan pats the soil with the tiny tomatoes tucked safely in the blanket of cool soil.

"I turned it over to God," she says. "When I was diagnosed, I began to worry about my children and grandchildren." She looks away for a moment. "There are so many things a person can worry about. I lay at home, worrying. One day I simply prayed that God would take all of my cares. I got up and came here. He will take care of it all."

I listen to the assurance in her voice. . . . "He will take care of it all."

I walk home thinking of all the cares, worry, burdens I carry. I look back toward the garden. Tomorrow I see Susan, my friend who tends to a wilted garden and leaves her cares to God.

Dear heavenly Father, I cast my cares to You, knowing You care for me. Reminding me that as You care for me, I too must care for others.

Dixil L. Rodríguez

Oh, What a Day That Will Be!

For our conversation is in heaven; from whence also
we look for the Saviour, the Lord Jesus Christ. Phil. 3:20.

We have a dog named Peaches, and like any good dog he likes going for walks. In fact, it's the highlight of his day. He's ready at any moment. You can hear the excitement in his bark, see the pure emotion in his movements: he jumps, he wiggles. He makes it very difficult to attach his leash, but once it's clicked on he quickly grabs part of it in his mouth, runs out the open door, and continues to run back and forth, jumping as well, until we get to the driveway of our yard. He goes through the same routine every time. He never loses his exuberance.

Sometimes we don't want to take Peaches with us. We want to enjoy a walk at our own pace, without the stop, go, and pull motions of a dog the whole time. When he sees us putting our shoes on and start to leave the back door, though, Peaches looks at us with great anticipation in his eyes; he is so eager to go with us. He starts to get all excited again like he is going for a walk, but when it doesn't happen and we leave without him, he barks in absolute protest. In the past when we have left the house without him, we find out he is still barking when we get back. It's that serious.

Now when one of us wants to go for a walk, we have to sneak out. My husband grabs his shoes from the back porch and leaves, using the front door as inconspicuously as possible. Peaches can hear very well, and if he gets the notion that someone is going for a walk without him, he lets you know about it quickly. The barking won't subside.

We take Peaches for a lot of walks, and it always brings a smile to my face to see his joy broadcast in every part of his being. He's like a little kid in a candy shop! Looking at Peaches and seeing his excitement makes me wonder if I ever get excited like that; it seems hard to remember. But there is an event coming that will be the most exciting of our lives! Soon the Lord will come and take us away to a most glorious place. Let's keep a watchful eye, let our ears be open, and may we be waiting in hope for His return. Our excitement will know no bounds when He arrives and will keep on going through all eternity. Another Bible version of today's text says, "And we are eagerly waiting for him to return as our Savior" (NLT).

Rosemarie Clardy

The Itch of Sin

*Submit yourselves therefore to God. Resist the devil,
and he will flee from you. James 4:7, ESV.*

While working at an orphanage for eight months, I spent hours holding the children there, but an unfortunate moment reminded me how easily infection spreads. Many of the children had ringworm, a fairly harmless fungal infection that can spread easily by just touching the afflicted area. Sadly, the ringworm often caused scars on the children's bodies and hair loss when it infected their heads. I caught this ringworm when a young one rested her head on my neck.

I had only one outbreak of ringworm, but that tiny spot was agonizingly itchy. At first, it was only a small red spot, but as I began to scratch it, the infection worsened and got larger. The spot grew from a tiny circle to the size of a bottle cap. It was so satisfying each time I scratched the area, so it was hard to stop. All day I was tempted to scratch. But once I realized it was spreading, I tried to stop, to will myself to stop.

Fearful of the infection spreading, I began new measures to stop myself from scratching. The children helped too by showing me some aloe vera plants to rub on my ringworm. The aloe vera was soothing, and the ringworm began to recede, but the healing seemed to take forever. When I waited for the infection to lessen without scratching it, I noticed that it healed much faster. After a few weeks of treatment and not scratching, I was healed of the ringworm.

The temptation and satisfaction of indulged sin is much like me scratching my ringworm. Even the tiniest sin, when indulged, can grow larger, and even when we rarely allow sin into our lives, it becomes that much harder to resist. Often it is so satisfying to be right in an argument or do things to have others think well of us. However, it then becomes more difficult to pause and think of others before ourselves. Trying to fulfill your desire on your own only perpetuates the problem instead of curing the infection. Instead, we need to take our ailments, worries, and temptations to Christ to ask for help. Just as I had to seek out and break off the piece of aloe vera, Christ wants us to seek Him, because He was broken for us. "What shall we say then? Are we to continue in sin [ringworm] that grace may abound? By no means! How can we who died to sin still live in it?" (Rom. 6:1, 2, ESV). Without Him, we can never be rid of the itch of sin and temptation. But with Him, we can be restored once more.

Brandi Mills

The Desires of Our Heart

Delight yourself also in the Lord, and He shall give you
the desires of your heart. Ps. 37:4, NKJV.

Growing up, I always wanted a Barbie doll. A "real" Barbie. The Barbie with the smooth legs and arms, big blue eyes, and long blond hair. But instead, I received two Barbie-sized dolls, with movable (nonsmooth) legs and arms that eventually became amputees when rubber bands broke.

I shared this "desire" at a women's retreat where I was speaking. The theme was Christmas, and I used the story of my growing up wish as I asked the question "What do you want?" At the end of the retreat, I received not one, but two "real" Barbies. A beautiful princess Barbie with long brown hair, blue eyes, and a sparkling blue-and-pink gown. And a California Barbie—tan and ready to go surfing in board shorts, bikini top, and crocheted hat. Two totally different Barbies from women who wanted to see that little girl dream come true.

The Barbies surprised me. I never expected anyone to hear the story that I just thought was funny and a good lead-in to my talk and take me so seriously that they would leave the retreat, go shopping, and buy a Barbie for me. It made me think. *If people who don't really know me—who meet me once and hear a dream of my little girl heart and want to make it come true, and go to that much trouble to make it happen, how much more does God want to fulfill the desires of my heart? A God who has loved me with an everlasting love. Who wrote my story before I was even born. Who so delights in me that it causes Him to break out singing about me. Who promises to give me the desires of my heart.*

When I look at the Barbies, sitting here on my desk, still in their boxes, they make me smile. Not just because they are so different from each other. Not just because of the women who took the time to care about this long-ago desire of my little girl heart. But because God knew. Because He cared. He knew that I no longer played with Barbies. I don't even have a daughter whom I can share them with! But He wanted me to know "I see you. I know your heart. I care about the desires of your heart—even those you've long forgotten." They cause me to delight in a God who knows me and cares about every desire of my heart.

Tamyra Horst

I Thought I Had More Time

And when these things begin to come to pass, then look up, and lift up your heads; for your redemption draweth nigh. Luke 21:28.

I did think I had more time. Needless to say, that was not the case. I decided to purchase an air card for my iPad. During conversation with the vendor, he reminded me—more than once—of the rebate expiration date. I nodded in confirmation, knowing that I would remember the exact date. Several weeks passed and I, again, made a note to send off for the rebate, which was a substantial amount. However, when I finally made time to gather all materials to mail in for the rebate, I discovered that I had missed the deadline. I was distraught. I thought it was set for the end of the month, when generally rebates are scheduled. This one, unfortunately, was set for another date within the next month. I was so upset with myself for missing the deadline.

On another occasion my husband also had a rebate application. When given to me, I reviewed it and said, "Oh, I have a good month." Then I forgot about it. (Not even conscientiously remembering that just two months prior I had forgotten to process my own.) Time and time again he reminded me to send off for the rebate and again I said, "OK, I've got this. I'll take care of it." I was becoming annoyed because he kept reminding me. However, when time permitted to send the application off, I realized there were only a few days left before expiration. Immediately I processed the application and thanked God for helping me remember.

I am reminded that God wants me to take care of matters as they are presented: praying, studying His Word, or taking care of important matters, and not just when it is convenient to me. He impresses upon my mind to act in the present and not at a later time when forces of evil can deter me from acting upon the will of God. God uses scenarios such as these to remind me of the present shortness of this age, the infinite value of time, and the misfortune of procrastination. So I ask myself, *What do I do with this knowledge? Am I learning to use time more wisely? Am I planning and preparing each day as God wants me to?*

As "time" is defined as the duration of all existence, past, present, and future, I must be careful to stay focused on the mark, lest taken by surprise because I failed to adhere to God's calling, His pleading, knowing that my redemption draws near.

Sylvia "Giles" Bennett

The Burial

When the even was come, there came a rich man of Arimathaea,
named Joseph, who also himself was Jesus' disciple: he went to Pilate,
and begged the body of Jesus. Then Pilate commanded the body to be
delivered. And when Joseph had taken the body, he wrapped it
in a clean linen cloth, and laid it in his own new tomb,
which he had hewn out in the rock: and he rolled a great stone
to the door of the sepulchre, and departed. Matt. 27:57-60.

The time that I worked at the homeless health-care clinic as an intern ended up being one of the most blessed experiences I have had. During that time I also began to volunteer at the community kitchen. To work alongside and serve homeless people gave me joy beyond words. At these two places I met many souls that would freely give of themselves to serve the homeless. Two of these great people were Jord and Brother Ron.

The time I spent with these men was always an uplifting and learning experience. They lived and breathed helping the homeless and others. They gave me a perspective of people and human nature that changed my vision and how I serve. There were so many meaningful experiences we had together.

One of the most touching experiences was the funeral service for a homeless man. He did not have any family that lived in the area. A burial service was held for him at a county cemetery for the poor. Prior to the service, I helped Brother Ron put flowers on other homeless people's graves. It amazed me how he and Jord could remember so many homeless people who had died and where they were buried. He would ask me to move grass or things blocking the grave markers. As we located the graves, he would tell me a little about each one.

The service that was held for the homeless man was simple but very well done. The casket was brought to the graveside by a hearse—both were donated. It was heartbreaking to see how other homeless people who knew him dealt with their grief at the service.

The experience helped me to see the value of all people no matter what their status, and that we are blessed when we care. I'm so thankful God cares about all people. What a valuable thing for us to learn. I want to see people, no matter what their physical or spiritual condition, as God sees them.

Mary Wagoner-Angelin

Living the Constant Life in Jesus

Since we are surrounded by so many examples of faith, we must get rid of everything that slows us down, especially sin that distracts us. We must run the race that lies ahead of us and never give up. Heb. 12:1, GW.

My husband, who is my best friend, has a ritual that he goes through. He goes on a diet, loses a lot of weight, gains a mountain of confidence, and gathers a basketful of compliments. Very soon, however, he discontinues the diet and returns to the same eating habits as before. I've found the repetition tedious at best and useless at worst. The last time my husband went through that process, I decided to express my opinion. "Why not change your whole lifestyle and eat the proper way all of the time?"

"Well, slim gym," he smiled, "you've never had to deal with weight issues, so you can talk."

I thought about his response. It is true that I don't have to deal with weight issues, at least not physically. But I do engage in a spiritual diet during which, for a period of time, I trust God, study His words, give Him my best, and obey His words. At other times I shoulder my burdens, doubt God's promises, ignore His counsels, and make my own decisions. I go back and forth through that process, alternatively flustered and frail or sturdy and spirited. This is a tiresome course of action at best and deadly at worst.

God is calling us to be faithful at all times. The Christian walk is not easy, but God has not left us alone. In fact, He has set life and death before us, and pleads with us to choose life so that we and our children can live (see Deut. 30:19). In addition He has given us His words, messengers, examples, and the Holy Spirit, the ultimate guide who is a constant help for us. There is no reason for me to go through spiritual diets, for God has already provided salvation. All I need to do is rest in Him and live a life that's constant and persistent by His grace. For truly, the race is not given to the swift or the battle to the strong (Eccl. 9:11), but he who endures to the end shall be saved (Matt. 24:13).

I now turn to God to help me stay attached to Him daily. He alone can help me not to live on a spiritual seesaw, and to let my Christian experience speak of a life that's been transformed and renewed until the day Jesus returns. You can do the same.

Rose Joseph Thomas

Underground

I praise you because I am fearfully and wonderfully made;
your works are wonderful, I know that full well. Ps. 139:14, NIV.

Next to the Bible, nature is to be our great lesson book. That's why it is important to spend time studying God's second book as much as we can and learn from what nature offers.

Over the years I have developed an interest in flowers that bloom in the desert under the most challenging circumstances. Why do I do this? Simply because we can learn wonderful lessons from them. We can be inspired as we see how they overcome all obstacles in order to bloom where they are, even in very hard places.

One of the most amazing flowers that I use as an illustration and inspiration in my own life is the *Rhizanthella gardneri*, also known as Western Underground Orchid. This was discovered in the spring of 1928 in the wheat belt of Western Australia. As Jack Trott bent to investigate an odd crack that appeared in the dry soil of his garden, he noticed a sweet smell arising from the ground. Scraping away the soil, he soon uncovered a tiny white flower, about half an inch across, growing underground. What he had found was an entirely new type of orchid, beautiful in all ways. According to the experts, this flower is a cute, quirky, and critically endangered orchid that lives all its life underground. It even blooms underground, making it virtually unique among plants.

The beautiful *Rhizanthella gardneri* has a lesson for us: we can bloom! Even under difficult circumstances. Even if no one notices. We can bloom where we are.

Today if you are thinking that where you are now is too dark and there is no light, remember this little orchid. If this underground orchid can find her way to bloom by God's power, you also can receive His power—to grow, to bloom, and to bless.

God lovingly plants us exactly where He wants us to bloom. He gives us the right kind of light to grow; He tends us well. We are pruned, fertilized, watered, protected from drought, and covered in His protective care. And still, with all that nurturing care, we sometimes fail to bloom. Blooming where you are planted is a choice, a challenge, and often involves change.

God is doing a transforming work in our hearts and lives right where we are. I encourage you to accept His challenge, embrace His plan, and bloom where you are planted

Raquel Queiroz da Costa Arrais

What If?

The Lord will watch over your coming and
going both now and forevermore. Ps. 121:8, NIV.

We were nearing the end of a 1,000-mile trip from our winter home to our summer home when it happened. We had just turned into our neighborhood when we heard the most horrible screeching, grinding noise. What in the world was going on, we wondered. We had never heard anything like it before, and it was not a sound like anything we had heard during the entire trip, but now it would not stop.

We pulled into our garage to unload all our things from the back of our minivan. Even though we have duplicates of most of our things in both places, there are still a lot of things we have to carry back and forth twice a year. It is like moving that many times in a year, but it usually is so lovely down South in the winter, it is worth it.

Our daughter and son-in-law took us out to eat that evening, and after discussing the matter of the noise, we had decided it must be the brakes making all that noise. But the brake shop was closed for the day, so the next morning my husband took our vehicle to see what was wrong. Later, while he was mowing the lawn, we got a call from the shop, and I was told that the brakes indeed were no longer any good. They would have to be completely replaced. Not only that, the two front tires were about to split open. I knew it had to be cared for, so I gave the man permission to go ahead with the replacement of the brakes and the tires.

As I hung up the phone, I said a prayer of thanksgiving to God for the safety of the trip. I could not help wondering what would have happened if those tires had split open as we were driving at 70 miles (113 kilometers) an hour along the freeway, or if the brakes had given out on a steep road or a corner.

We always ask God to go with us as we travel, and He always has, but we never realized it more fully than the afternoon we were coming home and the brakes gave out and the tires were about to split open.

So often we think we are in control, but things happen that remind us that it is really only God who is control, and He alone knows what we need at all times. As we pray and seek His will, He will watch over our coming and going, now and forever.

Anna May Radke Waters

Brave Little Bird

Whatever you do, do well. For when you go to the grave,
there will be no work or planning or knowledge or wisdom. Eccl. 9:10, NLT.

It was a battle of epic proportions. No matter how fast the enemy dodged, the tiny mother was right behind him. She was fearless. He chattered at her. She dive-bombed him, plucking hair from his back. He bounced around the tree trunk. She pecked his head. He raced up and down the tree. He even chattered at her from the top of her birdhouse. She flew at him, scolding his impudence. He wasn't ready to give up without a fight, but the red squirrel's offense was useless against the tiny, furious wren. There was no way that a squirrel was going to eat her babies. Finally the squirrel gave up and went looking for another dinner. The wren perched on her little house and sang her song of victory.

As I watched the fierce battle, I was reminded of the story of David and Goliath. The big bully looked at the youngster and not only mocked him but cursed him, too. He even threatened to feed David to the birds and beasts. David's response was "You come to me with sword, spear, and javelin, but I come to you in the name of the Lord of Heaven's Armies . . . whom you have defied" (1 Sam. 17:45, NLT). David knew that he was on the side of right. Goliath didn't have a chance. He paid with his life because of his dependence on himself. All it took to destroy Goliath was a faithful young man and a pebble that hit the target.

All too often we are faced with a battle. Our salvation depends upon us being more like that little wren. We must not give up no matter how mighty the enemy appears to be. He may threaten us. He may cajole us. We must hold firm. In the end we will be successful if we can just remember that the battle to save us was won on Calvary when Jesus bore the cross to save us.

We too can sing the song of victory. There is no chance that Satan will win the battle for our souls. No matter how hopeless things seem, sing the victory song. Hold fast to Jesus, and He will open heaven's door for you.

Every day I want to be sure to thank our Father in heaven for sending His only child to gain a victory for me and others like me. I want to be like the tiny wren, ready to die for what I believe in.

Patricia Cove

Time Is Precious

But of that day and hour knoweth no man,
no, not the angels of heaven, but my Father only. Matt. 24:36.

God has made us stewards over our money, time, and talents. In my opinion time has always been more valuable than money or anything that money can buy. As a child I was taught the value of money, and as an adult I've come to the conclusion that time is indeed the most important. Once even a second has passed, I will never be able to reclaim it. It is gone for good; therefore, I should be extremely careful how I utilize my time, especially since I am unaware of how much of it I have left.

I often think of the days of Noah. The Bible says that "Noah walked with God" (Gen. 6:9). This implies that Noah must have spent quality time with God, and it reminds me of my life today. How am I spending my quality time? Am I spending it with God? Am I spending quality time in worship, witnessing, fasting and praying, ministering to or meeting the needs of others? Or am I too busy spending time looking at TV, talking on my cell phone, listening to an iPod or MP3, or on a laptop, watching DVDs, or allowing some other device to distract me from spending quality time with God?

Although always busy, I have learned to create quality time to spend with God. I don't generally receive telephone calls in the wee hours of the morning, and since I am a morning person, I've discovered that the best time for me to spend quality time with God is in the wee hours of the morning. I refer to this as "God's time." It is important to give God His time.

God said, "Heaven and earth shall pass away, but my words shall not pass away" (Matt. 24:35). In His Word He has given us signs to look for prior to His second coming. God's Word is being fulfilled moment by moment. The world is in chaos, and only God Himself can fix it.

Some have set a date for when they believe that our Lord and Savior will return. My Bible reads: "But of that day and hour knoweth no man, no, not the angels of heaven, but my Father only" (verse 36). The next verse says: "But as the days of Noe were, so shall also the coming of the Son of man be" (verse 37). I look forward to meeting Him in the air when He comes! Time is winding down!

Cora A. Walker

Life's Roadblocks

And we know that all things work together for good to those who love God, to those who are the called according to *His* purpose. Rom. 8:28, NKJV.

I've moved a lot over the years. Whether as a military kid or a pastor's wife, I've never liked moving. It's life-disrupting, hard work with too many decisions. Since my husband and I have moved ourselves across the United States several times, you would think it'd get easier.

In all our moves I never really worried about my worst nightmare. But if you asked me, I could readily tell you what my worst nightmare would be about moving—to have something go wrong after the 27-foot truck is fully loaded, requiring us to totally unload and reload.

Well . . . in our latest move from California to Florida, transmission problems developed with our rental truck in Montgomery, Alabama. Good news—they had a 24-hour truck service center right there. We dropped off the truck in hopes they could fix it overnight and we'd be on our way. In the morning came the bad news—no can do! Must unload and reload. My worst nightmare had come true! We had driven more than 2,000 miles across the country without major incident. We were just a day away from our destination, and now this. My wearied heart sank.

Ah, but the rental company promised that contract movers would do the job. Nice. They should! The movers would arrive at 9:30 a.m. We were to be on-site to supervise. 9:30 a.m. . . . no movers. 10:00 . . . still no movers. My husband, Zell, wasn't waiting any longer. He backed up the new truck to the old truck and started moving our boxes himself. Two hours later the movers arrived. On that sweltering, steamy Deep South day, I have to admit that this unhappy camper was a bit steamed up herself, though trying to keep a lid on it.

As this miserable day dragged on, I reluctantly concluded there are worse nightmares than unloading and reloading a moving truck: travel accidents, injury, and death. Once my temperature cooled down in body and spirit, I realized a new "route" this roadblock had opened. Because of the vehicle breakdown, I now had leverage to negotiate more time with the truck rental agency before the truck had to be turned in once we arrived in Florida. This relieved the stress of rushing to find a rental house, paying extra truck rental fees, or hassling with storage issues.

Life's roadblocks. Are they really roadblocks, or can you find a blessing in disguise?

Heide Ford

God, Our Loving Father

Whosoever shall receive one of such children
in my name, receiveth me. Mark 9:37.

At first there were three boys, neatly dressed, faces smiling as they walked into the sanctuary. They were not shy at all, and anyone would have thought that they were a part of the regular group of children. But a couple of weeks later one boy was missing, and in his place was a little girl. And then she did not come one Sabbath, and in her place was a new boy. I wondered what was going on, so I inquired, asking the member who was responsible for them, and I found out that they were foster children. Presently, of the three who started, two of the boys are still here, and they have been joined by three new girls. The children are now regular Sabbath school members; they recite their Bible text memory verses during the special Sabbath programs and sing in the children's choir.

This experience has taught me many wonderful lessons. Furthermore, I now have a lot of respect for foster parents. It must be difficult to train so many children from different backgrounds with different personalities and habits. It must take a lot of love, patience, and commitment. After all, "Jesus said, 'Let the children come to me. Don't stop them! For the Kingdom of Heaven belongs to those who are like these children'" (Matt. 19:14, NLT).

I have also learned to appreciate my own parents more. They have long since gone to sleep in Jesus, but when I think of my mother bringing me up all by herself and giving me everything that she could afford, I am so grateful. She could have easily given me up for adoption or to foster parents.

Most of all, I have learned to love my heavenly Father more. It is so comforting to know that He loves all His children and that He is just waiting to take us all to live with Him forever in heaven. There are many reasons children are put in foster homes, but there will be no foster homes in heaven. You see, we will all be part of His family: "God decided in advance to adopt us into his own family by bringing us to himself through Jesus Christ. This is what he wanted to do, and it gave him great pleasure" (Eph. 1:5, NLT). We will all have one heavenly Father and live in the homes He has prepared for us. I say, *Thank You, Jesus*, but I also say thank you to those who lovingly care for foster children here on this earth, training them for heaven as well.

Gloria McDowall

Throw Away a Gift?

For God so loved the world, that He gave His only begotten Son,
that whoever believes in Him shall not perish, but have eternal life.
For God did not send the Son into the world to judge the world, but that
the world might be saved through Him. John 3:16, 17, NASB.

It was Mother's Day. Our home was adjacent to several acres of woods where wild-flowers grew profusely. My children, ages 3 and 6, bubbled with joy and exuberance as they sang "Happy Mother's Day to You" and handed me a large bouquet of pollen-drenched flowers. I answered with a sneeze, than another sneeze, and yet another.

It was hard to explain to them why I had to throw away their precious gift.

Many years later the older of the two wrote a no-thank-you note to me from her college. "Mom," she said, "the cookies you sent were covered with mold. I had to throw them away."

There were several occasions that my husband and I were missionaries in Russia that we had to painfully throw away a love gift. One gardener gave me flower starts to take home to plant in my American garden. I had to throw them away—they were not allowed to pass through United States Customs. That was painful to me.

And what about the stacks of thank-you and get-well cards crafted by grateful little hands? Eventually they, too, have to be discarded. When we were first married I saved baby announcements from friends, and I pasted greeting cards that we had received into a couple of scrapbooks. It wasn't long before it was obvious that that practice could not continue.

Currently I save unusual greeting cards from my children and grandchildren. That practice is also becoming overwhelming. I keep thinking that perhaps after we are gone, the kids will enjoy looking at them. (Probably not!) Then there are Christmas cards; what to do with them? Friends of ours select a Christmas card from their stash each day and pray for the person who sent it. A great idea that doesn't work for us more than a week or so. Some even take the time to write that person a note and tell them they prayed for them that day. Lofty actions all.

All of these gifts are trivial compared with the gift of salvation that our Lord Jesus Christ offers us. We must not discount that Gift, or think frivolously about it. It is the real thing. It's the only gift that really matters.

Barbara Huff

Counsels for a Transplant Recipient—Part 1

And my God will meet all your needs according to the riches of his glory in Christ Jesus. Phil. 4:19, NIV.

In 1977 my husband, Gaspar, was diagnosed with a polycystic kidney. His mother and several uncles, aunts, and cousins had already died from this hereditary defect. So through the years we were trying to brace ourselves for the inevitable: dialysis, deterioration, and death. Of course, if he could eventually have a kidney transplant, his future would look much brighter.

Life can be fairly normal for several years until the polycystic kidneys finally quit working. However, during this time the situation is like a ticking time bomb. At last, in December 2002, we were informed that Gaspar's kidney function was so poor that he should prepare for dialysis or a kidney transplant. Placed on a waiting list for a possible kidney donation, Gaspar knew the average waiting time to receive a kidney for transplant is about five years.

Knowing that it is best to skip the dialysis stage and receive a kidney transplant right away, I wrote in my prayer diary, "Lord, Gaspar needs a new kidney *now*. Work out this problem according to Your will. You have said in Philippians 4:19 that You will supply all our needs. Thank You for taking care of this urgent need in Your own time and in Your own way."

I decided to get tested to determine if I could donate a kidney to Gaspar. Even though the chances were slim that I, not a blood relative, would be compatible enough to be a donor, I went ahead anyway. Amazingly enough, I was compatible! (That is good to know after 33 years of marriage!) I donated a kidney to Gaspar on August 7, 2003. God supplied our need in a surprising way! We now feel an extra closeness to each other and are experiencing a deeper meaning of the biblical idea of "one flesh" (Gen. 2:24).

When Gaspar and I awoke from the surgery, I asked, "Are you being a good landlord for my kidney?" The answer to that question suddenly became a lifestyle for Gaspar. Preventing rejection of the new kidney *is* a matter of life and death. Accountability procedures, anti-rejection and anti-infection medications, plus other precautions, became a nonnegotiable part of Gaspar's daily schedule for preventing kidney rejection. A lesson in real-time that when God meets our needs, we are then responsible, by His grace, to be good stewards of those blessings.

May-Ellen Netten Colon

Counsels for a Transplant Recipient—Part 2

I will give you a new heart and put a new spirit in you. Eze. 36:26, NIV.

Preventing rejection of his new kidney has become a major priority for Gaspar, my husband. Just as my "new" kidney replaced Gaspar's defective one, God—who supplies all our needs (Phil. 4:19)—offers us a heavenly heart transplant (Eze. 36:26). All we have to do is receive it. And then ask God's help not to reject it. Preventing rejection of our heart transplant takes *intentional* measures. For example . . .

1. During the weeks following the kidney transplant, Gaspar had to take antibiotic and antiviral medications to keep him from infection. Taking time to foster a close relationship with God prevents spiritual infection and fights the germs of sin and evil. Jabez asked God to keep him from evil, and God granted his request (1 Chron. 4:10). Since Gaspar is immunosuppressed, he must be careful to avoid places of pollution and sickness, as we also must—spiritually.

Along with a healthy diet, multiple vitamins and prescription-strength calcium strengthen Gaspar's overall physical health and keep his bones from weakening. Spiritually speaking, trusting in the Lord with all our heart, acknowledging Him in everything we do, and shunning evil will bring health to our body and nourishment to our bones (Prov. 3:5). Strong physical and spiritual health prevent rejection of the new heart.

2. Gaspar must take his medication regularly. And in the spiritual realm we must regularly take time for heart antirejection measures. Having regular personal devotions and family worship are significant means toward this end.

3. Accountability to medical personnel is extremely important in preventing rejection of a transplanted organ. Gasper regularly takes—and reports—his temperature and blood pressure readings. Spiritually, we must regularly evaluate the internal environment of our personal lives, homes, and churches. Is the environment "hot" and full of pressure with criticism, argument, and gossip? Or are our personal lives, homes, and churches full of praise, affirmation, and thanksgiving? A healthy environment prevents rejection and nurtures the new heart from God.

As you think of my story, what other spiritual lessons can you draw about preventing rejection of God's gift of your new heart? What antirejection measures keep your heart healthy?

May-Ellen Netten Colon

From Pretty to Ugly

You are altogether beautiful . . .
there is no flaw in you. Song of Solomon. 4:7, NIV.

I love pretty things. I browse Pinterest for home decor ideas and use pretty filters on Instagram just as much as the next person. There's absolutely nothing wrong with being happy and having a good life, but sometimes life just isn't as perfect as home decor on Pinterest or heavily-filtered selfies on Instagram. In fact, someone recently told me her pretty-to-ugly story.

"I had every reason to succeed in life: a trust fund for my schooling, two wholesome Christian parents who loved me, and an amazing big sister who adored me. If I had followed the plan laid before me, by now I'd have a career and perhaps my own family. However, some really bad choices led me elsewhere.

"It all started in grade school. I was young, impressionable, looking for fun, and just wanted to have friends. At first I experimented with soft drugs, but it was never enough. Eventually I found myself knee-deep in major drug addiction, chasing highs that almost cost me my life more than once. I was sent to various programs to help me get clean.

"As a young girl experimenting with drugs, I thought I was invincible! Truth is, addiction doesn't see race, age, status, or religious upbringing. It doesn't know any boundaries. Once it finds you, it wants you dead. But lucky for me, God doesn't see obstacles or boundaries either.

"I have been clean for 16 months now, and I regularly attend NA (Narcotics Anonymous) meetings. Because of God and my support group, I have found a beautiful life. It's not perfect, but it's all mine. I try not to regret the past because, had it not been for this blessing-in-disguise disaster, I wouldn't have been humbled. I would never have seen my need for a Power greater than myself. With that brokenness, I have had the opportunity to lend a helping hand to the sick and suffering. My struggle with addiction has given me a new chance to develop inner beauty, and for that I am forever grateful."

Ugly can become pretty. Distressed furniture is popular on Pinterest. Instagram has filters to make things look gritty. We call skin defects beauty marks. God brings to life the things in our lives that are dead, scarred, and broken. Whatever part of you that you feel is too ugly for God, lay it at His feet today. You may be surprised with what He can make out of it.

Alison Brook

Baby Brother

You do not know what tomorrow will bring. What is your life? For you are a mist that appears for a little time and then vanishes. James 4:14, ESV.

An unexpected telephone call came, letting me know that my brother was gravely ill. His liver was failing so badly that he ended up in the hospital in a coma. Miles away in the snow-covered north, I skied to a favorite meditation spot, all the while praying and singing, "Great is Thy faithfulness, O God, my Father . . ." God does not change; He is the same loving God whom my grandparents and parents served. A deep peace invaded my soul, as I continued, joyfully singing, "Thy compassions, they fail not."

My baby brother, now a senior citizen looking forward to celebrating his seventieth birthday with his beloved wife, returned to us out of his coma, something very rare in such cases. God had performed a miracle. My brother was sent home under hospice care; I arrived at his bedside the following day. How frail he looked, but how dear.

As siblings we were close again. I told him about when he was born, how he nearly drowned in a tub and a pond when he was a toddler. I was not a mini-mother but a tomboy; still, I did my best to help our busy mother. While Mom cooked and the baby had whooping cough, I would function as an alarm system: "Mom, the baby can't breathe—he is turning blue."

Life was simple and happy except for World War II, with nasty planes passing overhead on their way to bomb the city about 20 miles (32 kilometers) away. We had been taught that God was living in heaven above, taking care of us. One day, looking at a war plane overhead, the only tangible, powerful thing he could see in the sky, my brother cried out, "Terrible God."

We reminisced about our childhood and sang hymns. My brother told me what he would do "if he made it." He looked at me and said, "Did it have to come to this before I realized the reality about God, and how many loving people there are?" His voice trailed off: "God is not a Santa Claus to whom you go only to ask for things. . . . He is different. . . . It is the reality of life. . . . God is in it. . . . all the time."

God does not always heal a person in this life, but He gave us a little window from heaven to share closeness and love and hope of eternal life. "Till we meet again, beloved baby brother." A hope for you and me each day.

Sinikka Dixon

God's Amazing Providence

And the Lord, he it is that doth go before thee; he will be with thee, he will not fail thee, neither forsake thee: fear not, neither be dismayed. Deut. 31:8.

My husband had been assigned to work in a new position in a faraway town. The time came for us to move, but we had heard that no homes were available for rent in that town. We had gone ahead, however, and rented our current house to a family who was expecting to occupy it shortly.

We wondered how we would manage, because our older son, who was in college, had made arrangements to live with us off campus within a month's time, and a house had not yet been found. The question was "When and where are we going to find a house?" My husband assured us that if God wanted us there, He would go ahead of us and prepare the house.

One morning we got up, prayed together, and decided to go in search of that house. This was a leap of faith, and we believed our prayers were already answered. When we reached the town we inquired whether there was any house for rent. The reply was that there were none. However, someone told us of a house that a man was building for his son who lived abroad, but he was not sure that the man concerned would be prepared to rent it. We took the man's name and proceeded to go in search of him.

On reaching the house under construction, my husband realized that he knew the man; unexpectedly, the man did not look surprised to see us. As a matter of fact, he told us that he recently had us in mind because his son had recently called and told him that he would not be returning home. He had heard that we would be moving to that town, and he felt that the house he was building would be the right one for us to occupy. There were just a few finishing touches to be done, and he would let us move in.

God moves in mysterious ways His wonders to perform. We were able to move into the house earlier than we expected. We were convinced more than ever that God means what He says when He tells us that "he it is that doth go before thee; he will be with thee, he will not fail thee, neither forsake thee: fear not, neither be dismayed." Blessed be the name of the Lord! Let us continue to put implicit faith in Him at all times, for His words are always true.

Shirnet Wellington

Queen of Quite a Lot

Very early in the morning, while it was still dark, Jesus got up, left the house and went off to a solitary place, where he prayed. Mark 1:35, NIV.

I was wandering around cyberspace somewhere when I came across a woman who called herself the Queen of Quite a Lot.

Cute, I thought. And then I realized that I myself am a queen of quite a lot. I am the queen of quite a lot of laundry, for example. In fact, Mount Washmore could almost qualify as a high peak in my state.

I am also the queen of quite a lot of dishes, I have sinks full of them. My kingdom is home to quite a lot of giant dust bunnies, which are secretive creatures that hide under the furniture until they grow so large they are mistaken for small dogs.

And there is quite a lot to be done every day, judging by my to-do list—most of which I never finish.

Yes, I think I qualify as a queen of quite a lot, and most days I would give my kingdom for a long nap and some peace and quiet.

There are days that it's difficult to see the blessings for the mess. Life can be so in-your-face that there's really no getting over, around, or through it in order to get any kind of perspective. In the middle of all the caterwauling, it's hard to hear yourself think.

Jesus must have had those kinds of days too, because He often rose early and went off by Himself to talk to God.

When the mess and the stress become overwhelming, it's helpful to follow His example and take a time-out to be with God so we can locate our center again.

Because there's one thing you can be sure of: When the mess and stress are worst, the spiritual battle is raging around you.

Get thee hence. It's time to retreat and regroup, spend some time with the King, and stock up on peace and power to carry on.

I've decided that I am happy to surrender my crown as Queen of Quite a Lot and relinquish the throne in order to become the Princess of Plenty.

Céleste Perrino-Walker

Traveling in a Bubble

Dear friends, let us love one another, for love comes from God. Everyone who loves has been born of God and knows God. 1 John 4:7, NIV.

In May of 2012 my husband and I went on a European river cruise up the Lower Danube to celebrate the completion of my master's degree. We had a delightful time on our cruise. The service was excellent. The food was wonderful. Our fellow travelers were extremely interesting. We enjoyed learning about and traveling through countries we had never visited before. However, despite our overall enjoyment of our experience, we were plagued with the oddest feeling. We felt as if we were all in a bubble. Our fellow travelers were all from English-speaking countries, so everyone we interacted with spoke English. On the cruise ship and on our tour buses we were cut off from the people of the countries we visited because we did not speak directly to them or interact with them. We were merely observing from a distance rather than immersing ourselves in the lives and culture of the people who lived in those countries.

While pondering this rather odd feeling, I was struck with the realization that I all too often go through life in my own little bubble. How often am I caught up with my own concerns and even joys to the point that I miss out on connecting with my neighbors, my coworkers, or even strangers on the street or in the store? God wants me to reach out to those around me. Each day I can be a blessing to others by sharing their sorrow, encouraging them when they are downhearted or rejoicing with them for all the blessings God pours down. In today's busy world it is all too easy to only brush the surface of each others' lives.

However, I believe that God is calling each one of us to more meaningful relationships with our friends, our family, our church family, our coworkers. We are to live out God's love. I believe that God first of all wants to have an authentic relationship with each of us, and then because of that relationship, we will be able to reach out to those around us with God's love.

I don't want to go around in a bubble. I don't want to be cut off from those around me—or at best only touching the surface of my friends' lives. I want more. I know God wants more for me and for you. Let's be God's love to those around us!

Julie Bocock-Bliss

Not Just a Cleaner!

Whatever you do, work at it with all your heart, as working for the Lord, not for human masters, since you know that you will receive an inheritance from the Lord as a reward. It is the Lord Christ you are serving. Col. 3:23, 24, NIV.

The downside of living in the beautiful country of Scotland is that we live a long way from our families. But being a writer means that my schedule is flexible, so I can visit them whenever my husband has meetings in England.

Our daughter, Beth, has a full-time job. So I spend my mornings at her home working as a freelance writer. After lunch I spend an hour cleaning her house and making supper, and then I collect little Zara from day care so we can play together before her parents come home.

I'm not particularly devoted to cleaning, but when I'm doing it for my daughter, it becomes a gift and a delight, and it makes a huge difference to Beth because she's so busy. When she's home, her priority is spending time with her little girl and husband, not cleaning the bath.

One day as I scrubbed her kitchen floor, the phone rang. It was from a charitable organization, and I didn't really want to get into a long discussion. So, rather than saying I was Beth's mother, I said I was "just the cleaner" and hoped the conversation would end quickly. After all, there I was, with a bowl of soapy water and a scrubbing brush, cleaning.

Suddenly it was "Don't put yourself down, young lady!" (That made me smile!) "There's nothing wrong with being a cleaner. It deserves as much respect as any other job. The world would be a terrible place to live if there weren't cleaners!" He continued for five minutes. It was heartwarming that a stranger would be so concerned about one who was "just a cleaner."

Today most of us will do something mundane, boring, dirty, or unappreciated. We may think we're *just* a cleaner, *just* a mother, *just* someone who washes the clothes—but we are so much more. Every tiny thing we do can be a gift of love for someone else, and therefore a gift of love for God. Our love turns the most basic task into an act of worship. When I'm scrubbing floors, I imagine I'm doing it for Jesus. I smile, my body relaxes, and I know my work is the most important thing I can do for God, right now. I am not just a cleaner—I am serving God Himself.

In God's eyes we are never *just* anything. Except loved.

Karen Holford

Sparrows and Evil

Jesus wept. John 11:35, NIV.

I sat in the back seat of the car. As we stopped at a red light on the highway, I looked out my window, and there on the highway was a dead sparrow. *Poor little thing*, I thought, *it probably was hit by a car.* Not surprisingly, my next thought was of the text "Are not five sparrows sold for two pennies? Yet not one of them is forgotten by God" (Luke 12:6, NIV). *How often does God's heart hurt because of fallen sparrows?* I wondered. *There must be thousands in a day!* And then I thought of other things that must pierce His heart, probably every minute. The list must be endless. In the news in the past few days there have been stories about children who have intentionally been starved to death—intentional abuse! That must just tear Jesus' heart! And then of course there are all the other types of abuse—all the horrible things that people do to each other, and often to people in their own family, people they supposedly love.

It did not take long for my mind to wander over all sorts of things that I hear about from day to day that just make me cringe, and God knows—and cares—so much more about them. Day after day we see pictures of people suffering from famine, from floods, from other natural disasters. Immorality is becoming rampant. And then there are of course the wars, and there are more than enough! And sectarian violence and terrorism that is being carried on in country after country—when will it stop? God must long for that day even more than we do.

Thinking this way, I can identify with Jeremiah, the weeping prophet. As he thought of the horrors of the destruction of Jerusalem, he wrote: "This is why I weep and my eyes overflow with tears. No one is near to comfort me, no one to restore my spirit. My children are destitute because the enemy has prevailed" (Lam. 1:16, NIV). But there is good news, and Jeremiah wrote about that too: "Yet this I call to mind and therefore I have hope: because of the Lord's great love we are not consumed, for his compassions never fail. They are new every morning; great is your faithfulness. I say to myself, 'The Lord is my portion; therefore I will wait for him'" (Lam. 3:21-24, NIV). Even though Lamentations is a book of weeping, it holds some wonderful promises as well. I encourage you to read it all. God wants evil to end, including the death of little sparrows, even more than I do—and I know you do too, don't you?

Ardis Dick Stenbakken

Charlie

He shall call upon Me, and I will answer him; I will be with him in trouble; I will deliver him and honor him. Ps. 91:15, NKJV.

I live on six acres and have a great love for dogs, so it has been a privilege over the past several years to meet some wonderful surrendered or abandoned dogs. That is until I met Charlie.

Charlie is a beautiful golden doodle who looks like a miniature of his golden retriever mom. The only thing he seems to have acquired from his poodle dad is his proud stance. He was given up by his family primarily because at the age of 2 he was too much of a "renegade" for them to handle. Despite my spending hours with him and gaining his cooperation when on a leash, the moment the leash came off he seemed to forget everything. He ran the opposite direction when called; he often appeared on the outside of the fence and never seemed to remember where it was that he had dug his way out. On a couple occasions he had traffic stopped in both directions on the highway while people tried to help me catch him.

One day when I leashed my other two dogs to go for a walk, I called Charlie, but he ran in the opposite direction. A few minutes later I saw him running (outside the fence) toward the highway. By that time I was frustrated with him, and I turned him over to God. I paused and said, *Dear God, he is Your dog; please take care of him one way or the other, and if You want me to continue caring for him, please have him back in the yard when I return.* With that I took the other dogs for our walk. When we returned about a half hour later, there was Charlie, sitting inside the yard looking at me quizzically. He seemed to wonder why we had left without him.

I learned a couple of valuable lessons that day. Why do we continue to try to "fix" things (or others) on our own when God is just waiting to be asked to intervene? He wants us to call on Him. Also, I realized just how much He cares for us; He will be with us in trouble and will deliver us. If He was able to save Charlie from being hit on the highway and to help him find his way home, how much better able He is to guide us safely home if we just ask Him.

I'm pleased to say that Charlie is now almost 7 years old and has become my best example for the other dogs. He is the first to come when called and the only one, at present, who can go for walks off leash, as he stays by my side and obeys every command.

Beverly D. Hazzard

Fruitful Blessings

O taste and see that the Lord is good:
blessed is the man that trusteth in him. Ps. 34:8.

Wait on the Lord: be of good courage, and he shall strengthen
thine heart: wait, I say, on the Lord. Ps. 27:14.

As I am standing in the kitchen by the sink, looking out the window, my quick glance is greeted by a joyous burst of peach-orange color. I had planned a weekend trip away to enjoy a much-needed mental repair to recharge my spirit; however, there were physical obstacles to obtaining that goal. Dwelling on the color I had just glimpsed, my thoughts drifted back to the acceptance of the gift of a storm-tossed fruit, a papaya.

The fruit tree had to be cut down because of serious damage from a severe windstorm. The green, premature fruit was, to say the least, unappetizing. There was no guarantee this fruit would mature now that it was separated from its source, the tree. My acceptance of the gift was with reluctance. *Why couldn't I be given a ripe fruit—I don't want to wait for it to ripen.*

Several weeks passed without a sign of change to this fruit.

My trip was unsuccessful and not as I had anticipated or planned. But on my return a burst of color streaming through the covering of the bag arrested my attention. I smiled widely because a gift awaited me, and I discovered as I tasted the papaya that I was more recharged and even better refreshed than I could have planned.

Without any reluctance I now enjoyed the sweetness of this fruit. And as I tasted the delicious fruit, I saw that the Lord is indeed good. Looking at the green, immature fruit, one could not have guessed at how good the ripe fruit could be.

The Lord our Father says to taste and see that He is good. There are times we accept His gifts with reluctance. We miss the pleasant and fruitful blessings when we hesitate and miss our opportunities to be recharged and refreshed—beyond our anticipation or expectation.

There are storms that approach one's life, and the effects are not always welcome. But these storms can also bring gifts, and these gifts do come with blessings if we wait on our Father and do it with courage.

Marjorie Gray-Johnson

Divine Strength

But he said to me, "My grace is sufficient for you, for my power is made perfect in weakness." Therefore I will boast all the more gladly about my weaknesses, so that Christ's power may rest on me. 2 Cor. 12:9, NIV.

As a teen I was always fond of telling my male friends that I was more than a pair of breasts. Little did I know that the day would come when this would be more than words but an actual fact.

When I was 25 years old, I had the first lump removed from my breast. It was a very large phyllodes tumor that was benign. Almost five years later, when I felt another large lump, I thought it was more of the same. I submitted myself to the required surgery and lost a good portion of my right breast. I did not worry about the histology results, as I was convinced that God would not allow it to be malignant because He knew I resided in Turks and Caicos Islands, and cancer treatment there was not an option. So I returned to work and awaited the results. After almost two months I had received no results and called the surgeon. He told me that the tumor was cancerous and that I needed further treatment that would include possible radiation.

In that moment my life started to change, as I resolved in my mind that if I was going to submit to the surgeon's knife again, I would have the breast removed totally. I asked God to open doors as to where I should have my surgery. I went home to Jamaica, and four days and two consultations after my arrival, I had a unilateral mastectomy.

The road has not been easy, as my mastectomy has affected many aspects of my life. I could have been angry that God did not heal me directly, but I have learned that joy is a state of mind. I choose to have joy. My illness did not break my spirit. What could have destroyed me has simply made me stronger mentally and physically because of changes in my diet and exercise activities. I have learned to depend on God. He not only strengthens me but helps me to minister to others through dietary reform and as a counselor to fellow cancer patients and their loved ones. Losing a breast does not define who I am—or who you are. Your circumstances do not define you. Regardless of what you face, know that God is there. He is an ever-present source of hope and strength. All we need to do is lean on Him, and He will be our strength.

Andrea Francis

The Salvation of the Lord

Tomorrow march down against them. . . . You will not
have to fight this battle. . . . Stand firm and see the deliverance
the Lord will give you. 2 Chron. 20:16, 17, NIV.

On the night before a court hearing, I read today's verses. It all started when, in my teens, I caused a traffic accident and was sued. Immaturity, inexperience, and lack of knowledge—especially in the ways of the Lord—allowed the enemy, and successive mistakes of malicious lawyers, to transform this incident into an open wound. I spent years running away from the problem, but the more I fled, the more it grew, becoming a bleeding wound.

When I returned to the arms of the Lord, His Spirit began to organize my life. "But seek first his kingdom and his righteousness, and all these things will be given to you as well" (Matt. 6:33, NIV). I hired a lawyer to find out the current status of the case. The debt was far greater than we could afford. My boyfriend started having Bible studies. We began to tithe, and we set a wedding date. I chose the simplest things and got 50 percent of the cost from relatives and friends. God blessed us in everything. After the wedding my husband and I were baptized (he for the first time and I for the second). Even after paying rent and the attorney, we started saving money. In one year we had saved two fifths of the debt. We hoped for a settlement of 50 percent.

I turn now to the beginning of this message. Even though God was speaking to me through His Word, I was numbed by anxiety and lack of faith. We lose the wonderful comfort of Jesus in our struggles when we don't put them in His hands and rest in Him. I got the victory that day. We got the deal, even with so much heartache involved. It happened as I read in the Word of God. I didn't have to argue. I just waited, and then I heard the words of deliverance: "Yes, I accept the agreement."

Today I am very thankful to God, for He not only gave me strength and resources to tackle this problem, but after a year my husband even won a raffle for a new car! What a miracle! God gave us back the amount used to pay off the debt.

I don't know what you're going through today, but it's worth serving and being faithful to our God.

Adriana Lúcia Bonatti

Singing His Praises

*O come, let us sing unto the Lord: let us make a joyful noise
to the rock of our salvation. Ps. 95:1.*

The church I love and belong to is on the campus of a Christian boarding high school, so much of the music features the praise songs the teenagers prefer. Those of us who miss the old traditional hymns and gospel songs find joy in singing them during the Sabbath evening vespers, attended primarily by the older members and the younger children. Unfortunately, I do not have a beautiful voice like some in my family, but I can make a joyful noise, and those sitting near me are kind enough to pretend not to notice when I hit a sour note.

There have been times my efforts have been appreciated. When our children were very young, they had a pet duck with a couple of peculiarities—she was afraid of water, and when put into a lake she would paddle furiously toward shore and safety. Happy on dry land, she would sit on the back steps and "sing" when I played the piano. She had an even more limited range than I do, but it didn't stop her!

Then there was our fluffy yellow cat. Once she seemed to have something stuck in her throat, so I put her in the car and headed for the veterinarian, who was many miles away. As I drove I started singing and was surprised that any time I stopped kitty would meow piteously until I started again, then she was content, and I was amused! (Some morsel had scratched her throat on the way down, but she did recover.)

Though my musical ability is limited now, I thrill to magnificent performances by others. I can't begin to imagine what the choirs of heaven must sound like. Even more amazing is the idea that I might join them in singing praises to the Lord of lords and King of kings!

My older son played piano and trumpet and sang in the school choirs. His brother played piano and trombone and sang in choirs in high school and college. My husband played a baritone, and we would have family musicals at home when I played the piano and they played their instruments. Perhaps in heaven we can have our little family ensemble again in some out of the way spot in the vast universe. We'd love to have you as an audience, and I promise you that there will not be one missed or sour note!

Mary Jane Graves

Heading North

To every thing there is a season,
and a time to every purpose under the heaven. Eccl. 3:1.

Our compass usually points north in the summer. Many years ago my husband, Larry, and I took our 4-year-old son to canoe the Bowron lakes in northern British Columbia, Canada. When Garrick was 9, we bought him a backpack and headed to Alaska to begin a 33-mile trek on the famous Chilkoot Trail. The next summer the three of us paddled 430 miles (690 kilometers) northward on the Yukon River to Dawson City, and then we drove to Inuvik, as far north as one can drive on a public road in summer in Canada—120 miles (200 kilometers) north of the Arctic Circle. When Garrick was in graduate school and could not take a summer vacation, Larry and I still took our boots and binoculars to Alaska to hike in Denali National Park in the shadow of North America's highest mountain, Mount McKinley.

Much to our delight, Garrick and his wife now work in Alaska. Usually the 1,925-mile (3,098-kilometer) trip to their home takes us three long days, but in 2011 we were in a bigger hurry than usual—we wanted to meet our first grandchild. We pressed on mile after mile. Despite the long days, we felt good. As usual, we made lists of animals we'd seen. We read books to each other and sang along with recorded music. Although we didn't stop for meals, we did visit the "Cinnamon Bun Center of the Galactic Cluster."

As we reminisced about our earlier trips north, we felt young, despite the fact that we were grandparents. When we stopped for gas, I filled the tank and Larry cleaned the windshield. We looked at the other cars and smiled. A canoe on a Jeep. Two kayaks atop a SUV. That was how we had traveled. And then we looked carefully at our vehicle. We carried no canoe. Our hiking boots and a flashlight were visible, but we transported no tent or backpacks. We saw a small suitcase filled with our clothes, but the rest of the car was filled with baby things: boxes of children's books, the basket our son slept in for the first few months of his life, and a rocking chair purchased 30 years earlier when he was born.

The contents of our car shouted that Larry and I are no longer young, no longer as adventurous as we'd been. But we looked at each other, laughed, and headed north filled with joy in anticipation of meeting our grandson. To everything there is a season—and we relish them all.

Denise Dick Herr

An Unforgettable Holiday

Trust in the Lord forever, for in Yah, the Lord,
is everlasting strength. Isa. 26:4, NKJV.

During the Whitsun (May 25) holidays our family traveled to the South Tirol to spend 10 days together enjoying the beautiful scenery. This was one holiday I probably will never forget—from the start I had a terrible toothache. On the second day of the holiday I could not suffer the pain any longer, and went to see a dentist. What I had already feared proved to be true: my tooth that had given me continual trouble since January had to be extracted. Now began the agony of the aching wound, and this suffering continued until the last day of our holiday. In spite of that, I am thankful to our Father in heaven that He carried me through.

Despite the dental problem, our holiday was very lovely; I also had no back pain from which I always suffer when sleeping in a strange bed; on reflection, I can say, *Thank You, Lord.*

On our way back home we went into a restaurant in Austria for dinner; it was very late in the evening when we arrived back at our house, and then found, to our horror, that our rucksack, which held our house key, was not with us. It must have been left behind in the Austrian restaurant. The rucksack also had our cell phone and digital camera.

So we called a neighbor who kept our spare key in case of such an emergency, only to find that she had been called to stay with her sick mother in another city. My husband had to drive to that city to get her key to enable us to enter her house to search for our house key.

At last, late into the night, we were able to get into our house; then the telephoning began in earnest. We had to call the telephone company to block our cell phone, and call the restaurant. The rucksack had been found, and they promised to post it to our home address.

I was so relieved. However, the rucksack did not arrive, so in the meantime I was pushed, at great expense, to have our house lock changed, as I did not feel secure anymore, as everyone knows that anything can happen when your house key is in unknown hands.

After three long weeks of waiting, the rucksack arrived safely with all our belongings intact. Thanks be to God! I can say only that the good Lord allowed us to go through a testing time of anxiety; we had prayed to our heavenly Father for help in time of trouble, and He heard us, and in His own good time He delivered us out of all our difficulties.

Sandra Widulle

Plain and Simple

But his officers tried to reason with him and said, "If the prophet
had told you to do some great thing, wouldn't you have done it?
So you should certainly obey him when he says simply to go and wash and
be cured!" So Naaman went down to the Jordan River and dipped himself
seven times, as the prophet had told him to. And his flesh became as
healthy as a little child's, and he was healed! 2 Kings 5:13, 14, TLB.

The cancer had encircled major structures, which prevented its complete excision. So the surgeon removed what he could and gave Dave* about three months to live. Two weeks later he and his wife, Ruth, came to see me. A farmer, keen hunter, and fisher, Dave ate meat at almost every meal. Despite medications, I found his blood pressure was extremely high.

I encouraged him to eat as much raw fruit and vegetables as possible (even juicing them to increase consumption), to exclude meat from his diet, and to replace it with legumes and whole grains. After Dave made the assigned lifestyle changes, I next planned to start hydrotherapy. As the couple left the clinic, I wondered when I might hear from them again. I had recommended many changes, but there was no point in compromising, not with cancer. Four days later Ruth called requesting the hydrotherapy. She happily reported that Dave had eaten no meat, was starting to juice, and was already exercising outdoors every day. So hydrotherapy began, initially limited by his blood pressure, which was now too low! The new diet and exercise regime had clearly made a major and positive impact in just one week. He was able to stop all medications.

Dave faithfully kept to his lifestyle and hydrotherapy regime. We prayed before and after every treatment, asking God's blessing and healing. Dave felt so good after just three months that he requested his doctor do another CT scan. In sharing the scan results, the bewildered surgeon looked at Dave and said, "I guess miracles still happen." The tumor was gone, leaving only a small area of fibrosis where the surgeon had left a large tumor just three months before!

Are you facing a health challenge? Is there something you can do, by God's grace, to improve your health habits? And then, like Dave, leave the rest to the will of your loving Father?

Following the plain and simple laws of health, Dave—a man in his 80s—is still living a healthy lifestyle. And he is still going strong!

Nerida McKibben

* names changed for anonymity

God's Thousand Ways

O taste and see that the Lord is good:
blessed is the man that trusteth in him. Ps. 34:8.

Our heavenly Father has a thousand ways to provide for us, of which we know nothing" (Ellen G. White, *The Desire of Ages*, p. 330). My heavenly Father has proven time and time again the truth of this quote and that He is capable of taking care of my every need. When I worry, I am saying that God is limited, and in my mind, to limit God is to sin. You see, my dear sisters, I am still under construction. Daddy is still working on me, helping me to learn to fully trust Him. Each day He lavishes fresh supplies of blessing along my pathway. He is not limited by means or ways; He has His thousand ways.

Some time ago while I was going to college and working as a home health aide, it was difficult to make ends meet. I was taking a writing class, and the professor recommended a certain book that would be helpful. I went into the bookstore and looked at the book, but could not afford to buy it.

Soon after, I went to work at my patient's apartment. For some reason I glanced over to where the newspapers and books were tied up and ready to be thrown out. I saw something that looked familiar. I drew closer, and to my surprise, there was the book that I needed! One could imagine my happiness. One of God's thousand ways showed up in the garbage. I believe that God has a sense of humor. After many years I still have that book to remind me of God's thousand ways. God does not always show up when you want Him, or how you want Him to, but He always shows up on time.

My sisters, take time today and allow God to reveal His thousand ways to you. I am sure you will not be disappointed. "Delight thyself also in the Lord; and he shall give thee the desires of thine heart" (Ps. 37:4).

There are so many good texts besides the ones for today. Here is a beautiful one to bless us in our walk today, reminding us of His thousand ways: "Lord, you are my God; I will exalt you and praise your name, for in perfect faithfulness you have done marvelous things, things planned long ago" (Isa. 25:1, NIV). Have you thought about His promises and His ways? If we have trust, we can count on Him, in a thousand ways.

Joan M. Leslie

The Prayer

But when you pray, go into your room, close the door
and pray to your Father, who is unseen. Then your Father,
who sees what is done in secret, will reward you. Matt. 6:6, NIV.

It was a Saturday night. I was very worried and anxious because each of my two young sons had gone to a different place. My younger son was the biggest reason for my concern and anxiety. He was a drug user, and I knew where he was. I did not worry so much about my older son, for he was a responsible boy.

But that night, I felt agitated, worried, and anxious. My older son and three other young people were riding to a neighboring town. It was not a tour of major risks, but an uncontrollable concern dominated me. Given this anxiety, I felt the need to talk to God, so I went to a place that I could be alone with God, and there I talked about what I was feeling. I asked God to protect my children and everyone they were with.

After the prayer I felt better and went to the bedroom. When the phone rang, I ran to answer and heard the voice of my older son. With a trembling, nervous, and scared voice, he told me bluntly, "Mom, we just had an accident, but we are all OK. A rear wheel came off, and we could see sparks of the iron touching the asphalt and the car sliding out of control. At the time of the accident, there were no other cars, and, thank God, my friend was able to stop on the side of the road—we do not know how. Fortunately, we're fine. We need Dad to come and help us and bring another wheel."

I praised God for having protected them and having led me to a prayer at the exact time of the accident. God, who loves us so much, heard my prayer and took care of the boys. As our text today says, He "will reward you."

As our car was the same make of car as the one the boys had been driving, we could use the spare tire and solve that difficulty. God not only provides protection, but fills our needs as well. I needed relief and certainty of God's constant care, and I received much more.

Even Jesus prayed for those He loved. In John 17 we read: "I pray for them. I am not praying for the world, but for those you have given me, for they are yours. . . . Holy Father, protect them by the power of your name . . . so that they may be one as we are one" (verses 9-11, NIV).

Vera Lúcia F. S. Ferrari

Supply All Our Needs

And my God will meet all your needs according
to the riches of his glory in Christ Jesus. Phil. 4:19, NIV.

I live in the driest state of the driest continent of the world, Australia, on a small property approximately three acres in size. The original farm was taken up by my husband's great-grandfather in the 1800s. We live in the township of Murray Bridge, located next to the river Murray, a very slow-flowing river that commences in the Snowy Mountains in New South Wales, traveling through three states, then emptying into the sea at Goolwa, South Australia.

We experienced a drought during the years 2008-2009. We have been married for more than 60 years and have lived here for 55 years, but had never known such dryness. There have been droughts before, but never to this extent. When we are having our morning devotional, approximately 500 Corellas and a few Galahs would come to our property for breakfast, systematically digging up the ground with their beaks and eating the bulbs of the nut grass, botanical name *Cyperus rotundus*. It is an introduced weed to Australia. Both humans and birds eat this small bulb, which has a thin, papery outer layer, with spear grasslike leaves, so the birds can locate it easily.

We have a marvelous God who supplies all of our needs, as well as for the birds. In the last days before Jesus comes we are promised that our bread and water will be sure. Remember how God fed Elijah with food brought to him by the ravens, morning and evening (see 1 Kings 17:2-6)? God supplies the needs of the birds, too: "Behold the fowls of the air: for they sow not, neither do they reap, nor gather into barns; yet your heavenly Father feedeth them. Are ye not much better than they?" (Matt. 6:26).

Twenty to 30 years ago an elderly woman of our church was stockpiling food for the "time of trouble," which the Bible says is to come on the earth before Jesus returns. She has since passed to her rest in the Lord, as has her only child and his wife. Was she trusting the Lord or trying to take care of things herself?

We are to trust in the Lord; only our heavenly Father knows the time and the hour for His coming. As a favorite hymn admonishes us, we are to trust and obey.

Joan D. L. Jaensch

Unity, Part 1

I ask . . . that they may all be one. As you, Father, are in me
and I am in you, may they also be in us, so that the world
may believe that you have sent me. John 17:20, 21, NRSV.

That a prayer for unity among His followers should have been foremost in the mind of our Savior just before His sacrifice on Calvary gives evidence of the less-than-ideal relationships among His disciples. Jesus' final wish for His followers was that they should get along!

The Epistles are full of exhortations for the brothers and sisters of the new Christian churches to get along with one another. And the advice was not limited to church members—it was also aimed at church leaders.

To the Romans He exhorted that they "welcome those who are weak in faith, but not for the purpose of quarreling over opinions" (Rom. 14:1, NRSV). Some believed in eating anything, and others, in limiting what they ate. No matter, says Paul—just don't fall into the trap of judging your brother or sister who doesn't do as you do or believe as you believe. Apparently that's just what the Roman Christians were doing. Just a few verses down in chapter 14, Paul is forced to ask rhetorically, "Why do you pass judgment on your brother or sister? Or you, why do you despise your brother or sister?" (verse 10). Eventually Paul concludes by exhorting: "Let us then pursue what makes for peace and for mutual upbuilding" (verse 19).

Again, this time to the Corinthian Christians, Paul points out practices and attitudes that were threatening the unity of the believers: "For as long as there is jealousy and quarreling among you, are you not of the flesh, and behaving according to human inclinations?" (1 Cor. 3:3, NRSV). The Corinthians were divided according to which apostle or church leader gave them the gospel. We can imagine them arguing that Paul was more "authoritative" than Apollos, since he had been called by Jesus Himself. Paul makes the point that no man is an island, that he could not have done his work without Apollos nor Apollos without Paul nor Peter without Paul and vice versa, concluding, "For we are God's servants, working together; you are God's field, God's building" (1 Cor. 3:9, NRSV).

Church unity is understood by Paul to be aimed at the holy purpose of building up the body of Christ, the church.

Lourdes Morales-Gudmundsson

Unity, Part 2

Holy Father, protect them by the power of your name, the name
you gave me, so that they may be one as we are one. John 17:11, NIV.

Anything that works against the building up of the body of Christ, Paul wrote to the Corinthians, must be eschewed: sexual immorality; taking each other to secular courts to resolve conflicts that could easily be resolved within the church; abusing the body that is the temple of the Holy Spirit; denying each other conjugal duties; lording it over those with less power; overstepping their newfound liberty in Christ to the detriment of the church within the community; and so forth.

What are the factors that contribute to the absence of peace among the members of the body of Christ, the church? Diversity, blessed diversity! We were all made different from one another, though one in purpose. We are different because God meant it to be so. Just as each member of the Trinity is different, they are one God. Each has a different yet invaluable contribution to make toward our salvation and well-being. Likewise, each of the members of the body of Christ has a different, yet indispensable, contribution to make to the well-being of the entire body and the promotion of the gospel. When the Holy Spirit distributes the gifts that will guarantee the good health of the body of Christ, He leaves the door open for men and women, boys and girls, rich and poor, people with Ph.D.s and those with three years of primary school, to hear the call of God to minister with their particular gift for the edifying of the church.

The glorious diversity of gifts assures that every part of the body will be nurtured and strengthened. Unity and diversity are not opposites—they are complements, like the two components of a plug. You can't have one without the other if you want that lamp to turn on or that toaster to work. In creating male and female, God established diversity as the context in which unity should flourish. Unity is not uniformity or lockstep. True unity recognizes the diversity of our gifts and creates a friendly environment for each unique gift to be exercised in blessing to the entire body.

Recognizing the symbiotic relationship between unity and diversity is the first step toward peace in our relationship with God, with each other, and with our own souls.

Lourdes Morales-Gudmundsson

Creation's Marvel

Then God said, "Let the land produce vegetation:
seed-bearing plants and trees on the land that bear fruit
with seed in it, according to their various kinds." And it was so. . . .
And God saw that it was good. And there was evening, and
there was morning—the third day. Gen. 1:11-13, NIV.

It's June again in the northern woods of Ontario where I live. My hubby, John, has been out in the gardens planting, pruning, and doing whatever else devoted gardeners do.

I don't care for gardening, but I do love the gorgeous warm-weather flowers that grace our yard, whether their blooms last for only a few hours or as long as a few weeks. Some people say it's a shame to go to the work of planting flowers for such a short growing time. But I'm a great fan of the seasons. In fact, after a seemingly endless winter of snow and barren ground, I truly believe one can appreciate flowers even more than if they bloomed year-round.

My neighbor knocked at our door on a recent June evening. "Please come see my moonflower," she invited. John and I tromped over to her yard where she had set up a lawn chair right in front of a furry little green plant sporting some pointy buds. My neighbor said, "Last night buds started opening around sunset. Five actually emerged before my eyes in the lingering twilight." Though dubious, I thought, *Well, that does at least explain the name of the moonflower.*

I noticed one bud that had pale yellow showing along one side, but I detected no noticeable movement. Yet, as time passed, the bud's increasing yellow tint seemed to announce it was starting on some type of journey. We suddenly noticed that the bud had opened ever so slightly. Curiously, though, we couldn't identify when that change had actually happened. Maybe at an instant when our weary gazes had wandered? I vowed to stare more diligently.

Then a green petal peeled away. Right before our eyes the flower started to move. Slowly, weblike, it spread apart as if in slow motion. Then all movement stopped. We too remained still. Suddenly the moonflower unfurled in all its glory as we watched in wonder.

What an awesome experience! One I shall never forget. To be given the honor of watching God's creation in action with my naked eyes—wow! What must it have been like during Creation week? Praise the Lord for His marvelous works!

Dawna Beausoleil

Painful Places

Beloved, think it not strange concerning the fiery trial
which is to try you . . . when his glory shall be revealed,
ye may be glad also with exceeding joy. 1 Peter 4:12, 13.

I can't do this alone, God. I need you to hold on to me." The words of Josh Wilson's "Savior, Please" came to mind as I opened my eyes and painfully rolled out of bed. It had been a difficult week. I felt drained—emotionally and physically. Not only was I struggling with my financial limitations—I was also trying to cope with physical injuries sustained from a major motor vehicle accident and its ripple effects in other areas of my life. Yet I was not the only person in a "painful place" that morning. I prayerfully remembered what some of my close friends were also going through: financial struggles, betrayal, divorce, brokenness. To myself I said, *God's people are going through tough times.*

I suspect the apostle Peter had similar concerns for his friends as I did for mine. In fact, using straightforward terms, he acknowledged the painful places being experienced by many early believers in Christ: grief, injustice, and suffering. Peter urged his fellow believers to see their struggles from the viewpoint of God's chosen people. In so many words he was saying, "Don't be surprised by Satan's attacks and the fiery trials you're currently undergoing. Just remember that God will vindicate your faithfulness when He comes back in glory."

This same encouragement holds true for believers today. Yes, the devil aims his darts at our most sensitive areas in our most vulnerable moments when we are at our lowest points. We sometimes struggle to understand the reasons for the fiery trials we go through. However, God is right there with us through our shattered dreams, wounded hearts, emptiness, grief, and loneliness. And He delights in our steadfastness and faithfulness.

Moreover, it is often in a painful place that God impresses His deepest truth upon our hearts. It's in our own brokenness that we better understand what Jesus suffered for us. We start to feel His agony and loneliness, endured in love for us. In our painful places, we find *Him.* And then, healing and peace.

He's promised to reveal His glory in us and give us joy—both of which will serve as godly witnesses to others who are watching us journey triumphantly through our painful places.

Stacey A. Nicely

Does God Care?

*For he will command his angels concerning you
to guard you in all your ways; they will lift you up in their hands,
so that you will not strike your foot against a stone. Ps. 91:11, 12, NIV.*

By the time you read this devotional, my heart will undoubtedly be aching for the loss of my sister Norka. Nine years ago doctors gave her a sobering diagnosis regarding symptoms she had been experiencing. She is suffering from two immunodeficiency diseases: lupus and scleroderma. Since diagnosis Norka has bravely battled these two illnesses that have practically consumed her. Norka's only life goal right now is to survive day by day. Since her diagnosis many people have faithfully and earnestly prayed for her healing. Yet she has not been healed.

So does God care? Is He listening to our desperate cries?

Without a doubt I can say, "Yes, He cares." Why? Because our merciful God has been lifting up Norka in His hands so that she will not strike her foot against the stone of despair. Though He has not healed her, He has divinely intervened on her behalf and provided for her.

God cares enough to have given Norka a faithful, loving husband who has also helped keep her alive during the ups and downs of this medical roller-coaster ride. He has tenderly met her needs as only a man who loves his wife with all his heart can. God cares about Norka enough to have put her in the hands of a doctor who considers her not just a patient but a friend and a member of his own family. This physician does everything he can to alleviate her physical pain. God cares so much for Norka that He gave her three young sons who continue to fill her life with joy and tender love. In His care for my sister, God has surrounded her with other supportive family members and friends without whom her tortuous experience would have been much less bearable. Furthermore, God cares so much for Norka that He has provided for all her physical, financial, and medical needs. In addition to all these blessings, God has cared enough about Norka to transform her, giving her His peace, which transcends all understanding.

Because of His care, Norka continues to be a testimony to the rest of us. A testimony that despite uncertainty and incomprehensible suffering in this life, we can yet be at peace in Him. We can trust that even if we face loss on this earth, He is still lifting us up in special ways. And one day He will reward us with eternal life. Yes, God cares!

Hannelore Gomez

I Can't Believe It!

Unless I see the nail marks in his hands and put my finger where the nails were, and put my hand into his side, I will not believe. John 20:25, NIV.

On June 27, 2010, the German soccer team beat out England's team 4-1 for the World Cup Championship in South Africa. In previous soccer matches the German team had not played very convincingly, so many people interested in the match didn't believe this team would easily win, if at all. However, the German team played hard and won in a surprising upset.

The day of that game my daughter, Saskia, was on duty at a gas station where she works from time to time. Though working, she was still able to catch reports of the match on the radio. Not being at the game or watching it on TV, Saskia obviously couldn't see the German team scoring their goals. After her shift at work, she returned home shaking her head. "I can't believe it! I just can't believe it unless I see it for myself!" Of course, as soon as Saskia watched replays of the game on the Internet, she was convinced that the German team had indeed won the match.

My daughter's experience with doubt brought one of Christ's disciples to my mind. Thomas. After the Lord's death and resurrection, most of the disciples were huddling behind locked doors in an upper room when Jesus suddenly came to them. Thomas was not present at this time, so he missed the opportunity to see Jesus for himself. When Thomas later joined the other disciples, they reported, "We have seen the Lord!"

As with Saskia, who'd only heard reports of the soccer match, Thomas found it difficult to believe that his friends were telling the truth about the risen Savior. He exclaimed, "If I don't see the nail marks in His hands, I can't believe it!" Since Internet didn't exist in those days, Thomas had to wait for further opportunity. A week later, when Thomas was together with the disciples, Jesus appeared again. This time the Master specifically sought out Thomas and showed him the nail prints, saying, "Because you have seen me, you have believed; blessed are those who have not seen and yet have believed" (John 20:29, NIV).

Our proof of Christ's resurrection is in His Word. We may be tempted to doubt or not trust. But if we are sincerely open to truth, Jesus will seek us out as He did Thomas. Then one day we will see Jesus with our own eyes. Knowing this, even now we can say, "I believe it!"

Hannele Ottschofski

The Fly

Strengthen the hands that are weak
and the knees that are feeble. Heb. 12:12, NASB.

I was suffering through the intense summer heat in the main auditorium at the British Columbia camp meeting in Canada. On this particular day of our church's annual weeklong spiritual retreat, I was trying to absorb deep concepts from the sermon being preached. But with the side tarps drawn up for ventilation, the buzzing of pesky flies disturbed my concentration. To make matters worse, I'd neglected to wear my glasses. As I squinted, trying to locate a verse the preacher was citing, one of those flies swooped down and lighted on my Bible. I didn't want to make a scene, since I was seated among hundreds of people. So I restrained myself from swatting at it. Then I noticed the fly was on the very verse I'd been searching for!

The next day I wore my glasses to the meeting. The speaker began his sermon with a short review of the former day's topic. I opened my Bible to the already-familiar passage he'd be reviewing. Then right before my eyes a huge fly again landed—and on the very same verse as the day before! Was it the same fly? Did it land there for a reason?

I don't know. But, having on my glasses, I was now able to study that fly like I'd never looked at flies before. I noticed that its visually beautiful and robust body reflected light in iridescent shades of green, blue, and gold. Delicate, airy shapes patterned its short wings. I allowed the fly to walk around on my chapter as I listened to the sermon. I sat still, not wishing to frighten it. Its large eyes appeared to move across the verses. Then it tiptoed along the margin, paused, and rubbed its front feet together as we would our hands, as if to say, "Look over here—see what I've found!" It was sitting on Hebrews 12:12, our text for today.

I mused how often I am consumed with the business of everyday life, and sometimes get annoyed with interruptions that might transport a touch of beauty into my life if I'd take the time to appreciate it. The Bible tells us (see Rom. 1:20) that God reveals what we *can't* see about Himself through things He has created. In other words, through the things that we *can* see. That morning at camp meeting God allowed a tiny creature, whose original created purpose has been distorted by sin, to still give me a visual reminder of His creative power. The same Power that will daily strengthen me when I feel discouraged, weak, or feeble.

Vidella McClellan

A Good Bad Hair Day

I will praise You, for I am fearfully and wonderfully made;
marvelous are Your works. Ps. 139:14, NKJV.

I wish people would just stop talking about my hair!" I muttered to myself as yet another person commented on how much they liked my new hairstyle. I didn't like it. I thought it was messy. I had told the stylist I didn't want layers. But layers I had. It was like my hair had a mind of its own, and it decided that it was going to be its natural curly self no matter how hard I tried to make it straight. I really didn't like how it looked. When one friend told me it was an old-fashioned haircut and made me look older, I agreed with her. She seemed to be the only one who thought that way. Throughout the weekend retreat people kept commenting on how much they liked it. I just wanted to scream, "But I don't like it curly!"

I really wanted the straight hair shown in all the current cute hairstyles. Straight, shiny hair that falls neatly and swings a bit. Hair more stylish and pretty than my curly mess. But with this new cut, I had no choice but to let my hair go the way it naturally wanted to go. When I tried to straighten it and make it look stylish and trendy, it just looked awful.

That's when God got my attention. Pointing out how often I want to be different than who I naturally am. How often I want to be like someone else, thinking that they have better gifts, are prettier, do things better than I do. Not really wanting to be the "me" He created me to be. I sometimes try hard to make me different, just like making my curly hair straight.

Yet He created me to be me. An introvert who prefers meaningful one-on-one conversation to a party filled with people and games. A teacher at heart who wants to turn everything I learn and experience with God into an article or sermon or blog. A woman with an empathetic heart that cries at commercials and the morning news—even at the gym on the treadmill. God longs for me to be the me He created me to be. He wants us to get up every morning, look in the mirror, and say, "I am fearfully and wonderfully made! Marvelous are Your works—including me!" Smile and walk away, being the best ourselves we can be.

To paraphrase a contemporary poet's thought, no other person on the entire planet can be a more authentic you than . . . well, *you!*

Tamyra Horst

Rainstorm

We depend upon the Lord alone to save us. Only he can help us; he protects us like a shield. No wonder we are happy in the Lord! For we are trusting him. We trust his holy name. Yes, Lord, let your constant love surround us, for our hopes are in you alone. Ps. 33:20-22, TLB.

Glorious springtime! A time of new beginnings! From the crocus peeking out under the snow to the flowering trees and newborn animals, it is a season of newness and beauty.

As a child growing up on a farm, I loved spring for another reason: baby chicks! The farm I lived on was a dairy farm, but for extra income we sold eggs to a small local grocery store in exchange for groceries. Every spring my mom purchased 100 or more chicks, and it was always a thrill to go along with mom to the hatchery and bring home those very cute chicks—a fluff of yellow with black beady eyes and long skinny legs. We had the chicken coop all ready for them with an enclosed area, a heat lamp, and feed and water troughs. Since the chicks had no "mom" to keep them warm, they depended on the heat lamp.

One late spring we had an extreme rainstorm—lots of thunder and lightning— even some hail! The electricity went out—a hard thing on dairy farms—no milking machines working, and also the heat lamp in the chicken coop was off. We all pitched in with the chores, doing the milking by hand. It was my job to go to the chicken coop and keep the little chicks separated. When chicks are cold, they gather together to keep warm, and many times they gather so tight that some end up suffocating. So my job was to gently keep those little chicks from gathering too close together. With a flashlight in one hand, with the other hand I gently kept those cute little chicks from gathering too close together. It seemed like a long time, but eventually the heat lamp came on again and the chicks were safe and warm.

When I think of that incident, I think of Matthew 23:37, in which Jesus says He would like to gather His people together as a hen gathers her chicks under her wing, but many times we refuse. To me, the picture of a mother hen drawing her chicks close conveys the truth of God's tender concern for His people. He loves us so and desires that we be willing to run under His wings for protection from the evils of this world.

When the storms and threatening thunder and lightning come in your life, do you seek the Lord? Jesus is with us always through those storms. Seek His tender loving care today!

Ginger Bell

My Provider

The eyes of all wait upon thee; and thou givest
them their meat in due season. Thou openest thine hand,
and satisfiest the desire of every living thing. Ps. 145:15, 16.

After praying for God's guidance and direction, my eldest daughter was accepted into a school that offered a combined five-year master's and medical program. Despite the astronomical tuition cost, God opened ways that only He could. She is now in her third year.

At the time she was accepted into the program, my prayer was that God would take us through debt-free. We had no savings, education fund, or investments to rely on, but trusted that God would provide the badly needed funds. When she got her first loan, I reminded God that we wanted to be debt-free when she was finished.

We were elated when she completed the first year magna cum laude and maintained a high grade-point average. She was set to enter her second year. God, however, had other plans. Her loan applications were rejected, so she did not return to school that year. At the end of the year God miraculously provided the funds to take her through the next two years. When those two years ended, we were again seeking God's direction and provision. We had seen over the years how instrumental He was in our lives, but now we weren't sure what to do. We didn't think our faith in God and what He can do was weak—in fact, in our view, it was stronger than ever. We just could not recognize His will at this time. So I took an inventory of God's goodness to us. That helped me put things in perspective. In addition to everything that He had already done, God kept us fed, clothed, and sheltered. The list was endless.

The tuition for the next term is due. While I am not sure how God will deliver, I will trust Him. He knows I need reassurance and strength to wait patiently on Him, so He sends me messages of hope from His Word every day: "They that wait upon the Lord" (Isa. 40:31); "The Lord is faithful, who shall stablish you, and keep you from evil" (2 Thess. 3:3); "Fear not for I am with you" (Isa. 41:10); "Hast thou not known? hast thou not heard, that the everlasting God, . . . fainteth not, neither is weary?" (Isa. 40:28).

God is our refuge, our strength, our ever-present help in time of need. I can hardly wait to see what He has planned for us next.

Joan Dougherty-Mornan

A Personal Pentecost

But ye shall receive power, after that the Holy Ghost
is come upon you: and ye shall be witnesses. Acts 1:8.

Ever have a mental disconnect between what God did for Bible characters and what you believe He can do in your life? I have. It's way too easy for me to let the "the care of this world" (Matt. 13:22)—and knowledge of my failures—weaken my faith in God's unconditional grace.

Once I allowed an early-morning chiropractic appointment to keep me from my usual devotional time. I'd been up late helping my husband put a sermon together and had overslept that morning. After my medical appointment, I decided to walk the strip mall sidewalk for a bit of fresh air before the drive home. I chastised myself for not having prayed enough about my day before leaving home—though I'd barely had time to get a brush through my frizzy gray hair (and it certainly showed!). *God, I look and feel frumpy today. Frazzled. Yet forgive my leaving You out of my chaos. I invite Your Spirit into my life to use me—despite my shortcomings.*

Just then something drew me through the doorway of a clothing store I was about to pass. An hour later I walked out of that store, having spent the previous 50 minutes listening to the pressing challenges of the tearful store manager (a total stranger). God had given me words of biblical encouragement for her. She'd even agreed to my praying with her about her situation.

After the next day's chiropractic follow-up, I stepped inside the clothing store, this time with an inspirational book in my hand. "Oh, it's *you!*" she cried, running up and enveloping me in a warm hug. "You're a real *person!*" Perplexed, I nodded. She explained, "Last night at my midweek service I told my Bible study class that God had sent someone to me at the very moment I thought I was 'going under' and needed a word from Him. I told the class that I didn't know if you were an elderly lady or an angel. That's because a light went on in my heart when you came through the door. So . . . you're *not* an angel—but I'm glad to see you anyway!"

Humbled, I marveled at the personal Pentecost experience God had led me through the previous day. *Despite* my frantic, devotional-less departure from home. And *because* the Father gives "the Holy Spirit to them that ask him"—anyway (Luke 11:13).

So go ahead . . . ask Him. Maybe someone will suspect *you* of being an angel today.

Carolyn Sutton

My Extraordinary Gallery

For he shall be as a tree planted by the waters,
and that spreadeth out her roots by the river, and shall not see
when heat cometh, but her leaf shall be green; and shall not be careful
in the year of drought, neither shall cease from yielding fruit. Jer. 17:8.

While returning home from work one day several years ago, I was gravely hurt by a car. My life changed dramatically. Even so, I have countless reasons to be grateful to God.

I consider myself privileged to have had the opportunity to learn many things in my life. But the most difficult one was to depend on others. Moving from my bed to the wheelchair, taking a shower, dressing, reaching for the pen that fell on the floor, getting a glass of water, paying for the bills that don't stop coming even as you can no longer work, opening a door—all these, the most simple things that we think we will always do, required help from others.

Nobody plans to be in a wheelchair any more than we plan on any other calamity. Even in the midst of the many difficulties that we will all go through sometime whether we want it or not, God places extraordinary people along our way to help us during those hard times. Today, at this very moment, He has already chosen someone's name to add to your schedule and give you the privilege of becoming immortal in that person's Gallery of Extraordinary People.

I have my own precious gallery. In it there are hundreds of names of relatives, friends, employers, children, neighbors, doctors, physical therapists, and even strangers who make up the Gallery of Extraordinary People in my life just because they agreed to be my hands and feet or my support and comfort during the painful healing process of recovering. Maybe these people will never know exactly how deeply they touched my heart and how they gave me the strength to continue. But I know very well. And I know that God also knows. And we are both forever grateful that even in today's world there are still people like this.

It is a great challenge to find time for others when our own lives demand so much of us. But even harder than this is being the person who needs the help. If by any chance that is you today, accept it. I guarantee that you will be grateful to have had the privilege of being touched by an angel in human form. You will discover that there are many wonderful people capable of doing for you what you never imagined!

Kênia Kopitar

Angels Watching Over Me

Count yourself lucky, how happy you must be—you get
a fresh start, your slate's wiped clean. Ps. 32:1, Message.

When I was a child living in England, about 7 or 8 years of age, I was walking home from church with my mother and older brothers. I held Mama's hand as we reached the main road. My brothers ran ahead and crossed the street, so without any thought I let go of Mama's hand and ran—without looking—into the main street. The next thing I heard was my mother calling my name; when I turned to look at her I noticed a car had stopped at the edge of my dress, and Mama was clutching her Bible to her chest. Angels were watching over me.

Approximately six years later, this time in the Bronx, New York, my brothers and I were crossing an empty street late at night when we all heard squealing tires. My brothers decided to run forward, but I stepped back. Something hit my right leg, and I landed on my face. Nothing was broken—just a few missing teeth. Yes, angels were watching over me.

Fast-forward 15 years. Through one conflict and one war my mother's prayers continued to go up for me, although I had stopped trusting in God. Then while I was driving home from New York to Oklahoma after Mama's funeral, exhaustion overtook my body somewhere in Missouri. When I came to, the vehicle I was driving had rolled over twice, my husband was ejected out of the rear door, and my mother-in-law and three children were trapped inside the vehicle. Many hours and phone calls later, and after being transported to the hospital, we all continued our journey home. Angels were still watching over me.

This time I listened as God spoke to my heart, and I had to ask how many times I must try God before waking up to follow His will. In the next two years I sat still and let the Holy Spirit take control of my life. He even sent a pastor and a field worker to my home. Eventually I was baptized, and several years later two of my children were also baptized. As Psalm 32:1 says in a different version, "Blessed is the one whose transgressions are forgiven, whose sins are covered" (NIV). As I personalize our text for today from *The Message*, I write, "Count myself, Heather, lucky, how happy I must be—I get a fresh start, my slate's wiped clean." All praises to the most high God—angels are *still* watching over me!

Hearther E. Overstreet

God Is Amazing!

Then you will call upon Me and go and pray to Me,
and I will listen to you. Jer. 29:12, NKJV.

The plane stopped at Gate E12. My heart was pounding fast. I looked at my watch again. My heart sank. Only five minutes before my next connection to Santiago, Chile! *How will I ever get to the next gate in time? It's impossible!* I thought.

As soon as the door of the plane opened, an agent was right there to meet me. He helped me with my carry-on. We ran as fast as our legs could carry us to Gate 25, the last gate in the terminal. As we ran, the agent reminded me that the plane was waiting for me but my luggage would not get on that plane in time.

I kept praying. *Lord, what could I possibly do without my luggage and its contents?*

My training program was to be held in a little town outside of Santiago. Yet the town was a two-hour drive from Santiago, where the late luggage would have to be delivered.

I would just have to leave this situation in God's hands. He would lead, as He knows what is best for me.

After our plane landed in Santiago, I waited at the luggage conveyor belt for an agent to assist me. As the bags and suitcases were being picked up by my fellow passengers, I approached the ground agent to explain my situation and also file a missing or delayed luggage report. Yet the courteous, attractive agent kept telling me to stand aside and just wait. *But why should I wait?* I thought. *There is no possibility that my luggage could have been transferred to my connecting flight in time. No possibility at all!*

After 15 minutes of waiting, the agent pulled out a form, asking me to fill it in. Just as I was looking for my pen, I happened to glance up at the previously empty luggage conveyor belt. My heart stopped! "I can't believe it!" I exclaimed. My one piece of luggage was moving slowly toward me. Yes, my heart leaped for joy! I don't know how that happened, and I don't have all the answers. Yet one thing I do know—my heavenly Father knows my needs!

Even in the little things of our lives, God is interested in us. Just like He cares for the little sparrows and the lilies of the fields, God cares for *us*. We have no need to worry about anything—just simply trust in our loving Father.

Linda Mei Lin Koh

The Heart of Amarelis

I call on the Lord in my distress, and he answers me. Ps. 120:1, NIV.

The unexpected ringing of the telephone abruptly interrupted my basking in the sunny beauty of that Dominican Republic morning. "Mrs. DeMattos," a young girl's voice pleaded, "Amarelis is dying! Please get over here as fast as you can. We need help! Quickly! Her bad heart is giving her terrible pain. We don't know what to do. Come help us!"

In shock I hung up the phone. Amarelis lived with two other students, Rebeca, and Belkis, next to where we were staying while serving as missionaries in that tropical paradise.

I thought, *Why did these girls call me—I'm not a doctor! And if Amarelis should die under my care, that would be terrible!* In anguish I prayed, "God, please help me! I don't know anything about how to care for the serious heart problem Amarelis has. So I ask You, dear Lord, to go before me and heal her."

Even as I prayed, I prepared to hurry over to the girls' house. Stepping out of my door, I again pleaded, "Lord, I don't understand why they called me. O Lord, have mercy on me and on Amarelis, too. May all be done according to Your will."

As I entered the students' house, I saw Amarelis lying facedown and obviously very sick. An open Bible lay above her head. Instantly I understood she had been reading it just before becoming so ill. My eyes rested on its open pages and then specifically on Psalm 120:1. "I call on the Lord in my distress, and he answers me." I read the verse aloud and continued reading aloud through the next psalm. With the Bible in my hand now I said, "God is very powerful, and there is not a being greater than He. Amarelis," I spoke with confidence, "we will pray for you now. Only God can help, because I can't do anything." We knelt and prayed. After we finished praying, I read more selections from Psalm 125 through Psalm 150.

When I finished the reading, Amarelis stood up and said, "I don't feel discomfort anymore. God healed me. He is very powerful." Again I invited the girls to kneel and thank the Lord for His great victory. I believe our prayers were answered immediately because, as His children, we trusted only in God's mercy. For our great God works wonders.

Praise this powerful Savior! We give thanks to Him for His mighty power.

Socorro Castro de Mattos

The Enemy Was Foiled

Through God we will do valiantly, for it is He who shall
tread down our enemies. Ps. 108:13, NKJV.

I was the new Bible worker in Tonopah. I asked Barry (not his real name), an elderly gentleman who attended our church sporadically, if he would like Bible studies. He did, and the studies went well, with his understanding and acceptance of everything on our visits. He also had many questions that I was able to answer to his satisfaction. I questioned Barry about our doctrines and asked whether he would like to join the church on profession of faith. "Oh, no," he replied, "I want to be rebaptized." We scheduled the baptism for the following Sabbath.

Since the church we rent does not have its own baptistry, we traveled 28 miles to a Baptist church. I called Barry on that Sabbath morning to finalize the arrangements. He sounded very angry on the phone. This was so out of character for him that I was stunned. He then told me that he had been up half the night in the bathroom, and the other half he had had nightmares—starring me! However, he said he would go through with the baptism because he had promised us. And so he did, making it to the church before we did.

All the way to the Baptist church I wondered if I had pushed him too far, too fast; however, I was reassured (I believe by the Holy Spirit) that he would be all right once it was over. At the church their pastor and his wife could not have been more gracious and welcoming, eating lunch with us, attending our entire service, and providing every help we needed. They also gave us yarn and other materials for our senior center work—we make lap blankets for wheelchair patients and quilts for needy children.

Two days later Barry said that he was very happy he had been baptized and was his usual self. His wife, Margaret, who resides in another state, had already accepted Christ and was ecstatic at the news.

I know the enemy was responsible for the disruptions. Praise the Lord that Barry went through with it; otherwise, he might never have been baptized. Praise the Lord also that the Baptist pastor went through with our service. Barry is now witnessing to others with Christian literature. I felt God's leading that His enemies were overpowered—valiantly.

Joyce Rapp

Magic Mirror Neurons

But we . . . beholding as in a mirror the glory of the Lord,
are being transformed. 2 Cor. 3:18, NKJV.

I'm in big trouble!" Melissa announced, skipping into the house from her music lesson. *"Big, big trouble!"* Setting my laptop aside I prepared to listen. Turned out that her *big, big trouble* involved a conflict between an upcoming piano recital in three weeks and a week at junior camp. "It's a very hard choice," Melissa said, real anguish swirling around her words. "I really want to go to junior camp and I really want to play well in the recital." She sighed. "My teacher says junior camp will seriously interfere with my practice time."

"Choose both," I said. The expression on Melissa's face showed she was both puzzled and intrigued. "You have some amazing neurons in your cerebral cortex," I said, "the outermost part of your brain. Located directly behind your forehead, they *fire* when you do an action in real time, when you picture an action in your mind's eye, and even when you watch another person's behavior. That may be the reason they're sometimes referred to as mirror neurons."

Researchers used brain imaging equipment to study the brains of two individuals: one who actually practiced the piano for two hours a day for seven days; the other who simply imagined playing the piano for the same amount of time. Both actual and virtual practice caused a similar reshaping of the brain's cortex. "Seeing yourself practice the piano in your mind's eye can speed up learning," I said. "Memorize your recital piece during the first week. That's actual practice. Take the music with you to junior camp and continue to practice in your mind's eye during the second week. That's virtual practice. When you're back at home for the third week, do a combination of both actual and virtual practice."

"My brain has magic mirror neurons!" cried Melissa, whooping with joy. She was so excited she hopped up and down, spun around in circles, and waved her arms. "I can use them for actual and virtual practice!" And that's exactly what she did. Melissa enjoyed seven days of junior camp, and she played her piano piece very well at the subsequent recital.

Have you tapped into your brain's mirror neurons? They are only too happy to help you. Follow actual practice with virtual rehearsal. When actual is impossible, picture yourself doing the task successfully. And then imagine something you have not yet seen—such as living in heaven.

Arlene R.Taylor

Jury Duty

For it is by grace you have been saved, through faith—and this not from yourselves, it is the gift of God. Eph. 2:8, NIV.

I was summoned for jury duty on a beautiful summer day. Because the courthouse is about 45 minutes from our home, my husband and I left early to miss the morning rush hour traffic. I checked in at 7:00 a.m. and proceeded to the jury lounge. Around 8:00 the court clerk gave us an orientation on what to expect and reminded us how important our roles were as potential jurors. She emphasized that today we were going to make a decision that would affect the life of another citizen.

There were about 400 people in the jury lounge that morning waiting to be assigned to different cases. We were assigned to a case in groups of 25 and waited for our turn to be called to the courtroom. About 10:00 our group was called to line up in numerical order as we waited for the bailiff to usher us in. As soon as the group was complete, we were suddenly told to go back to our seats, as the judge didn't need us just yet.

We waited all day to be called to serve but were never called upon again and were finally dismissed at 4:00 p.m. What a disappointment for us who had gotten there early to do our civic duty. What is worse than being summoned for jury duty than not being able to serve at all? I learned from this experience that there are no certainties in our earthly courts; anything can happen or change on a case-to-case basis.

As I sat in the jury lounge that day, I thought about the heavenly court where my life will be examined on the judgment day. I can visualize my Lord and Savior, Jesus Christ, pleading my case before the heavenly Father and acting as my attorney. I have faith that He will do what is best for me; having ransomed me from the bondage of sin with His blood shed on Calvary's cross. I am humbled to know that He loves me unconditionally and wants me to spend eternity with Him.

I am so thankful that mortal humans are not deciding my eternal destiny. Only the blameless Son of God can cover my faults with His righteousness. Are we willing to accept His gift of salvation?

Rhona Grace Magpayo

Lessons From the Water Lily

A joyful heart helps healing, but a broken
spirit dries up the bones. Prov. 17:22, CEB.

I am often inspired by stories of women who find strength to overcome big challenges in life, learning to experience a joyful, fulfilling life despite adversity. Recently the story of Fanny Crosby touched me. A poet whose written words became the lyrics of many beloved hymns, Fanny became blind as an infant because of poor medical care. Despite her difficulties, Fanny chose to focus on the sweet love of her Creator and Savior. She wrote "Blessed assurance, Jesus is mine. . . . This is my story, this is my song, praising my Savior all the day long."

Her disposition made me ask, Am I truly joyful? I realized I can easily mistake my perceived "needs" with "preferences" or "wants." I asked myself, *What do I really need to live a joyful life without anxiety?* You see, we can become miserable when something we perceive as bad happens, or when someone acts or doesn't act in the way we believe they should. Our perceived "needs" become imaginary requirements. How can we avoid this trap?

In my case I learned a lesson from the water lily. If you have seen them, although "surrounded by weeds and rubbish, strikes down its channeled stem to the pure sands beneath, and, drawing thence its life, lifts up its fragrant blossoms to the light in spotless purity" (Ellen G. White, *Education*, p. 119).

I learned that when I feel alone or rejected, or if I experience relationship problems, financial needs, loss, frustration, or pain, I can focus my thoughts on what is "true, noble, reputable, authentic, compelling, gracious—the best, not the worst; the beautiful, not the ugly; things to praise, not things to curse" (Phil. 4:8, Message). It takes work for the water lily to send its stem deep, the same way it takes work and practice to focus our thoughts on what is true. We need to choose to let God change the way we think (Rom. 12:2, CEV).

If you are surrounded by slimy waters of trials, or weeds of doubts, and rubbish of the cares of this world, I invite you to learn from the water lily too, and dig your stem deep beneath the stinky waters to the pure sands of the true, gracious promises of God. Like me, you will find renewed joy and physical, mental, and emotional healing, and, like the water lily, you will release a pure fragrance that will enrich your life and bless others along the way.

Katia Garcia Reinert

Spread the News

We cannot stop telling about everything
we have seen and heard. Acts 4:20, NLT.

My younger son could never keep a secret. Any news he happened upon was far too exciting to keep to himself. When he was about 3, he returned from a shopping trip with his daddy and older brother. As soon as he could he ran to tell me the news. With a sparkle in his green eyes, he exclaimed, "We went shopping, and we got you a present. But it's a secret! So I'm not going to tell you we got you a hanging lamp for Mother's Day."

As he grew older he never lost the excitement of sharing good news. The night he fought his first fire as a volunteer firefighter was especially exciting. It turned out to be the beginning of a career in firefighting. That night he sat in our bedroom telling us all the details from the moment the call came in from 9-1-1 until the trucks were able to return to the station.

His love of sharing good news reminds me of the scene in Acts 3 and 4. In chapter 3 Peter and John healed a lame beggar. Then they used the opportunity to share the story of Jesus. But they were arrested because of preaching the good news of the resurrection of Jesus.

The next day the religious council questioned the two men. They wanted to know by what power Peter and John had healed the man. The two disciples gave the credit to Jesus. The council could not deny the miracle, since the healed man was standing right there. Angry, they ordered Peter and John never to speak or to teach in the name of Jesus again. The followers' response to this order is captivating. "For we cannot stop speaking of what we ourselves have seen and heard" (Acts 4:20, TEV).

These two disciples were so excited and happy with the gospel message that they could not stop talking about it. What they had seen and heard while they were with Jesus had changed their lives. Now the good news bubbled out of them. They were unable to stop sharing their experience with Jesus.

Have you spent enough time with Jesus that the good news bubbles out of you? Do you, too, find yourself unable to stop talking about what you have seen and heard while you are sitting at the feet of Jesus? The good news about Jesus was never meant to be kept a secret. Never lose the excitement of sharing the best news ever.

Ginny Allen

Listen to the Little Voice

*Yes, I obey your commandments and laws
because you know everything I do. Ps. 119:168, NLT.*

One Friday morning after my morning devotions, I went back to bed, as it was still very early. I was thinking about the number of things that I was going to need to do before sunset in preparation of the Sabbath. As I relaxed there in bed, I heard a little voice reminding me I had decided to fast that day. I asked myself what to fast about as this voice was telling me to fast. After all, we as a group fast on Wednesdays, but that Wednesday I had not joined the group in fasting.

I then told myself, *OK, I will go ahead and fast for my own spiritual growth. It is the right thing to do, and I am content about it.* I told myself, *Today I will just consecrate myself to the Lord.*

A few minutes later my son called to tell me that he had received a phone call from the licensing examiner asking that since the weather was good, would he be able to take his pilot's licensing exam? He was to be prepared to take the exam at 3:00 that afternoon. My son asked if I could take his need for blessing to the throne of God in prayer.

It then dawned on me that God wanted me to fast for my son. God is great; His plans are not our plans. I felt that He planned the prayer program, and I started praying for my son. I told myself that I would break my fast after my son had done his check ride. I did my duties and Sabbath preparation and went to the homeless shelter to invite people there to attend Sabbath services as it was to be a guest day at our church.

At 5:00 p.m. I received a telephone call from my son; he sounded so happy, and he was proclaiming the goodness of our Lord. He told me that he had passed his check ride and was now a private pilot. I danced in happiness to the Lord and gave thanks and praises. Yes, God answers prayers.

And now I have a prayer for myself as well, that the Lord will teach me to listen to His voice and follow His will in my life. Sometimes He speaks through a still small voice, and sometimes He speaks through His Word. A text in Deuteronomy speaks to this need for all of us: "Oh, that their hearts would be inclined to fear me and keep all my commands always, so that it might go well with them and their children forever!" (Deut. 5:29, NIV).

Orpha Gumbo Maseko

Reminiscences of My Father

Train up a child in the way that he should go:
and when he is old, he will not depart from it. Prov. 22:6.

My father, whom we called Pa, was an ordained minister, but he opted to be a self-supporting minister to enable him to be with his family, and foremost, to have his 10 children obtain a Christian education. He moved his family so we would be near a Christian high school, and then when my older siblings started college, Pa moved the family again near the entrance gate of a Christian college. I fully believe this is the best legacy Pa left for his children.

Pa began to work for our church's publishing house, so after classes almost every afternoon, instead of playing with my classmates at the school playground, I ran to Pa's office and read anything I could find there until closing time; that is how I learned to love reading good books. Then, together, we walked home. To this day, I relish those father-daughter moments.

Pa submitted my name to the pen pal section of *Our Little Friend,* a church magazine for children. I answered the letters I received from other countries, and Pa mailed these letters. That started my love for letter writing and other writing.

Once while I was a college student my name was among the list of students who were not allowed to take the final exams until proper arrangement had been made with the business office. While waiting for my turn to sign a promissory note, I heard my name called; the man who handed me the financial permit slip said he was doing it to show his appreciation for the kindnesses my father had for years given to his family.

Pa did not try to impose his desires for his children on us, but he did it subtly so as not to create rebellion. When I was in elementary, and even in high school, whenever Pa was invited to preach in other churches, he took me along. I became a most attentive listener. To me, he was the best preacher. Needless to say, I made up my mind that someday I would marry a preacher, which I did. My husband and I agreed to name our first son Alva, in honor of my father.

Pa wrote a letter to each of his children on his fifty-eighth birthday; he humbly asked for forgiveness for having been overly strict while we were growing up. Pa ended his letter with "Press on in the fight of faith until the victory is won." Shouldn't that be the goal for each of us?

Filipinas Roda Bautista

A Wonderful Father

If a son shall ask bread of any of you that is a father, will he give him a stone? or if he ask a fish, will he for a fish give him a serpent? . . . If ye then, being evil, know how to give good gifts unto your children: how much more shall your heavenly Father give the Holy Spirit to them that ask him? Luke 11:11-13.

Special days are recognized and celebrated around the world as indicated on yearly calendars, but special days and times come to my mind as memorable thoughts begin to surface of my father. Memories of him will always be foremost to the three of us siblings who called him Daddy. I get a bit sentimental when Father's Day is celebrated, because of memories not only of my childhood years but of my adult years also.

My father always exemplified strength and love for God; this created within my brother, sister, and me a love for God also. My father loved working in various capacities for the church and was a hard, dedicated worker at his daily job to support his family; but he never forgot to spend time with us, finding out how our day had been. There were, of course, times we were disciplined, reminding us that consequences would always follow disobedience. We were taught that when we disobeyed him, we were disobeying our heavenly Father also. His favorite text was Ephesians 6:1: "Children, obey your parents in the Lord: for this is right."

Daddy was a praying father who believed with faith in our heavenly Father that our needs would be supplied. I remember the day our family was called together for prayer during a terrible storm; lightning flashed, rain poured down, loud thunder crashed as Daddy put his arm around me and each member of the family held hands. Amazingly, upon ending his prayer we heard him say, "Thank You, heavenly Father." The storm had begun to subside, and we looked out the window just in time to see lightning strike the large tree behind the house. The wind had also blown a smaller tree over the shed not far from the house. I heard Daddy saying, "Thank You, heavenly Father, for permitting the lightning to strike the tree. I still have my family and house."

I realize no earthly father is perfect, but how grateful to my heavenly Father I am for giving me my biological father (Daddy). I cherish happy memories; a father's influence does not have to end when their life does.

Annie B. Best

Before They Call

Before they call I will answer; while they are
still speaking I will hear. Isa. 65:24, NIV.

hey . . ." my husband gasped. "They," he wheezed. "They . . . peel lungs . . . in
. . . here." We'd been in the kitchen, and Gerald had said something funny. I
started jumping, and he started jumping with me. We held hands, laughing and
jumping, and then his breath suddenly came in ragged gasps, and he was choking
and struggling to breathe. Another asthma attack!

I quickly asked a neighbor to stay with our kids and called someone else to
come over, perhaps for the entire night. Then I bundled Gerald into the car, and
we rushed to the hospital. Two things had brought back his childhood asthma with
a vengeance: Michigan's cold winter and, as we now learned, physical exertion.
Hours passed as he lay on a narrow bed in the emergency department struggling,
I felt, for his life. The doctors tried one thing after another, but still each shallow,
ragged breath seemed ripped from his lungs.

We'd moved to Michigan for the school year so he could finish a graduate
degree in Old Testament while still working, off-site, as an editor for a religious
publishing company. It was not easy, and money was tight. These emergencies were
breaking the bank.

I called our apartment and had the children settled for the night with a God-
sent babysitter. I stayed by my husband's side, reading, praying, thinking, praying,
reading, praying . . . and the night wore on. Sometime before dawn Gerald began to
breathe easier and begged to go home. At last the doctors relented—around noon.
We stopped by a pharmacy to fill his new prescriptions. They cost $50, leaving only
a pitiful dollar or two in the bank. This was not good. We'd have to live on that for
the next couple weeks until his next paycheck arrived.

"I don't want to go home," he told me. "Let's drive to the mall and just go in
and sit for a while." I was fine with that, but since we were near our apartment I
stopped to get our mail. I was surprised to see an envelope with a South American
stamp—addressed to me. It was a check for $50. A Christian publisher was reprint-
ing an article I'd written and sent payment for it. This was a miracle! My work was
often reprinted by foreign publishers, but I was rarely notified and almost never
received anything but thanks. I could only praise God for His goodness and perfect
timing. I believed He gave these "miracles" to build our faith for the future.

Penny Estes Wheeler

Calla Lily

How precious also are Your thoughts to me,
O God! How vast is the sum of them! Ps. 139:17, NASB.

At our daughter's wedding the bridesmaids were in red and carried white calla lilies, and the bride chose red calla lilies for her bouquet. I'm not exactly sure just when calla lilies had become a favorite, but it was all very beautiful.

Fast-forward a few years: our daughter and our "son-in-love" became parents to a beautiful baby girl, Callah (and her doll's name is Lily). She is my little delight! I am so blessed to live less than five minutes away and have been privileged to spend many hours with her during her first year of life.

I find I absolutely long to visit Callah and spend time with her. I smile from the minute I get there until I am halfway home, and then again when I tell Grampa what cute things she did on our visit that day. Sometimes she dances her little jig as she pushes the button on her furry elephant as he sings "Sugar pie honey bunch, you know I love you, I can't help myself . . ."

We go for walks, stopping to blow the dandelion puffballs, and when we see flowers we sing, "Who made the beautiful flowers, I know, I know. God made the beautiful flowers because He loves us so."

She loves her dog, Charlie, so-o-o much, and he is the recipient of her sweet hugs. She calls him CharChar or Chardee.

I can (and do) go on and on about my little treasure, Callah. This precious relationship reminds me of our relationship with the Lord. I think we are His delight, and He treasures every minute we spend with Him, and He loves to see all our "baby steps." He uses nature, His second book, to tell of His love for us as we see the calla lilies and other flowers that He has allowed to wander from Eden to brighten our days. The little birds that sing their songs of cheer remind us that He takes care of their needs, and we will also be well taken care of.

I'm also thinking He smiles from the first time that He sees us! Don't you think He goes on and on about us also? Maybe He sings a song like furry elephant sings, "You know I love you, I can't help Myself . . ."

Gay Mentes

What Would Jesus Do?

Those who say they live in God should live
their lives as Jesus did. 1 John 2:6, NLT.

As I sat in worship and studied the Word of the Lord, my mind raced back to my unchristian behavior while performing my duties at the hospital the previous day. My colleague had asked me to assist in the transfer of a patient from one room to another. I went to prepare the reassigned room, and as I stepped inside, my disposition changed. Inside this room was another patient who frequently had run-ins with the staff. He was one of those patients whom you don't want to have on a bad day and wished you never saw on a good day. So I did what comes naturally to me—I completely ignored him while I transferred the other patient.

My conscience pierced me, and I could just imagine Satan smirking that he had gained the victory. I felt ashamed. My lack of self-control had inadvertently opened the door for the "adversary of souls" to come in and take advantage of my situation. I was reading an article recently on opening the door to the adversary, and the author's words summed up my situation: "As soon as an alienation of feeling arises, the matter is spread before Satan for his inspection, and the opportunity given for him to use his serpentlike wisdom and skill in dividing and destroying" (Ellen G. White, *Selected Messages,* book 1, p. 123).

As I reflected on my situation a deep sense of remorse covered me. *Tamar, is this what Jesus would do? Of course not!* I realized the constant battle over my soul, and in penitence I bowed before my Savior. I could relate to Paul's experience when he said, "For I know that good itself does not dwell in me, that is, in my sinful nature. For I have the desire to do what is good, but I cannot carry it out. For I do not do the good I want to do, but the evil I do not want to do—this I keep on doing" (Rom. 7:18, 19, NIV). Jesus, being the merciful and forgiving Father, quickly reassured me with His words in Romans 8:1: "There is therefore now no condemnation to them which are in Christ Jesus, who walk not after the flesh, but after the Spirit."

As situations confront you today, my sister, ask yourself, "What would Jesus do?" A favorite writer of mine said that we bear the name of Christian—to be a Christian means to be Christlike. Remember, it's not enough to accept Jesus as Savior; we must follow His example in our daily lives. God bless you!

Tamar Boswell

A Second Chance

If my people, which are called by my name,
shall humble themselves, and pray. 2 Chron. 7:14.

We walked into the Build-A-Bear workshop on June 30, 2011, to celebrate my daughter Cassandra's ninth birthday. The children ran from place to place, selecting an animal to stuff, bathe, dress, and call their own. Watching them, I could not help marveling at the joyful enthusiasm exuding from not only the 9-year-olds but the three teenagers as well. (My older daughter Lillian, had two friends with her.) Eventually each child had selected a bear and stuffed it. Then the bears were given an air bath and a through brushing. Once groomed, the children selected clothing to dress their bears. Finally it was time to name them and take a group picture.

While the children were taking their picture, I sat down at the naming center, naming my bear Billie-Beth, after two special friends. Seated next to me was an older woman who appeared to be having difficulty with the computer. Eventually she leaned over and asked for help naming her bear. I was surprised but asked her if it was a special bear. She explained that she was going to have breast cancer surgery in the morning, and this bear was going with her. I said, "Well, how about naming her Angel so you will remember that your guardian angel will be with you?"

Her eyes filled with tears, and we talked a little longer. I felt impressed to pray with her; so seated in the middle of a busy store, two strangers bowed their heads and asked God for His mercy. After we prayed, we hugged, and I returned to the birthday party, knowing that God had placed me in this store for a purpose.

We had originally planned to go to Orlando, but changed our plans. God knew that I could be of use to Him and thankfully this time I allowed Him to use me. You see, years before, I was in a position to pray for someone in public, and I didn't do it. I still regret not praying for that woman, and when she crosses my mind, I pray for her and her family. This time, thankfully, I have no regrets. I listened to the small voice telling me to pray where we sat. Meeting Lee, praying for her, changed me. I pray we meet again; if not here, then in heaven as sisters in Christ.

Today's entire text says, "If my people, which are called by my name, shall humble themselves, and pray, and seek my face, and turn from their wicked ways; then will I hear from heaven, and will forgive their sin, and will heal their land." This time I was healed as well.

Tamara Marquez de Smith

Above Dark Clouds the Sun Is Shining

But you will receive power when the Holy Spirit comes on you;
and you will be my witnesses in Jerusalem, and in all
Judea and Samaria, and to the ends of the earth. Acts 1:8, NIV.

Some time ago I had the occasion to fly to Berlin. Dark clouds hung over Munich, and it was raining. But as the airplane rose higher into the sky I was plunged into a wonderful world. The sun shone on top of the clouds and made them look like fluffy wads of cotton.

Sometimes we are discouraged, everything is dark around us, and the clouds hang deep in our lives. If you need hope, think of the bright sky above the clouds!

I wonder how the disciples felt when Jesus left them. All of their hopes for a better future on earth were shattered. They had expected Jesus to change everything and to liberate them from Roman oppression. "Then they gathered around him and asked him, 'Lord, are you at this time going to restore the kingdom to Israel?'" (Acts 1:6, NIV).

But Jesus gave them a clear answer: "It is not for you to know the times or dates the Father has set by his own authority" (verse 7, NIV).

Hadn't He understood them? Or had they not understood Him? They had been with Him for three years, had seen His wonders, and yet they had not understood His message. But Jesus did not leave them in uncertainty about the future. He gave them instructions and hope: "You will be my witnesses" (verse 8, NIV).

We may ask, "Is this still valid for us as followers of Jesus in our times?" We too are given instructions and hope: To receive the gift of the Holy Spirit! When Peter preached his challenging sermon, the people who heard him had an important question: "Brothers, what shall we do?" (Acts 2:37, NIV). "Peter replied, 'repent and be baptized, every one of you, in the name of Jesus Christ for the forgiveness of your sins. And you will receive the gift of the Holy Spirit'" (verse 38, NIV).

We have been promised the power of the Holy Spirit, and this will help us to proclaim the gospel. The Holy Spirit is given at baptism to the followers of Christ. You and I, who claim Jesus Christ as our Lord and Savior, have received this gift so that we can bring hope to the hopeless, joy to the joyless, and a vision for a bright future to those in darkness.

Ingrid Naumann

Not Mastered by Anything, Part 1

"I have the right to do anything," you say—but not everything is beneficial. "I have the right to do anything"— but I will not be mastered by anything. 1 Cor. 6:12, NIV.

An elderly teacher, with a pupil by his side, took a walk through a forest. Suddenly he stopped and pointed to four plants close at hand. The first was just beginning to peek above the ground, the second had rooted itself pretty well into the earth, the third was a small shrub, while the fourth was a full-sized tree. The tutor said to his young companion, "Pull up the first plant." The boy did so eagerly, using only his fingers. "Now pull up the second." The youth obeyed, but found the task more difficult. "Do the same with the third," the teacher urged. The boy had to use all his strength to uproot it. "Now," said the instructor, "try your hand with the fourth." The pupil put his arms around the trunk of the tall tree and couldn't even shake its leaves.

"This, my son, is just what happens with our bad habits. When they are young, we can remove them readily; but when they are old, it's hard to uproot them, though we pray and struggle ever so sincerely." Old habits are hard to break and even more difficult to uproot and eliminate. We all have some bad habits that are personally embarrassing, physically limiting, and spiritually convicting. That is the reason we must be courageous and deal with our habits as soon as they manifest themselves. Let us, therefore, not continue to make a lie of the truth of the power of the gospel or be a living contradiction of its liberating message. We can accomplish this by immediately dealing with our unwanted habits.

Someone has made the stunning statement that a Christian has no rights, only duties. It appears from Scripture that the apostle Paul would disagree since he argued passionately for our liberties, underscoring that there is no other human with rights as incontestable as a Christian. He also emphasized that these divine freedoms are to be cherished at all cost, especially in the face of angry opposition. However, having insisted on that course of action under inspiration, Paul then used his vast and wonderful knowledge of the human heart to flash lights of caution on the dangers and limits of this liberty in a couplet found in 1 Corinthians 6:12, NIV:

"I have the right to do anything" . . . —*but not everything is beneficial.*

"I have the right to do anything"—*but I will not be mastered by anything.*

Hyveth Williams

Not Mastered by Anything, Part 2

I can do all things through Him who strengthens me. Phil. 4:13, NASB.

Members of the Corinthian congregation were insisting that they
"have the right to do anything" (see 1 Cor. 6:12, NIV).

Paul argued with intensity, saying, ". . . but not everything is beneficial." He was asserting that Christians must be those who use, but never abuse, these rights by recognizing the limits set by God for the exercise of such liberties. We must also exhibit a willingness to forgo them for the love of God and peace in the body of Christ.

The debate seemed to have taken on aspects of a conflict when some of the Corinthian members retaliated with an equally strong reiteration that they "have the right to do anything."

Again Paul countered with this terse response: ". . . but I will not be mastered by anything." He held such an attitude to be utterly antagonistic to the spirit of the gospel.

The Greek word for "mastered" means to be held under the authority or control of something, such as a habit. This isn't a verse talking about something lawless or wicked, but something that is actually lawful or profitable and even good. However, lawful or lawless, we should not be controlled by anything and should be only under the total authority of Jesus Christ, our Lord and Master.

Jesus said to the Jews who believed Him and, hence, to us: "If you continue in My word, then you are truly disciples of Mine; and you will know the truth, and the truth will make you free" (John 8:31, 32, NASB).

You may be wrestling with habits as "accepted" and common as gossiping, overeating, exaggerating, cheating, suspiciousness, and procrastination. Others in our society might be trapped by the lure of lust, dependence on chemicals, addictions to any number of unhealthy activities and cravings—not to mention a pill for every ill.

Avoid using this oft-misunderstood scripture written by the apostle Paul: "Do not handle, do not taste, do not touch!" (Col. 2:21, NASB). This text does not have the power one wants or expects for winning the battle against the aforementioned, and a host of other unwanted, habits or temptations. Only Christ can give us the power to make right choices.

Hyveth Williams

Not Mastered by Anything, Part 3

Therefore if anyone is in Christ, he is a new creature; the old things passed away; behold, new things have come. 2 Cor. 5:17, NASB.

Paul's words in Colossians 2:21 were not inspired words but rather a repetition of some idolatrous commands used by his antagonists. Paul simply quoted them in his argument against said opponents when he said, "If you have died with Christ to the elementary principles of the world, why, as if you were living in the world, do you submit yourself to decrees, such as, "Do not handle, do not taste, do not touch!" (Col. 2:20, 21, NASB).

Let me share, from the writings of favorite authors, some helpful hints on shedding bad habits. If taken with Paul's assertion that believers in Christ "will not be mastered by anything," these hints will help bring sought-for success. I can prove it by the fact that I'm so over the physically exasperating and equally emotionally debilitating habit of worrying about everything.

First, stop rationalizing. Excuses take the edge off disobedience. They encourage us to diminish or completely ignore the Holy Spirit's work of conviction.

Second, start right now, today! Now is the very best moment to quit a bad habit. To put it off is an admission of defeat. To say you are "trying" is a sign of resignation. Just do it! Otherwise, rationalization will intensify and prolong the self-confidence battle.

Third, apply strategy. Take on only one habit at a time, one day at a time.

Fourth, be realistic. Change will not happen fast, neither will it be easy. Your resolve may lack permanence, and the results will definitely not come overnight. Yet starting the process is a clear indication you are breaking the chain of slavery to said habit.

Fifth, be encouraged. Recognize that you are on the road to victory, perhaps for the first time in a long fight against this habit. Remember, enthusiasm strengthens self-discipline and prompts attitudes of staying the course. (See Phil. 4:6.)

People who are watching our Christian life unfold—and they do—usually are not that impressed by our expertise in quoting Scriptures. But when they observe the changes in our lives, they stand up and take notice. They want, for their lives, that something special we possess. Let us show them that, in Christ, we will not be mastered by anything!

Hyveth Williams

Witnessing in a Cemetery

*"Our friend Lazarus has fallen asleep; but I am going
there to wake him up." His disciples replied, "Lord, if he sleeps,
he will get better." Jesus had been speaking of his death,
but his disciples thought he meant natural sleep. John 11:11-13, NIV.*

It happened at a cemetery near Brush Prairie, Washington, as I was on my way to visit some friends. As I drove, I happened to notice a cemetery on my right. *Could that be the one that my brother and sister-in-law are buried in?* I wondered. I drove into the cemetery and looked around, but did not find their graves. I tried to find someone who might know, but found no help.

I spent the evening visiting with my friends, and of course I told them about my experience at the cemetery. They said it was the correct cemetery. So after lunch on Sabbath the three of us went back to the cemetery and did more searching, but still did not find the graves. We even went to the mortuary in town to ask for help; the mortician was not at all helpful.

My friends and her sister came over, and again we went to the cemetery. A rather sporty car pulled in, and a woman got out and went over to the corner of the cemetery where we had earlier noticed a grave of a baby. She was kneeling by a grave looking very sad.

I am usually not an outgoing person, but I decided to go talk to the woman. As I walked over I said, "Cemeteries are a very sad place, aren't they?" I then asked her whose grave she was visiting. She told me that her son had been killed in an auto accident very recently. He was only 19 years old. Then she said, "I just wish I knew where he is." That opened the door for me to tell her how I believe that he is sleeping the sleep of death until Jesus comes to take us to heaven. He will at that time call all of the dead to life and take those who love Him to heaven to live with Him throughout eternity. "It is just like when he was a little boy; you tucked him in at night, and he slept till morning. Well, now he is sleeping and will be awakened when Jesus awakes him on the resurrection morning," I told her. She seemed so thrilled to hear what I told her about death. I then gave her a card about Bibleinfo.com and said that if she had any more questions she could contact them or even take Bible studies.

I have no idea whatever happened or if she ever took the Bible studies, but I do know why we could not find the grave until I had the opportunity to witness to her. Just after I had the talk with her my friends called to me and said, "We found the graves!"

Esther A. Castle

Plum Tree and Stinging Nettles

The Lord God planted a garden. . . . The tree of life
also in the midst of the garden.Gen. 2:8, 9, NASB.

hall I really do it? I wonder as I look at the old plum tree. It stands in an over-grown orchard by a wooden hut surrounded by fields, meadows, and hedges. In my childhood days I was often here. Back in those days this orchard had a fence and was kept in better shape. But now the fence is broken, the hut is rotting, and the trees have a whole retinue of wildly growing, stinging nettles.

But, Lord, the stinging nettles shall not prevent me from finally climbing a tree! Cautiously I find my way to a small, free space between the stinging nettles, and I reach up to the lowest branch and hold it with a strong grip. But unfortunately, with the first jump I do not manage to pull myself up, and I have to step back on the ground—into the stinging nettles! Shaking my head, I laugh. I've heard that sometimes it is healthy to get stung by stinging nettles as they can help against certain sicknesses. What a comfort!

But with the second try I am successful and climb up to the next branch. There I comfortably sit down and rest my head against the tree trunk. As a child, in the late summer days I often sat in such fruit trees and ate juicy, sweet plums. I felt safe and secluded from the world, and now again I feel that way. I am just together with God. Golden sunrays transform the roof of leaves above me in a shining green dome. Flies are buzzing around unripe green plums, and singing birds flutter from one twig to another. All of this is peace.

The peace in Eden must have been a little bit similar. The tree of life in the middle of the garden must have borne fruits that even the sweetest plums cannot match. Since ancient days humanity has searched for that legendary tree that gives us eternal life. But haven't I found it already? Jesus said that He is the Bread of Life and He Himself is life. When we receive Him, we receive eternal life. Therefore I am already able to claim that promise and climb onto the lap of my life tree, Jesus. I can sit there in peace with Him and eat the fruit of life He earned for me.

Today Jesus provides us with the best fruits of Eden. Even today we are able to find the peace of Eden and the tree of life—since Jesus is our Tree of Life! He is our wonderful Savior!

Jaimee Seis

The Power of Words

Gracious words are like a honeycomb, sweetness to the soul and health to the body. Prov. 16:24, ESV.

My friend Beulah, my husband, and I were on the Metro line from the convention center in St. Louis, Missouri, to our hotel after attending an international meeting sponsored by our church. As I sat reflecting on the dynamic and inspiring messages and melodious music, I couldn't help thinking of the rich spiritual blessings I'd received and the joy of seeing many of my friends of long ago. Fascinated by the beautiful clear-blue skies and fluffy white clouds gliding majestically in the air, I began to sing softly the chorus, "Walk with me, Lord, walk with me," unaware that amid the loud noise from the speeding train, a stranger sitting in front of me was listening.

When I stopped singing, a woman turned around and said, "Thank you." I didn't understand her reason for thanking me until she mentioned that the song I was singing had comforted her heart. She confided to Beulah, sitting next to her, that she had just experienced a broken relationship with her boyfriend, and was hurting deep inside. Beulah shared with her comforting words found in Isaiah 41:10: "Fear thou not; for I am with thee; be not dismayed; for I am thy God: I will strengthen thee; yea, I will help thee; yea, I will uphold thee with the right hand of my righteousness." She encouraged the woman to read the text when she got home.

A similar incident happened recently at my church. I was quietly singing the words to the song "Only trust Him, only trust Him; He will save you now," as I washed my hands in the ladies' room. The guest soloist for the worship service looked at me with a beautiful smile and said calmly, "I needed to hear those words." Another woman nearby, also washing her hands, chimed in: "I needed them too; thank you." Just a few simple words from a song, but they had touched the heart of two individuals. Wow! The power of words!

Words can have a tremendous impact on people! They have the power to make a difference. So what about your words? Do they bring peace, comfort, inspiration, joy, and hope, or discouragement, doubt, despondency, and despair? God grant that our words will uplift, bless, encourage, and inspire fellow travelers on the meandering road of life.

Shirley C. Iheanacho

Making a Difference

Therefore all things whatsoever ye would that
men should do to you, do ye even so to them. Matt. 7:12.

The foundation where I work raises money to support a medical mission project called Operation Walk. The doctors who participate in this mission activity go to developing countries and replace hips and knees for people who desperately need the surgery. Typically they replace about 70-75 joints in five days.

On a trip to Panama one year, during the first day of actual surgery, one of the team members walked out of the operating room and saw someone down a long dark hallway sitting in a wheelchair with a person standing beside the chair. When she walked down the hall, she found a young girl sitting in a wheelchair, her father standing beside her. When the team member asked if she could help her, the girl said, "I was hoping you could operate on me and I could walk again. I haven't walked since I was 9 years old!" She was 23 years old at the time, and suffered from pediatric rheumatoid arthritis.

The team member went and got one of the doctors from the operating room, and he knelt down in front of the girl and said, "I will operate on you tonight, and you will walk tomorrow!" He did just that, and the girl, named Maria, walked the next day.

The following year when the foundation hosted an event in North America to raise funds for Operation Walk, Maria walked out on the stage and thanked everyone, in broken English, for helping her walk again. She then handed the doctor $100 that she and her family had saved (a small fortune for a family living in the mountains of Panama) to help others with joint replacement surgery who, like her, were underserved and could not walk.

What a difference the doctors made in Maria's life, and what a difference she made that night by handing them $100. There was not a dry eye in the house.

This was one of the most beautiful demonstrations of the golden rule that I have ever witnessed. The doctors demonstrate this with each mission trip they take, because they give of their time and money to take these trips. Certainly Maria demonstrated that as well as she very clearly wanted to "do unto others" as they had done for her.

Karen J. Johnson

The Seashell on the Seashore

And my God will supply all your needs according
to His riches in glory in Christ Jesus. Phil. 4:19, NASB.

The water shimmers like diamonds on the Indian Ocean. My teaching year in Kenya is halfway over. It's time for vacation.

"I found more shells!" I holler to Chris, as I splash around in the low tide. I'm collecting them. Broken ones. Ugly. Small. Small and ugly broken ones. Any shells I can find.

I'd taught this past semester, every day seeing a gorgeous conch shell on the principal's desk—the biggest shell I'd ever seen, and it was from this beach. *What are the chances I can find that kind of shell?* I had thought. On the bright side, I could find a lot of little ones. I couldn't wait to go on this trip to start my collection, and here I am.

"Hey, Chris, want to check out those rocks?"

"Sure," he answers.

We walk, zigzagging between tide pools. The crabs part like the Red Sea as we approach our destination. Chris climbs the rocks, and I become intrigued with the little shells once again.

"Hey, Cassi, look at this!" I run over to him, and behold, Chris has a shell. *The* shell. His grapefruit-sized beauty shines in the sun like a trophy. I'm jealous. *Sigh.* He had never even looked for shells, so how does he end up with the biggest one?

My jealousy seems silly; but maybe this isn't about a shell. Throughout life I've repeatedly searched for my own answers. I end up settling for second best. The ugly side of a situation. Small dreams. Broken relationships. My self-image is painted in a skewed light because of guilt from the mistakes I've made. If I look deep enough, maybe I can relate to these small, ugly, broken shells, because they resemble who I think I am—or what I deserve. But you know what? God will meet all of my needs according to His glorious riches in Christ—my healer and provider. There is no broken heart, ugly past, or small hopes and dreams that He can't change into something beautiful and enriching. All we have to do is trust.

That day I prayed for a special shell—no more settling. God sent me the perfect one 30 minutes before our departure—a gift from a stranger on the beach. All I had to do was wait.

Cassi Alise Meelhuysen

An Honest Man

Leave all your worries with him, because he cares for you. 1 Peter 5:7, TEV.

When working in Chicago a couple of years ago, one of my son's customers had a test of honesty while on vacation; he told Jack of his experience.

His customer and a friend were on their way to Canada for a week of fishing in a remote area accessible only by boat. They had been traveling all night. It was now early morning as they were passing through a small town in Minnesota. Already on the outskirts of town, Jack's customer saw an object on the side of the road and asked his friend to stop. He jumped out of the vehicle and ran back to retrieve what turned out to be a bank deposit bag from a local church. Along with checks, there were hundreds of dollars in cash. His first thought was *Is this* Candid Camera?

He immediately called his wife to tell her, and then called the church and left a message on their answering machine informing them that he had found their bank bag. He explained when he would be back through town and gave his home phone number with instructions to coordinate a meeting spot with his wife, since his cell phone would not be transmitting from their remote location. The bank deposit bag stayed with him for the next six days.

Upon his return he called his wife. She informed him that he would be meeting the pastor and treasurer, but instead of at the church it would be at the local TV station. This was a surprise to him. After spending a week fishing in the wilderness, he certainly was not dressed or prepared to be featured on the local TV station.

When meeting the pastor and treasurer, he learned that the treasurer had put the deposit bag on the roof of her car, got distracted, and forgot about it. When she drove away from the church, the bag eventually slid off the car roof, landing on the side of the road. How upset and distraught the treasurer was when she realized she had lost the Lord's money!

I'm sure many prayers were offered to the Lord, and how thankful she was when Jack's customer returned this precious bag. Tears of joy and prayers of thanksgiving were sent up to our heavenly Father for His protection over His money.

What a witness of how the Lord watches over and protects His own. It's awesome to serve such a God, and to meet one who allowed the Holy Spirit to work through him to do right.

Patricia Mulraney Kovalski

Misjudged

Do not judge, or you too will be judged. For in the same way you judge others, you will be judged. Matt. 7:1, 2, NIV.

I had just arrived at the Hong Kong International Airport following a 16-hour flight. I had only 30 minutes to find the transfer desk, pick up my boarding pass for my next flight, and find my way through the airport and security to the train that would take me to the concourse from which my next flight was to leave.

Several minutes later, boarding pass in hand, I searched for a sign to lead me to the train, but I saw none. I asked several people, but they didn't know either. Finally I found the correct escalator and hurried toward the line awaiting the train.

When the train arrived, a Chinese woman and her daughter rushed to the front of the line to board the train. The rest of us boarded, but I couldn't help noticing that this woman seemed quite agitated about something and spoke in rapid Mandarin to those around. *She's probably late for her flight,* I thought. *But crowding in front won't get her there any faster.*

When the train stopped, the woman and her daughter pushed ahead of everyone else to get off the train. I was standing behind several people and didn't understand why they weren't exiting the train. *Perhaps they are going on to the next stop,* I thought, and I urged myself forward so I could disembark.

And then I saw her. The woman who had rushed off the train was kneeling beside a little girl who was sobbing inconsolably. Suddenly I knew what had happened. This "pushy" mother had lost one of her daughters. When she realized the little girl wasn't with her, she frantically reboarded the train to find her. Reunited again, the trio wept openly.

Forgive me, Lord, I prayed. *I misjudged this woman and her intentions. I'm sorry.*

It happens too often. Whether we can't understand the words or read the body language of someone, we sometimes misjudge their intentions. It is my prayer today that the Lord will give us patience to see the needs of others as He sees them. As another version translates part of today's verse: "God will be as hard on you as you are on others! He will treat you exactly as you treat them" (CEV). *Help us not to judge* can be the prayer of each of us.

Charlotte Ishkanian

Job's Friends

Trust in the Lord with all your heart and
lean not on your own understanding. Prov. 3:5, NIV.

For years I could not understand why God was displeased with Job's friends. They seemed to be sincere. After all, they spent a lot of time trying to console Job and help him discover areas in his life that may have been unacceptable to God. How many people do we know who will invest their time, effort, and thoughts with us the way that we see Job's friends devoting to him? So for a long time I was bewildered with God's response to Job's friends: "He said to Eliphaz the Temanite, 'I am angry with you and your two friends'" (Job 42:7, NIV). I thought well of Job's friends and wondered what could be wrong with friends as caring and concerned as they were. I would listen, ask questions, and ponder texts over and over, but it just wouldn't come together. What was wrong?

Gradually the light came on, and I gained insight as I continued to reflect on and listen to explanations regarding this biblical passage. Job's friends didn't know God's love; Job did. His friends did not have the right commitment to God; Job did. But, thank God, they had Job. Job's faith in God sustained him: "Though He slay me, yet will I hope in him" (Job 13:15, NIV). Neither did any of these men know what had actually happened between God and Satan.

So God told Job to pray for his friends: "Go to my servant Job and sacrifice a burnt offering for yourselves. My servant Job will pray for you, and I will accept his prayer and not deal with you according to your folly. You have not spoken the truth about me, as my servant Job has" (Job 42:8, NIV). They were trying to convince Job that God was punishing him for something that he'd done wrong. They were ascribing the characteristics of other gods to Job's God. Job knew "no other gods." He knew in whom he had put his trust and confidence. Perhaps they should have been quiet: "If only you would be altogether silent!" (Job 13:5, NIV).

We have to know God for ourselves in order to be sustained when trials come into our lives. Even though friends may have good intentions, we cannot lean on their understanding of God. Oh, to have an earthly friend like Job; or, better yet, to be a friend like Job. May we get to know God better each day by sitting at His Feet and letting His Holy Spirit direct us moment by moment.

Sharon M. Thomas

He Leadeth Me

In all thy ways acknowledge him, and he shall direct thy paths. Prov. 3:6.

I remember it very vividly even though seven years had passed. It was the beginning of the summer. The weather was so warm that the city center was crowded. For me it was a very special day. I had just left the mayor's office, where I had received a reward for being one of the best students in town. It was a great honor. Would you suppose I was happy? No, I wasn't. As I sat at a pastry shop with my mother, I felt bitter and disappointed. I had everything I dreamed of: I was a straight-A student, and so far I was successful; in just a few months from then I would be getting into the medical university. It was all going according to the plan. But I felt empty and hollow.

My mom tried to cheer me up. We were talking about a book when out of nowhere an older woman came over to us. I assumed she was my mother's friend, so I forced a polite smile. She greeted us and asked me if I wrote the book we were talking about. Confused, I said "No," trying to comprehend why she would assume that.

"But you do write short stories, don't you?" For a few moments I stared at her, thinking *How in the world does she know that?* Yes, I did write stories; I liked doing that, and deep down I always dreamed of becoming a writer. But I had never told anyone. Bewildered, I answered that I did.

The woman looked in my eyes and said: "You are going to write a book one day, and I would like to have a signed copy. Just don't give up. Keep writing, and you are going to succeed." And then she was gone.

My mom asked me, "Do you know this woman?" We spent the next 15 minutes trying to figure out who she was and how she knew me. I never got the answers. But that day something just clicked. I realized why I wasn't happy. I had never asked God what His plans were for my life. I started praying for God to take the lead in my life. I focused on writing, and when I got in college, I studied literature. And that decision brought me to theological seminary, where I am now a student. What I learned is that God is always near, trying to reach our hearts and lead our lives toward a better future, even if we sometimes forget to ask Him.

Tijana Tizie

The Wonder of a Seed

Whoever sows sparingly will also reap sparingly, and whoever sows generously will also reap generously. 2 Cor. 9:6, NIV.

My son carefully removed a tiny, shiny black seed from his pocket. I wondered what made him so attached to it. He was just 5 years old, too small it seemed to be interested in something as small as a seed. But even little plants or weeds caught his interest. One night, before going to sleep, he asked, "Mommy, how does a seed grow?" I tried to remember my basic science. I told him the best way to find out how plants grow was to put the seed in some soil and watch what would happen. I promised to help him with the experiment the following day.

For the next few days my son was very excited caring for the seed. Every day, before the sun was up, he was already checking the plant and ready with a glass of water. I remember his excitement when the first green showed up and finally the figure of a guyabano tree shot up into the sunshine. His joy was immeasurable.

As the little plant grew, I thought about the joy God must have felt as He formed us with His own hand. He referred to us as "the excellent ones, in whom is all my delight" (Ps. 16:3, ESV). God pays close attention to all our needs. He tends to even the smallest cares of our lives. He watches our growth with so much love and tenderness. He delights in our truthfulness. He finds pleasure in our prayers. He never gives up on us. He wraps us with an abundance of blessings so we may live in comfort and ease. When life seems hard, and trials and troubles come, He invites us to lift our heads for reflection and prayer. He provides all the materials that enable us to construct and create hope that may shine out into the lives of those surrounding us.

Several years ago now, that little seed that became a tree bore its first fruit, and my son was overjoyed to harvest it. As he watched the tree growing tall, you could see the joy on his face to know that once in his lifetime he made a tree grow, one that bears good fruit for health. It's worth reflecting that in our lives there is also a God who is constantly watching over us, finding joy in all that we do for Him. He is also rejoicing in every bit of kindness we offer to those who are in need. He is also delighted when we spread the seed of His love into our families, churches, and communities.

Leah A. Salloman

God Forgives

If we confess our sins, he is faithful and just to forgive us our sins,
and to cleanse us from all unrighteousness. 1 John 1:9.

Y ou will be in my fourth-grade class this fall, and should know about your country of Canada," I told my son, Mark. "When school is out, we will drive through the provinces as far as Newfoundland. It will be a great learning experience for you and should be fun."

And it was fun to view the prairie provinces, to pick up amethysts in Ontario, to cross the bridge led by a police car when we were lost, and to visit the Parliament buildings. We stood upon the plains of Abraham and swam in the St. Lawrence River. We even saw a whale spouting! We watched a carver carving and bought some carvings in Quebec.

Heading around the Gaspé Peninsula, we arrived at the town of Gaspé. We stopped, shopped, went birdwatching, and added new names to our yearly bird list.

At Agate Bay we collected agates. Then Mark went into the water but could not swim, as the waves were rolling in. They crashed over him, but he stood his ground. He was so young and could have been swept out to sea, I later realized, but he was having such a good time.

When Friday came, we left to find a motel and get settled before Sabbath.

The next morning we rose early because we wanted to go to the Pugwash camp meeting. A knock on the door surprised us. It was the motel owner. "Is something wrong? It is so early, and I heard you up."

"No," I responded. "It is Saturday, and we want to go to the camp meeting."

"But today is Sunday; yesterday was Saturday," she answered.

I was shocked, *really shocked!* Thinking about what we had done yesterday, I was horrified. We had lost a day, somewhere, while traveling! My son asked tearfully, "Mom, will God forgive us for breaking the Sabbath?"

"Yes, Mark. He will forgive, for we did not realize what day it was," I assured him.

Relief flooded his young face when we prayed and asked for forgiveness, for we were truly sorry. Peace calmed our troubled thoughts. How wonderful to know our heavenly Father understands everything, and we can trust Him always.

Muriel Heppel

What Does It Mean to Witness?

The angel of the Lord encampeth round about them
that fear him, and delivereth them. Ps 34:7.

What does it mean "to witness" in the Christian sense? I have always heard that it was giving people information, or telling people things, or doing things for people so that they would eventually be convinced or converted. It was my responsibility to do this witness thing in order to be a good Christian and make others into my kind of Christian. I have to admit that this kind of witnessing has not been a comfortable fit for me. Most of the times I tried it, it fell flat.

A few weeks ago I began to think about what the word "witnessing" meant. As I understand it, it means to see something; to be there, experience it, and be able to verify something because of what you saw, heard, or experienced. It dawned on me that the noun form of the word fit what I believe about God much more than the verb form. My "witness" is what I have seen and experienced regarding God and His care. It is about God and what He does—not about me and what I think I know or what I think that I should convince you of.

Why did I mention the word "witness"? I just heard a very amazing story and decided to check it out. I went to see Pastor Shin. He had gone to a hospital to visit two Korean girls who had received some injuries from being hit by a van on the highway. It was a couple of days before they were going to return to Korea, and they were on their way to the supermarket to get some things to take back with them. When the two girls crossed the highway, they both were struck. They ended up on the side of the road. The driver of the van stopped and quickly got out to check on the girls, very afraid that they were dead. The hood of his van was severely bashed in, as he had been going quite fast. He was surprised and relieved to see the girls get up from the side of the road—they were not dead after all. But he continued to look for the third girl dressed in yellow. He walked up and down the road and in the ditch looking for her, but he could not find her. The driver said that he had seen three girls, and he had hit the girl in yellow first! There was no girl in yellow, at least that anyone else but the driver could see!

It is gratifying to hear this story from a person who had a part in it—a firsthand witness. The story had not grown more fantastic with the telling. When we hear from a witness, we are much more likely to believe. I want to be that kind of witness.

Janell Brauer

All Things Work Together

And we know that all things work together for good to them that love God, to them who are the called according to his purpose. Rom. 8:28.

I was so happy to hear that our West African mission committee had selected my husband as a delegate to a church world convocation in the United States. Yes, a dream come true. I could also participate as a guest, but my joy was reduced by half when they said that we would have to contribute half of the total cost because of the financial constraint of mission.

Looking at our family financial difficulty, I knew I could not go to the session. Nevertheless, I decided to support my husband in raising his part of the necessary funds in order for him to attend.

But another terrible blow came when after some months we were called to serve in a different mission of our territory. Our home mission committee informed my husband that he could no longer be their delegate to the session, because he had been replaced by another person. I felt seriously disappointed, but quickly got comfort from the text of Romans 8:28, as I do believe all things work for the good of those who love God. We forgot about attending the world convention, but constantly prayed for its success, especially for the election of the officers.

Then good news came from the mission committee: they had decided that my husband should remain a delegate to the session and be fully sponsored. What good news! He would have to contribute nothing; he had a full sponsorship. And now I could also participate, with only my ticket fee to pay for. The burden had been lightened. Praise God.

God provided, and my husband and I attended the session of 2010 in Atlanta, Georgia. It was a great privilege to worship with thousands of the folks representing all the tribes and languages of the world.

I praise God for all that happened. Although it was painful when my husband was replaced, it opened another door, a better one indeed, that allowed me to also benefit. Sometimes we just have to wait and trust to see how God is going to work things out according to His purpose.

Dear sisters, do not give up when a door closes; trust God and believe today's text. God will open a better door for you.

Omobonike Sessou

Are You Healthy Inside?

Man looketh on the outward appearance,
but the Lord looketh on the heart. 1 Sam. 16:7.

I was 10 the summer we moved from the little rental house on Franklin Street to a larger house on Front Street, a house that would be ours. No longer was my bedroom in the basement. And the yard was full of trees. There was a flowering crab apple tree that bore small red apples. I remember trying to eat them (trying, but not succeeding). Another tree produced larger apples that my mother used to make pies, apple crisp, and other delicious things to eat. There were plum trees, silver leaf maple trees, elm trees, and green ash trees. But the grandest were the large cottonwood trees near the front door.

I would climb in the apple tree, but the lowest branches on the cottonwood trees were well above my head. Their trunks were so large I couldn't reach around them. I'm not sure how old they were, but they provided glorious shade and lots of leaves in the fall. (That last part was fun for me, but not my parents.) The trees appeared to have been there for nearly 100 years, and I expected they would remain many more.

After I had left home, my mother told me that the trees had to come down. On the outside they appeared healthy, but inside they were rotten and hollow. It was dangerous to have the trees stand because they could split and injure something— like our home—or someone. Their appearance was a facade.

I wonder if the same thing may apply to some Christians—if it applies to me? We attend church regularly. We have positions and duties in the church that we perform faithfully. We don't do the "don't"s and we do the right "do"s. But what does God see when He looks at us? When He sees our heart?

We may be able to fool our neighbor, fellow church members, even family, but we can't fool God. He sees what we are on the inside. He sees if inside we are healthy. He sees the hollow places that only He can fill. Unlike those old cottonwood trees, we are not doomed to be cut down. No matter how much hollowness there may be inside each of us, God has the remedy. God can fill us with His Spirit, His perfect character, His perfect love. All we have to do is ask. And accept.

Barbara Lankford

My God Moves Pages

Even before a word is on my tongue, behold,
O Lord, you know it altogether. Ps. 139:4, ESV.

When my sister and I inherited a commercial building our father had built many years ago, I had no idea how my heavenly Father would guide me through the problems of being a landlord. The tenant moved out without notice five months before the end of the lease, and finding a new tenant became necessary. By now the rental was not just the "extra" money in the budget, so we needed to find a long-term tenant.

The building had been occupied by several long-term tenants, so I had never seen it empty. I was shocked to see what we were dealing with: leaking roof, a large showroom floor that needed cleaning, and easements. We were blessed with an interest in our store from a large company that indicated they could solve these problems and have it back into a great *new* store. After all, the location was ideal.

The forthcoming paperwork didn't seem so promising, and as each day went by my stomach hurt more and more. I talked often to my heavenly Father about what to do and about making the right decision. One particularly hard morning I had to decide whether to return some documents, and as I read my morning devotional, God spoke to me with "Before they call, I will answer; and while they are still speaking, I will hear" (Isa. 65:24, NKJV). Peace flooded through me as I felt God take the burden of that day and help me make the right decision. I signed the papers and returned them.

Yesterday I received an e-mail that the company had revised that document and resent it to my sister and me for our final signatures. But I was in Kansas City to help my daughter with the family for a few days while she had surgery, so I didn't open the e-mail.

This morning I opened my *Renew* to November 29 and read "God Carries You and Me." God did it again. He moved the pages to just what I needed for the day. I don't know what the e-mail documents say. Maybe they are perfect for us. Maybe they are saying they have decided against our location. Whatever it says, God will carry me through, and He will do the same for you with whatever problem you are facing. Most will probably be a lot larger than renting a building, but large or small, if it is important to us, God cares.

Judy Gray Seeger Cherry

A New Way to Pray

The prayer of a righteous [woman] is powerful and effective. James 5:16, NIV.

Do you ever feel as if your prayers don't even get high enough to bounce off the ceiling? Do you have trouble concentrating on your sentences long enough to complete a thought? Is your prayer list so long that you can't get through it? Maybe you are a step from giving up on prayer. I was like that too—until someone suggested writing out my prayers, either longhand or on the computer. I write for a living, and the thought of writing more was abhorrent. But I gave it a try.

This was new, since I'd been prayer walking for years and found walking and prayer a delightful combination. Then I developed back problems and began biking. Biking and prayer weren't compatible. That's when I moved to writing my prayers out.

I purchased a notebook, divider pages, and lined paper. I divided the notebook into sections and pray for different topics every day. I use the principle of breaking a big task into several smaller more manageable ones. My prayer list proceeds as follows: Monday—personal concerns; Tuesday—husband or significant other; Wednesday—family and extended family; Thursday—friends; Friday—Sabbath readiness and missionaries; Sabbath—pastor and family, and church leaders; Sunday—country and leaders. I keep this prayer journal in a basket where I use it along with pens, Bible, and other study material.

My topics are listed on the first page. If a prayer has been answered I write it in a different colored pen, or underline it in color and move it to the back under "Answered Prayer." On a down day, start reading through the "Answered Prayer" file and you will be praising God!

I thought I would dread more writing, but I love it. It keeps me on task. My mind no longer wanders all over the place. I don't have to worry about grammar or spelling, as no one will read this but God, and He has the capacity not only to read my scrawling but to read my heart. The prayers aren't so much for Him—they are more practice for my walk on earth. God already knows what I want and need.

This style of praying has taken great pressure off me. God knows my heart every day of the week. It may take me a week to get through my requests, but I get it done in an orderly manner. Try this new way to pray. You'll like it!

Nancy L. Van Pelt

Healing Your Heart

If we confess our sins, He is faithful and just and will forgive us our sins and purify us from all unrighteousness" (1 John 1:9, NIV).

I'm still amazed at this promise. When God showed up in the drug house where I was trying to kill myself, He gave me a glimpse of what I'd be like the day after resurrection—an innocent child. I told Him, "I've never been innocent."

And He told me, "I've never seen you any other way." It was the first time in my life I'd ever felt loved. I just sobbed. I could hardly believe it. Maybe you're like me and you find it hard to believe that you can actually be clean. Or maybe it's been totally different for you. Maybe you relate to my friend, Fran.

At first, you might think there's no way Fran could understand anything about recovery. I mean, she's never used drugs or alcohol, never been abused, never had any of the darker addictions. She's a great Bible student, and she does tons of ministry. If anybody was ever an innocent child, she was probably it.

About a year ago she told me she had a hard time relating to this verse: "You say, 'I am rich, with everything I want; I don't need a thing!' And you don't realize that spiritually you are wretched and miserable and poor and blind and naked" (Rev. 3:17, TLB). She couldn't see herself as wretched. When she looked at her life, it seemed like the cross was a bit overkill in her case. "I mean, really? God poured out all of heaven and gave His Son to die because I'm impatient once in a while?"

But gradually, gently, God has been revealing to her the mess inside her heart. And it's the same junk we all have: wounded by other people; thirsty to be loved and valued, choosing foolish, selfish ways to get those needs met. Whether you choose drugs, sex, or achievement (as Fran did), the result is the same: you're still thirsty, and you're still a mess. God showed Fran it's as though she has a bad case of heartworms. Heartworms will kill you. The incredible thing is that God says, "I will give you a new heart, and I will put a new spirit in you. I will take out your stony, stubborn heart and give you a tender, responsive heart" (Eze. 36:26, NLT).

He's not only willing to forgive us, He longs to do it, and He delights to heal our hearts.

Cheri Peters

The Miracle Dog

For I know the thoughts that I think toward you, says the Lord, thoughts of peace and not of evil, to give you a future and a hope. Jer. 29:11, NKJV.

The call came about 4:30 the afternoon of July 17. "Yvette's house is on fire! Yvette, Tyrone, and Courtney are OK," Nikki said.

"Thank You, Jesus," I said. As I hung up, I thought, *She didn't mention Frazier, their beloved Schnauzer.* He was locked in the house at Camp Springs, Maryland.

I saw the raging fire through the trees as I came near the house. Yvette stood weeping. "I can replace the things, but I cannot replace Frazier. What a horrible way to die! He trusted me, and I failed him."

I hugged her and said, "I am so sorry," but that was so little consolation.

Family members arrived, and we watched as the fire continued to burn. We silently mourned the loss of Frazier. Yvette and Tyrone's neighbors came to comfort them. Finally, about 6:30, the smoke and flames died down, and two firemen were able to enter the house. They came back out, Frazier running from between their legs! Yvette screamed, "Frazier!" and ran toward him, fell to the ground, hugging and kissing him, tears of joy streaming down her face. He was soaking wet, licking her face, very much alive. What had been mourning became a celebration.

A neighbor offered to feed him. I took him to the woman's house, and she gave him dog food and water. He ate hungrily. One of the firefighters called him the miracle dog and advised that he be checked for smoke inhalation. So Yvette took Frazier to the veterinarian, who said Frazier was fine, but to watch him for signs of distress.

Around 11:00 that evening he seemed in distress, so they took him to the animal hospital in Waldorf. They treated him and kept him for observation. That night we prayed earnestly for God to heal Frazier. The next morning the veterinarian called to say Frazier was doing so well they would release him that night. And they did. Frazier has been doing well ever since then. He is now 15 years old and is our joy.

"The very trials that task our faith most severely and make it seem that God has forsaken us, are to lead us closer to Christ, that we may . . . experience [His] peace" (Ellen G. White, *Patriarchs and Prophets*, p. 129).

Wilma C. Jardine

Please Stop the Rain!

*If ye then, being evil, know how to give good gifts unto your children,
how much more shall your Father which is in heaven
give good things to them that ask him? Matt. 7:11.*

A few years ago Oklahoma had an exceptionally rainy spring and summer. We had at least some rain every day for a number of days. We Okies aren't used to that kind of rain and were beginning to wonder what was going on!

Every year we have our camp meeting in mid-July. This is a much-anticipated event in the Sagel household. In a normal summer we're likely to experience some of our highest temperatures in mid-July, so we usually have a pretty sweltering time at camp meeting. Sometimes rainstorms pass through, and it has become almost a tradition to get at least one good old-fashioned gully washer at some point during camp meeting, but we rarely have extended periods of rain then.

However, this year as camp meeting time approached, the rain did not seem to be slowing down! We camp meeting regulars know from experience how interesting life can get in a tent when it rains a lot, so we were hoping and praying that the weather would clear up. But it certainly didn't look like that would happen!

Finally it was the week for camp meeting to start, and it was still raining! I wrote to our camp director asking him what the weather looked like at the camp. It was rainy there, too.

We began packing as usual, but it did not look good. Monday. Tuesday. Wednesday. Thursday. Rain, rain, rain . . . Friday morning. Rain. We planned to leave Friday afternoon.

Then, about the time we set out for camp meeting, the rain stopped! It was clear when we got to Wewoka Woods. It stayed clear and sunny throughout the meetings.

We all had a wonderful time, but not long after we got home, it began to rain again. The next day I e-mailed the camp director and asked him what had happened at the camp. He replied that they had gotten all the camp tents taken down and put in storage, and then it had begun raining!

God's timing is always perfect, and He wants the best for His children. Maybe stopping the rain for camp meeting was a small thing, but it meant a lot to those of us who attended, and it encouraged this sometimes faith-challenged child of God!

Robin Sagel

A Mother's Comfort

As a mother comforts her child, so will I comfort you;
and you will be comforted over Jerusalem. Isa. 66:13, NIV.

Riding in the car to the pet store, my daughter squirmed with excitement as she envisioned her first fish. Once there, she viewed hundreds of swimming creatures before she finally found her favorite. Afterward, she watched as the small iridescent goldfish shimmered in the tank in her bedroom.

Unfortunately, the new pet failed to thrive. Later that day my daughter pointed at the aquarium. We watched as the goldfish pulled her lips in, circled to the top, and lifted her head out of the water.

"It's the dead dance," my daughter said solemnly. Sure enough, within a few hours the new fish had died. I glanced at the orange corpse on the brand-new pink rocks that lined the aquarium. Wishing I could erase my daughter's sad face, I contemplated a quick run to the pet store to replace the goldfish.

Pausing, I sensed God asking me to remain present for my daughter, letting her cry loud and deep; I hugged my little girl close as she rested her head against my shoulder. Eventually her sobs began to slow, allowing for an opportunity to talk about the experience of loss.

Like many moms, I wish I could protect my children from rubbing up against the challenges of everyday living. Often life turns out different than we expect. Relationships fail. Finances crumble. Health withers. The uncertainty of broken dreams leaves us feeling restless.

At these times we do well to reflect on our Lord's promise to comfort those who mourn. In Christ we have a Savior who experienced the deepest measure of suffering known to humanity. His sacrifice on the cross stands as a continual reminder of His abiding love for all people.

As women we can rest assured God cares deeply for our every need. We read in 2 Corinthians 1:3, 4 that our Father of compassion comforts us so that we can comfort others. Sharing our burdens with God enables us to release the strains and stressors of life. As Jesus fills our souls with His healing balm, we feel refreshed and ready to minister to those around us.

Bronwyn Worthington

Clear Out the Cobwebs

In the past God overlooked such ignorance, but now he
commands all people everywhere to repent. Acts 17:30, NIV.

Whatever you have learned or received or heard from me,
or seen in me—put it into practice. Phil. 4:9, NIV.

My husband and I had been married for almost five years before we could afford to buy our first home. But we soon discovered that a number of things in our new home needed our attention. Money was short, so for the first few years we concentrated on replacing the heating system, the windows, and other essential repairs. Eventually we reached the point at which we were able to refit our bedroom completely. As part of the new layout, we changed the lights from a single pendant bulb to six recessed fittings.

After a few months we noticed something odd about the new lights. For some reason one would go off, then come back on. A little while later a different one would go off and come back on—like blinking Christmas lights. This continued for a number of months until we got to the point at which we were operating with only two or three of the six lights most evenings.

My husband called in an electrician, who diagnosed a fault with the transformers. Within a matter of days the electrician returned with the parts and fitted them. What a difference it made! It was a joy to be able to see to do my ironing and sewing properly. At the same time I became aware of the dust and cobwebs that I'd managed to overlook when the lights weren't working, and quickly got to work cleaning all the areas where they had accumulated.

When Christ comes into our hearts, there is great jubilation. But as we learn more about our Creator and who He wants us to be, we realize there is a lot of junk and dirt in our lives that needs clearing out. Before we entered into God's light, that is, while we were ignorant of these faults, God did not hold us accountable. But once we know the truth, we are compelled to get rid of anything that prevents us from having a closer relationship with Christ.

It is my prayer that we will be less critical of those within our communities who are ignorant of God's truths. Instead, let us ask God to clear the cobwebs from our lives as we endeavor to walk in His light.

Avery Davis

You Look Like One

When they saw the courage of Peter and John and realized
that they were unschooled ordinary men, they were astonished
and they took note that these men had been with Jesus. Acts 4:13, NIV.

Leaving the airport parking lot, I was about to pay the parking fee when the man behind the gate's window looked at me and asked, "Are you from India?" I said no. Then he looked at me again and said, "But you look like one." I thought it was a very nice compliment because of my love for India. India is one of the places you will never forget—the colors, the food, the beautiful dresses, the jasmine flowers on the streets, the smell of curry and chapatti, the languages, the music, and the amazing architecture.

As I talked to the man behind the window, all these images and senses coming to mind, I thanked him for the compliment. I told him that part of me is in India. He smiled and offered to share his last chapatti with me.

As I drove home that day, his words stayed in my mind: "You look like one." Every day, many times a day, we look like something to someone. Every day we make an impression. The word "impression" means to stamp or form, or figure by impressing, or to imprint. So the question today is What impression are we leaving on the hearts and minds of those we come in contact with?

Our Bible text says, "When they saw the courage of Peter and John and realized that they were unschooled, ordinary men, they were astonished and they took note that these men had been with Jesus." Others saw Jesus in them. Many in cities, in small towns, on your street, in your place of work are looking for someone who has been with Jesus. Have you been with Jesus? Do you "look like one" who knows Him? How can you "look like one"? Here are three ways we can look more like Him: by loving to spend time with Him, by copying Him in everything we say and do, and by relying upon Him. In these ways we will be transformed into His likeness.

I do not know if I will encounter someone today who will look at me and say I "look like one"—Indian, Brazilian, Turkish. But I want to walk with Jesus so that when people look at me they will recognize that I "look like one," act like one, and speak like one who has been with Him.

Raquel Queiroz da Costa Arrais

Praying Boldly

If you remain in me and follow my teachings, you can ask anything you want, and it will be given to you. John 15:7, NCV.

I married my neighbor. For 10 years I lived across the court from a kind gentleman; I never knew he had his eye on me until one day he asked me out to dinner. I stood dumbfounded, because I would not have guessed that we could ever have become more than friends. However, over the course of two years of dating, my son gave me away in marriage to my neighbor Vondell as my daughter looked on as maid of honor accompanied by more than 100 guests.

It soon became evident that housing was going to be an issue. For a short time we shared his townhouse, and my young adults lived across the court in mine. But to better serve our concept of "family," we thought it best that we purchase a large home where everyone would have their own space. So the search began.

Housing in the Washington, D.C., metropolitan area is pricey, and finding something that is suitable at a reasonable cost is challenging. Then these two words hit me: Pray boldly.

Certain that it was the Holy Spirit, I immediately obeyed and asked God for a big house: at least five bedrooms, a family room, and a garage for my husband's "toys." A few days later Beverly, our real-estate agent, called and said she had found the perfect home. Of course our joint question was three words: "What's the price?" She quoted the cost, and in unison Vondell and I said, "Too much." She countered with "Come and see."

The words "pray boldly" continued in my thoughts. When we saw the house, we were convinced our real-estate agent was right: a colonial, five bedrooms, three baths, two family rooms, and a two-car garage, all on a shaded lot in a well-established subdivision. "But we'll have to sell our townhouses before we can make this move," we cautioned Beverly.

She assured us our townhouses would sell in a matter of days. Beverly was absolutely right again. She listed my house on Monday, and on Tuesday evening I had five strong offers. The same for Vondell; his house never made the listings.

Three weeks later we were in our new home. Lesson learned: Is there anything too hard for the Lord? Absolutely not when you commit your ways to Him.

Yvonne Curry Smallwood

Welcome Home

Start children off on the way they should go, and even when
they are old they will not turn from it. Prov. 22:6, NIV.

I haven't seen you since we attended the primary Sabbath school class together."
Who was this woman who had just addressed my husband? The study of the
Sabbath school class had ended, and there she was right in front of us. We were
visitors, so we didn't know who she was. My husband had to ask her name. "My
name is Gwen." It had been close to 60 years since he had seen her. She had gone
off to boarding school, met a fellow who turned out to be from a farm family, got
married, and had two sons. We had lost track of her after that. "I started attending
church four months ago and hope to be baptized at camp meeting," she told us.

"Do your brother and sister know that you plan to be baptized?" I asked her.
Her sister knew, but she wasn't sure that her brother did. Her sister had never left
the church, but her brother had. Ten years ago he felt drawn back to the Lord and
was baptized. He had wandered in the wilderness of the world for at least 25 years.

"Now he is in church every Sabbath helping out as a deacon. Occasionally he
has special music. Mother was still alive when he returned, but she had no idea that
one day her youngest child would also yield to the call of the Holy Spirit. Won't she
be surprised to see her daughter in heaven one day?"

Two weeks later while attending a small rural camp meeting, there she was
again enjoying the fellowship of Adventist believers. At supper we sat together, and
in passing I said to her, "Welcome home!" I learned later that she really appreciated
hearing that.

Soon it was time for the conference-wide camp meeting, and at the baptism
Gwen reconsecrated herself to the Lord. Her brother sang the song that had
touched her heart and drawn her back.

Jesus' wandering children are coming back just as He promised they would.
Recently while visiting with friends they excitedly told us that their daughter had
been attending church the past five Sabbaths. It takes a lot of courage to go to a
church where you don't know anyone. Let's be ready to greet these people with a
warm welcome and perhaps even sit with them.

Vera Wiebe

God Comes Through Every Time!

But my God shall supply all your need according
to His riches in glory by Christ Jesus. Phil. 4:19.

One morning I awoke at my usual time of 5:40 with an overwhelming feeling to wear sweats to work. Now, I always wear skirts to work, but the insistence of the voice in my head was very clear: "Wear sweatpants!"

Fine! I thought, *I will wear the sweats.* But I remember grumbling to God that if I got written up later that day at work, it would be His fault.

About an hour later, while driving on the freeway, I found myself next to an 18-wheeler. I was praising God and listening to my usual morning sermon on a local Christian radio station when I noticed that the truck was veering over into my lane. I couldn't believe it, so I started to honk my horn, but the truck did not stop—it just kept coming. I tried to veer to my right, but there was nowhere to go, not even much of a shoulder, just a downward embankment. To my dismay, our vehicles collided.

The impact sent my car fishtailing from side to side and out of control. I tried desperately to hold on to the wheel to steady the car, but it was not working. I felt my car go to the right toward the downward slope and hit what felt like a ditch, which then sent it back over to the left, toward the truck. It seemed as if I were going to go under the side of the truck. I remember the fear that filled my body, and all I could do was call out to God for help. "Jesus! Jesus! Jesus!" was all I could say. Then miraculously I felt my car being pulled away to the right and finally come to a complete stop. The car was badly damaged, but I was alive. Praise Jesus! I was alive.

Sometime after this, when the highway patrol and tow truck had arrived and I had to literally crawl out of the side of my car, I couldn't help smiling to myself and thank God that I was wearing those sweatpants.

God takes care of everything; even the tiny little details. In urging me to wear sweats, He was preparing me for what was to come; even though I didn't know it at the time. This is why it is so important to know God's voice and to obey. Even when it seems insignificant, obey! God does not fail us.

Sherilyn R. Flowers

I Am a Follower

"Come, follow me," Jesus said, "and I will send you out to fish for people."
At once they left their nets and followed him. Matt. 4:19, 20, NIV.

Throughout my ministry and leadership roles of almost 42 years, I have been extremely intentional to take advantage of leadership seminars. I have chosen to
consistently listen to or attend John Maxwell's LeaderCast Simulcast (now Chick-
fil-A LeaderCast Seminars) since 1998. When commuting from home to work, I
listened to CDs on leadership, underpinning my ministry life with excellence.

This past year God has infiltrated and interrupted my leadership life with an
attitude adjustment. I have recently completed reading a book by Leonard Sweet,
I Am a Follower: The Way, Truth, and Life of Following Jesus. The subtitle is: It's
Never Been About Leading. After I read this book Jesus showed me that through
His ministry life He was always about doing the will of His Father—following the
lead of God. John 17 portrays the relationship between Him and His Father, the
oneness of Jesus, the follower of God.

Jesus' final words to His disciples and His believers (us) are found in John 17.
These are the parting words He spoke before crossing over to Gethsemane before
being crucified. John 17:22 portrays the entire leadership life of Jesus as a follower.
"I have given them the glory that you gave me, that they may be one as we are
one—I in them and you in me—so that they may be brought to complete unity.
Then the world will know that you sent me and have loved them even as you have
loved me" (NIV).

As a follower of Jesus Christ, "you are a Jesus work of art." Your life is about
sharing the story of whom you follow. When you follow, people will view Jesus'
presence in your life because they cannot miss seeing Him. "When you merge your
story with Jesus' story, you drink the rushing and creative waters of life. You have
Jesus under your skin. You can feel Him in your bones. . . . Jesus is the artist, and
you, disciple—are so beautiful" (Sweet, p. 259). Being a follower of Jesus Christ is a
joy journey as long as He is in the lead!

"Come with me. I'll make a new kind of fisherman out of you. I'll show you
how to catch men and women. . . . They didn't ask questions, but simply dropped
their nets and followed" (Matt. 4:19, Message). Whom do you follow?

Mary L. Maxson

Are You Listening?

All scripture is given by inspiration of God, and is profitable for doctrine, for reproof, for correction, for instruction in righteousness. 2 Tim. 3:16.

For whatever the reason, I had failed to read the women's devotional for that particular morning. I went out to go about my daily obligations and, as always, when we fail to spend enough time with our Lord, even the little things of the day go wrong. Things such as asking for patience when patience is needed.

This particular morning was especially trying, and I ended up getting very upset with someone. Finally I gave up trying to reason with them, and said I was going home! I had had enough.

When I arrived at home and went into the house, my eyes immediately saw the devotional book that I hadn't read before I left.

God has ways of speaking to us, and that day He spoke to me.

The devotional text for that morning was Ephesians 4:31 and 32. "Let all bitterness, and wrath, and anger, and clamour, and evil speaking, be put away from you, with all malice: and be ye kind one to another, tenderhearted, forgiving one another, even as God for Christ's sake hath forgiven you."

I was humbled. I'm sure it would have helped if I had read that verse as a reminder *before* I went out that morning. I asked for forgiveness from God—and also the one with whom I had gotten so upset.

Our walk with God is not only a learning experience but a listening experience. How much better are my days when I start them out asking for God's guidance throughout each day, each step of the way. And this guidance comes through God's Word just as it did that fateful day. As another text tells us: "The word of God is alive and active, sharper than any double-edged sword. It cuts all the way through, to where soul and spirit meet, to where joints and marrow come together. It judges the desires and thoughts of the heart" (Heb. 4:12, TEV).

God spoke to me that morning with words from His Holy Word. I pray that we all will listen in whatever way He speaks to us.

Donna Sherrill

One Ringy Dingy

Let us strip off every weight that slows us down, especially
the sin that so easily trips us up. And let us run with endurance the
race God has set before us. We do this by keeping our eyes on Jesus, the
champion who initiates and perfects our faith. Because of the joy awaiting
him, he endured the cross, disregarding its shame. Heb. 12:1, 2, NLT.

When the phone rings and it's my vet calling, I have about 30 seconds to decide if I want to turn my life upside down for two months. I know he's calling because someone has dropped off orphaned baby cottontail rabbits that need to be raised by hand.

This means that for two weeks I won't sleep for more than two hours at a time. I will spend eight hours of every 24 feeding baby bunnies. I will perform distasteful tasks like stimulating their bottoms with a wet cotton ball to make them piddle and feeding them cecotropes, a type of feces that rabbits must reingest and without which they cannot survive.

I will fret and worry over them every day, weighing them to be sure they are gaining weight, fighting with them if they refuse to eat. I will be heartbroken if I lose any, and their survival is far from a sure thing.

And I will cry when they are finally released into the wild. I know all this, and yet I continue to pick up the phone and agree to take another litter.

As much as I love bunnies, and as satisfying as it is to raise orphans successfully, I still hesitate before I answer that call. I still feel a sinking sense of despair when I consider how my life is about to get complicated and how much I will suffer from sleep deprivation and anxiety.

And I wonder, How did Jesus do it? He didn't hesitate. He didn't take the time to consider how His life would change, not just for a couple months but forever. Before the call came, He answered. Before the need existed, He filled it.

And He continues to fill our needs today. He is there before we ask, waiting only for us to invite Him to take our burdens and support us through whatever trial or hardship we are facing. I'm continually amazed at how long it takes me to make that call to Him for help, and I resolve each time to call on Him sooner.

What about you? Will you call on Him today?

Céleste Perrino-Walker

Praying as a Warrior

They all joined together constantly in prayer, along with the women and Mary the mother of Jesus, and with his brothers. Acts 1:14, NIV.

In the past several years I have grown to understand what warrior means; before, the word "warrior" had stumped me. Why would prayer become a struggle or conflict, I ask myself? How could I learn to pray as a warrior? Then life began to come at me with more than I could possibly handle. I began to experience repeated, pleading prayer. Have you ever wanted something so much you would battle for it?

A recent devotional reading I read came from a church leader in North Korea encouraging his fellow believers to "pray as a warrior." He began with Colossians 4:12, 13: Epaphras wrestled in prayer, always laboring fervently in his prayers. He goes on saying that God uses this prayer to open doors. Yet sometimes it takes time to break down the barriers we hold onto and put between ourselves and God.

What do we discover when we struggle in prayer? We often discover God's will in the situation. To be a prayer warrior also means that we pray in a concentrated way, maybe for a long time. "I can do all things through Christ who strengthens me" (Phil. 4:13, NKJV).

A warrior prayer also includes the prayer of sacrifice. This is often forgotten when I want to do things myself. Prayer is the shortest way, not the longest! By sacrificing my time, myself, in prayer, God will open the hearts of people and break through their thinking, and often evil is conquered with good.

E. M. Bounds, writing on prayer, says: "Perseverance counts much with God as well as with man. If Elijah had ceased at his first petition the heavens would have scarcely yielded their rain to his feeble praying. If Jacob had quit praying at a decent bedtime he would scarcely have survived the next day's meeting with Esau. If the Syrophoenician woman had allowed her faith to faint by silence, humiliation, repulse, or stop midway its struggles, her grief-stricken home would never have been brightened by the healing of her daughter."

Just as Epaphras remained faithful to Jesus Christ until the end, I pray that we as sisters in Christ remain faithful in prayer wherever we are, even under dire circumstances as we walk the walk of faith in these end-times.

Nancy Wallack

This Is Your Season

He who dwells in the secret place of the Most High
shall abide under the shadow of the Almighty. Ps. 91:1, NKJV.

I grew up in a country with two seasons—wet and dry. Then I came to live in America, and there I found four seasons—spring, summer, autumn, and winter. I've discovered that life also has seasons. There are those that refer to the stage of life we may be in—childhood, adolescence, young adulthood, middle age, and old age. It seems to me that women have more seasons of life than men. I'm not sure why.

But there are also spiritual seasons that can also be called wet and dry. There are those times when our spiritual life seems to be parched, and we are always thirsting for God; and those times when we feel abundantly filled with the Word of God and the Holy Spirit. But I've found that the wet spiritual seasons don't last as long as the dry spiritual seasons.

I've spent many years of my life struggling with this change of spiritual seasons. Sometimes wet, most times dry. As I analyze the different seasons in my life, I find that my wet seasons come when I'm going through the most difficult trials in life. The dry seasons come when I feel that life is going well, and prayer is relegated to morning and evening times, and grace before meals. During times of trial I find myself praying without ceasing, claiming the promises in God's Word, and reading the Bible often to gain the strength I need for each day.

I used to complain about the trials in my life. I wondered why God allowed so many trials to afflict me. Many times I felt like a female Job. But I'm older now, and I realize how important it is to live in the wet spiritual seasons of my life. Spending time in the Word has become a habit, not something I must or should do or even need to do, but something I want to do. Why? Because I remember the dry spiritual seasons. Those times when I felt empty, and I knew what was lacking, but I allowed the business of life and the pleasures of this world to distract me, and so I thirsted and became weary in my Christian walk.

I don't know how it is for you. But I urge you to live your life in the wet spiritual season. Keep covered by the Word. Keep praying without ceasing. Keep claiming the promises in the Bible each day. Keep putting on the armor of God each day. But most of all, live your life under the shadow of God's wings.

Heather-Dawn Small

His Name Is Wonderful

Resist the devil and he will flee from you. James 4:7, NKJV.

As a child I never gave serious thought to angels. I thought all angels were good because of the pictures I saw when I went to church. They appeared to be men in white clothing but they had wings; often they were watching over children. Later, as I grew older, I learned that there were also evil angels or evil spirits who were able to deceive us humans by taking on different guises. They could also put thoughts into our minds and knew our weaknesses. Further study of God's Word gave me a background of Lucifer, who wanted to usurp God's position. "How art thou fallen from heaven, O Lucifer, son of the morning! how art thou cut down to the ground, which didst weaken the nations!" (Isa. 14:12). He was and is the father of lies (John 8:44), and deceived not only a third of the angels (Rev. 12:4), but our ancestors, Adam and Eve (Gen. 3). His purpose is to destroy humanity, but his time is short. He is well aware of the Scriptures and realizes Christ's coming is soon. The Scriptures describe him as a roaring lion seeking whom he may devour (1 Peter 5:8). Unless we have a close relationship to Jesus and trust His promises, all this is scary stuff.

However, in my old age I also learned that Satan tries to intimidate us by supernatural means. Here is my account of one of my experiences: One night in 2012 I was awakened by some strange noises outside my bedroom window. It sounded as though someone was stomping upon plastic bottles. I looked out the window, but there was no one to be seen, and the noise stopped. I didn't think I was dreaming, and a creepy feeling came over me. I tried going back to sleep, but after a while the same noises started once again. I woke my husband up, and with a flashlight we searched everywhere but found nothing. I said a prayer and tried going to sleep again, but to no avail. The noise began yet again, but this time I was convinced it was supernatural, and I yelled out, "Get out of here in Jesus' name, amen!" The noise went away.

There are many stories in the Gospels about Jesus casting out the devil, Satan, evil spirits, evil angels. After casting out the devil, the people responded in amazement, "For with authority He commands even the unclean spirits, and they obey Him" (Mark 1:27, NKJV).

I thanked Jesus that His name helped me resist the devil.

Aileen L. Young

Answer to a Prayer

I lift up my eyes to the hills. From where does my help come? Ps. 121:1, ESV.

After attending a church conference in the United States, my husband and I returned to our homeland, Cameroon, after serving for 20 years as missionaries in our regional headquarters based in Côte d'Ivoire. A lot of things had changed in our absence. My father and father-in-law had passed away; a lot of new faces in the church were unknown to us.

In our prayers after our return, we asked God to help us find a calm and peaceful place to live. God's response came sooner than we expected: a beautiful landscape, land surrounded by mountains. Because of this beautiful scenery we gave it the name "Mountain View." At the site we have pure and cool water from the rocks on the mountain; birds give us every day the privilege to be part of their music festival at the setting of the sun and at sunrise. Butterflies of all colors, flowers with their sweet fragrance give a happy mood to brighten our day. During the rainy season, we are witnesses to the change in guard as the clouds apparently take turns in guarding the mountaintops, an extraordinary phenomenon we call "the cloud dance."

The fertile soil, pure air from the mountaintops, intermittent rains to water the soil all give us the opportunity to harvest foods sown without fertilizers or pesticides. We take them directly from the garden into the kitchen. "Mountain View" is a stress-free zone. The climate is not harsh but very welcoming. I am short of words to vividly describe "Mountain View."

One thing that has impressed us tremendously at Mountain View is that whenever we are in difficulty, when we pray facing the gigantic mountain "Eloumden," we feel the presence of God close to us as we pray. And it seems we get almost immediate answers to our prayers.

When I am faced with challenges and I look up to the mountains around our home, I recall the words of the psalmist found in today's text.

The Bible says God will create a new heaven and a new earth. I will drink no more of the waters of Eloumden, neither fruits nor vegetables from my garden, for our Lord Jesus Christ will give me the water of life. I will eat of the fruit of the tree of life and will live eternally with Him in a stress-free land, where there will be no pain, no sickness, no pollution, neither death.

I hope you want to be a part of that wonderful world.

Angele Rachel Nlo Nlo

Walking, Jumping, and Praising God

He jumped to his feet and began to walk. Then he went with them into the temple courts, walking and jumping, and praising God. Acts 3:8, NIV.

One Sabbath, strongly tempted to stay home because of fatigue and not feeling well, I still couldn't help reflecting on all God had done for me during the previous weeks—in several areas of my life.

Family: our daughter's family had been able to spend an entire week with us. Being with my grandson was such a stress reliever for me!

Ministry: while planning a women's leadership training/certification convention in Bangkok, I got word that two of our invited speakers couldn't make it. Not only were replacement presenters soon found, but at the subsequent convention, more than 100 women earned their certification in Women's Leadership Training. How their testimonies inspired us all!

Finances: On a Monday afternoon my husband and I had gone to one bank only to be told that the adjacent bank, in which we'd recently made a significant deposit, had closed two weeks earlier. The only chance we had of getting the money back would be in six months at the bank's head office in Makati City (the financial center of the Philippines). Upon returning to the still-operational bank, I was handed two forms to fill out: one for withdrawing my deposit the next Friday; and the second, which granted my husband a special power of attorney since I'd be on my trip to Bangkok Friday for the (previously mentioned) women's leadership convention.

Witnessing: On Wednesday, as I boarded my plane, I asked God to let me share His love with someone on the trip. A Muslim couple joined me in my row. By the end of the trip, we'd shared common points in our different belief systems, talked about the importance of faith, and cordially exchanged contact information. After such a wonderful experience in my travels and at the women's convention, I was met at home by my husband who handed me a check, from the *closed* bank— refunding the full amount we'd deposited!

Yes, I *would* go to church this Sabbath, for I had plenty of blessings for which to praise God! My friends, when you feel tired, weak, or discouraged, reflect on God's blessings in your life. You will come forth revived and praising Him!

Helen Bocala Gulfan

God Protected Us!

The angel of the Lord encamps all around those who fear Him,
and delivers them. Ps. 34:7, NKJV.

I had been watching the 11:00 p.m. news, winding down a long day of deep-cleaning and doing odd jobs around the house. As I relaxed on the sofa, I looked up and saw a dark spot on the ceiling. Was that an insect? My husband was already in bed asleep, and I wasn't about to wake him, even though at only five feet two, I'd have to climb onto a chair with a flyswatter to take care of this situation.

A closer look revealed that the spot was moving. It appeared to be a spider. I took aim and swung, but apparently I only stunned the creature. It fell to the floor, behind the TV. I moved the TV and other pieces of furniture looking for it. No luck.

"What if this spider is poisonous?" I sighed. I didn't have enough energy to turn the whole house upside down to find it.

"Dear Lord," I prayed. "You know I'm only dust, and tired dust at that. Since I am not able to locate this spider, please protect us and our cats. Help me find it tomorrow before it bites someone. Thanks in advance for Your help. Amen."

I went to sleep. The next day, about 11:00 a.m., I opened a dirty clothes hamper. I felt creepy when my fingers brushed against a strand of spider silk. I quickly drew my hand back. Below where my fingers had been hung a brown recluse spider—a poisonous specimen!

O, God! I breathed. *Now make it stay put while I find something to kill it with.*

The spider stayed put. I wrapped it in toilet tissue and sent it to a watery grave in the bathroom. How glad I was that it hadn't hidden down among the dirty clothes!

I thanked God for His protecting care, for I had quite a story to tell Carl when he came home from work.

I will always believe in God and our guardian angels, who have saved me and my family from many dangers in our lifetime. Won't it be interesting when we get to heaven to talk with our guardian angels and find out about many other close shaves with trouble and danger we've had that we never even dreamed about?

Bonnie Moyers

There Is No Place Like Home

Let not your heart be troubled: ye believe in God,
believe also in me. In my Father's house are many mansions:
if it were not so I would have told you. I go to prepare a place for you.
And if I go and prepare a place for you, I will come again, and receive
you unto myself; that where I am, there ye may be also. John 14:1-3.

We're going home. After several weeks spent with one of our sons and his family in faraway places, we're going home. Our holidays have been truly blessed, and our children have spared no effort or expense to make our trip truly memorable. However, every beautiful experience eventually comes to an end, and now we are going home. Our feelings are mixed. We will miss our family for sure, but there is something magical about that word "home."

We bought our first house when we were in our 70s. It's an old building, virtually without a garden. Most of our furniture is older than we are, and almost all is secondhand, so it has no monetary value. Its worth lies elsewhere.

One of our sons visited Greece when we couldn't be home to welcome him, so he asked to spend the night in the house alone. He wanted to breathe the familiar atmosphere, to savor precious memories, to "touch ground" with his past. He has a beautiful home, large and airy, surrounded by lawns and shrubbery, so it certainly wasn't the house that drew him. It was the worn reminders of his childhood and youth, memories of caring acceptance, of laughter and the joy of simple pleasures that characterized his childhood and were forever etched in his heart.

Soon, very soon, we are all going home. We have no memories of heaven, as we have not been there before, but its exquisite beauty and breathtaking surroundings are not what make our hearts beat faster. It's the atmosphere of pervading love in our heavenly Father's home. It's the acceptance, the understanding, the warmth of His love that draws us. God Himself even plans to move to this earth of ours just to be with us (Rev. 21:3). Jesus will no longer be "only a prayer away," but our constant companion, together with His sweet Spirit, who has led us all the way. Jesus' sacrifice made our acceptance in His family sure, while His Spirit guided and counseled us so that we didn't wander far from the straight and narrow path. Here, too, we will get to know our guardian angels who so often intervene to save us when we are in danger. I just can't wait for that beautiful, homecoming day! "Even so, come, Lord Jesus" (Rev. 22:20).

Revel Papaioannou

Listen to Him

Write this down for the next generation so people
not yet born will praise God. Ps. 102:18, Message.

While I was driving to an appointment in a shopping mall recently, a man in an SUV decided that it was time for him to leave his parking spot. Without looking to see if anyone was behind him, he backed straight out and right into the passenger side of my car, causing more than $5,000 damage. When we both got out of our cars, the first thing he said was "I was almost finished backing out." I was rather stunned that he would make such an obviously dishonest statement.

After we took down the necessary information, I pulled ahead into a parking spot. Immediately a woman appeared by my side. She wanted to know if I was all right and not injured. She continued to stay by me until we were inside the office where both of us were going. After making sure I had a hot drink, she gave me her name and phone number.

A few days later I felt impressed to take her some flowers to say thank you. I told my husband I thought I would take her two roses, but when I went to the florist shop I decided that *no*, the roses just would not do. I looked at some of the other fresh flowers and then decided that pink and white peonies would be just right.

The woman, whose name was Lucy, and her husband own a specialty coffee shop in a very upscale part of town. Fortunately she was at the shop that day and soon came out to greet me. After taking a minute to thank her for her kindness, I gave her the flowers. She looked at them, then looked at me rather poignantly and said, "My mother used to grow these in her garden." She then went on to say, "Today is our twenty-first wedding anniversary, and my mother is dying of brain cancer."

I knew then why I was impressed to buy peonies instead of roses. How often have you been impressed to do something, or change your mind about something you had planned to do, and wondered why, but later you found that you had been led by the Holy Spirit? Have you found that as you have listened to Him, He has surprised you with what He has planned for you to do? Let us praise Him and share what He does for us each day.

Carol Stickle

The Battle Is the Lord's

Our God, will you not judge them? For we have no power to face this vast army that is attacking us. We do not know what to do, but our eyes are on you. 2 Chron. 20:12, NIV.

I had a cat we named Radar, and he used to love to play in the tall weeds that lined the greenbelt behind our apartment building. One day as I stood at the handrail outside of our apartment watching Radar chasing butterflies in the weeds, I noticed a very large dog approaching from the west. Radar must have heard him, because he assumed his stalking position and became very still. The dog just meandered down the path, making his way through the weeds, unsuspecting of any danger; after all, he was a big dog. Who would mess with him? Radar just patiently waited as the dog got closer and closer. When the dog walked in front of Radar, he pounced out beside the dog. The dog was so startled he yelped and ran for his life. Radar strutted after him a few feet just to let him know he'd better keep running. You could just see how proud the cat was. He had conquered the larger foe.

Second Chronicles 17-20 tells the story of how King Jehoshaphat prepared for war his whole life. He fortified his cities, built up his armies, and made his country strong, but when the armies of Moab and Ammon came to attack, he called for a fast and turned to the Lord. "Our God, will you not judge them? For we have no power to face this vast army that is attacking us. We do not know what to do, but our eyes are on you." God replied back to the king and the people, "'Do not be afraid or discouraged because of this vast army. For the battle is not yours, but God's. . . . You will not have to fight this battle. Take up your positions; stand firm and see the deliverance the Lord will give you, Judah and Jerusalem. Do not be afraid; do not be discouraged. Go out to face them tomorrow, and the Lord will be with you'" (2 Chron. 20:15-17, NIV). They went into battle singing praises. The interesting thing was, when they got to the place of battle, they found only dead bodies. The Lord had already destroyed the invaders.

It can be the same for us. When we face battles in our lives, the old stories show us how to win. We must be patient, like Radar, the cat. We must fast and pray, have faith, stand firm, and go into battle singing God's praises, for He has already destroyed the invaders and won the battle for us. It doesn't matter how large or small the battle is; our God can handle it.

Mona Fellers

Can You Take Me There?

Yes, I am the gate. Those who come in through me will be saved. They will come and go freely and will find good pastures. John 10:9, NLT.

I am at the Chicago airport, still panting from running a mile to catch my flight home after spending a wonderful weekend celebrating my grandson Benjamin's first birthday.

The weather was not good, and my flight had had a lengthy delay in South Bend. Because of this, I was afraid I might not make my connection in Chicago. As soon as we landed in Chicago, I rushed off the plane and into the airport. Explaining my situation to an airline employee at the gate, I asked, "Can you take me to the gate, please? Can you take me there?"

He replied, "Sorry. The doors will be closed in five minutes. You won't make it." But I persisted, pleading, "Could you take me there? I think if you help me we have a chance." But again he responded, this time emphatically, "The doors are closed, lady! There's no way for you to reach the gate and get home on that plane!"

What frustration! My heart sank! Running to my gate I was thinking about what I had said to him: "If you only could take me there." *If he had, I would have made my flight home.*

Wherever I go, wherever I travel, I meet women in different countries and cultures. There is always a cry for help, a "Can you take me there?" cry that—if you are willing to hear and respond to—you can lead someone—home.

I remember meeting the women in Malawi. After my presentation many women came to me. They all looked at me, searching for hope. I asked them what was in their hearts and why they were singing and crying at the same time. One woman answered, "We are all HIV positive. Could you help us?" I looked in their eyes, and the only thing I could do was wrap them in my arms, singing songs of hope as they tried to tell their stories. The cry was just that: "Can you take us there? We are sick, we are discouraged, we are dying . . . but can you take us there?"

Jesus says, "I am the gate. Those who come in through me will be saved." What a heartening promise. Run. The gate is still open. But above all, do not go alone. There is still someone asking for help: "Can you take me there? Can you help me?" My prayer is that you reach the gate that day.

Raquel Queiroz da Costa Arrais

Secret of the Rock

For in the time of trouble he [God] shall hide me in his pavilion: in the secret of his tabernacle shall he hide me; he shall set me up upon a rock. Ps. 27:5.

I was an avid caver 20 years ago. I knew all the safe caving rules including this one: at all times, maintain three points of contact with the rock surface. In intervening years, however, osteoporosis has injected another somber caving caution.

So a couple years back, while serving on the staff at a camp for troubled teens and their single parents, I had a private talk with a cave guide.

"I can't risk a fall at my age," I told him, "even in a beautiful limestone cavern."

"No problem," he responded, pointing toward a muscular, coverall-clad youth. "I'll assign you to Dave, one of my assistants." The young man gave me a thumbs-up as if to say, "No problem, Granny. I've got your back!"

Inside the cave we all began slipping in clay mud. Only our weak helmet beams pierced the thick darkness. Periodically I'd hear Dave's voice: "Ma'am?" and I'd take his hand.

The slimy surfaces grew slicker, the descent steeper. In the dark, ever-changing topography, I couldn't always hold Dave's hand and still keep my three points of contact with the limestone rock. Finally I said, "Dave, thanks, but let me ask for help only when I need it."

That's when it happened. And suddenly! Dave's legs furiously began backpedaling, his arms flailing. Then his long legs shot out from under him. The back of his helmet (and rear end) smacked into inches-deep miry clay as he barreled—feet first—down a rocky slope.

From my safe, secure position—maintaining three points of contact with the rock—I watched my husky bodyguard helplessly slam into the wall at the base of the slope.

The head guide called out, "You OK? Man, what happened?"

Dave responded, "I didn't have three contact points with the rock. So, guess I lost it."

We live in dark and slippery-slope times: temptation, spiritual deception. However, we don't have to "lose it" as Dave did. The secret of our spiritual safety is keeping three points of contact with the Rock of our salvation: (1) abiding in an attitude of prayer; (2) living daily by His Word; and (3) faithfully sharing with others what He, through Jesus, has done for us.

Carolyn Sutton

My Identity Crisis

Lo, I am with you alway, even unto the end of the world. Matt. 28:20.

Losing my voice for more than a month with the fear of never getting it back terrified me. It was all I had known for as long as I can remember. My entire life and career were wrapped up in those two little muscles that controlled all sound from my larynx. And now they were injured. This was the nightmare of all singers. One that could end careers.

And here I was . . . finally doing the Lord's work when it happened. I'd be lying if I didn't think about the timing. And why it had happened now, during such a strong year of proclaiming God's love in concert to thousands of people. Why hadn't it happened during my years as a young pop music singer?

When you must be silent for weeks, you have a lot of time to think. I did. Plenty of time.

What would I do if my voice didn't come back? What if it sounded different? What skills did I have other than speaking and singing? The truth is, my identity was on the line more than my voice was. *Who* was *I without my voice?* I feared I was on the verge of being stripped of everything I knew about myself!

Then during a moment of clarity amid all my prayerful questioning, I realized I was doubting God and His ability. Why? Hadn't He told me in His Word to trust and obey, to have faith the size of a mustard seed? Hadn't He promised that "all things work together for good to them that love God"? And, yes, I *did* love God and I *did* trust Him. I had seen Him work miracles in my life time and time again.

The strength of the Holy Spirit began to grow inside me, and I realized that I didn't need to know what would happen if this or that turned out differently than I had planned. My trustworthy God held The Plan. Not I. He had led me up to this silent moment without ever failing me, and He certainly wouldn't fail me now. The truth was that if God had chosen to take my voice at that moment, I still had the assurance that He would use me in a way I'd never imagined.

Oftentimes we make plans and build lives for ourselves and begin to think that is who we are. But it's not! Our identity is in Jesus, and our abilities are in Him too. All we need is His love. That's it—and the rest will fall into place. It always does.

Naomi Striemer

When "We" Becomes "I"

She who is truly a widow, left all alone, has set her hope on God and continues in supplications and prayers night and day. 1 Tim. 5:5, ESV.

One cannot realize the heartache it is for a widow or widower when death occurs. Some widows begin looking for new mates after the grieving period. Others grieve but never remarry. Research shows that becoming a widow is the top stressor in one's life, even beyond losing a child. I find little in the Bible regarding widowers. I suspect most just remarried.

We get used to saying "we" for years; we catch ourselves saying it long after the spouse is gone. We finally start to say "I" instead. I found myself saving a seat in church for my deceased husband for six months, not even realizing it.

Some widows are not prepared for financial decisions; sometimes the woman manages the finances, and the widower is not prepared. Widows may not be prepared to cope with house maintenance. Since some elderly women are more fragile; many must find inexpensive, trustworthy handymen who can do simple jobs. Widowers may not know how to cook. Widows may be more susceptible to telephone or Internet scams.

A young widow with low funds may have children to nurture. She may need to work; if she has been a stay-at-home mom, she may lack the education or training for good jobs. These factors affect the quality of family living. Or, what does a widower do with young children? He has to work and find care for them when he cannot be with them.

In 1938, when I was nearly 5 years old, with older brothers, 7 and 12, my mother passed away suddenly. At that age I never realized how difficult it must have been for my father. He was a garage mechanic who made little money. He found a 16-year-old girl to care for us. I now reflect on and admire the things he did to keep the family together.

I know the Lord is the best solution to many of the problems noted; He can guide each person. Your church family can be a source of help. There are funds such as Social Security for help with children; these funds were not available in 1938 when my mother passed away.

I also believe that our churches need to have a ministry for the elderly, whether widows or widowers, and often there is no such ministry in the church or in the community. I find that true where I live. I pray for all widows, for a change in the future.

Loraine F. Sweetland

The Presumptuous Bear

Yea, though I walk through the valley of the shadow of death, I will fear no evil: for thou art with me; thy rod and thy staff they comfort me. Ps. 23:4.

Camping gives me my sanity when work seems endless, with no relief in sight. What is it about nature that gives us such a relief from concrete?

The five of us set up our tents in a perfect arrangement to ensure that we would not see each other's "morning face" when opening our tents. We sat around warming ourselves by the open fire underneath God's canopy of stars. It was such a peaceful time.

Suddenly our tranquillity was disturbed by the neighbors on the hill directly above us. There were barking dogs, and lots of yelling and banging on pots. We brushed it off, thinking it was probably a party of drinkers who had a bit too much. However, I had the sinking feeling it was something more serious. I prayed for protection from my nameless fears, and tried really, really hard to forget it and trust everything with God. Just moments after the noise died down above, another camping neighbor directly across the street from our campsite came running to warn us about a bear. He described how his dog had protected him from the furry beast.

The next morning, in the campsite's community restroom, we met the neighbors who had been banging the pots. They explained to us that the bear had no fear of them. He had been leaning on the park bench taking a sip of water while watching these noisy humans try to shoo him away. When he finally tired of the song and dance show, he made his way down the hill toward our campsite. I was reminded of the story told in 2 Kings 6:8-23 of how Elisha was protected from the Syrian army by God's horses and chariots of fire that were sent to surround his home. Just as Elisha was guarded, we were protected by angels from this presumptuous bear seeking to do us harm.

It is times like this when I also remember some events David shared with us in 1 Samuel 17:34-50, when God gave him the power to overcome a lion, a bear, and the giant Goliath because of his faith in the God of Israel. Thank God for protection from seen and unseen dangers that surround us. The lions, bears, and giants in our lives have no chance against our living, loving God.

Gale Frampton

Ready to Ask Again?

Giving thanks always for all things to God the Father
in the name of our Lord Jesus Christ. Eph. 5:20, NKJV.

What good mother in any culture would not teach her child to say thank you when given something? The Shona mothers of Zimbabwe teach their toddlers to clap twice before receiving something, an action symbolizing thankfulness. Many parents may teach their children to say thank you; Christian adults, however, do not always practice the same habit when it comes to answered prayers. I was always eager to continue asking for things without expressing thankfulness and appreciation for what He had already given me or done for me. One morning at work one of my patients shared her extraordinary spiritual habit and changed my thankfulness perspective!

I thought it was a normal workday as I entered my workplace. I was not receiving tuition benefits for working part-time, but the joy of bedside caring for patients was priceless. Readers who are nurses will agree that working with ill individuals can be depressing and overwhelming. However, the fulfillment that comes with seeing them respond to your caring touch and comforting words as you treat them makes a huge difference! Seeing them go home healed makes your day! I try to imagine how many of those who came to Jesus and the disciples for healing were thankful as their lives changed. Not everyone is thankful. Consider the 10 lepers who were all healed after shouting "Jesus, Master, have pity on us!" (Luke 17:13, NIV). Only one gave praises and thanked Him. Happy in their success, the rest went on with their lives (Luke 17:15-19, NIV).

One day at work I was to discharge a woman whom I had cared for a few days before. In the process I asked Mary what could be attributed to her sudden recovery in the three weeks of several negative diagnostic procedures. She credited her recovery to her 3-year-old grandson's prayer for Nana: "Jesus, please make Nana feel better and come home." Mary obviously believed that God answered that prayer. Asking what she planned to do on getting home, she said her priority was to fast and pray for the answered prayer.

Ready to make another prayer request? First, thank Him for all that He has done for you.

Ruth Nyachuru-Muze

Forgiveness and Restoration

I will praise you, Lord, with all my heart; I will tell of all
the marvelous things you have done. I will be filled with joy because
of you. I will sing praises to your name, O Most High. Ps. 9:1, 2, NLT.

A while back I spent a getaway weekend visiting with a friend and her husband. During my visit I deeply offended them, but I didn't realize it until after I had returned home. They no longer stayed in touch with me. I knew this break in relationship was my fault. Sorry beyond words, I also knew there was nothing I could do to fix it. I even felt that forgiveness would be impossible. In these dark, dark moments I felt so totally alone, completely broken—like the proverbial Humpty-Dumpty. Nothing could fix me or the situation.

More than once I wrote my friend, expressing my sorrow for the pain I had caused. I begged for forgiveness. Finally, I got a response. But my own shame and guilt kept me from deciphering the heart behind her words.

In desperation I picked up my Bible. Then, probably for the first time in my life, I started reading God's Word for my own needs. The book of Psalms drew me. It is there David speaks so eloquently of his struggles, pain, and praise. No Bible writer lays out his emotions as does David. His words spoke for my heart: "Have compassion on me, Lord, for I am weak. Heal me, Lord, for my bones are in agony. I am sick at heart. How long, O Lord, until you restore me? Return, O Lord, and rescue me, save me because of your unfailing love. . . . I am worn out from sobbing. All night I flood my bed with weeping, drenching it with my tears. My vision is blurred by grief" (Ps. 6:2-7, NLT).

For several weeks I couldn't get beyond these verses. Eventually I shared them with my offended friend. She restated her earlier response to my pleas for forgiveness. This time I "got it." She *had* forgiven me, after all! Completely. Without reservation.

The harder part was forgiving myself. Yet God gently led me to the place of healing and restoration, filling me with joy. Where before there had been only intense grief, God filled my heart with songs of praise to Him. His love has restored the friendship I thought I had lost. It is better, stronger, deeper, and healthier than before. What an amazing journey forgiveness has been!

Sonia Brock

Be Wary for Nothing!

But godliness with contentment is great gain. 1 Tim. 6:6.

There was a construction worker, I will call Bill, who always had a positive attitude in life; and he was in the habit of praising God for everything he had and whatever happened in his life. In fact, his friends and coworkers would tease him about his constant optimism and gratefulness to God.

One day while the construction workers were taking their lunch break at the construction site, Bill sat down on a wooden plank with his coworkers, took out his lunch bag, and closed his eyes to say a blessing for his food. Before he could finish his prayer, a stray dog snatched his lunch bag and ran off with it. Bill chased the dog to get his lunch bag back, and had to run quite a distance. Just then he heard a loud noise behind him. When he looked back, he saw a huge cloud of smoke and debris flying all over at the construction site. Apparently there was a big explosion, and most of the workers nearby were badly injured.

Bill was very sorry to see his buddies badly hurt. He immediately thanked God for protecting him from getting hurt in that explosion. If the dog had not taken away his lunch bag, and if he had not had to chase after it, he too would have gotten hurt and suffered much pain.

Friends, please remember that when we put our faith and trust in the Lord, no matter what happens in our lives, there is always a reason God allowed it to happen. And you can be assured that at the end it was for our good. In life we may never know or understand why we had to go through certain trials and face tragedies, but in heaven we will understand and praise God for causing us to go through those trials and tragedies. We will then know they were ultimately a great blessing in our and our loved ones' lives.

Paul, who had suffered ups and downs in his ministry life, has some good advice for us in Philippians 4:4-7 where it reads: "Rejoice in the Lord alway: and again I say, Rejoice. . . . Be careful for nothing; but in every thing by prayer and supplication with thanksgiving let your requests be made known unto God. And the peace of God, which passeth all understanding, shall keep your hearts and minds through Christ Jesus."

What a beautiful promise we can cherish through tough times!

Stella Thomas

Left Behind

Train up a child in the way he should go:
and when he is old, he will not depart from it. Prov. 22:6.

We were seven carefree people, taking our annual road trip with camper in tow, this time from small-town North Carolina to Baxter Park in Maine. Our five children ranged in age from 3 to 13. A brief stop had been made at a country store, and the trip resumed, when, a few miles farther on, one of the children cried, "Where's Marie?" She had been left behind! Panic and prayers ensued, along with a frantic trip back to the last stop.

Six solemn people spilled out of the car and into the store. Relief flooded over everyone when our precious 3-year-old daughter was found, her little face starting to crumple, having just realized there were no familiar faces around. We resumed the trip, a little more subdued, but with prayers of thankfulness on our lips and in our hearts.

Just this morning I read on the Internet more than one horrifying instance of fathers rescuing their young daughters from would-be molesters. The youngest was a blond, curly-haired 2-year-old who was at a playground, and the would-be abductor had the nerve to argue with the father, claiming the child was his. In another instance, if the toddler had not dropped her sippy cup on the porch of the molester, where her father spotted it, her life would have ended tragically, as have countless others. Had our carelessness happened in a more dangerous setting, and the worst happened, our lives would have been forever haunted by guilt and remorse.

All this points to the fact that vigilance is vital in guarding our young ones in this world that has become alarmingly dangerous for children. Above and beyond this, how earnestly and perseveringly we should teach them of Jesus' love and care, and the danger and resulting tragedy of falling into Satan's snares. I urge you, mothers, grandmothers, family, and friends, to point these young ones in the right direction. The early years are the formative, impressionable years; the passing of the days and years is unrelenting, and all too soon characters are formed. What could be more urgent than having them so grounded in the love of Jesus that nothing could turn them aside? We have the assurance that He is coming to take His own out of this world of sin to everlasting joy. It is my prayer that we might all be there as families, together with Him.

Lila Farrell Morgan

Submission

Say to God, "How awesome are Your works!
Through the greatness of Your power Your enemies
shall submit themselves to You." Ps. 66:3, NKJV.

The puppy grew up, the gentle, big-chested boxer named Maverick. He protected the family and cleaned up the crumbs after the children ate, and on occasion even cleaned the baby's face. Mav was a fawn-colored beauty and adored by all the family. But the years passed and Maverick showed signs of aging.

The family decided to get a puppy in hopes that Maverick's good behavior would influence a new generation. The children searched the Internet and found a brindle boxer puppy with a good bloodline. All the family made the trip to Chicago to pick up Gunnar. Puppies are cute, but they're a lot of work, and Gunnar was no exception. The big sister took him to obedience school, and Gunnar learned gradually to sit on command, but there seemed to be other flaws in his learning curve.

As he grew bigger, mother Marla decided she would need to be the one to train Gunnar to behave on a leash. I went walking one day with Marla and Gunnar. As he kept jerking on the choke chain Marla sternly said, "Gunnar, if you'd only submit it wouldn't hurt!"

My quick comment was "I'll bet God would like to say that to us!"

The tendency for humans to pull against God didn't start this year. When the Israelites returned from the Babylonian captivity and rebuilt Jerusalem, Nehemiah got the Israelites together and rehearsed with them how God had led their ancestors—even bringing them out of slavery and giving them the land of Canaan. He recounted their rebellion, their disobedience, and not being mindful of God's wonders; you know—how they jerked against the choke chain.

Sadly, that behavior didn't end with the Israelites. We're still guilty today, I'm afraid. But then Nehemiah pointed out to the Israelites—and us—that God is ready to pardon, gracious and merciful, slow to anger, abundant in kindness and does not forsake us (Neh. 9:17). Now, that's the kind of God that's easy to submit to!

You know, there's a real peace in allowing God to be in charge. Fortunately for Gunnar his human family is gracious and merciful, and he still has a home!

Roxy Hoehn

Finding Fitness

I can do all things through Christ who strengthens me. Phil. 4:13, NKJV.

I stood in the bathroom looking at the reflection in the mirror, wanting to cry. I was turning 30, had just had my second baby, and was deeply discouraged with myself. My clothes didn't fit right, I felt self-conscious about the extra weight, and was noticing more fine lines than ever before. *It's all downhill from here,* I thought darkly. *Looking good is never going to be easy again.*

I had fantasies of someday getting into a regular, hard, workout routine and getting all tough and slim. But people don't change very often, and I knew it. I looked in the mirror that day and thought, *If ever I can believe in the power to change, it must start with me.*

First, I started praying seriously for discipline in my life, and God answered. Second, I joined a gym with a friend. I discovered the warm, satisfying rush of a good workout. I was inspired by women friends who were losing weight, and others who were very athletic.

One day a friend showed me a few simple pointers for running, and to my utter astonishment, I ran a mile without difficulty! That mile changed my life. I'm not saying running was always fun—it was uncomfortable and required me to push myself. But when I came home from a run, I was on a high. I never wanted to be without it again. Along with prayers for discipline, I started challenging myself to give up sweets and simple carbohydrate foods that I already knew were affecting my blood sugar. I found it easier and easier to deny myself things that weren't good for me and challenge myself to things that were.

By my thirty-first birthday I had discovered what it was like to push hard and sweat and want to do it again the next day and the next. I had found a strength I'd only dreamed of. In less than a year I not only lost a significant amount of weight, but I was running 7.5 miles at a time and feeling capable of things I'd never dreamed of. Even my marriage was improving.

Still, I kept thinking of the words to a hymn, "All the fitness He requireth / Is to feel your need of Him," and I knew I needed to prioritize spiritual fitness. This year God is helping me to do that. He has given me wings, and I only wish I could convince every other woman that the fitness she dreams of is definitely possible!

Adel Arrabito Torres

Luggage Lost . . . Yes

And he shall be like a tree planted by the rivers of water,
that bringeth forth his fruit in his season; his leaf also
shall not wither; and whatsoever he doeth shall prosper. Ps. 1:3.

While at a marriage retreat we were encouraged to look for a marital lesson from nature. In my search I came across a plant that was struggling to survive. It was covered with its own dead leaves, and other vines had taken it over; some were dead, others were still alive, but the plant was a great big tangled mess. It was then that the Holy Spirit brought the message to me: Sometimes in marriage we can become just like this poor entangled plant. We keep a lot of our old luggage hanging around us, and they become a means through which our marriages are stifled. Luggage of distrust, disloyalty, past experience, attitudes and behaviors—that we feel we should be entitled to keep—and a host of other unpleasantries. The marriage then struggles to survive. And just like the plant, we think that because we have leaves we are healthy, when the truth is that we are dying. In addition when we allow our own issues to build up, it makes room for other things to grow and fester. The old leaves around the plant made room for vines to grow, and vines made room for the harboring of insects and other things to live. Imagine how a marriage already tied down by its own luggage now endures the weight of other issues. Using another metaphor, that marriage would be a war zone, a constant bombardment of bombs and missiles, grenades, and other similar ammunition capable of causing serious harm, even death.

The remedy is so simple: lose the luggage. It may take some time, some counseling, some hard introspection, some putting of heads together, some working it out, but the result is a marriage that is actually healthy and growing. A plant that is unencumbered makes room for bigger leaves, fruit bearing, bigger fruit, and longevity of life. If we remain unencumbered, we too will have good growth, a well-working relationship, proper fruit bearing, success in family projects, longevity, and a long and happy marriage.

This lesson can be applied even if one is not married. In order to have a healthy, prosperous life, one needs to do a bit of cleaning in one's own life first; then cleaning up of relationships. It may take time and effort, but the end result is worth it. Are you ready to lose the harmful luggage in the relationships of your life?

Kezlynn Daisley-Harrow

Angels Living in My Home

*For he will command his angels concerning
you to guard you in all your ways. Ps. 91:11, NIV.*

When I became a mother, my heart was filled with joy, but at the same time filled with fear! Bad thoughts came to my mind: *How are you going to protect this child? You are not good enough! What if something bad happens to him? You can't watch him 24/7. What are you going to do?*

I started to pray, asking God to take those awful thoughts away from me and at the same time give me peace. I knew I couldn't protect my child, so I asked God to take that little baby in His hands and send angels to guard and protect him. It was when my son Joseph was 2 years old, and for the first time, I actually felt the presence of an angel in my home

It was a hot summer day in New York City. I left to go to the supermarket, but before I left I told my husband that the fire-escape window was open and to watch our 2-year-old son so he wouldn't go near the open window. We live on the fifth floor of a brownstone building, and when it got hot, I would open that window, but I always watched my little one so he wouldn't go near. As I walked to the supermarket a voice in the back of my head kept telling me, *Go back home!* I thought to myself, *Why go back home? I didn't forget anything. I have a credit card with me, and that's all I need.* However, that voice didn't leave me alone! *Go back home!* It kept bothering me all the way to the supermarket. The voice became so real that I decided to go back even though I didn't know the reason.

As soon I walked into the apartment I couldn't see Joseph. My heart almost stopped. I just knew he was at the open window! I ran into my bedroom, and sure enough, there he was hanging out over the fire escape! He was about to fall. I knew that if I said a word he would get scared and certainly fall. Slowly I approached him and grabbed his little feet that were already up in the air! I held him and cried!

I thank God for sending His angels to protect Joseph. I have no doubt that His angels were holding him until I got home! I praise God for giving us angels to protect our children! As a mother I can't be with my child all the time or protect him from all harm! However, I know he has angels guarding him, and I can have peace. There are angels living in my home right now!

Andrea Rocha

Hit the Road!

All things work together for good for those who love God,
who are called according to his purpose. Rom. 8:28, NRSV.

In August of 2011 I was preparing to go back to work at a local university for the fall semester. Then I received a phone call from the department chair. She asked me to come see her. When I went to see the chair on Friday morning, it was as if a bomb exploded in my mind. The chair told me they had decided to hire someone else to take my teaching position in the department for the coming school year. This was the beginning of August, and school began mid-August. I was living in Maryland with no family or close friends near. I didn't know what to do. I felt abandoned and rejected.

About this time my daughter, who lives in Alabama, told me that her husband was going to Afghanistan for a year, and he should make enough money so they could buy a house. I said that was great for her and her family. The thought never occurred to me that I should go to Huntsville and help. As the days turned into weeks and weeks turned into months and still no work, the Holy Spirit began to impress me that I should go to Alabama. I told the Lord that I liked my single, unattached life and I really didn't want to move to Alabama. As the days continued with no work, I began to succumb to the Holy Spirit's promptings. I put notice in at my apartment, rented a truck, and drove to Alabama.

I have learned over the years that it is best to go with God's plans. I know now that being let go from my job in Maryland was God's will because I wouldn't have made the move otherwise. God wanted me in Alabama. He has used me here. My oldest grandchild has accepted the Lord Jesus Christ as her personal Savior and been baptized. This past year I was able to pay for her to go to Oakwood Academy, a Christian high school. She is active in children's activities at church; she loves going to church on Sabbath; and she is a witness to her family and friends. I know God sent me to Alabama, and now I would have it no other way!

Although I felt rejected and abandoned when I was let go from my teaching position, I know it was God's plan. He promises in today's text that all things work together for good for those who love the Lord, and I found that He keeps His promises. Have you discovered that?

Eva M. Starner

Prearrangements

The devil said to him, "If you are the Son of God,
tell this stone to become bread." Luke 4:3, NIV.

On a recent Thursday evening after working in the garden all day, my husband and I were tired and wanted to take a shower, eat, and rest. Brother E., a church member, called to inform us of a member who was gravely ill and in need of a pastoral visit. Brother E. stated, "I will come now for you, Pastor." My husband told the member we had just come in from the garden and were dirty and sweaty; we would go in an hour after the much-needed shower.

My husband got ready and headed for the health-care facility, which was only about a 15-minute drive away. I received a call about 10 minutes later and knew he could not be there yet and that something was amiss. There had been a collision with a van; it tore up the front end of our car, but there was no damage to the van. I whispered a prayer and immediately drove to the scene. Upon arrival, I did not see my husband, but saw a fire truck, tow truck, two police cars, and the EMT van. After I parked safely and ran over to see my husband on a stretcher, my heart began sinking with fear. I managed to get to see him; hearing him respond to me was beautiful. They rushed him to the emergency room, and he was released eight hours later, walking.

Our insurance agent was notified, and prearranged the rental car, estimates, and towing.

Friday evening we got dressed again and went over to the health-care facility to see our dear member, and he was most delighted to see us. After prayer and conversation, we went home, happy that we had finally completed what we had set out to do the day before.

Our church members were sad that the accident happened, but happy we were fine. The devil's plan is to stop our progress all of the time. The devil tried to have Jesus killed as a baby. The devil knows he has only a short time, and he knows about the prearrangements for him in a lake of fire. Trust in the Lord at all times, as the devil will throw all kinds of curves to try to stop you from doing the Lord's work. But if you are strong, it will slow you down for only a time.

Jesus said, "I go to prepare a place for you" (John 14:2). We cannot allow the devil to stop us from our journey to heaven. He may try to slow us daily; keep your eyes on the prize, and by God's grace we shall claim heaven as our future home. John 14:1-4 is a promise for each of us.

Betty Glover Perry

Trapped

Stand fast therefore in the liberty wherewith Christ hath made us free,
and be not entangled again with the yoke of bondage. Gal. 5:1.

As caregiver of my husband, who sustained a traumatic brain injury when he was in his 50s, I was somewhat prepared for his recent senile dementia that has been manifesting itself in his 60s. However, I now call it "dementia on steroids."

Short-term memory loss has been a way of life for him, but I am also reminded of other skills that people with dementia can lose. For instance, one day Dean was unable to open a loaf of bread. He couldn't seem to twist that little bread tie just right to open the wrapper. He had to ask me to do it. And he's the man who used to fix anything that broke. No problem was without a fix when my handyman husband was around.

I recently had a little taste of what his ineptness feels like, though, when we both got in the car one day after grocery shopping. I had lowered my window visor earlier, but as I rushed to get in the car from the frigid cold outside, the hair on the top of my head got caught in a zipper on the visor.

I was totally trapped in my vehicle in an awkward position and unable to free my head from that visor without pulling my hair out. Dean, trying to be helpful, mentioned scissors, but of course I wasn't about to consider chopping off what little granny hair I have left, especially since that would mean losing hair down to an inch on the top of my head.

Fortunately, I had the wherewithal to think of taking the bun out from the back of my head. Sure enough, when I loosened my locks, I could slide the hair right out of the zipper.

My next thought, though, was of the parking lot video camera, plus any curious passersby who may have been watching this comical scene. Thoroughly humbled and embarrassed, I was so glad that home was our next destination. I had had enough public notoriety for one day.

There are so many things in life on which we can get snagged. Sometimes caregiving feels like entrapment. And there's only one way to free ourselves. Ask God for liberty, and when He guides us with the proper moves, He'll allow us to slide right on through our difficulties, and we'll be totally free.

Teresa Thompson

Transition Point

*The thief comes only to steal and kill and destroy; I have
come that they may have life, and have it to the full. John 10:10, NIV.*

I was born in Holland, so when I came to Australia with my family at the age of 14, I could not speak a word of English. Some local young people indicated they wanted to help me learn the English language. As I spent time each week with them, they taught me many words.

I faithfully practiced the words, but one day as I practiced my English I was in the garden, and the next-door neighbor heard and understood some of the words I was saying. She soon knocked on our door to speak to my mother. My dear mother was less able to speak English than I was. However, Mom very quickly picked up my name and that the woman was very disturbed, concluding I had done something very wrong!

I had no idea what I had done wrong, so together my mother and the woman next door went to another Dutch woman who lived around the corner. They learned that these "friends" had taught me every bad and dirty word they could think of. I became very discouraged.

I then met another young woman about my age who also wanted to help me and indicated she wanted to be my friend. I naturally was a little wary after the last experience. This girl took me to her home, which was only around the corner from mine. I met her very nice mother and father, who invited me for meals, gave me clothes, and took me on my first holiday. Then one day, after a few months, they asked if I would like to go to church with them. I said yes.

They made arrangements to pick me up, but when the mother said Saturday, I said, "Sunday?" She said, "No, Saturday." This didn't worry me, because this family had almost adopted me, and I was happy to go to any church to which they belonged. The young people there were quite different from the ones I had met the year before. From the very first visit I felt accepted and happy. I asked if I could go with them each week; I was loved into the church. I have never forgotten that.

When Jesus chose His followers, He was looking for real people who could be changed by His love. Caring, showing genuine love and friendship, are powerful ways to touch other people's lives; it certainly was a transition point in my life as a teenager, and from then on.

I want to keep following Jesus on a daily basis, and serve Him faithfully.

Sibilla Johnson

The Apple of His Eye

Keep me as the apple of Your eye; hide me under
the shadow of Your wings. Ps. 17:8, NKJV.

One Wednesday of each month I travel to a nearby town to meet with my ophthalmologist for an injection. That should be a relatively simple task except for the fact that I have to get the injection directly into my right eye. Naturally those particular Wednesdays are not welcome. I usually spend some time in prayer the night before, asking God to help me to be brave.

Although the procedure takes only three seconds and the technologist has already desensitized the area, when the ophthalmologist comes into the room where I'm lying on the table, I tense up. When I see the needle, no matter how soothing her voice, no matter how calm I try to be, I flinch, and my eyelids clamp shut. "Breathe deeply," the doctor reminds me. I breathe, and in a flash the much-feared situation is over.

When I described my trauma to my daughter one day, she suggested jokingly that I have the medical team put me in restraints. That idea definitely did not appeal to me, so she advised instead that I repeat Bible texts that include the word "eye."

After some research, I found out that there were more than 550 such verses, including those with such words as "eyelids" and "eyebrows." Sometimes the word has a literal meaning. At other times, however, the meaning is symbolic, referring to such ideas as intelligence, focus, understanding, or presence.

Today's text is my personal favorite. Somehow that word picture—a tasty red apple—speaks to my individual situation. In it I hear my God saying that with His attention focused on me, I need not fear a single thing.

We must wait patiently for His return when all will be joy and peace. Jesus left us with a promise. "And God will wipe away every tear from their eyes; there shall be no more death, nor sorrow, nor crying; and there shall be no more pain, for the former things have passed away" (Rev. 21:4, NKJV). I long for that day. Don't you?

It would be a good idea for us to spend more prayerful, soul-searching time preparing for the Great Physician to cleanse us from all sins. Let us search the Scriptures for the blessed hope and wait patiently for His return. I hope to meet you on that special day.

Carol J. Greene

I Was Thirsty

Come, you blessed of My Father, inherit the kingdom
prepared for you from the foundation of the world: for I was hungry
and you gave Me food; I was thirsty and you gave Me drink;
I was a stranger and you took Me in. Matt. 25:34, 35, NKJV.

After being single for eight years, and my children grown, I began finding that life didn't seem to have the same fulfillment it once did. I was preaching most weekends in different churches, running women's ministries programs and retreats, and speaking in the remote areas of Papua New Guinea. Yet my heart wasn't at rest.

To turn your life upside down, resign from your job, and leave all that is safe and comfortable and fly 24 hours to a life that is very much unknown takes either courage and dedication, or insanity. I am still unsure which is the better description. Living in a country and with a people whose culture and lives are so very different from everything you have ever known and believed in has its many challenges, both emotional and physical.

Yet when I flew over Kenya and looked down at the land below, I knew in my heart that God was bringing me home as He had promised. This was where He had a work for me that would give me "the desires of my heart."

Little did I realize before this that my whole life, with its many challenges, dark days, and heartbreaks, as well as amazing opportunities of growth, was God preparing me for the task He now had for me to do. He had been preparing me to be able to help the Masai people, especially the women and girls, to a better and more healthful way of life. My new life began by living very poorly and simply on a small farm with very few modern conveniences, looking after animals. To cook a simple meal or heat water for my "dish bath," I must first light the fire in a small "eco stove." I carry my clothes to the river to wash them. Now as I sit in my mud-walled, dirt-floor home in the middle of the forest in Kenya, I marvel at my ability to be comfortable, and that I have grown to love this simple life.

Even though some days are fraught with depression, frustration, and loneliness, yet they are the most fulfilling of my life. As I took hold of God's promises, stepped out in faith, I knew I serve an amazing God who sees us and knows the true desires of our heart.

Barbara Parkins

I'm Living a Dream

Do not judge, or you too will be judged.
For in the same way you judge others, you will be judged,
and with the measure you use, it will be measured to you. Matt. 7:1, 2, NIV.

As I drove from our home to the doctor's office, my mind was filled with questions. Lab work had been drawn earlier that week, and I was anxious to hear the results. I hoped that my triglycerides and cholesterol had improved with the help of the new medication the doctor had advised me to try.

I pulled into a parking space and noticed a red pickup backing slowly into the handicapped parking place in front of me. A man in his mid-30s carefully stepped out with the help of a cane. He was dressed in a tank top and khaki shorts; the sun reflected on his shaved head and I noticed the numerous tattoos on both arms and legs. I felt unsure if I should speak to him, but felt impressed to ask a polite "How are you today?"

He smiled sweetly and replied, "I'm living a dream." I was puzzled by this response and told him that I was living a dream also. I explained that I had worked as a nurse for 45 years and now was retired and able to help my aged mother. I said, "The Lord is good," and he responded by saying, "All the time." I then opened the office door, checked in at the desk, and found a seat. He did the same, and we were the only two in the waiting room. I felt the Holy Spirit impress me to talk to him, but questioned what we could have in common to talk about. Before I knew it, I blurted out, "How many tattoos do you actually have?" He laughed and said, "Oh, I think about 25." He paused and said, "I got those when I was young and stupid; I was thinking only about myself and what I wanted. But I found Jesus and now I have a wife and precious family, and there is no money for such foolishness." I was touched by his honest reply and told him I was happy for him and wished him well. The nurse then called my name, and I smiled and turned to follow her.

He called out, "Thank you, lady, for talking to me."

As I followed the nurse down the hall, I felt ashamed that I had ever hesitated to speak to him. I said to myself, *He may be a little different from me, but he is still one of God's precious children.* Today's Bible text also came to mind: "Do not judge, or you too will be judged."

Rose Neff Sikora

God Never Forgets

As an eagle stirs up its nest, hovers over its young,
spreading out its wings, taking them up, carrying them on its wings,
so the Lord alone led him. Deut. 32:11, 12, NKJV.

I have had a very challenging life; you see, I was born an albino on the island of Jamaica. This might not sound like the biggest problem in life, but in my country of birth, society was not very kind to anyone who was different. I watched as many other boys and girls were admired for their beauty, but I always felt like the ugly duckling. And that's the way I was treated.

Oh, yes! I had a loving, caring family; my parents taught us to love the Lord, and we had devotions each morning and evening. We were also taught to love and respect others regardless of their circumstances. Home was a place of joy and love, but I was terrified when I had to leave that boundary. The taunts and jeers were difficult for me; I had constant emotional pain.

I cried silently to God, especially at night, when no one could see me. As I grew older I became angry with God because I believed He could have prevented this tragedy: no color, reduced vision. I wanted to drive a car, to be free as a bird; I wanted to be admired by all, not with that look of rejection. Psalm 139:16 was a challenge for me. Paraphrased, it states that all my members were written in God's book and were fashioned when as yet there was none of me. I cried out, *God! If You knew me before You formed me, why did You not change the defect before I was born?*

After many years of struggle God pointed me once again to Psalm 139, especially verses 14 and 17. "I will praise thee; for I am fearfully and wonderfully made: marvellous are thy works; and that my soul knoweth right well." "How precious also are thy thoughts unto me, O God! how great is the sum of them."

God opened my spiritual eyes to see beyond the color of my skin, beyond the desire for social acceptance. I cannot physically drive a car, but God has given me the ability to steer others to His wonderful promises in the Bible. With great happiness I have watched many enter the watery grave of baptism. This is my joy. I have counseled many who have been abused.

Reader, whatever your challenges in life might be, remember that God has not forgotten you; you are precious to Him.

Sonia Kennedy-Brown

Protection of Angels

For he shall give his angels charge over thee,
to keep thee in all thy ways. Ps. 91:11.

One summer evening my husband and I were driving on the Capital Beltway, I-495. We had picked up a car in Virginia for his friend, and we were headed home in two separate vehicles. We had just come over a hill, and I started to change lanes. The man to my left had the same thing in mind. I panicked and hit the brakes, and the brakes locked. I could not turn the wheels, and all I could imagine were piles of cars surrounding me and my car being hit on every side.

I was able to slowly turn the wheel toward the Jersey wall and managed not to hit anything in my path. I came to a full stop facing the northbound traffic. My husband had gone on ahead of me, not knowing what kind of dilemma I was in.

In a short while a state trooper came to my side of the car and asked me what had happened. I explained that my brakes locked, and I ended up facing the traffic coming over the hill. Thankfully he did not give me a ticket, but told me to turn off my lights and wait while he stopped traffic so that I could turn my car around and face traffic in the right direction.

In the meantime, my husband called. I started to cry, thinking of the mess I could have been involved in, with all those cars piled up beside me. It was such a relief to know that my heavenly angels had protected me from any damage to my car—or to anyone else's.

My husband returned to the area where I was parked. He saw all the police cars flashing their red lights, and he was relieved that I was all right.

I still had to drive the car home, but now I was shaking and crying at the same time. I thanked my heavenly Father over and over for sparing my life and the lives of others. Surely His angels had been with me through the whole ordeal.

When I arrived home, I was so thankful and overwhelmed at God's goodness to me. The situation could have turned out to be a disaster with lawsuits, injuries, and other unforeseen complications. But Psalm 4:8 promises, "In peace I will lie down and sleep, for you alone, Lord, make me dwell in safety" (NIV). How good our God is to each one of us, and I praise Him for His wonderful care.

Nancy Heller

The Unequal Ways of God

*For my thoughts are not your thoughts,
neither are your ways my ways, saith the Lord.*

*For as the heavens are higher than the earth, so are my ways higher than
your ways, and my thoughts than your thoughts. Isa. 55:8, 9.*

I can prove to you that God's ways are "unequal"! Yes! Throughout my life I have been amazed at how He does it—and consistently, too. When I was about 6 years old, my uncle would take me to church. Oh, how I was enamored with everything that I heard and saw.

As I grew older the thing that impressed me most was the fact that the people were allowed to be so involved in the service of the Lord. I began to ponder: *Could God use me like that? Maybe I could just lead song service; that would be so exciting!* I was shy, nervous in front of people, and very self-conscious, but I had a heart's desire to serve the Lord.

One day Sister Roole came and invited me to be in the choir. Eventually they called upon me to lead song service (I had not told anybody about my desire). That beginning led to me serving in several capacities, and eventually spending a year in Thailand as a volunteer youth missionary. As I read today's text, I was living its truth. I began by simply desiring to do something small, yet God multiplied and expanded His assignments for me beyond what I could have imagined. Many times I told the Lord, *I'm overwhelmed. I asked for something small, and You gave me something excessively large.*

That's what I mean by the "unequal" ways of God. When we have our heart's desire to make ourselves available to Him, He reveals plans that are limitless. He makes what seems impossible to us possible and real. After all, He turned a fisherman into an apostle; He turned a shepherd boy into a king; He turned an orphan into a queen. That's unequal. God acts way out of proportion to what we deserve.

Perhaps you have a dream or thought about what you want to do for God, what you want to do with your life. It might seem small, but give it to God. You have no idea what He plans to do with your life if you are willing to surrender everything to Him.

Oh, and by the way, just to emphasize my point, I recently graduated with a degree in theology and am now serving in Barbados as a ministerial intern. How is that for unequal?

Deborah P. Spooner

He Knows Best

*Ask me and I will tell you remarkable secrets you
do not know about things to come. Jer. 33:3, NLT.*

Did you always know what you wanted to become when you grew up? Somewhere at the beginning of high school I made up my mind to study psychology. And I decided to work hard and get excellent marks so I could study what I desired after finishing high school.

I started preparing for my exam for entrance into the psychology program. I expected the best results because my studies were going very well. Of course, I asked God what I should pick for my studies after high school, but I had already decided what it would be.

The test results shocked me! I didn't pass! Until that moment I hadn't had any failures in school, so this was amazing and totally unexpected. I was even a bit angry with God. With September and time to enroll in some college coming closer, my panic grew. I didn't know what to do. I didn't have a plan B. Despite my desperate prayer, it seemed that God was silent.

And then one day in late August I begged God to show me what to do that very day. In less than a half hour the phone rang. It was my grandmother with a proposal: I could spend one year studying theology in Belgrade. I realized this was God's answer to my prayers, but it wasn't an expected one. I wasn't excited about it, but in the end I agreed to do it for one year.

I kept asking God why I was where I was. I even asked Him to tell me what I should study through people I didn't know so that I would know that it was objective. He did it twice. But I was stubborn, and I decided to try once again to enroll in psychology. I said to God, *If I don't pass, I will come back to theology.* I failed again! I was persistent, but God was more persistent.

Finally, I accepted the fact that He has something better for me. I don't know in which direction I will go, but I can see clearly that God has a plan for me. I can see it even through the way He takes care of my scholarship. Meanwhile, I spoke to some psychology professors and they advised that it would be best to combine theology and psychology in order to help people. So I am trying to follow His plan—He knows best.

Almost every day I can see why God brought me here. It's amazing how He works. He can fulfill dreams for each one of us and do great things through us, if we just let Him do it.

Jelena Pavlovic

He Is Always on Time

Martha said to Jesus, "Lord, if you had been here,
my brother would not have died. But even now I know that
whatever you ask from God, God will give you." John 11:21, 22, ESV.

Over the years I have come to the conclusion that God has a very interesting sense of humor as it relates to how He does things. But even more interesting is God's sense of humor as it relates to His timing.

Have you ever been in a difficult situation in which you saw no way out? It may have been that time you needed money to do something very important, or a time you needed the right solution to a problem. Whatever the situation may have been, you were able to see the divine hand of God work wonders for you in the end.

When we look back at the story of Lazarus' death, we see a grieving Martha cry out to Jesus. When Jesus finally arrived to see Martha, she was not quick to ask a question but to make a declaration! In one breath she declared that she knew Jesus could have healed Lazarus, but she also expressed her faith in the fact that whatever Jesus asked of His heavenly Father at that point would be honored. I think Martha's faith can inspire us to believe that God is a powerful God who is always on time. There may be those times we make requests of God and we expect those requests to be honored in a specific time frame, but we have to remember that God is ultimately in control and whatever He does is well done and always on time. I am immediately reminded of the words of the song "Four Days Late" in which the author says, "But His way is God's way, not yours or mine. When He's four days late—He's still on time."

We might be facing many giants in our lives at this time. It may be that we are waiting for the healing our bodies need, the arrival of that husband, or we are awaiting the birth of a child of our love. Some of these giants may be much older than four days. The waiting time may be four months, four years, or what may be a lifetime to some of us—four decades. But rest assured that God is always on time, and He will rescue you from these giants (if He sees fit) at the right time. He has the power to control time, and our heavenly Father is never late. So despite the challenges you may be facing now, rest assured that your heavenly Father knows what is best for you and will deliver you on time.

Taniesha Robertson-Brown

Keep Dancing

You have turned for me my mourning into dancing; you have loosed my sackcloth and clothed me with gladness. Ps. 30:11, ESV.

I heard a story that has taught me a life lesson. Once there was a man, thin and graceful. He wandered through many towns and villages, searching. In one village the townspeople went to church every week. That was the only constant in their lives. When the man came to this village, he observed the people. For two weeks he watched. The third Sunday he stood in the town square as the townspeople left the church. After they had all entered the square, he began to dance. His legs moved his body back and forth with a beauty that captivated the people. His arms spread wide, he reminded each person of an eagle soaring freely through the skies. He danced silently, cheering the hearts of all who watched. The next Sunday he did the same. And the next, and the next. Soon the villagers accepted him into their community. Word spread, and soon people came from miles around to watch this man dance. Every week, without fail, he danced; he awed and inspired many.

But soon the jealous king heard of the amazing dancer. He sent his men to cut off the "heathen's" legs. They did. The villagers mourned the loss of the dancer's legs. But the next Sunday the man sat on a chair and smoothly swung his arms about. He entranced the villagers once again. But again word reached the king, who sent his men to cut off the man's arms. They did, and again the villagers mourned. But still, the next Sunday the man danced. His head weaved and bobbed gracefully on his neck. The king had his head cut off. Still, the man danced until he died.

We, too, should dance until the end.

How do we dance? We do it through our attitude, the joy we show in our activities, the joy we bring to other people in our day-to-day life. We dance as we play with children, as we bring joy to those who are elderly, as we reach out to the ones who are vulnerable. We can dance even if our legs and arms don't work the way we would like. It is a matter of outlook, of attitude. Ecclesiastes talks about "a time to dance" (Eccl. 3:4). David danced for the Lord. The psalms call us to sing and rejoice with voice and instrument, and dance (see Ps. 150). So why stop?

Marielena Burdick

Sharing the Journey

Help carry each other's burdens. In this way
you will follow Christ's teachings. Gal. 6:2, GW.

After traveling long road-trip distances with my husband, Keith, I've come to understand the importance of sharing a journey. There have been opportunities that have challenged us, not just for each other, but those we've met along the way.

Many times we have pulled over to check on a traveler whose vehicle has broken down; subsequently, how thankful we've been when someone has stopped to help us. Just recently a couple camping next to us were cooking in the dark, and we were able to lend them a light. Another camper had an electrical failure, which Keith was able to fix. It's not always big things that confront us, but the small and needful personal matters that each of us bear in everyday struggles during life. We don't know what God can do through a little love in action.

As today's text says, let's not forget to do good and to understand and help one another. This is the most pleasing sacrifice you can give to God (see also Heb. 13:16).

Jesus' life here on earth was an example of selflessness in helping others in all ways. It's only by taking hold of Christ that we can do unto others as we would have them do unto us (see Matt. 7:12). God is calling us to share and care, and I pray that I may be alert to accept this call to serve and honor Him.

Listening to someone is all that's needed at times. I believe, too, that God can place you in the right place at the right time to share another's burden. I was hiking through bush country in Kakadu, northern Australia, when I met a woman sitting by a waterhole. Joining her, I listened as she unfolded a tragic story about her family. If anyone needed an ear, it was this woman.

As we have traveled around I've found there are a lot of people searching for comfort and support. As a counselor I try to offer as much as I can. My husband, being an electrician and handyman, has been very welcome in remote places. To be able to give just a little of your time can make such a difference, not only for them but for your own relationship with God.

Whether it is traveling or at home with family and neighbors, there will always be burdens to bear. Sharing life's journey makes a tremendous difference, especially when we accept the importance of the message our text for today imparts.

Lyn Welk-Sandy

God Is My Refuge

God is our refuge and strength, a very present help in trouble. Ps. 46:1.

Every morning I go into the presence of my Lord. There I spend time and enjoy being with Him. God speaks to me through His Word; He comforts and strengthens me for the day. He helps me remain connected with Him all the time. I keep praying for the needs of my family, friends, and neighbors. I ask Him even for little things, such as help for finding my keys or getting rid of a headache. I praise and thank Him for the tangible help, in one way or another, that He gives me each time I ask Him for it. In the midst of all my blessings, I started worrying for my daughter, Priya. She has been living in the United Kingdom for the past six years without a job. As a mother I pleaded with God about her situation. I knew God would not refuse to hear my prayer. But at times my prayers seemed to be empty. I knew His Holy Spirit was still with me, and that, somehow—in His ways—He would surely answer my prayers.

Whenever my daughter called me, I would advise her, "Don't worry. Just go to your knees and give your problem to God."

"Oh, Mama! I am tired of praying," she admitted during a phone conversation. "Besides, how much longer should I keep praying about this?"

"Pray until God gives you a job," I answered.

That day Priya broke down in sobs and said, "Mama, I have no hopes of getting a job. I have given so many interviews, but no one responds." I assured her that her situation was secure in Christ. Then I prayed with her over the telephone and read Psalm 46:1 to her.

"God will not let you suffer for a long time, Priya. You are His daughter, and He is your refuge and strength. Just rely on Him." That day I too pleaded with God as never before. And God spoke directly to me through His Word: "Therefore do not worry about tomorrow, for tomorrow will worry about itself. Each day has enough trouble of its own" (Matt. 6:34, NIV). I understood what God was saying to me.

The next day Priya phoned me, uncharacteristically, in the afternoon. "Mama, I got a government job. Praise God for being my help in trouble!" How true that is! When we wait and trust, in patience, we will experience His answers in His time.

Premila Masih

Encouragement From Joshua

Have I not commanded you? Be strong and courageous.
Do not be afraid; do not be discouraged, for the Lord your God
will be with you wherever you go. Joshua 1:9, NIV.

Years ago at a women's retreat I attended, the speaker suggested we personalize Bible verses by inserting our names into them. Doing that, I found that Joshua 1:9 read, "Have I not commanded you, Carol? Be strong and courageous. Do not be afraid, Carol; do not be discouraged, Carol, for the Lord your God will be with you wherever you go." I wish I had learned that lesson years earlier.

I attended three semesters of college and then quit to get married. I worked while my husband attended college and until our second daughter was born. A few years later we moved to a different city when my husband got a new job. As I worked full-time and attended classes at night, graduation seemed far off; I felt discouraged. When my college adviser suggested I take two classes each semester so I could finish in five years rather than 10, I followed his advice.

Marital problems led to a divorce, and I was a busy single mom. I enjoyed learning, but I partially dreaded working full-time and attending classes for another five long years. Then God inspired me to investigate attending college full-time. Imagine my surprise when I learned that I could get enough funding to cover college and our regular living costs! I filled out financial-aid papers and planned what classes to take the first semester.

My employer granted me a year's leave. Coworkers organized a goodbye potluck, and offered advice, hugs, gifts, and best wishes. Although I'd been attending the very same college for night classes, I felt nervous as I moved closer and closer to being a full-time student.

After a year my employer asked if I was ready to return to work. I chose to finish college rather than return to my job. God blessed me again: I received company stock after my job ended. I graduated the following May, and am so thankful I acted strong and courageous, just as God commanded me. He truly was with me all the way!

As I think back on my life, I realize God has never left me. He has been prompting me, leading me, and patiently waiting for me to hear and follow, and helping me understand what He wants me to do.

Carol Jean Marino

In His Arms

*I spread out my hands to you; I thirst for you
like a parched land. Ps. 143:6, NIV.*

When I was about 11 years old, I tried out for the chorus at my elementary school. I was surprised to be chosen because, quite frankly, I didn't think I had a very good singing voice. Our school was chosen to be part of a Christmas show that would be video-recorded and played on our local television station during Christmas. We had to do the dress rehearsal and recording on a warm September day at the television station. What I remember most about that rehearsal now were the hot lights.

Being one of the taller girls, I was put on the top row of the risers that were about six to seven rows up near the lights. We had just finished the rehearsal, and it was time to start recording the actual performance. I remember feeling hotter and hotter, and before I knew it, all I remember before everything went dark was looking at the girl to my right and saying, "I don't feel so good."

When I woke up, I was being carried off in the arms of a man—I think he was the principal of the school. I remember being told that I was a "very lucky young lady" because there was someone there to catch me when I fell from the back of the platform.

I would say that I was very lucky and blessed! It wasn't until years later that I realized how badly I could have been hurt if someone hadn't been there to catch me.

We have Someone else who is always watching over us and is there to catch us when we fall. Our wonderful Lord Jesus is watching over us every moment of every day. He sees us while we sleep, while we go through our day, and He is always there for us. All we have to do is turn to Him and pray to Him. He longs for us to need Him and to be a part of our lives.

I remember that after my mama died I had a hard time sleeping. A friend said, "Let yourself rest in Jesus as if He were holding you in His arms." I loved the visualization of that: our King and our God holding me in His arms.

So no matter what you are going through today, whether you are in a great time in your life or are facing challenges, His hands are reaching out to you. Take His hands, climb into His arms, and rest. It's the most wonderful and safest place you will ever be.

Jean Dozier Davey

God Is in Control

Cast all your anxiety on him because he cares for you. 1 Peter 5:7, NIV.

I had recently moved from the United States back to my homeland of Brazil. After having lived in the States for seven years, I was not certain that I would be able to adapt to living in Brazil once again. For this reason, when friends offered me puppies as a gift, I had to reject them even though I have always loved animals. And I especially loved dogs.

As I struggled to make the decision to stay, God showed that He had plans for me in Brazil, using various situations to tie me down. One of them was Lili, a beautiful dog that I found abandoned on the way to church on a Saturday morning. She was always cheerful, coy, and very friendly. I was very happy with her.

One Christmas Day I had just come from a lovely Christmas cantata and, as usual, I stroked my Lili, who greeted me. *But what is this I am touching?* I felt a lump the size of a marble. *Oh, no! What is that?* On Monday, very early, the veterinarian reassured me and provided some medication. Relaxing, I went ahead with a planned trip to the university for a monthlong postgraduate course. In January, when I came back, the lump was 10 times bigger! *Help, God! Mercy!* The next day she would have to have surgery. This time the vet scared me. Several tests verified alarming hormonal alterations. A month later the tumor was back! I cried again to the Lord, who created me and also the animals. *God, I don't want to see my Lili suffering.* I ached, seeing a once-happy-and-playful animal prostrate, full of pain. That's when the Lord told me to go to another veterinarian.

That May, Lili was operated on again. The sarcoma had returned, and some organs had to be removed, together with the tumor. The vet was concerned. On the night of the surgery I needed to hear God's voice. It was a Friday, and for my evening devotions I opened my devotional book to the meditation of November 4 and read, "Are you worried about a disease?" I was! But the Doctor of doctors was in control. To His honor and glory, Lili recovered well, and I was able to witness and do missionary work in the clinic where she was. Now it's September again, and she is doing very well. We continue doing tests and treatments to control the hormone levels. The region where the tumor attacked twice is now clean. Glory to God!

Eloisa da Silva Monken

Rescue Needed

I have redeemed you; I have called you by your name;
you are Mine. Isa. 43:1, NKJV.

The speeding car raced on, leaving behind a small crumpled pile of fur in the street. A kind passerby picked up the little broken body and carried it into the nearby animal clinic.

The veterinarian carefully examined the little cat and shook his head. "It is very badly damaged," he said. "It will be too much to repair; it has a microchip, but is not registered to anyone." The vet tech Melissa had taken to the little animal, and pleaded: "If you will fix him, I will be responsible for his care and help him as he heals." The vet considered her offer until a blood test revealed that the kitty tested positive for FIV (feline immune deficiency). "No shelter will take him; it is not worth it to repair the damage." But Melissa pleaded, "Let me have him; I will take care of him."

And she was as good as her word. After two years the little cat she named Mikito had developed into a handsome fellow with soft, cream-colored fur and brown points. His alert blue eyes really caught one's attention!

Circumstances changed, and Melissa brought him to live in Maryland. The home where he was expected to live turned out to be a disaster, as he fought with the other cats. What to do? He couldn't stay there any longer. He needed another new home. Who would take him?

Since I was grieving over the death of my cat Ginger, I was not interested in a new pet, but reluctantly gave him a chance. Good decision. He has become my special companion, a reserved, dignified animal who seems to love few people besides me. I thank the Lord for Mikito's comforting presence every day. He has found a forever home with me!

When the Lord found me, I also was broken. Many foolish decisions and actions had taken their toll, and I was down in spirit. Jesus said, "Come to Me. I will fix your brokenness and give you a new spirit and a new hope." But I cried out to Him, "You don't understand—I am also diseased and not worth Your care or Your attention."

Jesus replied, "I am a Redeemer, and that is what I do—redeem those who are broken. I am the Healer, and I heal diseased sinners and make them whole again. Believe on Me, and I will give you a forever home with Me!

Marilyn Petersen

Oh, How I Need Him!

*Let the wicked forsake his way, and the unrighteous man
his thoughts: and let him return unto the Lord, and he will have mercy
upon him; and to our God, for he will abundantly pardon. Isa. 55:7.*

It is easy to get caught up in the rush of the daily routine: get up and get ready before the 16-year-old has a shower and uses all the hot water, get the 4-year-old up and listen to all the reasons he doesn't want to go to the babysitter's. Then it is the baby's turn: change his soiled diaper and get him dressed. Coats, scarves, mittens, special toys, and, of course, don't forget the snacks. Breakfast? Don't have time; we need to be in the car and on our way. Drop the kids off and kiss them goodbye. Another day they grow, play, and learn without me.

Off to work where I have students waiting for me to be the example of professionalism, tact, and calmness. Time to hand back yet another assignment marked at 2:00 that morning and share my "infinite wisdom" about business—which I polished up on the night before.

The day concludes with picking up the kids and groceries, making supper and cleaning up, bathing the little boys, conversing with the teenager about his day and the injustice of his world, preparing and marking for the next day, throwing in a load of laundry, kissing my tired husband good night, and closing my eyes for a short night's rest.

I had convinced myself that there was no time for devotional and prayer time for far too long. Oh, how my need for God's strength and guidance was felt and not realized! The gracious Father that I serve brought me—ever so gently—to the understanding of my need for Him with gentle encouraging whispers—until I gave in.

Oh, how much better it is to rest in the Lord, to spend time with my Savior. My daily activity hasn't changed much. I still have far too many demands on my time, but now I give it to God, and somehow He takes care of it all. Life is far more manageable when I give it to the all-powerful, almighty King of kings. I have discovered that with just a half hour of devotion and prayer each morning and an intimate prayer each night, so much more can be accomplished in that same amount of time and with far less stress and anxiety.

Thank You, Lord.

Tammy Jamieson

Permission to Say "No," Lord

Thou shalt love thy neighbour as thyself. Matt. 19:19.

*O*K, *how much is enough?* This is a question I keep asking myself and, ultimately, God. So I've got to let you in on my conversation with Him.

How much giving to others do I have to do? I read in Psalm 112:5: "Happy is the person who is generous with his loans" (TEV), and I wonder why, when I share, I grumble. We know "God loveth a cheerful giver" (2 Cor. 9:7), and "It is more blessed to give than to receive" (Acts 20:35), but I'm challenged with this "giving" thing. *Come on, God, there must be a limit. I can't give to every cause. I can't help everybody. My returning love to You does not require that, does it?*

I'm struggling with this because just the other day a friend needed funds to keep her utilities on. She asked me to lend her the money. Now, I'm a single person solely dependent on my income for support. I have no one to cover my back, and when it's gone, it's gone. I've been dipping into that to meet my monthly expenses. I responded favorably to my friend because I did have the amount she requested, and she did need it worse than I did. So I shared. But it was "grudgingly, or of necessity" (2 Cor. 9:7). So I'm struggling with this concept of "love thy neighbour as thyself" as in today's text.

Actually, Lord, I do know what it means. Back in my really lean times, when I literally lived on a shoestring, I was forced, for much too long, to ride on the doughnut—you know, that pretend tire strategically hidden in one's car. It looks like a toy and doesn't match any of the other tires. I'd been riding on mine so long that I was putting air in it! I just didn't have the funds or the credit to buy even one tire.

One evening, as I drove home from picking up my children from school, some friends were following me. They saw the predicament of the car and sized up my financial status. They flagged me over and told me to follow them to Sam's Club. There they bought me a tire. What makes this an act of love is that a few days later the store called to say the check had bounced. I imagine the bank called my friends, so they made it right, and I never said a thing to them. The point: they were obviously as short as I was—yet they loved me enough to give of their little means. They loved me as themselves!

OK, God, that's my answer. I've got to love others as much as I love myself.

Elizabeth Darby Watson

When You Think
God Does Not Answer

*So do not fear, for I am with you; do not be dismayed,
for I am your God. I will strengthen you and help you; I will
uphold you with my righteous right hand. Isa. 41:10, NIV.*

My brother told me over the years that I must work for the "Jesus Temp Agency," because I could always get a job. Whether I left voluntarily or the position was downsized, I would have a job the next day or week. But that all changed in 2010 when the economy went belly-up, and I was without a job for more than a year. In fact, I'm still without one. I went on interviews but never got a job. Since this was something completely foreign to me, after a few months I began to wonder why God was allowing this to happen, and after my morning worship I began to write to God for understanding.

I (God) will never leave you. *Really? Then why can't I hear from You? I don't have a job. I go on interviews, and nothing happens. Even Walmart won't hire me!*

I (God) will never leave you. *Really? My family and those whom I thought I could depend on don't help. In fact, I believe they fast and pray that You won't bless me.*

I (God) will never leave you. *Really? I have fasted, prayed, memorized, and recalled all Your promises, attend church weekly, try to obey Your commandments, even pray for my enemies and confess my sins.*

I (God) will never leave you. *Really? Bills are overdue and sent to collection agencies; phone, cable, and Internet have been disconnected; my car has been repossessed, and I need my hair trimmed.*

I (God) will never leave you. *Really? My boyfriend's family doesn't like me. He pays my rent, and they call him a fool.*

I (God) will never leave you. Really! When I died on Calvary's cross, I thought of you and your present situation. When I rose from the dead, I thought of you and your present situation. "Do not be dismayed, for I am your God."

All I have ever needed His hand has provided, great are His promises. I thank Him for understanding my lonely, needy, egotistical, sinful self!

I (God) will never leave you. Really, truly, that's a promise!

Andrea Walker

Being Held by God

*As one whom his mother comforteth, so will I comfort you;
and ye shall be comforted in Jerusalem. Isa. 66:13.*

It started out as an ordinary day. However, before the sun went down that evening, I found myself crying out to God like never before. My whole world was caving in around me, my children were getting into trouble in school, bill collectors were calling, and my marriage was unraveling. I had already tied a knot at the end of my proverbial rope, and now the knot was slipping loose. I took my children to my grandmother's home and asked her to keep them for a few hours.

I grew up in the church. In fact, I'm a fourth-generation Adventist. I've given Bible studies, taught Sabbath school, and participated in practically every facet of our church. And with all that background, I still found myself in utter despair. That day, after leaving my children with my grandmother, I went home. I didn't even have the will to turn on the lights. In a state of despondency I walked to my bedroom and lay facedown across my bed. I cried until physically I couldn't cry anymore. The tears had now become my enemy, and I couldn't gain any solace from them.

Somewhere deep within my soul I was able to muster the following thought: *Lord, I've talked about You all my life; I've studied and shared You with others. Lord, at this time I need to know that You are near. I need to feel You.* Without warning, the area where I was lying sunk. But I felt myself being held. I was being held by God! I didn't imagine it. I wasn't asleep or dreaming. God was holding me in His arms, and I felt safe, secure, and confident that I could face anything.

Here, some 20 years later, I believe that God is still holding me. Sure, problems still arise, but no longer do I allow them to shake me or my faith.

Have you ever noticed a small child fall down and immediately run to her mother? Her mother quickly embraces her and comforts her as she assures the child that everything will be all right. As you read my story, be reminded that your heavenly Father will also comfort you as a mother comforts her child. You too will be held by God!

Cheryl P. Simmons

Discovering My Gift

For as the body is one and has many members,
but all the members of that one body, being many, are one body,
so also is Christ. For by one Spirit we were all baptized into
one body—whether Jews or Greeks, whether slaves or free—
and have all been made to drink into one Spirit. 1 Cor. 12:12, 13, NKJV.

Raised in a Christian home, I remember the discussion of gifts or talents that God has given each of us. It seemed to me that I didn't have any of the gifts mentioned in 1 Corinthians 12; it made me feel inadequate, and I questioned my relationship with God. I was envious of the obvious talents of others who had the gift of music, academic achievements, healing, or leadership skills. During my early years my gift never seemed to be defined or apparent to me.

While in my first year of college, my first time to live away from home and being a bit homesick, I decided I would collect personalities. I made it a challenge to find something in common with every person I met during my daily routine. Because of that goal, I have been so blessed to be involved and of assistance to persons with a variety of needs. Through my relationship with God I have developed instincts for when to help.

As a result I have met people from all different cultures, religions, ethnic and social economic status; I am honored to have met Benjamin Netanyahu in Denver, and Shimon Peres while visiting in Jerusalem. I made a visit to Cuba on special visa to take in medical supplies. All around the world I have met the most interesting people, and I've been in a position to help when needed. Sitting with sick and dying family members and friends; intervening to help resolve relationship issues for friends and neighbors.

My life experience has taught me that if I stay true to a daily relationship with God's guidance, I have been rewarded with the most wonderful adventures and opportunities to be of service in His name daily and with everyone with whom I come in contact.

As it says in 1 Corinthians 12, we are all an important part of the body, and one is not more important than the other. I am proud to have learned to use my gift of comforting and generous sharing, and with God's grace, practicing it at every opportunity. I would encourage each of you to ask God to help you discover and use your talents/gifts daily.

Jan Wall Rosen

Do Unto Others

Do to others what you want them to do to you. Matt. 7:12, NCV.

Years ago my oldest son worked for a truck farmer picking corn, driving a tractor, and running errands. In the course of working for this farmer he would often come home sopping wet from the early-morning cornfields and then drop his wet, dirty clothes down the laundry chute. Several times I cautioned him, "Please don't do that; some of the towels were stained by you doing that." And the last person he, as a teenage boy who had his first job (being a "working man"), needed to take orders from was his mom. He was even able to buy some of his own clothes.

As time passed, I found a yellow dress that was perfect for Sabbaths. I loved it and received compliments on it at church. I took good care of it. However, one day while doing laundry, I pulled my dress from the laundry to wash it separately. I found it was full of dirt, stains, and what looked like mold.

On top of the dress were my son's dirty clothes still wet from the day before. I was furious. *How many times have I talked to him about this!* I prayed, *Lord, how can I show my son how disrespectful he is being by not following my directions?*

It was a rainy day, and I had promised my son I would pick him up from work. While driving there, I had an idea of how I could teach him how I felt about his disobedience and disrespect.

After some small talk, I casually mentioned, "Oh, I'm sorry, but you know that new blue shirt you bought? The one you love so much?" He nodded. "Well, one of the kids threw a wet towel down the chute; it landed on your shirt, and it has mold and stains on it. Not sure it will come out."

He was furious! After a time of seething and muttering about having bought it with his own money, I told him, "Son, I'm sorry, but what I just told you isn't quite true." He swung his head around and looked at me with disbelief. Then I told him, "I know that if I had told you what had really happened you would not understand the loss and frustration I feel after so many times of telling you to put your work clothes in the laundry room." He hung his head, "I'm so sorry."

My point: we have heard it at Bible study, in sermons, and yet we disobey our parent, God the Father. I wonder how hurt He is when we willfully disobey Him. That's why He put today's verse in His Word. I learned something as well that day.

Marge Vande Hei

God Cares

Casting all your care upon Him, for He cares for you. 1 Peter 5:7, NKJV.

It was time for my children to start school, and I had been working 3:00 to 11:00 for 20 years. As I was a single mom, I interviewed for a recovery room position so that I would be able to work days. I don't interview well, and I wasn't able to promise to work on call because of child care, so I was not seriously considered. I applied and interviewed for a home-care job, which involved shadowing a nurse for four hours. They decided they needed a psychiatric nurse instead of a medical-surgical nurse, so I didn't get that job. A while later I broke my leg. About the time I was recovering and able to work again, a friend called to say that the home-care job was again available. I looked for my résumé but was unable to find it. I looked everywhere that I could think of. Two or three weeks later, when I thought it was too late to apply for the job, my résumé was right where I thought I had put it.

After I went back to work 3:00 to 11:00, the recovery job became available. The nurse, Judy, had leukemia. They were going to save the job for six months for Judy, but they needed an interim person. I interviewed along with several others. The conditions for the job were that if you took it and the nurse came back, you would be out of a job and would not be able to have one at that hospital. Even though there might have been another job open at that hospital, they were not going to let you have it. That was what they said. I got the job.

A while later I found out that no one else wanted the job under those conditions. A month or two after getting the job the thought struck me, *Something bad is going to happen to Judy.* I was worried, and prayed hard for God to take care of her. I didn't believe I had received the job for it to be taken away from me. God took care of Judy. She was able to come back to work, although not to her previous job. She had had a stroke, so she went to the job of interviewing patients presurgery, which wasn't as active. Since I was doing the recovery job at the time, I interviewed for it again; I received it. Years later I crossed paths with the nurse I had interviewed with for the home-care job. She said the company was long gone, and everyone had had to find other jobs! God had provided the work I needed when I needed it, where the pay was better, and I wouldn't have to change to a new environment. I praise and thank God. He cares for you, too.

Ruth Middaugh Goodsite

Calm, Soft, Serene, Peaceful

Blessed be the Lord, because He has heard the voice of my supplications! Ps. 28:6, NKJV.

These words of today's title were whispered to me in a hospital bed by the Holy Spirit to console me. I had already been admitted for four days, waiting for a surgery, but it seemed that my wait had been in vain. I did not know what to do anymore as I prayed, cried, read the Bible, listened to praise. But that day I was deeply uneasy, nervous, and tired of waiting. I cried out to God to calm me down, but God remained silent. And in that silence I received extra comfort.

What happened to me was an experience similar to Elijah when he was fleeing from Jezebel; while alone in a cave, he thought that God had forgotten him, but in a soft breeze God revealed Himself and granted him the strength necessary to accomplish his goals. I was alone physically, and despite thinking that I was spiritually alone as well, God in His mercy sheltered me, and I heard His voice through music whispered in my ears, saying: "Calm, soft, serene, peaceful is the voice of my dear Jesus./ Calm, soft, serene, peaceful is the voice which calls me with love./ I should answer the gracious invitation and answer the tireless call,/ For calm, soft, serene, peaceful is the voice of my dear Jesus./And His voice will not be in the strong wind, earthquakes, or intense fire./ But in the peaceful, whispering breeze, I know that the voice of God is there."

Accompanying these chords, I was lulled further by a few words from the psalmist David, but just with three psalms: 27, 28, and 29, and at the end of the reading I found myself completely different; I was calm, peaceful, serene, and confident in God. I thanked God with a prayer, and a few hours later my family arrived, and I had my surgery.

To God's honor and glory and my increased sense of calm and tranquillity, the surgery was quick and successful. And throughout the surgery I felt *His* presence calming me and assuring me that all would go well.

Therefore, if the difficulties of this life want to overshadow the presence of God in your life, or if the noise of this world wants to impede you from hearing the soft voice of the Master, stop, and stay in silence, and thus you will be able to hear and feel the presence of Jesus comforting you.

Carmem Virgínia dos Santos Paulo

Give Thanks in All Things

*Giving thanks to God the Father at all times and for everything
in the name of our Lord Jesus Christ. Eph. 5:20, NRSV.*

In troubled times I have often heard people say, "Why does God allow this to happen?" In my own life I have always tried to trust in God, leaning on Him and seeking His answers to life's problems. As I look back over my life so far, I can see that God has never let me down.

When my first daughter was born 24 years ago, I was told by the doctors that she had a heart murmur. Devastated by this awful news, I prayed for God's healing; the next day when my daughter was reexamined, no heart murmur was heard! On another occasion my mom was told that she had breast cancer; again I prayed for her to be healed, and when a further biopsy was done, there was no trace of the cancer. On facing my husband's unemployment, I prayed that God would sustain us, as we had a mortgage and other regular bills to pay. Although jobs were difficult to find, he was offered further employment without a gap and on a higher salary!

The New International Version's rendition of Ephesians 5:20 reads: "Sing and make music from your heart to the Lord, always giving thanks to God the Father for everything, in the name of the Lord Jesus Christ." In the big problems and smaller ones God has always provided. In fact, on many occasions He has not only answered my prayers but has given far more than I asked Him for. This has reminded me of the words in Ephesians 3:20 that "God is able to do far more than we could ever ask for or imagine" (NIrV). I now also make a conscious effort to give thanks and praise to God for trials and problems, realizing they can only serve to strengthen my relationship with Him as I lean on Him completely during those times.

God, in His wisdom, does not always answer in the way I expect, but He supports and encourages me as He carries me through the difficult times. I am just like you—not perfect, and I know I make many mistakes in life—but over and over God has demonstrated His love for me, reaching out in His grace to forgive and help me. He wants to do that for you today if you will allow Him. Whatever your problem, however big or small, God cares about it because He cares for you. Don't be afraid to approach Him; just lift up your heart, ask, and God will not let you down. He has promised!

Karen Richards

The Road Home

Surely your goodness and love will follow me all the days of my life,
and I will dwell in the house of the Lord forever. Ps. 23:6, NIV.

It had been a familiar driveway for years. It had been home. We were moving to a new town, job, and school. The moving company had cleared the rooms of furniture and loaded every box. Yet the rooms were still full to the brim with memories upon bountiful memories. Each wall and window of our home spoke warmth for our story there; each room held a piece of us. We had packed school lunches on kitchen counters, raced down hallways dripping pool water, prepared the Christmas tree in its living room spot, taken too long in the bathroom in the morning, and watched the weather forecast in the family room. As lady of the house, there was part of me that felt like our home was my special domain. My husband spent weeks at work, and my daughter spent weeks at school. I spent weeks caring for every nook and need at home. My domain was changing now, and I was unsure how to change with it.

One of the movers came and said, "I think we got it all." I looked at them, then at the huge semi that united every room of the house into one large irreverent rectangle on wheels. Despite my polite "Thank you," I wanted to say, "There's no way you could get it all, for this is home." They explained they would travel and meet us at the new address the next morning.

Filth coated our jeans and the smell of cleaning supplies owned the air as we tearfully wandered our home. I ran my hand across my stove and then again across my favorite dining room wall. It was time to go. It was time to trust Jesus and forge on to a new chapter. It was time to walk forth in faith. It was time to let go in bravery. It was time to grow.

I look back, believing it was past time for me to surrender all earthly domains and to engage in a deepening walk with my immovable Jesus. He could have never moved in if I hadn't moved out. May the words I hear each staying or changing moment be in humble serenity of His: Your spirit will be most at home if you build your domain within Me. Ask Me to bless your earthly home and help you. Trust Me with the movable emotions in your life. And know that wherever we journey together, I can use you if you let Me. Daughter, I alone am the real road home. Jesus.

Heather VandenHoven

The Sin of Unforgiveness

And be kind to one another, tenderhearted, forgiving one another,
just as God in Christ also forgave you. Eph. 4:32, NKJV.

As far as the east is from the west, so far has He removed
our transgressions from us. Ps. 103:12, NKJV.

Jesus taught us in the model prayer to forgive others even as we need to be forgiven by our heavenly Father. For me this can sometimes be difficult, since my human nature wants to get even with those who hurt me.

Whenever I experience this difficulty, I become remorseful and uncomfortable, which drives me to do a close examination of myself. I am always reminded of the many times that I hurt my heavenly Father and how He freely forgives and forgets what I have done. He tells me that as far as the east is from the west He has forgiven my sin. He reminds me that no one has ever been hurt as much as He was, and yet He forgave His murderers. When I consider how my Lord, the Creator and Sustainer of heaven and earth, the King of kings and the Lord of lords, humbled Himself to the point of forgiving and praying for His enemies, then I am constrained to follow His example. And as hard as it is for me to do, I must.

I am reminded that God's forgiveness of my sin is contingent on my willingness to forgive others; this is brought out in the Lord's Prayer: "And forgive us our debts, as we forgive our debtors" (Matt. 6:12). This means that I must cultivate a forgiving attitude at all times. When my life is hid in Christ, my whole attitude will change, and I will be willing to do the things He did. I will then be able to sincerely say to someone who hurts me, "I forgive you."

When we truly forgive someone, we will not harbor a grudge or ill feelings toward them. We will not forget that a wrong was done, but we will want the very best for the one who has hurt us. I will no longer let it control my life, either. Proverbs 20:22 admonishes, "Do not say, 'I will repay evil'; wait for the Lord, and he will deliver you" (ESV). What freedom that promises!

My prayer is "Lord, it is not my will, but Thine be done. Change my heart with its unforgiving nature and give me one like Your own. Amen." It will be then that I become more like Him.

Kollis Salmon-Fairweather

My Way Versus God's Way

Now to Him who is able to do exceedingly
abundantly above all that we ask or think, according to the
power that works in us, to Him be glory in the church by Christ Jesus
throughout all ages, world without end. Amen. Eph. 3:20, 21, NKJV.

Have you ever prayed to the Lord about a problem and told Him how to solve the problem? I have, and He must have pitied how I underestimated His power.

My family had just finished a short-term language study in France and prepared to leave for Cameroon for mission work. As I filled suitcases and boxes, I worried about the weight, as the packing seemed endless. Language books, pots and pans, clothes—each item took space and added to the weight. My husband and two of our children (our other son had left for France earlier) could take only 80 free kilos on the plane. That night I prayed earnestly, "Lord, we have too much baggage. Tomorrow at the airport, would you send another passenger who has no baggage to check in, so we can use his weight allowance?" At least it would reduce our excess baggage expense. I went to bed, conscious of a peace that filled my heart.

The next morning, when the school administrator came to drive us to the airport, he looked at all the baggage. "Did you weigh all these?" He probably wanted to be sure he had brought enough money to ship everything. I shook my head.

At the Geneva airport check-in counter, the woman's head turned from side to side as she surveyed our load. "Is this all?" she asked. As we piled the luggage on the scale, I held my breath. The needle stopped at 176. I mumbled something about needing the things in Africa.

"Well," said the woman, "I can give you another 20 kilos each." When I expressed surprise, she said, "I can add another 20 kilos for each passenger, making it 160. Then you will have to pay for only 16 extra kilos."

"Thank you very much!" I exclaimed, meaning it both for the woman and the Lord. But God wasn't done just yet.

"Excuse me a minute," the woman said, then left and returned a couple of minutes later. "That's all right. The manager says you don't have to pay for the 16 kilos," she informed us. I could have hugged her. I admitted to God that His solution far superseded mine.

Bienvisa Ladion Nebres

My Angel Artist on Kilimanjaro

For He shall give His angels charge over you,
to keep you in all your ways. Ps. 91:11, NKJV.

That Friday dawned perfect, and our group of 13 missionaries (ages 18-57) from Kenya, Malawi, and Zambia was ready for a five-day climb of Mount Kilimanjaro in East Africa. A snow-covered mountain on the equator, Kilimanjaro rises 19,340 feet (just under 6,000 meters) and is on the bucket list of climbers around the world. Our path to the world's highest freestanding mountain began in a dusty village on the Kenyan border. Beyond the village, the path narrowed and wound through vegetation that changed with the altitude as we climbed higher.

After spending Sabbath in a cave, we began our climb Sunday more slowly to Kibo Hut above the tree line. On Monday morning at 2:00, clad in numerous layers, we trudged up the scree; some climbers were feeling the result of the thin air. Two steps forward, one step back, two steps forward—up the switchback path. My husband encouraged me from ahead, and little by little we made it to the rim. The sun burst with breathtaking splendor above the clouds and sparkled on the glaciers as we reached our goal.

Soon we began our descent back through the landscape flung with train-car-sized boulders. Dehydrated climbers still on the mountain needed water and medicine, and my husband hurried ahead to the cave for help. Reaching a long plateau, he went on, and I plodded along slowly. As the path veered left and down, he waved and disappeared over the side.

Following the trail alone in silence under the big sky now turning dark, I suddenly lost the path! Startled, I looked around with a sinking heart. But then I found some stick pictures— smiley faces, hearts—drawn along the trail each time I deviated from the path. *What a great husband I have*, I thought, *drawing pictures along the path to show me the way*!

The sun set as I limped along the trail; cold dew dropped on the vegetation. I sat on a rock to await his return. When he returned, we scrambled down through the bushes together. "I can't believe you drew those pictures for me along the way," I gasped as we stumbled along.

But he had neither drawn nor seen the pictures! He had only turned and waved as he disappeared. No one had passed between us. But surely my artist angel walked ahead of me, delighting to show me the way, guarding my missteps, taking charge over me.

Beverly Campbell Pottle

An Incredible Knock at the Door

Ask, and it will be given to you; seek, and you will find;
knock, and it will be opened to you. Matt. 7:7, NKJV.

It was summer 2007 in Waterloo, Ontario, Canada. After our morning devotion, my husband, Albert, told me that the Holy Spirit told him that something was missing in his spiritual walk. He asked if I would pray with him to search for the truth before he died. I agreed, but I did not comprehend the "die" part. He was not sick.

That September we went to Freeport, Bahamas, our winter residence for 23 years. One day while we were walking on the beach, Albert cried out to the Lord: "Father, please show me the truth before I die." I was stunned. When we got back to our condo, we decided to rest and watch TV before lunch. That afternoon I turned on the TV and heard a preacher saying, "If you love Me, keep My commandments; if you break one, you broke them all."

These words hit us like a hurricane. We both fell on the floor weeping. I said, "This is the truth we waited for! Thank You, Lord." When Albert stood up, he said, "We must start attending the Seventh-day Adventist Church." So he called Ted Rahming, who had invited us to their church service 21 years earlier; he was also an assistant pastor. Albert kept phoning, but there was no answer.

A few minutes after he hung up, someone knocked at the door. It was Ted Rahming and his wife, Carmen. What a divine appointment! They told us that they had been at our place that morning to invite us to their camp meeting, but they missed us. We told them we had better news. Had they come before we were convicted, we would have told them what we had said 21 years ago: "Leave us alone, for you are a legalist." With tears of joy they told us that they had not stopped praying for us for 21 years.

The following year we were baptized. The next September we went back to the Bahamas. About six months later we had a flood in our unit, and Albert over-exerted himself fixing the place. The following Sabbath evening he collapsed, and died shortly after. Before he took his last breath I said, "Goodbye, my love. I will see you in the morning!" And I will. Albert died knowing Jesus had died to save him! Praise God!

Nena A. Wirth

You Did Give Me Chives!

For who has despised the day of small things? Zech. 4:10, NKJV.

It had been a balmy day at the seaside. In spite of His lack of rest the night before, Jesus felt invigorated as the breeze rustled His hair. Clearly the Spirit ministered to Him as He ministered the words of life to the throngs who had come seeking Him that morning. Perhaps this would be the day Jesus would declare His right to David's throne!

As the sun sank low, His disciples begged that the people be sent to their homes to get something to eat. Jesus said, "You give them something to eat." Apparently the disciples had been thinking about their own stomachs as much as anyone else's as they had been scoping out the crowd and spotted a boy with an uneaten lunch before they had come to Jesus.

Of course, Jesus already knew what He was going to do. Accepting the boy's lunch, He blessed the small offering and fed a multitude of 5,000-plus people! They came expecting a king that day, but were fed lunch; but in Jesus they got a king and so much more, if they had only opened their spiritual eyes.

There may be times in our lives when we feel our need is great. We are praying for some important blessing. It may or may not be God's will for our lives, and we continue to wait and pray. Meanwhile, God comes by with little blessings to show He hasn't forgotten us.

The fall had come bringing a chill to the air, and I was craving a bowl of warm apple-squash soup. While shopping I was torn, trying to decide whether or not to get chives for garnish, but decided it was a luxury I couldn't afford and bought only the apples and squash.

With the soup cooking, I decided to take out the trash. Sitting on a low wall beside the trash can was a deteriorating pot a friend had given me. The survival of its contents of rosemary and thyme was rather doubtful, but I had been watering it some. Passing by the pot, I glanced at it—and stopped in my tracks. Right there in the middle of the pot was—you guessed it— chives!

"The Lord is good to those who wait for Him" (Lam. 3:25, NKJV). As I pray for what seems like forever for what I perceive to be a major need, God is continually surprising me with little blessings that tell me He has me on His mind. When tempted to lose hope, I am reminded of these blessings and say, "Lord, You *did* give me chives!" and my faith is renewed.

Sylvia Stark

The Bottle of Perfume

Truly I tell you, wherever the gospel is preached throughout the world, what she has done will also be told, in memory of her. Mark 14:9, NIV.

One Saturday morning I was visiting Nairobi, Kenya, for business, and as I entered the hotel lobby, the hotel butler asked, "Where are you going, dressed so lovely?"

I said, "To church." I started to walk away, then asked him, "Can I pray for you?"

"Yes, please pray for my sister Beth. She is in the hospital dying of cancer."

One evening, returning to my hotel room, I remembered the spiritual devotional books my auntie Stella had given me. I wrote in one for Beth, then Felix. Then I remembered I had a new, expensive bottle of perfume. I thought, *I should give this to her!* Then I rationalized, *This is expensive, and I've never met her. Maybe it would be better suited for someone I know.*

Then the story of Mary Magdalene came to my mind. She didn't think twice before pouring expensive perfume before Jesus' feet. Grieved by my sins, I longed for that moment with Jesus and thought to myself, *If only I could pour the perfume before Jesus' feet, maybe I could be set free like Mary Magdalene.* Excited, I presented the books and the perfume for Beth to the butler, who humbly accepted them as if he had never received a gift before.

He placed the bottle of perfume on the podium, but a moment later the perfume bottle rolled off and broke before his feet. With shock, he knelt down, picked up the broken glass, and with his uniform unintentionally soaked up the perfume. Embarrassed, he didn't know what to say. I reminded him of the story of Mary Magdalene and shared with him how I felt before giving him the perfume. Speechless, and with tears in his eyes, he hugged me tight. In that moment I was finally, truly free from the guilt of my sin.

The next day he told me, "I read Mark 14, the story of Jesus being anointed." Then he added, "Sometime ago I walked away from the church, and my sister does not believe, but today my life has changed. My sister Beth called me crying, saying 'I didn't know, Brother, you were praying for me, I didn't know you had others praying for me.'" Beth thought God had forgotten her. The day I left Kenya, I was given a note from Felix with today's text and "I will always tell the story of an angel called Aimee, and the perfume that broke for the both of us."

Aimee Seheult

Facing Death With Peace

Yea, though I walk through the valley of the shadow of death, I will fear no evil: for thou art with me; thy rod and thy staff they comfort me. Ps. 23:4.

I vividly remember the morning of September 23, 2011. My husband, Jonathan, and I had just finished our morning exercise on our community jogging trail. Then we had gone to get groceries when all of a sudden he started shivering and feeling chills. He had gotten a prostate biopsy the previous day, which had gone smoothly. However, I was alarmed when he started shaking vigorously and breathing rapidly. We rushed to the nearest hospital. On the way there, he became delirious. As a physician myself, I realized the gravity of the situation and became quite concerned. Soon after we arrived in the Emergency Department, ice compresses were placed all over his body to lower his temperature, which had gone up to 105°F. The monitor showed that his blood pressure had gone down to 70/40, and it stayed persistently low. He had gone into septic shock, which could result in organ failure and death. The prognosis was bad, and I realized that I could lose my husband. This was truly a walking "through the valley of the shadow of death" experience for me. However, in the midst of apprehension for what might happen next, my mind was at peace. I knew that God was in control. His "rod and staff" comforted me.

Efforts were made to raise Jonathan's blood pressure by giving him four liters of fluid. When this was insufficient, vasopressors were started. After what seemed like a very long time, Jonathan was finally stabilized and transferred to the intensive-care unit. Unfortunately, all the fluid given for resuscitation had put him into congestive heart failure. Diuretics were then given to flush the excess fluid from his body. This resulted in a severe electrolyte imbalance that needed to be corrected. After a five-day hospitalization, he was discharged home. I had to give him intravenous antibiotics every eight hours for 10 days to make sure he had gotten rid of the multidrug-resistant bacteria that had placed him into sepsis. I praise the Lord for my husband's recovery and the negative prostate biopsy result.

You may face challenging times and walk through the valley of the shadow of death, whether it be physically or spiritually. These moments may be filled with uncertainty and anxiety. Be of great comfort, for God truly can give you peace.

Kathleen Kiem Hoa Oey Kuntaraf

This Is the Way; Walk in It

Whether you turn to the right or to the left, your ears will hear
a voice behind you, saying, "This is the way; walk in it." Isa. 30:21, NIV.

Have you ever wondered how to discern the voice of God and know what His will is for you? I grew up in Malaysia, and upon finishing secondary school I found myself among the many thousand 17-year-olds in the National Service. We would have to attend an army camp for a period of three months, during which we would undergo several different types of training such as marching, shooting, obstacle courses, and survival techniques.

These were the first few months I spent away from home, isolated from my computer and mobile phone while being thrown into a world of dodgy facilities, unpalatable food, and interracial drama. The first week the dorms were infested with locusts and frogs, and our showers didn't work until the third month. I remember half our camp being rushed to the hospital in a mass ambulance convoy because of food poisoning; fortunately, I had not eaten dinner that night.

However, what was most amazing was that God had found me in all of this and taken this opportunity to call my name and speak His will.

In the first week the Christian students were told to elect a leader. The duties were to gather the students for the weekly church excursion as well as organize Christian activities two nights a week. Among us I saw many confident Christian youths with eager looks on their face, some of whom had been Christians for many years and were leaders in their churches. As for me, the only time I had set foot in church had been the odd Christmas that my parents agreed to go.

Then a girl whom I had never even spoken to before suddenly said, "Lianne should be the leader." Oddly enough, the decision was unanimous—and I knew I had heard the voice of God.

I was thrown into a new world, one so amazing that I wished I had known God sooner. The Lord blessed me with great support from those who taught me, guided me, and prayed with me. Together we planned fellowship and outreach activities to nurture the Christian youths.

I left the National Service camp feeling rather sad, as a small part of my journey had to come to an end. However, I knew it was time to continue my walk with God. Over the years I have heard His voice many times, telling me that "this is the way; walk in it." I pray that you too will hear His gentle prompting and may be able to walk in the way He has prepared for you.

Lianne Zilm

The Seize

Entrust your efforts to the Lord, and your plans will succeed. Prov. 16:3, GW.

It was in October 1982 when my call to serve as English teacher in Wollega Adventist Academy, Ethiopia, was finalized. I was then working as secretary to the dean of students at Philippine Union College (PUC) (now Adventist University of the Philippines).

Every now and then I would go to Manila to process my papers. One Friday afternoon I was delayed coming back to PUC, which was at least two hours from Manila. I reached Balibago, the barrio before the college, at past 7:00 in the evening. Normally there were still jeepneys (the local Philippine transportation) available at that time. However, when I asked people about a ride to my destination, they said the last jeepney had left just a few minutes before my arrival.

Two military men who were eating in a restaurant heard my inquiry, and they came to offer me a ride. Camp Castaneda is only a few kilometers away from the college, and they had a car. I respectfully refused their offer and prayed to God for a safe ride back to the college.

Pretty soon a young man called me. He was a student at the college and was also waiting for a ride. I told him about the offer from the men, and he told me to ask the men if they'd be willing to give him a ride as well. So with mounting courage I called the men and asked them to take my student with me. One of the men grabbed my bag and said that the ride was only for me. I seized my bag back, and for a few seconds my bag went back and forth. Then the student spotted the PUC truck and hailed it, saying that he and I needed a ride. He then ran to my rescue, and we both boarded the truck.

Was I scared! I'd never been that scared in all my life. I couldn't imagine what could have happened to me had I ridden with those drunk men. Back in 1982, all the way from Balibago to PUC tall sugar cane grew on both sides of the road. When I think about it, I am convinced that it was not only my plan but God's plan as well that I serve Him as a missionary in Ethiopia, where I served for 18 years as English teacher, librarian, and choir director. Praise God for rescuing me from trouble and giving me the opportunity of serving Him in a foreign land. I entrusted my plans to God, and He did make me succeed.

Forsythia Catane Galgao

Is It Over?*

Even so it is not the will of your Father which is in heaven, that one of these little ones should perish. Matt. 18:14.

My favorite weekends include a visit from our grandchildren. While Heather still prefers to stay close to home, her 3-year-old brother, Ryan, is always eager to spend the night at our house. He has a bedroom that he calls his own, but lately he's become conveniently convinced that there are wolves upstairs. He's "heard" them growl, and he's even seen their *big* eyes! No amount of convincing has erased his fear of a night visit from the wolves. So we came up with the idea of using the mattress from the guest room crib to make him a bed on the floor beside Grandpa and Grandma's bed. Need I say that this was a very popular decision? One night the three of us knelt to pray that the wolves would be kept at bay. We had showered Ryan with hugs and kisses. I had just tucked in his covers when I felt a little hand reach out for mine. "Let's hold hands, Grammie," he said. So we did.

It seemed that only a short time had passed when I opened my eyes. Through streams of morning light creeping in around the shades, I saw Ryan watching me. He was kneeling on his bed, and his big blue eyes just cleared the top of our mattress. He asked me a simple question: "Is it over?" Now, in his mind that meant "Is the long, dark, dull night over?" That period of time when play ceases, and Grandpa lies still in his bed instead of playing hide-and-seek? To a 3-year-old, the arrival of morning is incredibly wonderful news! As for me, I can't remember a night that felt too long! But I couldn't help smiling at my grandson.

"Yes, Ryan," I said. "It's over!"

Sometimes, like little Ryan wishing away the danger and darkness of night, I feel like crying, "Lord, is it over?" Because I'm tired of the pain I see and the separation and the hurtful situations people experience in this world. But then, when someone I love isn't walking with the Lord, or when I sense my own need to come closer to Him, I want to plead, "Lord, wait a little longer." Our heavenly Father alone knows the best time for our "night" to be over. In the meantime, He's given us today to get ready for the glorious morning of His soon coming.

Rose Otis

---

*From *Among Friends* (Review and Herald Publishing Assn., 1992), pp. 353, 354.

Judge Not

*Do not judge, or you too will be judged. For in the same way
you judge others, you will be judged, and with the measure you use,
it will be measured to you. Matt. 7:1, 2, NIV.*

Some years ago my husband and I visited the United States. While there we decided to take a bus to visit a Christian bookstore. We had never been on an American bus before, so when we got on we asked the woman bus driver for a ticket. She was rather rude and didn't seem to realize we were from abroad; she pointed to a big piece of machinery where we were supposed to insert a dollar. After such a welcome, I hardly dared to ask her to let us know when we reached our stop.

We sat down and waited for her call. While we were in the bus it started to rain, and then the rain came down harder and harder by the minute. It was nearly torrential by the time our stop arrived. We stood and prepared to leave the bus, and as we did, we thanked the driver. But she called me back, and I thought, *What have I done wrong now?* But she turned around and rummaged behind her and handed me an umbrella and then called my husband and gave him a cap, which had obviously been given to her; it had an inscription of bus driver of the year 2007. She showed us where to get on again for the return journey and showed us where the store was.

After a bad start I found to my shame that I had totally misjudged this woman. She was not awful at all—in fact, she went above and beyond to help us.

Sometimes we make snap judgments about people without really taking time to get to know them or give them the opportunity to prove otherwise. This whole experience was a learning experience for me. When dealing with people in life, we need to be patient and kind and give people the benefit of the doubt. People can end up surprising us that way. That is what I love about Jesus: He was always giving people the benefit of the doubt. He didn't judge people, but accepted them for who they were.

It is interesting that James writes: "Don't grumble against one another, brothers and sisters, or you will be judged. The Judge is standing at the door!" (James 5:9, NIV). It is only Christ who can judge rightly. My prayer for each and every one of us is that we will not judge but be more like Jesus, who loved people for who they were.

Clair Sanches-Schutte

Stacey

I can do all things through Christ who strengthens me. Phil. 4:13, NKJV.

There she was, all 45 pounds of her, lying in the upper part of a recliner. Her thin little arms flailed a bit, swinging tightly curled tiny hands. One look told me something had gone terribly wrong in her small body. I was shocked to learn she was 22 years old.

As a hospice caregiver, I soon learned that this was not a hospice case. A friend had given my name to a mother desperate for relief care. Cheri, her mother, had cared for Stacey from birth, but the 24/7 care was taking a toll on her. She shared with me the sad story of Stacey's condition: spastic quadriplegic cerebral palsy with severe scoliosis.

I had had patients die while holding their hand, but this was more than I thought I could cope with. How could I graciously retreat and escape the whole situation?

I heard myself say, "I've never worked with anyone like Stacey. You'll have to be patient with me while I learn to care for her." A glimmer of hope crossed Cheri's face as I suggested a two-week trial, with the stipulation that if I could not give Stacey proper care, other arrangements would need to be made. Cheri's broad smile left me no option but to try, and try hard.

The next two weeks were a blur of learning to hold, diaper, and position Stacey while trying to keep the feeding tube from popping out of her stomach. Though she'd never spoken a word, Stacey's flashing smile meant she was comfortable while her grimaces indicated she was not. For the next three years Stacy became my weekly focus. She won me over with her extreme needs. My apprehension of caring for someone so deformed lessened. My attitude toward people with handicaps dramatically changed. Stacey was just what God knew I needed.

In a world where we're attracted to beautiful babies, flawless skin, and healthy, well-formed bodies, people who are wrecked and broken can repulse us. I was guilty. Those who are unattractive are often overlooked and ignored when they are the very ones most in need of compassion. The world is in need of people who will love the unlovely and give attention and smiles to those who least expect it.

I am eager to see Stacey in heaven, all made new. May God give us the ability to love both the lovely and the unlovely.

Marybeth Gessele

Mercy Came Running

*The angel of the Lord encampeth round about them
that fear him, and delivereth them. Ps. 34:7.*

I work as a home-care nurse in New York City. Two of my experiences have profoundly impacted me as I went home-to-home caring for patients. These experiences were moments of great praise to God and humility at the awesomeness of the God I serve.

After exiting the home of a patient in a not-so-nice section of town, I immediately felt in my pocket for my car keys—they were not there. Immediately a sense of panic gripped me, because I knew it meant I had misplaced them. I looked in the car; the keys were in the cup holder. *What do I do?* I had no one to call who could come immediately to help me, and I foolishly neglected to renew my automobile emergency policy. After a few minutes I saw a well-dressed man exiting a home two doors away. I immediately approached him and asked for help. He turned away saying he could not help, got in his car, and drove away. I went back to my car; as I stood there I started to pray.

A car pulled up, pumping hip-hop music. A young man exited the home talking on the phone and using very colorful language. He got in the car; both men looked at me, pulled up beside me, and asked me if I needed help. I related my dilemma. They immediately got out and ran inside to get some apparatus to help. After struggling for some time, some of their friends pulled up in a car with a fragrant odor. They started helping until they successfully opened my car door. As I stood there I realized I did not have much money on me, and I wondered what they would ask for. I took all the money in my purse and offered it to them, but they walked away; they didn't want any money! I was floored. I prayed a blessing on their lives.

On another occasion I pulled out of a parking spot on a narrow two-lane street. In going around a car I scratched a parked car. *How am I going to pay for this*? I then saw a young man across the street. He asked me if I hit the car. When I said yes, he said it was OK, it was his and don't worry about it! It brought tears to my eyes; I thought, *Who does that in New York City?*

The grace, mercy, and protection God affords is amazing! He sends angels to deliver and shield me—and you. What an awe-inspiring God!

Mitzie Knight

Who Are You?

And then will I declare to them, "I never knew you." Matt. 7:23, RSV.

Many years ago, as a junior member of a symphony support group, I was asked to help host a backstage reception for season ticket holders. I barely knew one instrument from another, a bass from a bassoon, but I loved the concerts and really enjoyed the company of other music lovers. So I easily agreed to this pleasant assignment, never guessing the embarrassment in store—and the important lesson I would learn from it.

As I mingled among the guests, I noticed an elderly couple standing off to one side, clearly out of their comfort zone in the jovial, milling crowd. I was drawn to them, touched by their wide-eyed awe and humble hesitancy. They seemed genuinely grateful as I smiled my way into conversation and in due time they were at ease enough to surprise me with an unexpected request: "Is there any way we can meet the maestro?" It was a subject not covered in the brief orientation I had received earlier.

Feeling now the weight of their unwarranted confidence in me, I quickly assured them that I would be happy to arrange their introduction, and set off through the crowd to fetch the maestro, a particularly daunting task since I didn't know him any better than they did.

I'm not sure if they sensed my clammy discomfort as I feigned breezy familiarity through the formal introduction, but they could not have missed the telling words that followed. At the conclusion of those several cordial, if awkward moments, the maestro turned to face me squarely and with a crooked grin asked lightly, "And who are you?"

My chagrin eventually faded, of course, but the unexpected insight it fostered has continued to burn brightly through my latter years of Christian service. How many of us, I have wondered, are risking eternal embarrassment as we embrace the church and all its lively functions without actually knowing its Master, Jesus Christ?

Do you remember the story of the 10 virgins found in Matthew? These young women were looking for the Master, but when they knocked on the door, he had to say, "Truly I tell you, I don't know you" (Matt. 25:12, NIV). How eternally sad. Oh, to know Him as a friend and bring all seeking hearts to Him!

Patricia Kay

The Gift of Waiting

But they that wait upon the Lord shall renew their strength;
they shall mount up with wings as eagles; they shall run,
and not be weary; and they shall walk, and not faint. Isa. 40:31.

I have never really liked waiting . . . waiting for the doctor, the dentist, the bus, the security check in the airport. I was too busy getting on with my life to waste time waiting! I was impatient, and delays were just frustrating. But something has changed. Maybe it's because I'm getting older. Maybe it's because I've learned to appreciate the gift of waiting. Maybe it's because we are renovating part of our old Victorian house and our home has been disrupted by dust, workmen, and a fair amount of chaos. And now I find waiting is no longer an irritating obstacle in my busy day—it's an unexpected treasure, an oasis, even a delight.

This week I intentionally booked a flight with a long stopover in a basic airport. There is just one simple café and an hour of free Internet connection. For the first time I found myself looking forward to spending a few hours there. It even feels a little luxurious to plan this waiting time—a clear space where I can work on a writing project that I'm really enjoying. No interruptions, no expectations, no dust nagging away at me in the background. Surprisingly peaceful and delightful . . . A gift.

I am learning that waiting time gives me space to be still, to think, to pray, to untangle the overbusy parts of my life, to breathe, to be refreshed. I can choose to be stressed and annoyed by waiting, or I can accept it as a gift from God to bless me with His love. I can be irritated when an appointment runs late, or I can use the time to let God's love soak through my tired and aching heart. I can be stressed when my bus is delayed, or I can look at the tree next to me and be filled with wonder at God's creation. Or talk to an elderly gentleman who is alone in the world.

As a human being I need to have waiting rooms, stopovers, and delays. I need some unfilled spaces in my diary where I can come up for breath and be reenergized. I need to stop rushing from one activity to the next, becoming tired and irritable. I need to learn how to wait for God's timing in my life. I need to experience the strength I gain from the gift of waiting on the Lord, so that I can experience the joy of learning to fly with the power and strength of an eagle.

Where will you wait for God today and then fly with Him on your eagle's wings?

Karen Holford

Choose Weakness

But he said to me, "My grace is sufficient for you, for my power is made perfect in weakness." Therefore I will boast all the more gladly of my weaknesses, so that the power of Christ may rest upon me. 2 Cor. 12:9, ESV.

I am a recovering perfectionist. As a true Martha Stewart "wannabe," I saw to it that every dinner event, birthday party, or play date was planned perfectly, and the napkins folded just so. A few years ago God knew it was time to launch an intervention in my life, but He did it subtly over the course of more than a year.

In the fall a few years ago I listened to one of my colleagues deliver a convocation address entitled "Choosing Weakness." In his presentation he reflected on his experiences needing and accepting help during a long illness, and he posed the question "What if, rather than pretending to be strong and hiding our weaknesses from others, we embraced it, chose to be vulnerable, admitted and owned our own and others' limitations?" Several months later, as I sat waiting my turn at the hair salon, I absentmindedly picked up an issue of *Architectural Digest* and came across the words of Gil Schafer: "True authenticity is a lack of perfection." Finally, my "aha" moment came in October of 2012 as I sat listening to the keynote by Brené Brown at a women's conference in Denver. In her remarks Brown suggested that vulnerability is not weakness; it is at the center of meaningful human experiences. Right there in that conference hall I wanted to shout out: "Lord, I get it!"

Thank You, Lord, for teaching me that our loved ones do not need perfection from us. Rather if we are strong enough to let go of the facades and reveal our authentic selves, that is where we can make the deepest human connections. In choosing to be vulnerable, we break down walls that get in the way of real intimacy, walls that suggest that I am somehow better than you, more beautiful, or even more righteous. What if, instead, we humbly admitted our flaws to others, admitted that we too make mistakes, that on some days the laundry remains undone, dirty dishes pile up in the sink, and our house is a mess? What if we choose today to be the first to say: "I was wrong" or "I am so sorry I did that"? What if we presented ourselves to each other simply as a fellow traveler in need of a Savior? Will you choose weakness today?

Kathy-Ann C. Hernandez

Dinosaurs, Cliques, and Other Quirks of Nature

When I was a child, I spoke and thought and reasoned as a child. But when I grew up, I put away childish things. Now we see things imperfectly, like puzzling reflections in a mirror, but then we will see everything with perfect clarity. All that I know now is partial and incomplete, but then I will know everything completely, just as God now knows me completely. 1 Cor. 13:11, 12, NLT.

As a group of high school friends sat around my picnic table, eating and chatting, Sarah* turned to me and said, "Bonita, my daughter loves dinosaurs. While she was at summer camp, some kid told her dinosaurs were created by Satan. What do you think?"

After discussing archaeology, antediluvians, and amalgamations, we were all in agreement on one thing: the idea of Satan creating dinosaurs was ludicrous! Which spawned, of course, a discussion about extremes in the church.

My other friend, Mary,* elaborated on how she's decided not to send her kids to the school associated with her church. Her friend, who is also sending her children elsewhere, said, "You know, that church is so large and unfriendly. I've never felt as though I belonged there." Mary looked at me and said, "You know, I always considered her an 'insider.' I'm shocked."

Sarah and Mary were part of our class's clique. Adjectives to describe The clique could include loud, boisterous, *intimidating*. This group created "names" for everyone on campus—and not always flattering ones. Even though almost 30 years had passed, the little child within me needed to know *my* name. So I asked, "Mary, what was *my* name? What did you call *me?*"

She looked at me, paused, and said, "We didn't have one for you. I think we respected you too much." I pondered that for a few moments.

"You know, Mary," I said, "that reminds me of the church situation we were just talking about. I thought *you* were the insiders. You thought your friend was an insider. She thought others were the insiders. But we're all just trying to find a place to belong, aren't we?"

Whether we see dinosaurs, cliques, or other quirks of nature that we don't understand, know, or see, we tend to place labels on them: "They were created by Satan" or "They're loud, intimidating people." But when we put aside our childish thoughts and insecurities and grow into maturity, we can seek to understand and know others as we ourselves want to be understood. Our mirror becomes less puzzling, and we begin to see ourselves, others, and God more clearly.

Bonita Joyner Shields

*not their real names

Wrongly Accused

Stand therefore, having your loins girt about with truth,
and having on the breastplate of righteousness. Eph. 6:14.

To be wrongly accused is a most painful experience that one can endure for any reason; it causes hurt and pain, and often damages the character. Sometimes a person will accuse others to protect themselves, to present a better picture of who they are, or, out of spite, to hurt and destroy because they believe they have been wronged. The individual on the receiving end is left with burdens to bear, tarnished character to clear, and wounds to heal. Sometimes the circumstances are such that words cannot be spoken to explain or create a defense to redeem one's self. It takes the grace of God to break through barriers, and a will to succeed to move forward. It is therefore comforting to know that the Holy Spirit intercedes on our behalf and knows our groaning that comes from the depths of our hearts.

As I consider the words "wrongly accused," I immediately think of Jesus. What better example is there for us? There are many persons among us who have endured the burden of being wrongly accused, but because Jesus Christ bore the shame and agony on the cross to redeem us, we have hope of being healed and delivered. Jesus was wrongly accused out of selfishness, greed, and a push for power by the leaders and followers in the Jewish community. We read of His experience so often that if we are not careful it becomes a mockery to our ear, and we are encouraged by such a spirit to reject the very nature of God. When we cannot understand the circumstances in which we are wrongly accused, when we have to accept and love those who accuse us wrongly, when we are burdened and oppressed by cares after our character is tarnished and our pride broken, it is only in our favor to fall on our knees before God and beg for mercy as we seek His help to bear the cross placed upon our lives. Not everyone's cross is the same, but Jesus bid us, "If anyone would come after me, let him deny himself and take up his cross and follow me" (Matt. 16:24, ESV). Will you follow Jesus today? Remember He too was wrongly accused.

It is when we have been falsely accused that we are led to seek God's help and grace. We find comfort and solace and understanding in the experience of our Lord and Savior.

Elizabeth Ida Cain

Breathe

*I am the one who has seen the afflictions
that come from the rod of the Lord's anger. Lam. 3:1, NLT.*

Have you held a child's last breath? A soft whisper that you can't quite hold on to. Holding your breath, waiting for just one more of theirs. Just one more.

Have you heard the piercing, gut-wrenching cry when the parent realizes it was the last? A sound that shakes your very soul and you do not know if you can breathe through their pain. A sound that drains the entire room of hope and air.

A lament is a cry of suffering. Jeremiah is crying, screaming with his whole being at the suffering of his people. He holds the dead child in the street and wails with that gut-wrenching sound of loss that you can understand only if you have lost. Then he walks to the next body and brushes the hair back from the gaunt face, and his grief is a wellspring that has no end. His own beatings and pain are nothing; it is for the people he loves that his heart breaks.

From his heart he cries out to God who has allowed all this suffering, and I can hear him bellow from between every heartbreaking line, "You are God." Over and over he tries to accept that God is God, and all things are His. Good and bad. Lamentations is a book reciting the pain and suffering of Jeremiah's time, and he says, "The Lord's love never ends. His mercies never stop."

In the dirt Jeremiah sits beside a crumpled body half eaten by the hot sun with the stench of decay all around him. He is bruised and sore from his last beating, and the tears flow from a swollen, blackened eye, as he whispers: "It is good to wait quietly for salvation from the Lord" (Lam. 3:26, NLT). In the heat and dirt and decay he has learned to breathe. To breathe in and breathe out, and even here God is. Jeremiah ends by exclaiming, "I will never forget this awful time, as I grieve over my loss. Yet I still dare to hope when I remember this: The faithful love of the Lord never ends! His mercies never cease. Great is his faithfulness" (verses 20-23, NLT).

I do not know where you are today, but I know where God is, and He knows where we are and what we face. There are times I know nothing else. My heart beats and my lungs fill and I only know, God is.

Selena Blackburn

No Birthday Cake With Candles

Whosoever shall receive this child in my name receiveth me: and whosoever shall receive me receiveth him that sent me: for he that is least among you all, the same shall be great. Luke 9:48.

It was a birthday never to be forgotten. My two daughters wanted to do something exceptional for my special day. What could they do that would be different? Days later they came up with the idea that would never be forgotten. By letters, telephone calls, e-mails, Facebook, any form of communication, they contacted people; each person contacted would have ample time to get a card in the mail to prepare my ninetieth birthday surprise. My girls set a goal of 90 cards, one for each year. Everyone contacted was delighted to take part. I had no idea what they were planning and expected an ordinary day to be spent with family, a few birthday cards from friends, and a big birthday cake.

However, when the big day arrived, I opened many, many cards from friends, family, relatives, church members, neighbors, acquaintances who were having as much fun as I was. My girls had contacted so many people that the results surpassed their expectations.

There were cards from people I had forgotten, now grown up, who recalled incidents from years gone by, schoolmates, relatives, business acquaintances, neighbors—all happy to take part in a birthday celebration for a 90-year-old. Cards continued to arrive for days afterward, making each day special.

One incident stirred a memory as a friend remembered the annual corn-husking day. Every year I bought several burlap bags of fresh corn from the farmer's market to be prepared for the freezer. We called every available child in the neighborhood to help us get the corn ready for the freezer. Each child was allowed to eat as much corn as they wanted as it came from the steamer. What was left was packaged and put away for winter use. It was such fun reminiscing about the corn fest and learning about families and friends from their notes on the birthday cards.

I wonder if Jesus Christ knows how special He is as we wait for His special day to arrive. What a day that will be as we wait in expectation. Because God is keeping it secret, we will all be surprised.

Laurie McClanahan

Legacy of Kindness

Put on then, as God's chosen ones, holy and beloved, compassionate hearts, kindness, humility, meekness, and patience, Col. 3:12, ESV.

Gifts of compassion, kindness, humility, meekness, and patience are wonderful blessings we acquire from individuals who cross our path. My mother, now deceased, has left me with wonderful memories. They are worth more than all the gold of Ophir, greater than precious onyx or lapis lazuli. Many years ago I watched her care for the downtrodden—or outcast as they are called at times. We ourselves were poor, but we had the wonderful love of God to share.

On one particular day a man who everyone called Mr. T came to our home. His speech was odd because of a cleft palate, and people made fun of him. Complicating his situation, he had a very large wound on his leg that had been there for a while and no one seemed to be taking good care of it. The wound had lots of rotting flesh; it actually smelled. I watched my mother pour water with disinfectant in a basin and proceeded to clean and dress the wound. I was 15 years old when she ministered to this unfortunate soul, and this left an indelible impression on me. After she completed this act of kindness, she proceeded to give him a nutritious meal, because she sensed that he was hungry. He expressed gratitude for all she did for him; and I know that Mr. T did not forget that act of kindness because he came frequently thereafter.

Today I find myself rendering care and assistance to individuals because I learned that valuable lesson from my mother. She cared dearly, she gave her all; and, while doing so, she wore a smile. This is what Christ wants us to do. He ministered to the sick, maimed, lame, blind, deaf, mute, and whatever other kinds of ailment beset individuals. Christ still ministers to individuals today, and there are times He comes in the form human agents. Our task is to follow His example, to have compassionate, humble hearts. Because we are God's chosen ones, we should never let an opportunity for service pass us by. He has promised that He will give us a heart to do His will; He will not force Himself on any of us. The Holy Spirit is at our heart's door prompting us to do His biddings. Will I, will you, listen and do what He wants us to do?

I will never forget the legacy my mother left me: compassion, kindness, humility, meekness, and patience.

Eveythe Kennedy Cargill

For the Love of Sisters

For it is God who works in you both to will and to do
for His good pleasure. Phil. 2:13, NKJV.

As a woman—even though I'm long past childbearing age—I possess a maternal instinct to aid my sisters, especially those who are younger. I've enjoyed many opportunities to do so over the years. And my life is joyful as a result.

The opportunities arise in unexpected ways. It's not that I go out seeking a particular sister; she simply comes into my life the same way that buds appear on the trees in springtime. Though I know the trees are there and that they bloom every year, I'm still amazed when a particular tree becomes mine to nurture. Of course, I do pray always for God to send someone I can mentor if it's His desire. He knows exactly the kinds of blossoms that I need to tend.

Sometimes we women get so busy that we may think we simply can't help with anyone else's life. We struggle enough to keep ourselves on track. Yet I find that busy or not, growing older or not, that when I'm involved mentoring another woman, my life also blossoms anew.

Light bearers is what today's section of Philippians 2 is subtitled in my New King James Version of the Bible. It doesn't refer to woman or man, but to "My beloved," as Paul calls his fellow Christians. With this consideration of other women, we women can serve by being a sister-friend, teaching, and bearing light for Him.

For most of us, the best way to mentor another is to use our talents. As a writer, I find that passing the torch of writing skills is rewarding: to see someone else learn to use words to bless others. So what is your talent, your skill? Do you share it with other women? Do you pray for someone to share it with?

One instance: following a tornado in our area of northwest Georgia, Jessi and I, a newly transferred member to the area, became acquainted when she started a free clothing ministry at our church to help victims of the twister. I was covering her story for the local press. She showed an interest in my work. In short, I taught her my writing class, and she found herself with two new ministries: *God's Closet*, and as my capable press writer assistant for the church and church school. We're two generations apart, but sisters in Christ, bearing light.

Betty Kossick

The Bell-shaped Cistern

So they drew up Jeremiah with cords . . . up out of the dungeon. Jer. 38:13.

Without outside intervention, it is virtually impossible to climb out of a cistern, especially one that is shaped like a bell. It was in a bell-shaped cistern that Jeremiah (the crying prophet), found himself. He was thrown into a dungeon because of his depressing and unpopular message. Though directly from God, his message was not accepted by his people. There was a famine raging throughout the land, and the people were dying of starvation. They wanted to hear something positive and uplifting, even if it meant Jeremiah telling lies.

Sometimes we find ourselves mired in the muddy depths of life's cistern, often through no fault of our own. We try to pull ourselves out and up one leg at a time only to find that the imbalance causes us to sink deeper with every attempt we make. When Jeremiah's enemies threw him into the cistern, it meant certain death, or so it seemed. All appeared hopeless. Everyone was fighting for his or her own survival. Who would remember a condemned prisoner? God did. God had other plans for Jeremiah that did not include his dying in a cistern. God often provides help from the most unlikely source. Sometimes glorious deliverance comes to us like a beautiful gift that is roughly packaged. Jeremiah's help came through Ebed-Melech, an Ethiopian eunuch employed in King Zedekiah's palace. It was neither Ebed-Melech's duty nor responsibility to aid Jeremiah. In fact he risked not only his employment but his very life in doing so.

When we find ourselves in life's cistern, as we surely will from time to time, we must hold tight to God's lifeline. God is able to hear our cry from the deepest pit of our despair. He is further able to use the most unlikely medium through which to answer our prayers. Inch by inch He will lift us up and out of the cistern.

We in turn must throw a lifeline to others. Like us, their cistern might be filled with sickness, loneliness, broken relationships, shattered dreams, or financial woes. A lifeline that connects to God will bring hope and encouragement. Having compassion for others will in turn help us to climb out of life's cistern of despair to face a new and brighter day. By God's grace I pray that this will be your goal today.

Avis Mae Rodney

God's Faithfulness

Before they call I will answer; while they are
still speaking I will hear. Isa. 65:24, NIV.

During a very stressful time in my life, God provided what I needed. As the nurse in the family, I had promised my mother that when she couldn't care for herself, I would care for her. When that time came, I took off work and cared for her until she died. As I prepared to get her house ready to sell, I prayed that God would open up a position of His choosing for me, and if possible, in the line of nursing I had done before, as I needed to return to work. I had worked in a nurse-family partnership in which nurses mentor first-time mothers, and I loved it.

Three months later I called the program site developer in Denver and asked if there were any new openings in Tennessee or Arizona. The program had not yet started in those areas, but that was where we were living. A message from the site developer that told of an opening in Prescott Valley, Arizona, gave me goose bumps! After appropriate phone calls, sending my résumé, and an interview, I was valued for my previous experience in the program and was hired for this new site. When I found out that the position had first been placed online in February, the time my mother passed away, I *knew* that God had provided for me before I asked! What a remarkable God!

During this time my marriage was also failing, and I didn't know the outcome. I moved to Prescott Valley alone. While praying and trusting, my days and adjustments were challenging and painful. One day as I drove around town, trying to find a place to live, I became aware that I was feeling "happy." *What am I feeling?* With everything going on in my life, I thought, *Why would I be feeling happy*? Then I remembered the verse "But the fruit of the Spirit is love, joy, peace . . ." (Gal. 5:22). Suddenly I knew that God was reassuring me that He would be with me in this new place. With tears I burst out with "Thank You, thank You, thank You!" What an awesome God we have!

There were many days when tears came quickly, but also days of feeling God's joy and His peace! I experienced— and am still learning day by day—that "the joy of the Lord is [my] strength" (Neh. 8:10). I don't remember where I heard this, maybe the words of a song: "The joy of the journey is God's faithfulness." It is really true regardless of the source.

Eileen Snell

Dusty, Grimy, and Calloused

How beautiful are the feet of them that preach the gospel
of peace, and bring glad tidings of good things! Rom. 10:15.

I was the guest speaker at the first-ever Trans-Pacific women's congress in the Fiji Islands. The opening ceremony would begin momentarily, and numerous invited government officials were participating. The Fiji heat and humidity was at its peak as we waited to be seated on the outdoor platform. Admiring the women's lovely native attire, I was surprised that they were almost all barefoot. I glanced at the platform guests, and not one of them had shoes on. *Am I supposed to have bare feet, too?* I wondered. *My feet are unsightly!* I was panic-stricken.

The host approached me and whispered, "Keep your shoes on. It's OK; you are a guest." Relieved, I nodded and quickly followed her to my seat, embarrassed that she had seen my distressed look. I tucked my feet under my chair, glancing closer at the dusty, grimy, and calloused feet of the platform guests and the attendees—far from pretty by American standards.

During the week I met women from Samoa, Tonga, Eastern Solomon Islands, Fiji, and other Pacific islands. They welcomed me with genuineness, warm smiles, and generous hugs. To enjoy fellowship with their Christian sisters, they had walked long, dusty roads or traveled by small boats. A wave of guilt swept over me as I recalled my initial perception of their feet: ugly!

Every morning the women, up before dawn, sang rousing songs as they walked happily to the prayer sessions, the oppressive heat already evident. During the day some checked on me briefly at my air-conditioned guest quarters on the hill to make sure all was well, then walked the path back to their cramped, non-air-conditioned rooms with thin mats on the floor. The women treated me lovingly and showered me with handmade treasures still close to my heart today.

In the six days we spent together, I was blessed immensely. I saw real humility, beautiful godly women, and true Christian spirits unmatched by any other women I'd met. Yes, I was sent to preach the gospel to them, but the loveliness of their spirits ministered to me, drew me closer to God, and allowed His Spirit to take control of my thoughts.

I praise God that we—dusty, grimy, and calloused—can be beautiful from our heads to our feet as we let His Spirit dwell in us.

Iris L. Kitching

Grandma, Granny, and G-Ma

Behold, children are a heritage from the Lord. Ps. 127:3, NKJV.

I have three beautiful granddaughters, and they each have a different affectionate name for me. Tyra, age 14, calls me Grandma (rolling her "r"); Najja (Ni-ya), age 17, calls me Granny; and Ammi (Ah-mee), 21, calls me G-Ma. They feel special having their own cool name for me.

Our monthly Granny 'n' Girls luncheons and shopping sprees are very special. This is a time of bonding, telling stories, and catching up on what's going on in our lives. We talk about their moms and what they were like as children. They like to hear stories of how their moms were just like them. We have lots of fun!

My grandchildren love me with all their hearts as evidenced by their lack of inhibition to talk with me about anything! Some of the things we talk about I would never have talked about with my mother.

In all honesty we older folk enjoy many of the techno-tools that they "just can't live without." They can't imagine life before remote controls, color TV, computers, and cell phones. They get a good laugh when I tell them about the good ole days, and I get a good laugh too. Actually, I'm thankful that I get to enjoy these modern conveniences and that some things of the good old days are gone.

Friends ask why I allow them to call me G-Ma, Granny, and especially Grandma (makes them feel old). They prefer cuter names like Nana and Mimi. Grandparenting is the best! You get another chance to get it right and, in most cases, you can always "send them home" LOL ("cool" new acronyms).

Displaying the character of Christ, helping them understand Bible principles as a guide for their lives, and giving them unconditional love is the best of what I can give. Regardless of whatever else they call me, my prayer is that they will always call me a woman of God.

God never changes, and His Word remains the only principle by which we are to raise our children. We must do so understanding the present-day environments in which they live. Theirs is a world of vast instant information and technology. Always remember that your children and grandchildren are first and foremost "a heritage from the Lord." That's a great place to start.

Edna Thomas Taylor

God Cares

He healeth the broken in heart, and bindeth up their wounds. Ps. 147:3.

The year 2011 was not a good year for me. The ringing of my phone woke me up in the middle of one September night. It was the nursing sister in charge of the old age home where my husband was a patient. She said, "Your husband has breathing problems, so we're rushing him to the hospital. Please don't phone till after 11:00 a.m." Now I was wide awake.

At 11:00 my cell phone rang, and this time the sister told me to which hospital he was admitted. I phoned my son, and we rushed to the hospital. We were too late. There were no goodbyes.

I notified the family immediately. My youngest daughter arrived from the United States a month later. Unfortunately, she had experienced a crash of her once-happy life, and the shock of her father's demise was like the last straw. She had suffered a psychotic breakdown while still in the States. I didn't realize how ill she was until she arrived at my home. I suffered weeks of trauma.

Psalm 55 was my daily prayer as I cried to the Lord. I questioned, *Lord, why do I have to go through all this? First my husband's illness and demise, and then the trauma of my daughter's mental illness. Why, Lord?* Life deals us all different blows, but in all its perplexities there is one constant that we can depend on: Jesus, our Savior. And He came through so amazingly. After my daughter got a month's treatment in the hospital she was her sweet, loving self again.

The holiday period with its special days came. Our wedding anniversary was not to be. The memories came flooding back as I thought of our wedding day, December 13, 1970.

I had to get my thoughts in a new direction. I tried my hand at gardening. I bought packets of zinnia and portulaca seeds and planted them to border the path. Pretty soon the zinnias bloomed in all their bright beauty, but I saw no life from the portulaca.

I was feeling so sad thinking of 2011 and all its problems; I thought, *What will the new year bring?* Then I saw my first portulaca flower bloom. A very pretty pink blossom on the first day of the new year here in the Southern Hemisphere. I said, "Thank You, Lord, for sending this long-awaited pretty flower to show You love and care for me. Teach me patience to wait on You. Your timing is always perfect. May I always trust You."

Priscilla A. Adonis

Perfect Peace

You will keep him in perfect peace, whose mind is stayed on You, because he trusts in You. Isa. 26:3, NKJV.

I've never been closer to God," my husband reassured his brother, "so if it's my time to go, I'm ready." He said his goodbyes, hung up the phone, and closed his eyes. Sitting next to his hospital bed, I wanted to scream, "I'm not ready! Don't you dare speak about dying!" Instead—with the robotic efficiency I had exercised over the past several days—I rose, silently pulled the covers over his shoulders, and kissed his fevered forehead. This was his third battle in 20 years with a baffling condition of sudden-onset septicemia. Strep B resides in his body—hiding from the best infectious disease specialists. It nearly killed him twice before. Now, my precious J.D. hovered over death's threshold again. Well-meaning friends said, "J.D. is doing too much for the Lord. God won't let him die!" Their words provided no solace. For six months I had prayed with a young pastor's wife regarding her husband's slow dance with death. He too was a mighty warrior for God. He had a 7-year-old daughter. He died.

The weekend J.D. fell ill I was speaking at a church in Alabama. I delivered a three-part message on faith and "earnest" prayer. But, facing this emergency, I managed only to offer constant little gasps of prayer—simple cries for help. When I returned to my hotel room late that night, God wouldn't allow me to stay at arm's distance any longer. Praying an earnest and lengthy prayer, the dam broke and I sobbed uncontrollably, begging God to save my husband. Following 30 minutes of frantic pleas, I was surprised to hear myself say, "Father, You know the end from the beginning. I don't. If you see that by raising J.D. from his sickbed, he might someday drift away from You, please take him now. I know You have his eternal benefit in mind. Forgive me for not trusting You." My focus was returned to the Author and Finisher of my faith. A sudden calm came over me. Trust in God provided complete comfort. No matter what happened, His loving arms were beneath us. The battle raged on for more than two months, but God raised my husband to health once again.

What is your emotional struggle? I counsel you to let God be God. Trust Him, and He will keep you in perfect peace.

Shelley Quinn

My Naturalization

*But while they were on their way to buy the oil, the bridegroom arrived.
The virgins who were ready went in with him to the wedding banquet.
And the door was shut. Later the others also came. "Lord, Lord,"
they said, "open the door for us!" Matt. 25:10, 11, NIV.*

The district we live in is one of the few districts in Germany where each year the newly naturalized citizens are invited to a reception. Receiving German citizenship is not just a bit of paperwork. It is the expression of the wish to become part of the life of the country with all its different aspects and the intention of bringing a contribution.

I received an invitation from the district magistrate to a reception in the Stauffenberg castle, because I had received my German citizenship during the past year. The ceremony began with German punctuality at 5:00 p.m. The door was closed, and a brass ensemble played. Then there was a knock at the door, and belated invitees entered. They had missed the beginning of the ceremony and were a disturbance. After that there was peace for a while until there was another knock at the door, and another, and another as the last people came in very late. I considered it a lack of respect toward the magistrate and his staff. I wished they had locked the door.

As I listened to the speech I mused about the parable of the 10 bridesmaids. The young women who were ready and waiting for the bridegroom were able to enter the wedding room with the groom. Then the door was closed. The other bridesmaids were not there at the right time and could not enter later however hard they knocked at the door.

At this ceremony my naturalization became more than a piece of paperwork. I had become part of a new people. I was inside. I now have to identify with my new nation. I realized that I could no longer say, "You Germans . . ." It was such an emotional experience for me that tears rolled down my cheeks and my voice failed when the national anthem was sung. Finally I belonged. I had lived in Germany for more than 40 years as an alien, practically like an observer.

A question arises in my mind. Do I really identify myself as a Christian belonging to God's people or have I kept the status of the external observer? Do I still speak about the church from the perspective of the observer? Do I really want to belong to God's kingdom with all its privileges and duties? Am I an active part of God's people?

Hannele Ottschofski

Always in Service!

Before they call I will answer; while they are
still speaking I will hear. Isa. 65:24, NIV.

"May I check for voice mail messages?" asked Melissa, her little face turned up toward me, her expression hopeful. She loved checking for messages on my new iPhone, and she was waiting for a call from her parents. Since I was driving, my response was "Certainly. My cell is in the outside zip pocket of my purse."

Melissa was busy for a few moments finding the phone. I heard her murmur under her breath, *Slide to open.* A sigh of contentment escaped her lips as the screen lit up appropriately. She continued murmuring to herself: *Press phone. Press recents. Press voicemail.* The little girl was so earnest. I smiled to myself and thought, *I'll just bet her next Christmas wish list has an iPhone on it. Not that any of us think she's really old enough to have one of her own.*

A moment later I heard another sigh, not of contentment, along with the words: "Oh, no! It says No Service! That's extremely unfortunate!" Melissa emphasized the last two words. I glanced at her face. Now it was wreathed in disappointment. I kept my face solemn. (Well, I tried to!) Melissa's love of big words was a constant source of amusement and pleasure for me, but there were times to chuckle and times not to. Melissa gazed out the window.

"We could play one of our games," I suggested, breaking the silence. "While we wait for service." No response. "How about 'What am I thankful for'?"

"That's easy," said Melissa, brightening. "I'm thankful God's iPhone is always in service. There's no wait to communicate!" (How Melissa loved rhyming words! This was yet another of her spontaneous little lines. If I had only started writing them down the first time one crossed her little lips, I'd have quite a collection by now.)

Fifteen minutes and several rounds of the "I'm thankful for" game, service was restored. And joy of joys, there was a voicemail message from her parents.

As Melissa chattered away, part of my mind was on driving, part was pondering her words: "There's no wait to communicate." How very true. God's iPhone is always in service, ready for our call. Blessing of blessings. When did *you* last communicate? How about now? There's no waiting.

Arlene R. Taylor

The Faith of a Child

"Assuredly, I say to you, unless you are converted and become as little children, you will by no means enter the kingdom of heaven." Matt. 18:3, NKJV.

Not long after pondering this text during my devotional time one morning, I learned this lesson from my very own child. While cleaning house one day, I decided to give my two parakeets a break from their cage. As I often would do, that morning I let them perch on our floor-length wicker mirror. Delilah, true to her routine, climbed down to the bottom and sat gazing into the mirror serenading herself. Samson, true to his routine, stayed at the top. With chest held high and singing at the top of his lungs, he proclaimed, "Hey, look at me—I'm king!"

But this particular day I heard more than their normal enjoyable singing. As I was about to finish my duties upstairs, I heard a shrill scream. My dog had happened upon the parakeets and decided it was time for a picnic lunch! By the time I removed Delilah from the jaws of death she was in terrible shape. Her tail feathers and part of her back end were missing. She had an apparently fatal gaping wound to her chest. Humanly speaking, there was no hope for this poor bird. The kids and I were all crying. Kaylie, my 7-year-old daughter, was sobbing pitifully! Between the wails of grief, my husband said that in mercy we should put the parakeet out of her misery. That's when Kaylie piped in, "No, Daddy! God can do miracles. I know He'll do it, Daddy. Let's pray!" We all knelt in a circle.

"Father," I prayed, "You said in Your Word to become as little children. I believe You meant for us to trust You as little children do. So we are going to trust You as Kaylie trusts You right now. In the name of Jesus we ask You to heal this bird. We thank You for it now. Amen."

We then padded a shoebox for the stricken Delilah and supplied food and water. Kaylie said she'd put a stick atop the box in case Delilah felt better in the night and wanted to stand on it.

I thought, *Wow, Lord, that would be a huge miracle!* The next morning that miracle became a reality! Delilah was perched on the stick, her chest wound completely closed and her back end totally healed! God honored our faith that day. I am here to testify that He delights in giving good gifts to His children when we come to Him in faith, believing as a child.

He will carry out what you've asked—according to His will. Have a faith-filled day!

Vonda Beerman

It's All About Grace

But He gives us more grace. That is why Scripture says: "God opposes the proud but shows favor to the humble." James 4:6, NIV.

While driving on Michigan State Highway 57, I was stopped by a policeman for speeding. He asked, "Do you know how fast you were going?" I told him, adding, "I thought that was the speed limit." He informed me it was 10 miles less than I thought. After going to his car and checking my registration and driver's license, he returned with just a warning. He granted me grace. I deserved a ticket.

Another day, while shopping, as I picked up an item to examine it, I accidentally broke it. At the checkout counter I presented the broken item to the clerk so I could pay for it. When I told her that I had accidentally broken it, she refused to let me pay for it. Again I received grace. I should have had to pay for that item.

Because I was very grateful on both occasions, you can believe I avoid repeating the actions that made grace necessary. In our daily lives we may be fortunate enough to meet people like the policeman and sales clerk who are charitable and understanding, making it possible to sometimes avoid severe consequences. However, that is not always the case.

God's grace is even more wonderful. His grace endures and has eternal consequences.

By nature we are sinful beings. When left to ourselves, we make choices that lead to death. Without grace we are forever running the race and forever losing. His grace, when accepted, greatly alters the outcome. Accepting it, we head in another direction—one that makes it possible to enjoy an intimate relationship with the God of the universe.

God's pardon of unholy sinners is because He secures our acquittal from guilt based on Christ's death. His divine grace then gives the gifts of repentance, forgiveness, and salvation. Thus grace is a gift from both God the Father and Jesus the Son. When our lives are transformed by grace, we become like them. In our earthly families we see similarities in actions and mannerisms between parents and their children. God's grace enables us, His children, to grow and become one with Him in thought, purpose, and actions.

Grace: such a full and precious gift; it is hard for us to grasp its magnificence.

Marian M. Hart Gay

October 19

Teaching for Jesus Anywhere, Anytime!

And though the Lord give you the bread of adversity,
and the water of affliction, yet shall not thy teachers be removed into a
corner any more, but thine eyes shall see thy teachers. Isa. 30:20.

If You move the roadblocks, I'll do it, God. I'll still teach." These were the words I sobbed to my Father. I'd been teaching in church schools for 35 years. Already preparing for the incoming school year, I learned the school's supporting church had just voted to close the school where I taught. In the meantime my 88-year-old mom was dying just a couple of hours away, and I was recovering from two double-hip replacements within one year's time. Parents and students alike were pleading with me to start a new school even "if you have to teach students at your house, Mrs. Wilson!" The only other teaching offer from my previous employer was at a school eight hours away. Neither the drive nor the move would have been possible.

Then, in response to my heavenward cry, God went to work. In just eight days He provided me a beautiful 7-year-old facility at the church of another denomination—free of charge! Great-grandparents of one of my students helped facilitate this miracle and said, "God prepared this building for a school. We are honored to have you here." God lined up all the inspectors' permits (fire, building, sanitation, and zoning), licenses, and state certification. Boom! Boom! Boom! One after another, God knocked the roadblocks out of my way. In the meantime I'd lost most of the 22 students from my previous school. Like Gideon, however, I went back to the Lord, telling Him I needed students. A still small voice said, *Sylvia, you don't need students; you need* Me!

"Wow, God! Whew! I'm sorry," I repented. Since then, as with Queen Esther, God has provided everything I need "for such a time as this." Not always cash. Sometimes materials, supplies, equipment, support, prayers, encouragement, the light bill—but everything I needed.

My daughter Danyielle asked, "Ma, why did you doubt God?" I had done just that. Now I just enjoy His blessings, His lessons, and His goodness. I named the school Prince of Peace Christian Academy after God's Son. And He has given me peace that passes all understanding.

God will bless us in ways that we would not have dreamed. He will move the roadblocks out of our way even if we are our own biggest block. I'll teach for *Him* anywhere, anytime!

Sylvia Jackson Wilson

He Has to Go! Part 1

For we wrestle not against flesh and blood, but against principalities,
against powers, against the rulers of the darkness of this world,
against spiritual wickedness in high places. Wherefore take
unto you the whole armour of God, that ye may be able to withstand
in the evil day, and having done all, to stand. Eph. 6:12, 13.

Polly Elrod and I were swapping war stories, as we occasionally do. She's well below five feet, 80, with sparkling eyes, white curly hair cascading over her shoulders, and a good replica of what Dolly Parton might look like at her vintage.

From the first women's ministries retreat where I had been her guest speaker, we connected, and our paths subsequently crossed from time to time. Her passion for Jesus is palpable, and her retreats have attracted many bruised and broken. You might find a biker babe doing praise and worship, and a smoker in the backyard struggling with her last cigarette. Broken women feel safe with Polly. She shared with me about an encounter with the enemy at one of the retreats I attended. It reminded me how powerful any daughter of God is when she puts her faith fully in Christ and His power.

Polly was attending a recovery seminar for abused women conducted by her daughter, Marie Fisher, a former abuse victim and elder at an Adventist church in Ketchum, Oklahoma, where they both worship. She was sitting with a young woman named Desiree, who had brought three friends to the seminar. Then she noticed something out of the ordinary. One of the women—"girls," she called them—was behaving strangely. Polly described to me what happened next. "The girl was jittery, restless. She showed another girl long scratches across her back. During a seminar break, this girl went out on a knoll in the backyard. I felt the Holy Spirit tell me I should go have prayer with her, so I told Marie we needed to have prayer together first. A vial of olive oil in her purse, Marie headed over to the young guest with me and a couple of other attendees in tow. As I reached the girl, she fell backward to the ground. I soon realized, when I tried to hold her, that her head wasn't touching the ground—because she had levitated off the ground."

Lord, when we realize we are caught up in the midst of spiritual warfare, remind us that You are our strength. Clothe us in Your armor, for You vanquished the foe at Calvary. Amen.

Cynthia J. Prime

He Has to Go! Part 2

The Lord thy God in the midst of thee is mighty;
he will save, he will rejoice over thee with joy; he will rest in his love,
he will joy over thee with singing. Zeph. 3:17.

Marie chimed in with the next chapter of the story as I listened. "The girl's eyes and mouth got green and sort of iridescent, and she was fighting us. As I reached for the vial of olive oil in my purse, I struggled to keep the young woman's head still, forcing her levitating body to the ground. There was no time for fear, as we were focused on the battle at hand. Then Polly commanded, 'In the name of Jesus, get out of her!'

"A snarling voice from the troubled girl's throat laughed and shouted, 'I'm not going!' Polly's firm, determined voice said, 'When I call Jesus' name, *he* [the enemy]—*has to go!*' With a final ugly screech, the young woman dropped to the ground. The storm was over. She became quiet. She stood up and asked, in a normal voice, what had happened. When we told her, she asked if this is what we do at our retreats. I told her, 'Only if Jesus asks us to.'"

What I liked about Polly is the matter-of-fact way in which she shared God's intervention. "I wasn't afraid," she said. "If Jesus is with you, you don't need to be afraid. He makes Satan scared of you," and this from a woman who is on familiar terms with grief and loss.

As I reflected on Polly's experience as well as on some of my own, it occurred to me just how physically present God is in the midst of the human experience. I grew up sometimes intimidated by bullies and, at times, scared of my own shadow. Then Jesus drove the truth of His promised presence, protection, and provision straight through to me, particularly during my mission work in Africa. Polly might be 100 pounds soaking wet, but Lucifer, a supernatural being capable of great evil, *had* to flee at her command.

The battle for our souls is not ours; it is God's. The warfare between good and evil already has a declared Champion who is on our side. Any woman, no matter how frail, is equal to the enemy if her Champion, Jesus, is at her side—for at His name, the enemy trembles.

"He's just a big bully," Polly remarked, describing our mutual enemy as one would describe a ferocious dog. Satan can't go anyplace where God keeps the gate. God is with us. He celebrates each time a child of His leans on faith in Him and puts the enemy to rout.

Cynthia J. Prime

It Wasn't a Coincidence

And I, if I be lifted up from the earth, will draw all men unto me. John 12:32.

As I do almost every year, I started packing a barrel of household supplies—clothing, bedding, and foodstuff—to send to my nephew, who delivers the contents to the needy in his community in Jamaica. The barrel was almost full when I realized that something was missing. My nephew had three young children, and I'd never ever sent them a present. Going to a nearby department store, I picked out some clothes I thought the children would wear.

When the cashier handed me the receipt at the checkout counter, I marveled at the amount: "$18.44! That's a special date for me." I must have said it louder than I intended, because a woman who had been in line behind came up to me later and said, "1844! Are you a Seventh-day Adventist?"

Surprised, I turned to her. Not many people recognize the significance of the year 1844. They don't know that Jesus was expected to come in that year. They don't know why Seventh-day Adventists refer to 1844 as the Great Disappointment. Most haven't even heard of William Miller, who realized later that the events in Daniel 8:14 had been misinterpreted. (The sanctuary to be cleansed was in heaven not on earth. October 22, 1844, was therefore the beginning of the investigative judgment in heaven.)

Most people wouldn't know the beautiful words Ellen G. White penned when she described that experience: "Those whose faith was based on a personal knowledge of the Bible had a rock beneath their feet, which the waves of disappointment could not wash away" (*The Great Controversy*, p. 394). Most people would not know all that history, but my new friend did.

Delighted, I listened as she told me that she had become an Adventist, had moved to my town, and was looking for a church family. Gladly I invited her to my home church, and she really liked it. We live in the same neighborhood so we can pray and study the Bible together. And she can drive me to church meetings at night—something my aging eyes no longer allow.

I know God has been arranging encounters in human history since the beginning of time. He must have smiled when the cashier rang up my bill that day. He knew the blessings my new friend and I would receive, and we could give. He knew our meeting was no coincidence.

Hazel Roole

The Endorsement

For God hath not given us the spirit of fear; but of power,
and of love, and of a sound mind. 2 Tim. 1:7.

My to-do list wasn't long: I needed to do some banking before going to help my friend Glena. She was selling her home, getting married, and moving to the United States. It was my joy, along with several other friends, to help her prepare for the move. It had been two years since Glena lost her husband to cancer, and now she was ready to begin a new chapter in her life.

At the bank I handed the friendly teller my convenience card along with the bills that needed to be paid. We've done our banking at the same CIBC branch for more than 30 years, so almost everyone there knows Sonny, my son, and me. I then endorsed a check that a friend had sent me in the mail. The teller examined the check, then she looked at me. I could detect a puzzled look in her facial expression, so I asked, "Is there something wrong with this check?"

"Oh, no," she said, "it is just so sweet of you to write this note."

Beneath my signature and account number I had written, "Thank you; God bless you." Together these five little words are empowering, and I use them often with heaven's blessings.

I then had an opportunity to share with the teller a little more about our family ministry. I told her that I believe that the Lord is connecting His people together in amazing ways. I read aloud an excerpt from the note that came with the check. "Dear Deborah and Sonny, God bless you as you carry on with your work of love for others. So good to keep in touch. I share your readings with others. Love and sincere best wishes and prayers, Edythe." I used the money that Edythe sent to buy postage stamps.

The gift was sent with love from a senior citizen who attends the same church as my daughter and son-in-law. This kind woman and her husband befriended my children and took them under her loving wings a decade ago when they moved to Victoria, British Columbia, to start a new chapter in their lives.

For more than 21 years I've been uplifted and blessed by such Christians as Edythe, who have prayerfully and financially worked with me in sharing the gospel message. I believe that Jesus is coming soon, and that He is preparing His children for Paradise, forever.

Deborah Sanders

I Did Not Tell You When

Trust in the Lord with all your heart, and do not rely
on your own understanding. Prov. 3:5, HCSB.

My husband's diagnosis was complicated during his final illness. I am sure that he understood the gravity of his condition much better than I, since he was a physician.

The day after admission to the hospital, he lost consciousness while having a procedure done and was "coded." He was brought back to consciousness, and then three hours later, while in the intensive-care unit, he again lost consciousness and was coded a second time. As his life hung in the balance, I found a quiet place and asked the Lord to do what was best. I kept repeating to the Lord, "Not my will, but Yours." I hoped, however, that he would be restored to health.

Over time he seemed to be recovering and was transferred to a second hospital where he had an up-and-down course. Since God brought him from the edge of the grave, I was sure that He would restore his health. Before going to bed one night, I saw my old promise box that I'd neglected, and reached to take a promise. Instead of one, three came up: Matthew 7:7: "Ask, and it shall be given you"; Ephesians 3:20: "To him who is able to do exceeding abundantly above all that we ask or think" (NKJV); and 2 Chronicles 20:15: "For the battle is not yours, but God's" (HCSB). I was greatly encouraged.

The next day I reassured my husband that he wouldn't die and told him about the promises. This lifted his spirits, but he continued to have an up-and-down course. He was transferred to a third hospital. Throughout all this, his mind was clear. However, he did succumb to pneumonia and other complications.

After his death I asked, *What happened, Lord?* Instantly I received a clear understanding in my mind: "Did you not ask that My will be done?" I answered, "Yes, Lord," and said no more. But I was also thinking of the other two promises; they were not fulfilled. I never talked to the Lord about those but often ruminated on them in my mind. *Were they from the Lord? Did I deceive myself? Did I use the promise box as a fetish?* I wanted to throw out the box or give it away. The Lord was silent.

About two months later, around 4:00 a.m., I was thinking about "able to do exceedingly above all that you ask or think," when a clear understanding came into my mind: "I did not tell you when this will be." Immediately I understood. I expected it in this life; God has it for the future. The battle for my husband's soul He has won. God always wins!

Thelda Van Lange Greaves

Ice Cubes

My soul thirsts for God, for the living God. Ps. 42:2, NIV.

One October day I experienced a difficult test, and that was to live without water. Or rather, with a small quantity of liquid.

It began after I acquired a chronic degenerative kidney disease; I was warned constantly that at any moment my kidneys could stop functioning, making it necessary to replace them with a machine that performed a similar role. I would have to survive on a dialysis machine.

During this period I had to learn some strategies for satisfying my thirst with little water. Living in the jungle of Bahia, Brazil, things always seemed a little more difficult, but I learned to substitute a glass full of water with a few ice cubes. During the day these ice cubes softened my desire to drink water, but it was far from truly satisfying my thirst! My body was thirsty for water, water in abundance! As time went on I discovered that this liquid, so often rejected by some, and substituted with other drinks by others, is extremely precious!

My whole body complained about the lack of water; I was thirsty. My skin darkened, becoming limp and dry, not to mention the damage that I would eventually suffer. Living like that made me see the need that we have for water, living water. Jesus is the living water; without Him our life is a desert; everything in us suffers.

Once the Creator of the sources of water was sitting next to a well, without a bucket or cord, and He offered living water to a woman. It took awhile for her to understand that the water He offered was not physical, but eternal: "Everyone who drinks this water will be thirsty again, but whoever drinks the water I give them will never thirst. Indeed, the water I give them will become in them a spring of water welling up to eternal life" (John 4:13, 14, NIV).

Unfortunately, it takes us awhile to understand that a "cup of ice cubes" will never satisfy our real spiritual need. We seek what we think is important, but Jesus offers us that which is really important. He says, "Daughter, are you thirsty? If you drink of the water that I give, you will never, ever be thirsty again!"

If this is what you are really searching for, try taking time today to "drink in" Christ, allow Him to fill you, and do not be content or comfortable with small ice cubes!

Jussara Alves

My Foolish Prayer

I say to the Lord, "You are my Lord;
apart from you I have no good thing." Ps. 16:2, NIV.

My mother was dead. My joyful, friendly, funny mother was dead. I was now back in Tennessee with my husband and family. But it was not supposed to happen this way.

I was pregnant with our fourth child, and my mother joked that she was going to have to make beds for my kids in dresser drawers because she'd run out places to put them. That summer the company my husband worked for was sending him on a five-week trip, so I and our three kiddies were going to spend that time back home. In fact, I'd give birth there. But things had gone terribly wrong. Suddenly my mom was in the hospital. Unknown to her, she had been diabetic for years. Not one of her doctors through the years had done that simple blood test. And now she had gangrene in her foot and sepsis throughout her body. We bundled up the children and went to Texas. I arrived in time to spend a day with her in the hospital before she had "minor surgery" to remove the gangrenous toe. However, under the light anesthetic her heart stopped beating. The doctors revived her, but she died two weeks later. She never woke up.

As planned, my husband went on his trip. Our baby was born in Texas. My husband returned. We went back to Tennessee, and life continued, as it does, despite tragedy. But daily I prayed, "Lord, I can't do this on my own. Hold me up. Give me strength." And I managed pretty well, given that there was no help to be had. That I had a newborn baby and three little girls. That my husband was gone almost 12 hours a day.

Then I thought of my father and sister in their deep grief. I changed my prayer. "Dear Lord," I said, "I'm doing pretty well now. You needn't worry about me. But please comfort Daddy and my sister. Give them strength to cope." And that was my prayer for the next several days. Then the strangest thing happened. I plunged into the deepest, darkest depression you can imagine. It sapped my energy. Days passed. Darkness and pain consumed me. Suddenly I realized what I had done—I'd told God I didn't need Him anymore and could manage on my own. "Forgive me, Lord," I pleaded. "How could I be so foolish? And thank You for showing me my great need of You and that You were holding me up all those weeks. Please, hold me again."

And He did.

Penny Estes Wheeler

Weak Yet Strong

But His answer was: "My grace is all you need, for my power
is greatest when you are weak." I am most happy, then, to be proud of my
weaknesses, in order to feel the protection of Christ's power over me. I am
content with weaknesses, insults, hardships, persecutions, and difficulties for
Christ's sake. For when I am weak, then I am strong. 2 Cor. 12:9, 10, TEV.

As a college student, I experienced a lot of struggles and hardships with school life. There were problems with academics, finances, roommates, extracurricular, health, and a lot more. At one time I experienced headaches and fatigue. My sleeping pattern was disrupted, and I thought of giving up. *Why do I need college, anyway? It's just making my life miserable.* Term papers, research papers, reaction papers, and other required papers started piling up. Even projects for minor subjects demanded time and energy. And on top of it all, a lot of information and knowledge had to be kept in mind.

I looked for comfort from friends and even from my religious support group in school. They did help, but it seemed incomplete. I cried. That was one thing I could resort to—crying.

I felt helpless and weak. But as I prayed to God, I told Him all that troubled me, all that pained me. It was as if God was silent and not listening. *Hey, Lord, speak up. I'm hurt, You know. You're the one who put me here, so it should be Your problem, not mine.* I blamed God but still poured out my heart to Him. *Lord, I don't know about my life. Please do stay with me.* That's all I could utter.

Though God seemed silent at that moment, He taught me a lesson—He did listen. No blaming. No arguing. No criticizing. His presence was there though I felt it not. When we focus more on ourselves than on God, we become narrow-minded individuals. We tend to consider problems as a big whale swallowing us up. That misconception often leads us astray.

My encounter with God taught me that when we ask wisdom and strength from Him, He often gives problems for us to solve. From experiencing the sways and twists of problems in our lives, we can gain wisdom and strength as well as faith. I realized how weak I am, but God let me know that He's strong enough to carry me. Problems are always there—and will always be— so, what's the solution? Just turn to God, and He will take care of things. We have a strong God!

Grachienne L. Banuag

Repairing the Damaged

Create in me a pure heart, O God, and renew a steadfast spirit
within me. . . . Restore to me the joy of your salvation
and grant me a willing spirit, to sustain me. Ps. 51:10-12, NIV.

A few years ago I bought a bright-red blazer with a black velvet collar. My husband has always liked it when I wear the color red, so I was happy to have found a garment that would please him. We were going to western Nebraska for the weekend, and instead of putting the jacket in a garment bag I just laid it in the trunk, where it wouldn't wrinkle. I looked forward to wearing it when I was speaking at a special meeting.

The next morning when I put the blazer on, I noticed what I thought was a soiled spot on the sleeve. To my consternation, it was not dirt but instead small holes with grease around the edges, evidence that it had been caught in the latch of the trunk. I chastised myself for being so careless and thought the jacket was ruined.

After thinking about the situation, I formulated a plan to disguise the damage. Going to the store, I bought a few yards of black soutache braid and a black tassel. I placed the braid around the sleeve near the cuff, blindstitched it in place, and did a second row up a half inch. I did the same to the second sleeve. Where the holes were, I designed a circular design with the braid and attached the tassel, thereby covering the area where the holes were. No longer was the jacket useless. I was always conscious of my "holes" and felt that the garment was diminished in value. Then one day I met a friend who had an identical jacket. When I remarked to her that we had the same jacket she said, "Yes, but yours is much more expensive." She thought because mine had the braid and tassel it was more costly. We shared a good laugh as I told her the story.

In our lives we sometimes do foolish and thoughtless things and mar our reputations. We may be embarrassed and ashamed of what we have done and label ourselves as "no good." The negative thoughts take over. We need to remind ourselves that there are ways to repair our lives and restore our reputations. In fact, we can go on to do good deeds and make our lives more beautiful and attractive to others than before. Everyone has made mistakes, and some mistakes show more than others. Use your creativity to formulate a plan to change your ways and become the person you would like to be. As with my jacket, in Christ your life will be even more beautiful.

Evelyn Glass

A Thousand-Year Therapy Session

And the Lord God will wipe away tears from all faces. Isa. 25:8, NKJV.

I believe heaven will feature several, dare I say, therapeutic reunions. Imagine:
Uriah: David! My king! Praise God! It was my honor to lay down my life for my God, my king, and my country!

David: Uriah! I'm glad to see you too (embrace). But, uh, we need to have a chat. There's something you don't know. Remember Joab's command that you fight in the forefront of the hottest battle? Uriah, there's something I must confess . . .

Or apostle Paul and the martyr Stephen . . .

Stephen: Wh . . . you? You're here, Saul? You?

Paul: Yes, me. And it all began with seeing your face, Stephen. No shred of resentment on it though we rained down rocks upon you while you saw Jesus at the right hand of God.

Paul: I saw Him too, a little bit later on the road to Damascus. Do you have a minute? I'll tell you about it—oh, and call me Paul.

Heaven will be a time of great rejoicing. But some things will need to be "processed." The conflicts that eat away at our peace beg to be resolved now before Jesus comes. For will we avoid each other in heaven? Say, "I forgive you, but I just can't trust you!"?

While we shouldn't postpone our duty to "live in peace" (2 Cor. 13:11), if death or distance or other factors prevent reconciliation, God has planned a therapy session. It's called the millennium, the 1,000 years between the coming of Jesus and the earth made new. Read about it in Revelation 20 and 21. Satan will be incarcerated (Rev. 20:2); the resurrected just will collaborate with God in reviewing the cases of the lost and the fallen angels (verse 6; 1 Cor. 6:3). I personally believe God will sit down with those of us who have wounded feelings and patiently help us to resolve those issues for time and for eternity. It is *after* the 1,000 years that "God will wipe away every tear from their eyes" (Rev. 7:17).

If I, as a counselor, held a thousand-year therapy session, I would earn about $438 million. Jesus will do it like He does everything—without money and without price. Praise our heavenly Therapist, our divine Psychologist, our wonderful Counselor!

Jennifer Jill Schwirzer

Failed Registration

With men this is impossible; but with God all things are possible. Matt. 19:26.

My nursing reregistration was due the end of October. I always complete everything, including payment, before the due date. This time was no different—or so I thought. Registration is important to avoid a lapse in nursing practice. I paid online as before, then left for a two-week holiday, expecting all would be well for resuming duties on returning. As I often did prior to leaving, I arranged with one of my colleagues to cover the day I was due to resume, just in the event something happened, and I could not report.

I returned home exhausted and checked my e-mails and spoke with my colleague, and confirmed I'd be ready for work the next night. Later that evening, I saw a stack of letters and was prompted to check through it. Lo and behold, there was not one, but two letters stating my registration fee had not been received, and I was given one week "grace period." It had passed.

I was horrified that all this time my payment hadn't been processed. Not knowing why it hadn't, I had to act fast. I double-checked the registry online, and yes, my fear was confirmed. There it pointed out that registration had to be done online. I thought, *No way!* The office was closed. Again, I contacted my colleague and explained the situation; she readily agreed to cover my shift, and I informed my manager of the situation.

The next morning I rang the nursing council office and explained what had happened. Fortunately, I was able to pay via phone. I was told it would take five working days for full registration, and I did not have five days without disrupting other colleagues' work schedules. It was now Thursday morning; I had Friday night off, but was due to work Saturday and Sunday nights. I prayed, asking the Lord for one thing: "Please allow my registration to come through by Friday morning if it is Your will." That was considered only one working day.

Friday morning I checked the registry. God had answered the prayer of a desperate woman! I was fully registered. Feeling overjoyed is an understatement. I felt very special and thanked the Lord for making what seemed impossible, possible. Faith in God is indeed very vital to the Christian life. This experience makes me think of the magnificent love of God and how much He cares for us. May we, by God's grace through faith, trust Him in all things.

Donette James-Samuel

Hidden Items

A faithful person will be richly blessed,
but one eager to get rich will not go unpunished. Prov. 28:20, NIV.

I sometimes helped a friend take care of her twin boys; then God blessed her with a lovely baby girl. Her husband asked me to help him shop for the newborn while they were still in the hospital. We filled two shopping carts with baby items. The twins chose to sit by the items in the carts, so we pushed them around as we shopped.

At the checkout counter the cashier said the playpen was too heavy for her to lift, so she checked it from the cart. We paid and left the shop. While we were loading our truck with the purchased stuff, we realized that the playpen had been lying on some bibs and one of the twins was sitting on some mittens and socks, so we had not paid for them. Mike suggested that I run back to the shop and pay for those hidden items while he strapped the boys into their seats. As I was explaining the unpaid items to the checkout clerk, she called the supervisor to bring a bag.

You may not believe it, but about half of the things we had paid for were in that bag; we had forgotten to take it. I was happy that Mike and I decided to be honest. The bibs, mittens, and socks were just $12 while the forgotten bag was worth more than $400! Besides that, we saved ourselves a second journey to the shop by being honest.

Michael was moved to tears when I came back with the big bag. All he said was "It pays to be honest." The fact is, he would not have noticed that he had left some stuff behind till Ruth and the baby were home; and it would have cost them extra money to buy new baby stuff. It is said that "Honesty is the best policy" and today's verse reminds us that we will not go unpunished if we use wrong means to get richer. I remember that Proverbs 28:6 says, "Better to be poor and honest than to be dishonest and rich" (NLT).

I think that Paul summed up the matter of honesty very well when he wrote "that in this matter no one should wrong or take advantage of a brother or sister. The Lord will punish all those who commit such sins, as we told you and warned you before. For God did not call us to be impure, but to live a holy life. Therefore, anyone who rejects this instruction does not reject a human being but God, the very God who gives you his Holy Spirit" (1 Thess. 4:6-8, NIV).

Mabel Kwei

The Mighty God

You who sit down in the High God's presence,
spend the night in Shaddai's shadow. Ps. 91:1, Message.

I love to study the names of God. Each name reveals something new about God's character. There was a time in my spiritual experience that I yearned to learn more about God. I knew He was a God of love, but reading through the Bible, especially the Old Testament, I found myself challenged to see God as loving, caring, and compassionate.

Then a number of years ago I came across a book titled *The Names of God*, by Ann Spangler. I found myself absorbed in the book. Each week she presented a new name of God in the Hebrew or Greek. There are readings for each day of the week, all based on that one name of God. I was thrilled and amazed as I delved deeper and deeper into a study of God's names.

Many of us already know some of these names: Jehovah Shalom—God is peace; Abba—Daddy; and Jehovah Rohi—God is my Shepherd. But the name I love the most is found in Psalm 91:1, our text for today. El Shaddai—the mighty God. The God with whom nothing is impossible. Oh, how I love this name. How precious the name has become to me.

Through the past decade of my life there have been some major trials that I have faced, both personally and within my family. This name, El Shaddai—the mighty God, has given me strength because I know that no matter what my trial, God is able to see me through. Whether He chooses to solve it, remove it, or leave it for a while—sometimes a long while—it matters not. I know He is in control.

You see, the El Shaddai is the God who calmed the raging seas, who saved Daniel in the lions' den, who gave David victory over Goliath, and who parted the Red Sea for the Israelites to walk through. There are so many stories in the Bible that show us the power of the El Shaddai. Do you want that power in your life today? Then all you have to do is to spend time each day under His shadow. Learn to lean on God. He will never let you down. If you want to study more about God's character and have access to the Internet, do a search for "the names of God," and you will be amazed at the information that is available. Use this information to help you develop a deeper understanding of the character of God. He is a God of love, caring, and compassion.

Heather-Dawn Small

Christian Witchery

So they were filled with all injustice, wicked behavior,
greed, and evil behavior. They are full of jealousy, murder,
fighting, deception, and malice. They are gossips. Rom. 1:29, CEB.

A hesitant hand slowly rose above the other heads. I looked toward the back of the class and nodded "Go ahead."

"Why do church women gossip so much?" the owner of the hand asked.

The question had come from our class discussion on a poem entitled "Le Loupgarou," by Sir Derek Walcott. This poem artfully described the life and demise of the main character, Le Brun, who sold his soul to the devil and was turned into an Alsatian hound. He was betrayed by those whom Walcott calls the "Christian witches." The effect of this cleverly woven tale is that the villagers shunned Le Brun and closed their windows on him as he passed to sell his fruit.

Perhaps it was Walcott's oxymoronic description or maybe it was observations of her own church that prompted the student to ask this question. Either way, it was valid, and there was no easy way to answer it. *Gossip is defined as "the inappropriate communication of unflattering, embarrassing, hurtful, or humiliating information about a person to another person. Truth is irrelevant."* This pernicious phenomenon is used to denigrate the different, denounce the dissident, and defame the disliked. And yes, this happens—even in church.

Many have been victims of direct slanderous stories or more indirectly, predatory prayer. "Let us pray for Jill whose husband is sleeping with Mary." Sometimes it is not hard to spot the faint smirk of smug satisfaction in the prayer group announcer. Paul addresses this in 1 Timothy 5:13, and thousands of years later—things are still the same.

The answer to this question at its root was very simple: godlessness. Sadly, the Christian women in the poem who spoke of Le Brun's demise were equally as evil as they rumored him to be. If Le Brun did not know God, these women did not show God to him. As ancient Israel missed the time of their visitation, many are without God—right next to His available presence.

None who engage in this practice will go to heaven. It hurts people and weakens the body of Christ. Our deepest need is to surrender our hearts to the Lord and our tongues will follow. Only with His grace can we exterminate this vile sin of Christian witchery.

Judelia Medard-Santiesteban

Risk-taking, Part 1

*Have I not commanded you? Be strong and of good
courage; do not be afraid, nor be dismayed, for the Lord your
God is with you wherever you go. Joshua 1:9, NKJV.*

In her book *Women Who Don't Wait in Line*, Reshma Saujani tells how, from her
childhood, she always longed to be a public servant. She tells how the day came
when she decided to run for Congress. She worked day and night raising funds and
getting the word out about her platform for change; she got endorsements from the
likes of the *Wall Street Journal* and other prestigious organizations and individuals.
There was no reason she should not win this congressional election—except that
she didn't! Stricken and confused, she wanted to lie down in a fetal position and
never get up—never again! But when she did decide to face her defeat, she found
that her supporters, rather than being disappointed in her, were congratulating her
for having the courage and conviction to do what she believed in. She was stunned!
What had seemed to her the end of her career as a public servant turned out to be
only the beginning.

In my own experience I have walked in brazenly where wise men and women
fear to tread and have gotten trounced and humiliated. I have always believed that
there is no person so important that they cannot be approached to do me a favor.
That is what brought me one day to the Harvard University office of a political
science professor and former U.S. ambassador to the United Nations to request
that he speak at an event I was planning at my little Christian college. He was
most courteous, but turned me down. I walked out of his office unable to believe
that he wouldn't have immediately said yes to my invitation. I promised never to
try that again, until I was teaching at the University of Connecticut, Stamford,
and approached a very distinguished and world-renowned professor of Latin
American literature to join the board of a literary magazine we were starting up in
Connecticut. Again I was received with much courtesy, but when he realized that
one of his archrivals was already on our board, he stared daggers at me as I backed
gingerly toward the door and made a run for it!

Thus is the fate of the brave who often can be seen as foolhardy by those who
never dare to do anything for fear of failure. Yet God has instructed us not to be
fearful or dismayed by setbacks. For He has committed to be with us in whatever
risk He leads us to take.

Lourdes Morales-Gudmundsson

Risk-taking, Part 2

Whatever your hand finds to do, do it with all your might. Eccl. 9:10, NIV.

But the day came when my brazen ways paid off—big-time! My work in the area of forgiveness and peacemaking brought me in touch with the work of Oscar Arias Sánchez, who was awarded the Nobel Peace Prize in 1987 for bringing the warring nations of Central America to the table to sign a peace agreement. I wanted to interview him. When I called his office in San José, Costa Rica, who should answer the phone but a former student who had joined my study-abroad group years before in Spain! Working now for Dr. Arias, she'd be happy to intervene to ask if he would be the graduation speaker at my university. He accepted both the invitation to speak at our graduation and to be interviewed by me—what a coup!

The Bible tells of women who stood up and walked brazenly into difficult and even dangerous assignments that were blessed by God. Deborah took a chance with Barak; Jael took on the difficult assignment of "dealing with" the enemy of God's people; Esther risked everything to save her people; an adolescent Mary risked social ostracism to say yes to God, and another New England teenager refused to listen to the voices that would hold her back from teaching and preaching because she was a woman. Theodore Roosevelt once said the following about critics who stand on the sidelines waiting for risk-takers to fall on their faces: "It is not the critic who counts. . . . The credit belongs to the [woman] who is actually in the arena . . . who strives valiantly; who errs, who comes short again and again, because there is no effort without error and shortcomings; but who does actually strive to do the deeds; who knows the great enthusiasms, the great devotions; who spends [herself] in a worthy cause . . ." (quoted in Resha Saujani's *Women Who Don't Wait in Line* [Boston: Houghton Mifflin Harcourt, 2013]).

That is what Christian women are called to be—risk-takers for the cause of the gospel—unafraid to move forward to use the gifts that God has given them to glorify His name. There will be the cautionary advice from those men and women standing on the sidelines, reminding you that you can't do what you propose, or that it's not appropriate, or that God will disapprove. Pray and then listen only to what is in your heart, and you, like the godly women of old, will know what it feels like to be blessed by God.

Lourdes Morales-Gudmundsson

I Am Free

Therefore if the Son makes you free,
you shall be free indeed. John 8:36, NKJV.

It took more than 40 years for the Lord to bring me to my knees—for me to understand what total dependence is all about. Of course, I have been on my knees before to pray like everyone else, but that physical gesture does not mean a full realization of the meaning of "depend on Him." The judgment and expectations I had of myself as a Christian, a wife, and mother were way too high.

My divorce in 2005 caused my world to come crashing down. As a fourth-generation Adventist Christian, I knew all the right things to do and say. My faithful giving of tithes and offerings, weekly church attendance, and church responsibilities made me feel as if I were a good Christian. When my marriage failed, I struggled to understand the why and how. What I should have been doing was searching the Scriptures. Instead I was angry—not at God, just angry. When people would inquire as to what went wrong, my frustration built up with the need to explain. And then there were these nagging thoughts: *Is the Christian community judging me? Do my friends and family think I am a bad mother?* These thoughts would occupy my mind, and they made me feel worthless as a person. Ultimately I pushed God away.

For several years I literally felt lost. That feeling can be described as just wandering around in the woods, flip-flopping between decisions. *Should I go this way? Maybe not. Maybe I should pitch my tent here. Should I start a fire, or should I just lie down and rest my weary bones?* While stumbling along life's way, I clung to what I needed to do for my children; what I needed to do just to survive.

It wasn't until 2012 that I sought God consistently. It was then I started asking Him for guidance in every little decision I made. Once I did that, it was such a relief! There were no more worries, no need to defend myself against the evils of this world. I am able to face each day with happiness, because now I know God is looking out for me, and I do not need to judge myself. If I fall, I can pick myself up again. When hurting, I know He is only a prayer away. What a joy my newfound love has been! "You will show me the path of life; in Your presence is fullness of joy" (Ps. 16:11, NKJV). Free indeed.

Viola Ruth Poey

Clothed in Honor

Strength and honour are her clothing;
and she shall rejoice in time to come. Prov. 31:25.

I don't know about you, but sometimes I read Proverbs 31 and it just seems impossible to be *that* woman. I mean, what couldn't she do? She cooked, she cleaned, she worked, she was wise, and her husband actually trusted in her (go figure). As a woman it's easy to feel the weight of the world on your shoulders and, make no mistake about it, you have to be cute while carrying that weight. I have more days when I am just trying to make it than days when I am rejoicing. "She shall rejoice in time to come." When will that time come?

However, I am learning more and more that being a virtuous woman has nothing to do with how much I can do and how well I can do it but, rather, how much I fear the Lord.

You see, this is an important revelation, because if you are anything like me you spend most of your time trying to convince your boyfriend, your husband, your children, and yourself that you can do it all! And that you can do it all without needing one word of affirmation or appreciation. You make plates, you wash clothes, and you work hard for your family, and—don't get me wrong—all of that has its place.

However, you begin to find your identity in how many pair of underwear you can fold per minute. OK, that may be a bit extreme, but you get lost in what you do, not in who God is. This is precisely why your time of rejoicing has not come yet.

Being a virtuous woman is a mind-set, not a to-do list. This is what it means to be clothed in honor. This mind-set comes only from being lost in God, who will give you wisdom on how to handle today, how to manage your household, how to raise your kids, how to deal with your boss (the one in your house and on your job), and how to bite your tongue.

"Favour is deceitful, and beauty is vain: but a woman that feareth the Lord, she shall be praised" (Prov. 31:30).

You better believe your time of rejoicing will come when you learn to fear God and stop trusting in your own abilities! Those words of appreciation will flow in.

You will be praised!

You are virtuous.

Rebecca Davis

That's Not Fair

For it is commendable if someone bears up under the pain of unjust suffering because they are conscious of God. But how is it to your credit if you receive a beating for doing wrong and endure it? But if you suffer for doing good and you endure it, this is commendable before God.1 Peter 2:19, 20, NIV.

It was a simple question, but it could have been anything—a look, a word, an action. Instantly I was ambushed by strife masquerading as an incredibly rude person. After a flurry of e-mails I felt as though I had unwittingly stumbled into a tangle of barbed wire. I wondered what I had done to deserve such treatment. The answer was . . . nothing.

I've been there before, and you probably have too. It doesn't matter if it is the betrayal of a friend or loved one, mean-spiritedness from someone you don't even know, or becoming the victim of malicious gossip.

Being treated unfairly hurts no matter which form it takes. It's easy to cry, "Why me? What have I done to deserve this?" And that is precisely what Satan is hoping we'll ask. Using our pain, he tries to focus our thoughts right where he likes them to be: on us.

But there's far more to these unfair situations than meets the eye. Each one is a divine appointment, chosen specifically for us by our loving Father, who promises to hold our hand throughout each excruciating circumstance. We have His word on that. "No testing has overtaken you that is not common to everyone. God is faithful, and he will not let you be tested beyond your strength, but with the testing he will also provide the way out so that you may be able to endure it" (1 Cor. 10:13, NRSV).

When we suffer unjustly without resorting to retaliation in kind or venting, we bring honor to our God, we vindicate His character. We prove His power because we are acting contrary to human nature. No one can do that without His strength. We're on a mission for God!

It's sad that life is not fair, people are not always nice, and the good guys don't always win. But in spite of this, God will prevail in unfair situations as long as we rely on Him completely to get us through them.

We are His ambassadors, and our victory is sure.

Céleste Perrino-Walker

Faith on Earth and Inside the Bus

However, when the Son of Man comes,
will he find faith on the earth? Luke 18:8, NIV.

One Saturday afternoon my husband and I went out for a saunter along the beach. We took a bus to get there. As we rode, I wondered, *How many people in this city where I live are interested in God?* And I thought of the words of Jesus in today's text. In the state of mind that I was in, I think I would have answered, "No, Jesus, You will not find what You are looking for here."

In the seats in front of us I noticed two women talking. The older woman seemed to be advising the younger one. Curiosity won, and I began to pay attention to their conversation— they were talking about God. What a discovery! I wanted to tell them, "Look, I also like to talk about God. It's good to find that other people are noticing that God acts in their lives." But it was only a momentary fantasy. I stayed quiet in my seat.

Immediately after, another woman entered the bus. She was slovenly, but seemed good-tempered. She stopped near the bus driver and walked down the aisle saying that she was religious, that she was passing through difficult moments financially, and that she was asking for help. Nothing different about that. But then she began to give a personal testimony of her life with God. With simplicity she spoke about her escape from God and her return to Him. She commented that she had asked God if He loved her, as she was Black and had bad hair (her own words). God answered, "My daughter, do you love Me?" And she answered, "Yes, my Lord, I love You." Then God replied, "For I love those who love Me, and for Me you are beautiful."

She said it with such conviction that she impressed me. This dialogue continued resounding in my mind a long time after she left and a long time after I left the bus. I realized that inside that bus I did not know anybody, but I had found proof that there is still faith on earth. Even with evil and selfishness increasing, God still has His children here, children who cry out to Him. They are around us, but not always in churches.

The simple woman's faith shook me. She spoke with conviction of how much God loved her. It forced me to change my imaginary dialogue with Jesus. He asked, "Will the Son of Man find faith on the earth?" Then I answered, "Yes, You will, Lord. These are Your children."

Iani Dias Lauer-Leite

Got Lotion? Part 1

And if you spend yourselves in behalf of the hungry and satisfy the needs of the oppressed, then your light will rise in the darkness, and your night will become like the noonday. The Lord will guide you always; he will satisfy your needs in a sun-scorched land and will strengthen your frame. You will be like a well-watered garden, like a spring whose waters never fail. Isa. 58:10, 11, NIV.

A few years ago I was on a flight departing from Baltimore, Maryland, traveling to Denver, Colorado. The airplane was full except for the middle seat next to me. As the flight attendant announced the closing of the doors, I could hardly contain my elation at the prospect of having an armrest for myself and not having to make small talk to the stranger next to me. Of course, I would say a quick greeting to my seatmate on the aisle, then turn my face toward the window, sink my face into my pillow, and sleep for the duration of the almost four-hour trip.

As I was making my glorious plans and thanking God for this wonderful blessing, the final departure proceedings were interrupted, the doors reopened, and a tall (like six feet four inches tall) young man in his 20s, with unkempt shoulder-length hair, entered the cabin with a huge snowboard and an overstuffed backpack. My heart immediately sank as I realized that my well-made plans were about to go awry! *Dear God,* I silently pleaded, *please hear my humble cry, and find him a seat other than the one next to me.*

Once situated in "my" middle seat, the lanky young man realized that he couldn't fit both his legs and his bag under the seat in front of him. So he looked over at me with a questioning smile and—before I could respond—dumped his backpack under the seat in front of me. Now, not only did I not have room for my arms, my legroom was also taken. I tried to be civil and muttered an almost grumpy hello. He greeted me back with a big grin, slumped down in his seat, and went to sleep. I decided I would make the best of the situation and proceeded to go to sleep as well—not with the same joy I had earlier, but with a need to put myself out of my misery. An elbow intentionally pressed into my side awakened me. *Now what?* "Got lotion?" he asked.

God never promised life would always be convenient. But He did promise He'd use us as lights in darkness. He said He'd give us strength for His tasks and refresh others through us.

Elaine Oliver

Got Lotion? Part 2

"For I know the plans I have for you," declares the Lord, "plans to prosper you and not to harm you, plans to give you hope and a future." Jer. 29:11, NIV.

I slowly opened my eyes and turned in the young man's direction.
"Got lotion?" he repeated cheerily. Before I could answer, he asked again, this time pointing toward my purse. "You got any lotion? I know you do in that big bag. My mom always has lotion in her bag, and you look like a mom, so I'm sure you have lotion somewhere in there!"

I couldn't help smiling as I retrieved my lotion and handed it to him. He slathered his face, hands, and arms with the lotion while telling me how nice it was. I just nodded and smiled some more. He was not put off at all by my less-than-friendly disposition. "Where can I get some lotion like this? I think my mom would love it." As he mentioned his mom I caught a sudden glimpse of sadness and confusion on his face. Instantly my heart softened, and I realized that this young man needed something more than lotion. I then invited him to share more about his mom.

For the duration of the flight I listened as my young seatmate poured out his heart. His parents had divorced a few years back. His mom had recently moved to another state with her new boyfriend. His dad, with whom he'd been staying for several months, had just asked him to move out—and had refused to pay the overweight fee, telling his son to go find another way to support himself. My seatmate had shifted some items from his check-through luggage into his backpack. He was on his way to a ski resort in Colorado where he'd been able to get seasonal work as a ski lift operator. His girlfriend had recently broken up with him, claiming that his future looked hopeless.

When my seatmate found out that I was a marriage and family counselor, he asked me if I thought there was hope for him. I assured him that there was and that God had great plans for his life. He told me he wasn't sure he believed in God, but he felt he could trust me. That day Jeremiah 29:11 wasn't just for the young man's encouragement. It also reminded me that I'd nearly missed the opportunity to be the real "lotion" needed by the young man that day.

Dear Lord, help me to work off of Your plans in my life today and not by the plans driven by my fleshly needs. Frustrate my plans and desires that are not of You and fill me with Your peace and Your joy for my journey today. Amen.

Elaine Oliver

Pay It Forward!

*Let your light so shine before men, that they may see
your good works, and glorify your Father which is in heaven. Matt. 5:16.*

I have been blessed to have strong women in my life who have inspired and motivated me to be the best woman that I can be. They have withstood hardships from miscarriages to alcoholic husbands, from struggling to make ends meet to loneliness. They have shown that being a woman is a blessing and a victory. They never buckled, they never dropped their standards. They squared their shoulders and pushed through, singing as they went.

One such woman that stands out for me is my mother. What really warms me is her support and example. Through all the ups and downs in my life she has been there. When I didn't do so well in school in the beginning she chided gently, then sent me back to get it right. She never missed a parent conference or award ceremony. When I completed my first degree (largely because of her making sure I always had tuition) and started painting, then writing, she cheered me on. From the start of to the dissolution of my first marriage, the birth of my daughter, my second marriage, and everything in between, she has been there—and is still there.

What an inspiration! She recently found out that she's diabetic and hypertensive. Instead of succumbing to artificial drugs, she challenged her doctor to give her a chance to get it down and managed. She changed her diet, exercised, and rested properly. Her next checkup blew the doctor away. He was so impressed with what she had done that he wanted her to come and lecture. By observing how she has dealt with the challenges of her life, I learned how to square my shoulders, look straight ahead, and push forward.

I wanted to share this with you because we have all encountered exceptional women; women who have inspired us with their great works—or seemingly small accomplishments. Women who have succeeded in spite of insurmountable odds: the Rahabs, the Naomis, the Hannahs, the Priscillas. God places them in our lives for a reason, and that is for us to pay it forward and become the next inspiration, the next group of women to inspire greatness or kindness or just the desire to overcome. You and I are to be the inspirations unto righteousness for the next cloud of witnesses. Pay it forward!

Greta Michelle Joachim-Fox-Dyett

GodPods

Therefore all things whatsoever ye would that men should do to you, do ye even so to them. Matt. 7:12.

Oh, it was so exciting! Sunday morning we had gathered at our church and were now ready for business: making pies! My job was to use a strange gadget that peeled, cored, and sliced apples. Soon I caught on to the knack of it, and off I went. Others did likewise. Soon the pans were filled with sliced apples, ready for "sugar, and spice, and everything nice."

It was fun to see how everyone seemed to enjoy themselves. There was much laughter and conversation, but the hands kept working. Men were on the job: loggers, elders, a treasurer, a contractor, and even our medical doctor. Children who came with their mothers were pressed into service to wash each of the 1,000 pounds of Macintosh apples. Mothers made and rolled dough; others filled pie pans while others bagged them. The assembly line worked smoothly and efficiently.

At lunchtime soup and buns renewed our energy, and then we continued our job, rejuvenated. The morning had gone so quickly. We continued all afternoon, and when finished, 313 pies and 56 apple crisps covered all the tables. Next morning everything was sold!

Why all the pies and apple crisps? In our congregation we have a couple who have been helping REACH (Render Effective Aid to Children), getting an orphanage started in Tanzania. Last year they took a few iPods in the Swahili language. Many people cannot read or write in their language, but they can listen to the iPods, only now we call them "GodPods," as they can hear the good news of Jesus' love in their own language.

A goal was set: 1,000 GodPods at $46 a piece—$46,000. Quite a sum to raise in a few months for Beryl and Darrell. There was much work to do. Many friends from far and near rallied to support. The money began coming in but not fast enough. Then someone suggested selling pies. The plan began moving. Brenden and Janelle drove more than 466 miles (750 kilometers) one way to secure fresh Macintosh apples. That was when another pie session began the next Sunday.

Our goal of $46,000 was realized, and we praised God for helping. It was so exciting to realize how a church family could come together and work for the Lord. Nothing is too big for our Lord if we go forward in faith.

Muriel Heppel

Hoarding

Create in me a clean heart, O God, and put a new
and right spirit within me. Ps. 51:10, NRSV.

Recently I surfed the TV cable guide and found a program called *Buried Alive*. Out of curiosity I clicked "Select" and was thrust into the most disgusting house that I have ever seen. It was filled with items that at a glance were unidentifiable; they covered furniture, shelves, anywhere that they could be stacked—even on the floor. There was little room for living or even walking. Although I was disgusted, my curiosity kept me glued to the screen. I discovered that this house belonged to an elderly woman, formerly a lawyer, who was grieving for her deceased husband. This led her to hoard mostly useless things, to the point that they had become a hazard to her health and life. She was given an ultimatum by the authorities: clean out the clutter or have the house condemned.

I self-righteously thought, *This could never be me.* But then I thought again (or was it the Holy Spirit speaking to me?): *What about my spiritual house? Is there a comparison?* I began to think, and I saw my mind cluttered with hurts that I have remembered for years. I remembered past disappointments, unkind acts that I have suffered in my professional and personal life. I remembered unkind words that have been spoken. I was libeled more than 20 years ago, and still get an adrenaline rush when I remember. Even more at risk to my spiritual health were past sins for which I have asked God's forgiveness, but evidently I had not forgiven myself, as I remember with remorse. My excuse for remembering all this garbage is that I am protecting myself from any recurrence, but the fact is that I am hoarding, and need to do some housecleaning.

Today my spiritual house is at risk of being condemned. I beg Jesus to clean out the useless and destructive clutter, to help me truly forgive others as well as myself. I ask God to give me selective amnesia to the many hurts in my life that have passed, and those to come. When God has cleared the clutter, I ask Him to create mental spaces for me to place the countless blessings that I do not deserve but God has constantly sent my way over the years; they far outweigh the hurts. I want to give the Holy Spirit unhindered access to live within me. I remember that Jesus endured far more suffering than I can ever imagine, and which He did not deserve, yet some of His final words were "Forgive them."

Cecelia Grant

There's a Devotional in This

Shew me thy ways, O Lord; teach me thy paths. Ps. 25:4.

My mother was my first Bible teacher. I loved listening to her tell me all the wonderful stories from the Bible. Then when I was older, in kindergarten, she was also my Sabbath school teacher. Each Sabbath we'd all troop down to the basement of the church and sing songs such as "Jesus Loves Me, This I Know" or "Jesus Wants Me for a Sunbeam" with our faces stuck through giant sun cutouts. Then off to the lesson study, where we sat around sand tables. She would stick paper figures in the sand to tell about the lesson. I still have some of those figures in my keepsake chest.

As I grew older, lessons became more detailed, and Mom didn't do the teaching, although we did study at home every night. Through those lessons she would ensure that no matter what we would be going through, someone in the Bible had gone through the same thing sometime or another. With that we knew we could go to the Bible and pray for counsel and comfort in our situation. Of course, in my youthful state in life, it took awhile for me to really understand that.

As I am now older, I see what she meant. I am so happy for the times we shared; I greatly miss being able to call her just for a few moments of prayer to get through the tough times.

But I have found an added dimension to being able to find answers and comfort in life situations. Now when I go through something, I hear my mother's soft voice saying, "Look to the Bible to find the answers," and I get to add to that with "There's a devotional in this!"

I feel very blessed to be given lessons to learn from, as well as to be able to write them down and find ways to share with others. I am not what some might think of as the best one to relate these lessons. Somehow, my sense of humor has developed in such a way that I have a different way of looking at things. But that is OK. Life lessons are not the very same for everyone. Just like snowflakes or people, no two are alike; nevertheless, they are special.

Remember, everything that happens to you is for a special reason. Some of them are not so pleasant, and others are the happiest moments in your life. Just remember there is a special lesson, a devotional, in there just for you and you alone. Relish it. Cherish it. Write them down. It's God's little sweet message just for you!

Mary E. Dunkin

Love Returned*

If anyone acknowledges that Jesus is the Son of God,
God lives in [her] and [she] in God. And so we know and
rely on the love God has for us. 1 John 4:15, 16, NIV.

It had been a day to remember. When less than 24 hours old, our newest grandson, Eric, had come home. For the first few hours we all took turns examining his tiny toes, button nose, and funny-looking tummy button. His 4-year-old brother, Ryan, and 2-year-old sister, Heather, were his most devoted fans. Finally at bedtime my daughter offered her two older children a reward for getting ready for bed without delays. The reward—one last chance to hold their new brother! It was a prize they couldn't resist. Soon they both reappeared bathed and pajama-clad.

When it was Ryan's turn to cradle the newest member of the family, his mother suggested that because he was the "big brother," he could hold the baby on his shoulder—the way she did. So with one hand supporting tiny Eric's head and the other around his waist, Ryan rocked the baby. All of a sudden the baby began to awaken. Arching his neck and drawing up his tiny legs, he squirmed in Ryan's arms. When Ryan felt his brother moving against him, he called out excitedly, "Look, Mom, he's loving me back!"

Many times since, I've thought about this simple exchange between two brothers and Ryan's delight over Eric's unconscious movements—accepted as his own love returned. How wonderful to be "loved back" by a loved one or a friend. How we search for this response in even the simplest acts!

In a beautiful book entitled *The Desire of Ages* I found a moving description of how our Savior longs to be "loved back": "Our Redeemer thirsts for recognition. He hungers for the sympathy and love of those whom He has purchased with His own blood. He longs with inexpressible desire that they should come to Him and have life. As the mother watches for the smile of recognition from her little child, which tells of the dawning of intelligence, so does Christ watch for the expression of grateful love, which shows that spiritual life is begun in the soul" (p. 191).

What an incredible truth—the Savior of the world longs for His children to "love Him back," in simple ways—every day. Today, how will you love Him back?

Rose Otis

*From *A Gift of Love* (Review and Herald Pub. Assn., 1994), pp. 389, 390.

Getting Rid of Junk

Therefore you shall be perfect, just as your Father
in heaven is perfect. Matt. 5:48, NKJV.

I do not remember where the motivation came from, but I found myself clearing out my home. We were moving to another house. As I packed our stuff, I noticed that my family and I had a lot of items we had not used for many years. We even had stuff that was still unpacked even though we had now lived in Harare, Zimbabwe, for many years. But now it was time to relocate; my husband received a call to serve in his home country of Botswana. As I was sorting out what to pack and what to give away or throw away, I was amazed at how much stuff we did not need. Some of the things were in good condition and therefore we could easily give them away; others were not in good condition at all and were fit to be thrown away.

After working in Francistown, Botswana, for a year, my husband received a call to serve in another area about 280 miles (450 kilometers) away. As we packed our stuff, it was amazing to notice again how many cartons were still unpacked. Six years later my husband received yet another call to work in a different capacity. Each time we moved, I noticed that there was a lot of junk that we were holding on to, and some of the stuff had never been used in six years.

It is not easy to sell, give away, or throw away some stuff that actually is no longer useful in our daily lives. That stuff will probably become junk, and it is easy to get comfortable living among junk. There can be a lot of unwanted items in our homes, offices, churches, tool sheds, and garages. Once in a while now I try to get rid of junk, either from my office or from my home. I am always delighted to have so much space and order when I get rid of junk.

My dear sisters (and brothers who may read this), it is very easy to harbor junk in our hearts as well. We need to ask Jesus to help us get rid of the rubbish that takes up precious space in our hearts. It is easy to harbor junk such as hatred, envy, jealousy, selfish ambitions, pride, contentions, greed, grudges, and covetousness. Instead, let us allow Jesus to fill our hearts with the fruit of the Spirit found in Galatians 5:22, 23.

One day Jesus will come to take us home. On that day we shall realize that everything we own in this world, whatever we consider precious, and all that we consider to be of great value, will suddenly become junk. Today is the day to get rid of junk!

Priscilla Matimba Ben

Blessings

All of you be of one mind, having compassion
for one another. 1 Peter 3:8, NKJV.

I would like to purchase this bolt of flannel from the clearance rack," I told the clerk at our local Walmart store.

"OK, I will measure it for you to see how many yards there are. You want it all? Do you mind if I ask what you are planning to do with so much fabric?" I was proud to tell her that our Secret Sister group at church planned to make flannel baby blankets for newborns in a developing country. The clerk went about her duties and I added several additional bolts to my order. As I loaded my shopping cart with the entire yardage she reached into her pocket and pulled out some cash. "Here, take this. I want to have a part in this worthy project too." Wow! That was such a blessing to me even as we were in the process of blessing others.

Our example, Jesus, went about doing good while He walked on this earth. He healed the sick, fed the hungry crowds; He even helped with the drinks at a wedding and visited in many homes, cheering people one at a time or in a group. He was always a blessing to those around Him. We are His feet and hands in the world today as we find ways to help others. Jesus shines out of our hearts, and we all receive a rich blessing.

On another occasion our group chose to minister hands-on to an elderly woman who had just arrived in this country. We did not speak the same language, but smiles can be understood in all languages. She was a wheelchair user, but that didn't stop us as we figured out a way to touch her life. One of our group who is a nurse did foot care, while someone else did her nails, then a professional cut her hair. We also gave her several gifts, such as new slippers, a lap quilt, and all the products we had used for her makeover. To end the evening we sang her favorite hymns, which she of course recognized by the tune. There were smiles and happy tears from her and her family. You just have to feel good after a session like that!

Jesus once said, "Whatever you did for one of the least of these brothers and sisters of mine, you did for me" (Matt. 25:40, NIV). Today, think about where you can lend a helpful hand, say an encouraging word, or do a kind deed while expecting nothing in return except to receive the blessing that comes with giving.

Rosemary Byrd Hickman

The Dreams of Your Heart

Delight thyself also in the Lord: and he shall
give thee the desires of thine heart. Ps. 37:4.

Henry David Thoreau, writer, poet, and American philosopher, wrote that castles in the air can become a reality if only we put forth the effort to build their foundations in reality.

We human beings normally dream in our sleep or in wakefulness through daydreaming. Daydreaming can also include thinking about our aspirations. Thoreau was referring to the latter. Though an individual cannot spend all her life daydreaming or building castles in the air, dreaming about our aspirations can be useful. After all, everyone dreams of fulfilled desires, plans, projects, and dreams. The psalmist called them "the desires of thine heart."

Bible scholars claim that the Bible contains more than 3,000 promises. Therefore, every believer can see from God's Word that many of these promises have already been fulfilled in their life. Something interesting happens when we read these promises in the Bible: hope is revived. And the context of hope is a good place to be when we start talking to God about having our dreams fulfilled. To speak to Him of our dreams is to speak to Him of our faith . . . in *His* wisdom and power. Faith in His promises is necessary if we want to maintain hope that He will fulfill the desires of our hearts, according to His promises and His will. Faith will also sustain us during those difficult times when we wonder if God is really going to fulfill those promises.

The dream of Hannah's heart was to have a son. According to God's promise in the Temple through priest Eli, Hannah's dream became a reality in Samuel. Hannah made two choices toward her dream becoming reality. First, though her dream was in her heart, her knees were on the ground. "And she . . . prayed unto the Lord, and wept sore" (1 Sam. 1:10). Claiming victory on our knees opens our hearts to God's will in our lives. Second, Hannah had faith, with its accompanying sense of security, in her loving God. The biblical account continues: "So the woman [Hannah] went her way, and did eat, and her countenance was no more sad" (verse 18). If we trust our hearts' dreams to the Lord, He will honor our prayers and efforts.

So today is a good day to envision a dream. A good day to work toward victory on our knees. A good day to banish worry and sadness. A good day to put our faith and hope in the Lord, moving forward in confidence. And in trust that He will fulfill the dreams of our hearts.

Cecilia Moreno de Iglesias

God Answers Our Prayers

Call unto me, and I will answer thee, and shew
thee great and mighty things, which thou knowest not. Jer. 33:3.

All of us wait for answers to our prayers from God. Sometimes He gives the answer to our prayer right away, but often we don't expect the things God will give to us. I would like to tell about those blessings and about that great love that the Lord presented to us.

When my daughter was 17, she had gynecological surgery and the doctor said she would never have children. We were concerned but decided that if she married, they could adopt a child.

Not long after, I became an Adventist Christian. And I started to learn to pray. I had been reading books about prayer. Following the advice in one of the books, I cut pieces of paper and wrote on each a prayer request for my daughter, and put them into her Bible. I asked God for a good son-in-law and a granddaughter. I wrote to God: "I ask You give me a granddaughter. I really want two granddaughters, but give me at least one."

Concerning the son-in-law, God answered immediately. I met a woman who told me how she prayed for a husband: "Lord, give me a husband of whom I would be worthy!" I told my daughter, and she started to pray this way. Four years after the surgery, she got married. The choice was very interesting: the man has no parents, no work, nothing by the measures of this world. When I asked her: "Why Zhenya? He has nothing. You have rejected good boys."

"Mom, he is kind; he would be a good family man, and he appreciates a family. I prayed. And when I told him that I may not have children, he told me, 'But we will be together.'" In 2002 they married, and in 2003 Katya was born. Two years later Eve, and in 2012 God gave them a son, Damir. These children have everything, especially love and understanding.

Fathers such as is our Zhenya are difficult to find—he does everything. God blessed my children so much! And the miracle is that when Aliona was waiting for the first child she had an ultrasound. The doctor looked at her medical records and couldn't believe her eyes—everything was as if no surgery had been made; there was only a scar. The doctor who did the surgery said only God could have done this. And we agree. And we thank God above all!

Alla Shumilo

God Meant It for Good

And we know that God causes everything to work together
for the good of those who love God and are called according
to his purpose for them. Rom. 8:28, NLT.

One week before Thanksgiving 2005 I received a call from the world church headquarters requesting that I take charge in establishing a Bachelor of Nursing program at Valley View University in Ghana. My husband and I had returned the year before after spending six years in Kenya, so a call again to the motherland was exciting, but this time seemed a bit more challenging.

I listened carefully and prayed about the offer. Everyone felt that God was calling me to this task. My husband was promised a position in the university's Counseling Department.

Mission service requires physical examinations and health screenings. During one of these screenings the doctor told my husband to schedule follow-up visits every six months.

The next year I made my first visit to Ghana with a team of nursing consultants for two weeks. We arrived in Ghana to live later that year and received permission to begin the program. The first group of students began classes in September 2007.

My husband continued his biannual appointments, but it was taking a toll on our resources and creating anxiety for the administration. After three years I requested to return home for the sake of my husband's health. We were again required to have physical examinations and screenings. My mammograms previously were all normal. In 2010, during Breast Cancer Awareness Month at our church's weekly prayer meeting, I was impressed to remind the women that they should all have routine screening for breast cancer. I also told them that whenever I am scheduled for any medical test I ask God to reveal anything abnormal. Sure enough, that very week when I went for my routine mammogram I was told that something suspicious was found and further evaluation was necessary. Be careful what you ask for!

I thought we left mission service because of my husband's health, not knowing that God was looking out for my health as well. My husband's health is now stable. Today's text continues to strengthen me as I see God working in every facet of my life. What a mighty God we serve!

Lydia D. Andrews

Unclean

But we are all like an unclean thing, and all our righteousnesses
are like filthy rags; we all fade as a leaf, and our iniquities,
like the wind, have taken us away. Isa. 64:6, NKJV.

I walked into the kitchen but stopped in horror. The floor was dirty! Why hadn't I noticed that before? There were crumbs and spills all over. Why could I see it now and hadn't seen it before? Sunshine. That was what was revealing the dirt.

I thought of other kitchen floors I have had that had never gotten any sunshine, and I thought of the dark tile kitchens in government quarters. Had I been living with dirty floors all these years and not seen it? Oh, I had cleaned—regularly—but I had not seen the dirt before or after I swept and mopped. I even remembered the last house we lived in—all-white tile floors. What had I been thinking? We had a black cat! I now live in a house with hardwood floors and lots of windows and sunshine. But today, even after I had recently cleaned, I could see every crumb and even flecks of dust. Why? Because of the sunshine. What a difference it makes!

I could not help thinking about my life. I think I am doing a pretty good job keeping my life clean and in order. But then the Son shines in. Horror of horrors! There is filth everywhere.

I love the story of the woman bleeding for 12 years as found in Matthew 9 and Mark 5. Because she was bleeding, this poor woman was unclean. And according to the beliefs, when she touched Jesus He should have become unclean as well. But that made no difference to Jesus, and when He healed her she became clean—clean spiritually, physically, socially, and emotionally. It cannot get any better than that! That is what I need personally—never mind the floors!

I like how David described the situation for us when we realize how dirty our hearts and lives really are. And it makes no difference how serious our sin, as David's own life exhibited. Here is how the New Living Translation records David's cry: "Don't keep looking at my sins. Remove the stain of my guilt. Create in me a clean heart, O God. Renew a loyal spirit within me. Do not banish me from your presence, and don't take your Holy Spirit from me" (Ps. 51:9-11, NLT).

This is not the time to draw the drapes, turn out the lights, or pretend there is no dirt. Today let us cry out to our Savior, asking for the Son, seeking a clean heart and life.

Ardis Dick Stenbakken

I Can Choose

You will keep him in perfect peace, whose mind is stayed
on You, because he trusts in You. Isa. 26:3, NKJV.

Something's wrong!" My husband's voice was strained and quiet. Glancing at him, I saw the apprehension and tension on his face. "My hands and arms are numb and tingling."

We were sitting in a small crowd; my eyes quickly searched for a physician or nurse. My friend, a nurse, sat a few tables away deep in conversation. Ignoring the rules of proper etiquette, I unceremoniously burst into their discussion and whispered into her ear, "Edith, come. Now!"

She came, asked questions of my husband, and then summoned another friend who also works in the medical field. The 9-1-1 call went out, the police came, then the emergency medical technicians with an ambulance, and my husband was whisked off to the emergency room.

Another friend, also a health-care professional, accompanied me as I followed the ambulance to the hospital. Various tests were given, vials of blood were drawn, an EKG and CT scan were administered, and a diagnosis was made. After hours of tension and waiting, we were finally on our way home, shaken and exhausted. Another crisis had passed. And then—then we were left to deal with the aftermath of my husband's medical problems.

I found myself filled with foreboding, the tears very close to the surface. As the days progressed I felt fearful to even have him out of my sight. My back and neck ached from tense muscles, my stomach cramped with worry, my head felt as though it would burst. After more than 50 years of marriage I've gotten accustomed to having my husband by my side, sharing life and pain, sorrow and laughter. I didn't want to lose that.

I am free to choose if I wish to continue living in this fearful state of turmoil. Or I can choose to put my trust in God, believing He has both my husband's and my best interests in mind. We believe He will take care of us in every situation—maybe not in the way we want, maybe not in the time frame we want, but in His own way, in His own time and wisdom. I realized that our heavenly Father had already shown His loving care for us in this situation. And so I choose to put my trust in Him and to entertain a calm outlook in my life. We know God is good; He has proven that to us in the past, and He will take care of us in the future. He wants only the best for us. I am at peace.

Barbara J. Reinholtz

Matchless Blessings

Let everything that has breath praise the Lord. Praise the Lord. Ps. 150:6, NIV.

One morning my mother woke me up. Not the usual "Kimasha, get up and get ready for work; it is 6:00!" (Or whatever time she realizes that I am still asleep.) That morning she was frantically searching for a matchstick in all corners of the house. I got up to help her when I understood that she was getting more and more perplexed as her search proved in vain.

"I just want to find one," she was saying.

Hoping that I could find at least one, I asked her to push me up onto the kitchen counter so I could look in the shelf above the stove. There, in the crack of the shelf, I found one. I felt victorious! I turned to her to ask for a knife so that I could pull it out. She was still searching, however, and not knowing that I had found that one matchstick, she said, "Well, Father, You said in everything, give thanks." As soon as she had said those words she found a new box of matches on another shelf. She was glad, and indeed, I was happy too. Nonetheless, I insisted on getting out that one match I was so careful to find. I also insisted that she use it too.

This experience taught me how important it is to praise God in advance. Just as the text that my mom had partially quoted says: "In every thing give thanks: for this is the will of God in Christ Jesus concerning you" (1 Thess. 5:18), so we give thanks even before we see the answer to our prayers.

God knew that I did not need to find that one match, because there was a box of matches in the kitchen waiting to be found. Sometimes we go through so much trouble on our own, trying to find a way out of the unfavorable situations we find ourselves in. Yes, we may find a way out, but how lasting is it? If we praise God in advance and trust Him to provide for us in spite of our efforts, we will surely see Him working things out for us in ways that are much more promising than one lonely match in the crack of a shelf.

When I compare that one match to a full box of matches, I think of God's unforeseen promises to me. I know that they will surpass much more than that which I can ever do for myself or think should be granted to me. It is because of His unmerited mercy that I am going to praise Him today and always. I am going to praise Him in advance.

Kimasha Pauline Williams

Thanks

In every thing give thanks. 1 Thess. 5:18.

"Thanks" is such a small but important word, but I wonder how many of us rarely use it.

First, we need to be thankful to the Lord for all His blessings. Each day that we wake up, it is reason to give thanks. We are alive. Give thanks for food, clothing, shelter, and the many things we take for granted. Then there are the birds, the trees, the sun, the stars, all nature for our enjoyment and benefit. Do we ever think to thank God for these? And what about answered prayers? "It is good to give thanks to the Lord" (Ps. 92:1, NKJV).

If we practice being thankful, we will find less time to complain. I once heard a woman say, "When I am tempted to complain about a sink full of dishes, I sing and give thanks. At least it is a sign that I had food to eat."

How do we relate to others? When someone opens the door, do we say thank you with a smile? People like to know they are appreciated. That one little word could help to lift someone's self-esteem, or brighten their day. We all like to be thanked when we do some good deed. Do we thank the Lord only in the good times, when things are going well? Today's text says, "In every thing give thanks." This is not easy. Someone destroys your property, robs or hurts you in some way, and you are to give thanks? Remember, it could be worse, but if you have a close and trusting relationship with the Lord, He will see you through.

I heard a story of a man who heard about a famous poet whose words were valued at $100 each. He went to the poet and said to him, "I heard that each of our words is worth $100; I would like to have one of those words." He handed a $100 bill to the poet. The poet took the bill, put it in his pocket, said "Thanks," and walked away.

Saying thanks is very important. In the cleansing and healing of the 10 lepers, Jesus noted that only one thanked Him. David, in Psalm 118:1, says, "O give thanks unto the Lord; for he is good." As we near Thanksgiving Day, it would be good to remember that Thanksgiving should be every day, and not just one day.

Christ came to this world and died to save us from our sins. Let us never forget to thank Him constantly for His great sacrifice on our behalf. So I say, "Thank You, Jesus."

Ena Thorpe

My Thanksgiving Miracle

Trust in the Lord with all your heart and lean not
on your own understanding; in all your ways submit to him,
and he will make your paths straight. Prov. 3:5, 6, NIV.

Another Thanksgiving was fast approaching, and I was hoping that my sisters and I would all be able to spend it together in New York. Two of them lived there, another two lived in the Caribbean, and I lived in Wales, so I believed that it would be a great time for us to be reunited. I was also secretly hoping and earnestly praying that with the help of my friend I would find my long-lost godmother, whom I had last seen some 35 years before when I was a child. I knew that she resided in the big United States, but where? I had tried several times before to locate her, but they were all unsuccessful.

I had recently moved to a new house, and thieves had broken into the garage and stolen some stuff that I stored there. My friend reminded me that "in every thing give thanks" even though I couldn't think of any reason to do so, since I was so upset. She had moved the remainder of the things stored in the garage into the house and decided to sort it out. She pointed to a bag indicating that I should sort it. I was not in the mood to do it, but decided just to have a peek in the bag. There I stumbled on an old address book, and my eyes were soon fixed on the name and phone number of the mother of my godmother, Aunty "Wellese." I called, but the number was no longer in service. *What do I do now? Where do I start to look? Lord, I need Your help!*

I ran to the computer and Googled the address of Aunty Wellese and recognized the names of some of her other daughters, but I could not reach them. I solicited the help of my sister, Karen, in New York, who had just phoned me. She found the number, and I dialed it. A distinct Caribbean accent flowed into my ear. I asked, "Are you Aunty Wellese?"

"Yes." After some questions and introductions, I impatiently blurted out, "I'm looking for my godmother, Norma." She gave me the number, and I soon heard a soft "Hello" from Norma, my long-lost godmother.

Thanksgiving was really the time for me to give God thanks for meeting my sisters and by a splendid reunion on Thanksgiving Day with Norma and her family members in Virginia.

I had lots to thank God for, since He'd blessed me with my Thanksgiving miracle!

Roxanne Girard

How Could I Have Forgotten?

He that dwelleth in the secret place of the most High
shall abide under the shadow of the Almighty. I will say of the Lord,
He is my refuge and my fortress: my God; in him will I trust. Ps. 91:1, 2.

November 26, 2011, cannot and will not be erased from my memory. No one enjoys going through such an experience even when surrounded by friends and family, much less if one is alone. And that was my situation when Hurricane Tomas hit St. Lucia that Sabbath morning. It began to rain around 8:00 in the morning. I was home alone since my sister with whom I lived at the time had gone to visit my mom in Dominica. I woke up, thanked God for another Sabbath day, and started preparing to make my way to church.

However, the rain came down even heavier. I was aware of the storm approaching the islands, but unaware of its exact path, and whether or not it had developed into a hurricane; I turned my radio on. The announcement was made: there would be no church because of the inclement weather. All there was left to do was to sit meditating on God's goodness, waiting for it all to calm down. But it never did; it got worse until about 6:00 the next morning.

I could only imagine how the disciples felt on the sea while the storm raged. But like the disciples, there was something important that I forgot. The many calls from my mom and family members could calm my fears only temporarily. I had forgotten that Jesus was right there, riding out the storm with me. The many possible things that could happen that night plagued my mind. *What if the wind took my roof away?* The neighbor's was already gone, and we shared the same apartment building. Where would I run to? So many robberies take place at such a time—what if my apartment was a target?

How could I have forgotten Psalm 46:10, 11? "Be still, and know that I am God: I will be exalted among the heathen, I will be exalted in the earth. The Lord of hosts is with us; the God of Jacob is our refuge." How could I have forgotten how the winds and the waves obeyed Him? How could I have forgotten that my Jesus is the same yesterday, today, and forever (Heb. 13:8)? In the dark I whispered a prayer and was reminded through that still small voice that He was there with me. Only then was I able to fall asleep, comforted that my Jesus was right beside me.

Amanda Isles

Taking Nothing for Granted

Always give thanks to God the Father for everything. Eph. 5:20, NCV.

When life is good, we seldom think about the many blessings we receive from the Lord each day. Such as the brand-new day we're given, during which we can choose to be God's representative.

So many things to be thankful for. Here are some examples:

The weather: I have lived in safe areas all my life; no ice storms, tornadoes, or hurricanes! How blessed!

Good health: I'm reminded of this every time I visit friends and family in the hospital or rehabilitation. For some, that's just their way of life.

Life: I like to say, "Every day aboveground is a good day." We celebrate birthdays and the life God has given us for the new year! The more years we add to our lives, the more we see friends and family whose lives end; some older, some at our age, and some younger. This reminds me to live every day to the fullest, without any regrets.

Friends: I've been blessed down through the years, and I'm truly grateful! I have moved so many times during my lifetime that I often joke that I will know most of the people in heaven. We just attended a large church convention in Tennessee at which we met many former friends from all over the United States. It was awesome!

Freedom: what a blessing to live in a country in which I can attend church openly each week. I'll never take that for granted. I am truly thankful to worship with fellow believers. The great preachers I can watch on television are also blessings. There's a blessing in Christian radio stations over which people can hear great music and God's Word each day. I praise God for Adventist World Radio, which can take the gospel to countries that don't have religious freedom.

Take a minute to think of the things you are thankful for: a quiet neighborhood; a nice, comfortable bed to sleep in; a warm shower; plenty of food for three meals a day; that you can taste your food; a rewarding job; funds to keep the bills paid and help ministries around the world; that you can keep in contact with your friends; for the trials God sends our way; and the special angel He gives us. Where would we be without God's love? Give thanks with a grateful heart, and never take even the smallest things for granted.

Louise Driver

May God Give You According to Your Faith

As Jesus went on from there, two blind men followed him, calling out, "Have mercy on us, Son of David!" When he had gone indoors, the blind men came to him, and he asked them, "Do you believe that I am able to do this?" "Yes, Lord," they replied. Then he touched their eyes and said, "According to your faith let it be done to you"; and their sight was restored. Jesus warned them sternly, "See that no one knows about this." But they went out and spread the news about him all over that region. Matt. 9:27-31, NIV.

Here in Russia I learned about a satellite program during which every person who wished could write a prayer request on a piece of paper; you could write about any problem you wanted to have prayed about. I also wrote out a prayer request. I pleaded that God would have mercy on my brother who had not been able to see during the previous year.

Until the time he lost his sight in both eyes, he could see with one eye; the other eye had been blind for three years. When the second eye started to lose its sight, he underwent many surgeries; unfortunately, none of them were a success.

When the second eye lost its sight, he asked God for two things: that God would let him see his wife—even if just a little bit—because of course he wished to see her, and his plate, because he had been having difficulty eating.

When I wrote the prayer request note, I started to pray earnestly, and I believed that the Lord would answer my prayer and my brother's prayer.

Finally, as a last resort, the doctors proposed another surgery on the eye that had been blind for several years. And the surgery finished successfully! Today my brother can see a plate with food and his wife! These are a very narrow span of sight possibilities, but it was the answer to our prayers. As much as you asked—as much you received!

There was nothing magic about the satellite prayer request program; we are told, "If you believe, you will receive whatever you ask for in prayer" (Matt. 21:22, NIV), but sometimes we just need to ask. John 16:24 says, "Until now you have not asked for anything in my name. Ask and you will receive, and your joy will be complete" (NIV). Praise the Lord for His love and mercy, and the wonderful miracles that He continues to show in our lives!

Raisa Ostrovskaya

Protected

The Lord will protect you from all danger; he will keep you safe. He will protect you as you come and go now and forever. Ps. 121:7, 8, TEV.

It was early Thursday morning when I was awakened by some noise outside my house. Because I was tired from working the night before, I ignored it and went back to sleep. About a half hour later I heard shouts coming from inside my house, "Police, police!" Opening my bedroom door, I faced two police officers on my stairway. The police officers asked, "Is this your house?"

I responded with a confused "Yes." They then asked me to come downstairs and turn off my alarm. *How did two police officers come into my house when my doors were locked?* I asked the officers what was going on. They explained that my alarm had gone off, and that the security company called them when they could not get in touch with me. My phone was on "silence" from the night before while I was working, and I had forgotten to turn it back on; therefore, I did not hear my phone ringing when the alarm company called me.

The officers explained that they had found my back door unlocked, so they came in and searched downstairs and were preparing to search upstairs for intruders. I was not aware that my back door was unlocked in the first place, and the strangest part of it all is that I did not hear my alarm going off. Even though I am a light sleeper, I had slept through the alarm. The police officers cited me for a false alarm, but a week later my neighbor informed me that when they examined their security camera's film from the night of the incident, they saw two men running away from my house. The police department took the film, and later the officers were able to find and arrest the burglars.

Sometimes we pray, thanking God for His protection and asking Him to keep us safe through the night. We may say these prayers as a routine, but that night I know it was God who protected me. *Why didn't the alarm wake me up?* I know that God allowed me to sleep through it. He knew that if I had awakened, I would probably have gone downstairs and been faced with the intruders. This story could have had a very different outcome. Let us not take God's protection for granted!

Agnes Vaughan

A Journey of Faith

I tell you the truth, if you had faith even as small as a mustard seed,
you could say to this mountain, "Move from here to there,"
and it would move. Nothing would be impossible. Matt. 17:20, NLT.

Leaving your life in one city, moving across country, and starting over in a new place is never an easy decision to make. However, my husband and I felt convicted that it was time to again make such a move. We were both working in very demanding and stressful jobs that no longer held much appeal. We wanted to experience a better quality of life than we currently had.

We decided to make the move a matter of prayer. We considered moving south, but we also wanted to be open to God's leading. We prayed for several years, and there seemed to be no response from God. There were a few opportunities that presented themselves, but they did not come to fruition. I must admit that we became discouraged at times and sometimes even wondered if God had heard our prayers and what His will was for us.

It was during a Bible lesson study at church that I really felt God speaking to me. We were discussing Abraham's call from God to leave his homeland and relocate to a new land that God would show him (Gen. 12:1-4). A woman in the study group pointed out that Abraham packed and got ready to leave without even knowing where he was going. He trusted God to lead him. As she spoke, I began to realize what God was calling us to do. This was not our regular congregation, but I believe God had led us to visit there so that we could receive that message.

I shared my conviction with my husband, and he agreed with me. And so in faith we began to pack our belongings and place things in storage. For a while nothing happened. However, our jobs continued to get more stressful, even causing us to develop health problems. We both felt led to quit the jobs and trust God to open doors for us. Friends thought that we were crazy to quit jobs during a recession, but that's when God began to move. In a matter of months He had opened up several opportunities, and then He narrowed it down to one. We did end up moving south, and throughout the move and resettlement process we saw God work miracle after miracle as we continued to put our faith and trust in Him. God wanted us to exercise faith before He answered, and it has truly been a journey of faith!

Karen Birkett Green

Financial Crises

This is what the Lord says: If you will return, I will take you back. If you will speak what is worthwhile and not what is worthless, you will stand in my presence. The people will return to you, but you will not return to them. I will make you like a solid bronze wall in front of these people. They will fight you, but they will not defeat you. I am with you, and I will save you and rescue you, declares the Lord. I will rescue you from the power of wicked people and free you from the power of tyrants. Jer. 15:19-21, GW.

While we see the collapse of nations and the financial structure crises all over the world, I am reminded of something I read years ago.

When my husband was designing Rio Lindo Academy (a Christian high school that in 2013 celebrated 50 years since construction was completed), a provider of the built-in furniture for the dormitories gave us several thank-you gifts. One was a subscription to a book-of-the-month club. I remember one book, written as a novel, talking about a coming financial crisis. It was back in 1960 when I read the book. The one thing that stuck in my mind was how interdependent all the world finances were, so that if one country failed, it would topple all the others like dominoes.

Now we have seen terrible financial crises in so many countries. No wonder people talk about a one world government! Here in the United States where I live, a few years back our financial situation became critical. People who thought they were financially secure are finding those securities wiped away or greatly reduced.

We are learning that nothing is secure, and we can depend only on God to give us wisdom to make good choices both spiritually and economically. Our only security is in God, and with Him we have nothing to fear. In Him all things will work together for good! (Rom. 8:28).

Only God can give you and me the peace that can come only from Him, our dear heavenly Father. We must claim His promise to provide us with our necessities as He did for the Israelites wandering in the wilderness, while we wait for His return—may it be soon. Our world and the things that are happening around us show that we cannot survive without His intervention. We pray today for His blessings alone.

Peggy Curtice Harris

People > Projects

And the King will say, "I tell you the truth, when you did it to one of the least of these my brothers and sisters, you were doing it to me." Matt. 25:40, NLT.

I t's done. The recording project started four years ago—putting the book of Revelation to song—has moved from our hands into others' who will refine, polish, and package it until it returns to us in a two-CD unit filled with the creative blood, sweat, and tears of more than 20 singers, writers, musicians, artists, and engineers. Whew! Now other hands will pop its ever-changing types of devices designed to move the music from disc to ears that will hear and nervous systems will feel pulse, chord, and tune. Hopefully, brains will comprehend the poetry. Then reactions will flow in—ringing affirmations; but also the criticisms of everything from that particular vocal to the instrumental treatment of such and such to the cover art to the artistic choices to "too tame" to "too wild" to *this should have been done like this . . . what were you thinking?*

By the grace of Jesus I'll ride these things out peacefully. The music, as important as it is, isn't as important as the souls who made it. See, I've learned that people are bigger than projects. Yes, God told us to occupy ourselves, work in His vineyard, stay busy, and bear fruit; and I believe God led in this creative endeavor. But in the middle of the marathon He taught me that the ones I ran beside mattered more than the finish line, the trophy, or the headlines. In fact, they *were* the finish line, the trophy and the headlines. Despite tediums and aggravations inherent in recording music. Despite inevitable disagreements arising, especially with my producer, Delon Lawrence, who worked long hours day and night. He mattered more. I'd find myself saying over and over, "I'd rather flush every one of these 45 tracks down the toilet than lose your friendship." And I meant it. Because Jesus has taught me what really matters, I meant it.

Religious zealots like me love to work, work, work for God. Actually, by virtue of a driven temperament I'd work, work, work—regardless. My bloodlines set me up. If God didn't have hold of my heart, the same drive that runs Christian music projects might run a large brothel or meth house. But in and of themselves, great works—even great religious works, mind you—don't indicate the presence of God. Love does. Without love, I am nothing. People > projects. People are more important than projects. Amen.

Jennifer Jill Schwirzer

The Tollbooth

As he was going into a village, ten men who had leprosy met him.
They stood at a distance and called out in a loud voice, "Jesus, Master,
have pity on us!" When he saw them, he said, "Go, show yourselves
to the priests." And as they went, they were cleansed. One of them,
when he saw he was healed, came back, praising God in a loud voice.
He threw himself at Jesus' feet and thanked him. Luke 17:12-16, NIV.

It was late afternoon when I pulled up to the unattended tollbooth with a carful of family. I gingerly inserted my $5 bill, listened to the change drop, scooped it up, and pulled away. The red light seemed stuck, and without thinking I stepped on the gas, ignoring my husband's complaints from the back seat that the light was still red. Meanwhile my sister-in-law, who was sitting next to me, picked through the change I handed her to verify the toll machine had taken the $2.25 I thought I had paid. But to her surprise, Claire counted $5 in quarters; I had only gotten change! By this time I was beyond the tollbooth and didn't know how I could right the situation.

For the rest of the afternoon I chided myself for being such a weenie of a Christian. I thought I had a firm hold on living right, but in one brief moment of inattention I broke the law. We went on our way to our destination and then headed back to the toll road to drive home. As we rolled up to another tollbooth, my husband leaned over to me and gently encouraged me to confess to the tollbooth attendant. Anything was better than the heavy burden of guilt hanging over my head.

The attendant listened and quickly handed us a card titled, "Missed a Toll?" As soon as we arrived home, I went to the Web address and read these words on the opening page: *"Enter your license plate information to verify your eligibility for a one-time courtesy toll payment without penalty."*

I was overcome with relief, and my heart turned to my heavenly Father. "Lord Jesus, thank You for lifting even the little burdens in my life. You have given me so much more than a one-time pass on a highway fine, but thank You for reminding me in this anxious moment that all You ask for is a grateful heart."

Nancy Neuharth Troyer

One Cold Night

*Have not I commanded thee? Be strong and of a good courage;
be not afraid, neither be thou dismayed: for the Lord thy God
is with thee whithersoever thou goest. Joshua 1:9.*

Indiana can be very cold in December, and this day was no different. I had taken my car to have the brake fluid checked, and I was in a hurry to pick up my car because I had an evening class to attend. When I arrived at the garage, I asked the mechanic if he had checked to make sure that I had enough brake fluid in my car. "Don't worry; it will be just fine," he reassured me. Usually I would check my fluid levels myself, but I was running late to meet my carpoolers to go to class.

Soon I reached our meeting place, but to my surprise my car pool riders were gone! So I had to drive a total of 54 miles by myself. This highway wasn't the most traveler-friendly, either. Plus, there were not a lot of stops along the way. Finally I made it to the university and sat through the three-hour lecture. Then it was time to head for home. I had seen my carpoolers leave before me, so I started out on this dark journey alone.

As I drove, I heard a loud rubbing noise. The only thing that came to my mind was that my car had thrown a rod. The car began to slow down and coasted over to the side of the road, as if an unseen hand was placing me in safety. I was afraid and cold, but I began to pray—wondering if my steps had been numbered to this very night. I put on my car blinkers, thinking that I saw a police car that would stop to help me. But the car didn't stop! I thought, *I should walk to that truck stop I can see in the distance. But it is too dark! And besides, I am wearing dark clothes, and that wouldn't be safe.* I stayed in the car and prayed, because I didn't want to risk getting hit.

Finally a car pulled up behind me. *Oh, no, this could be a murderer.* Then the Lord spoke to me and said, "The Lord would not send a murderer to help you." I was so excited to see that it was my carpoolers!

I immediately asked them what happened, because I had seen them leave before I did. They said that they had, but one of them had forgotten a glove and went back for it.

God is *still* in control! Praise the Lord!

Bertha Hall

God Is for Me

What then shall we say to these things?
If God is for us, who can be against us? Rom. 8:31, NKJV.

In every moment of my life God has always been there for me. In happiness, despair, unworthy, inadequate, best, worst, skeptical, doubts, negative, God has always and will always be there for me. Every moment of every day God is for me; nothing can be against me. I do tell myself repeatedly that God is for me; it helps me to appreciate Him for creating, protecting, and guiding me through life. It is His infinite mercy, grace, and love for a sinner like me that I am where I am today.

Twenty years ago a blessing turned out to almost devour my health and life, but by God's love and grace, I survived to testify the goodness of God in my life. It was my eighth pregnancy, and it turned out to be ectopic. I could not understand. The resident doctors were on strike, and I knew nothing about ectopic pregnancy, but God knew all about it. The hospitals that examined me refused to operate because my blood level was very low, so that ectopic pregnancy lasted for 21 days with heavy bleeding, fainting, and severe pains. A non-Christian doctor was the one who finally took the risk and operated; the wound healed primitively, but God saved me.

Another ugly incident in my life happened in December 2004, when a misunderstanding occurred between my children and my neighbors on Christmas Day. It was settled, and I thought it was all over and left on a trip December 26, to be back two days later. When I returned, the kids were again quarreling; once more it was settled, only to be attacked a couple hours later by the same neighbor, her children, and thugs hired to kill me and my oldest daughter.

To God be the glory, He's always there for me. I was attacked in front of my house, with heavy chains and cables, which landed me in the hospital that night to receive stitches all over my face and head. The policeman who handled the case, a non-Christian, pleaded that I not take the case to court, but forgive and allow God to take charge. That I did, although I didn't want to. God is for me, and today I have peace, moving freely, but my neighbor can't.

God saved and preserved my life to testify to His goodness in my life. That is God for me. Nothing shall separate me from my God. What has God done for you?

Ziri Palu-Amala

Word Pictures

But Jesus immediately said to them: "Take courage!
It is I. Don't be afraid." Matt. 14:27, NIV.

Have you ever had a picture in your mind that describes an experience that you were going through? When I went through my divorce, I was forced into some very extenuating circumstances that I had to face. A few of these were finding a new place for our family of five to live, getting a job after being home for 15 years with my children, and wondering where we would find our next meal. It was very difficult balancing my emotions and trying to spare the kids from any stress I could in an already trying situation.

During the years of this trial, my mind kept conjuring up the picture of me in a large swimming pool. I was standing on my tiptoes with my nose barely out of the water. There were many times I would go under and then struggle to get above the water line once again. I knew my survival instinct had kicked in, and this was the reason for the word picture formulated in my mind. I became frightened that this water would overtake me and that one day I would drown.

As a Christian, I remembered the Bible verse that God would never leave me or forsake me (Heb. 13:5). He never left Peter when this disciple climbed out of the boat, confident in his ability to walk on the water. Jesus, waiting in the distance, saw Peter sinking. This happened in the very moment Peter became frightened and took his eyes off his Lord. Peter then cried out, "Lord, save me!" (Matt. 14:30, NIV), and Jesus immediately stretched out His hand and took hold of him. Jesus then chastised him saying, "You of little faith, . . . why did you doubt?" (Matt. 14:31, NIV).

Yes, indeed. Why do we doubt that the Lord could stretch out His hand and rescue us from our situations? Instead, we let our minds create pictures that present a hopeless situation, and we believe the lies that the evil one presents to us. We delay asking God for help. Because of the frailty of our faith, our situation sinks us instead of lifting us up.

The next time we face trials, let's focus on the fact that our God is viewing it from above, taking hold of us, and out of His great mercy and love lifting us out of the waters into the safety of His arms. That's what our word picture should be.

Karen Phillips

Be Ready Yourself

Therefore, you also must be ready, for the Son of Man
is coming at an hour you do not expect. Matt. 24:44, ESV.

It was time for the first women's congress in our part of Africa. I was excited to attend and to network with women from other countries. As a church area director, I had to mobilize women from my region, many who had not traveled outside our territory, so I made sure I sent communication every month to remind them of preparations to make in order to have smooth travel. In the back of my mind, I knew I had no passport, and at that time it was very difficult to acquire a passport in my country, but I was too busy helping everyone else to get ready myself.

Two weeks before the event I finally visited the passport office. While in the process of presenting my application, a young man told me he could help me have my application processed in a short time. Knowing time was short, I accepted his offer. Three days before travel day, I made a follow-up only to discover that my application had not been processed, and there was no record whatsoever to show that there ever was such an application. I filled in another application form and paid more money. The normal time to process the application was three months, and I had only three days. I was told to go the next day, which was a Friday, to have a travel document processed because it was not possible to have a passport issued in three days.

Early Friday morning I reported at the passport office. I waited the whole day without success. Women from the faraway districts were arriving, as we had made arrangements to have the delegates meet together on Sabbath for worship. The sun was setting, and I was still waiting. Finally I was told to report again the following day—Sabbath. By this time, I was in tears.

I reported to the passport office the next morning. I did collect my travel document, but I missed the gathering of all the delegates. I was told later that the women had prayed for me.

As I sat on the bench waiting for my passport, a lesson came out very clearly. I was busy preparing other people for the journey, but neglected my own personal preparations. How true it is that in this life we may be busy preparing other people for the coming kingdom and yet we are neglecting our own personal preparations. On that day we will be in tears when we see the people we have been preparing ready for translation as we remain behind.

Caroline Chola

Welcome Home

So he returned home to his father. And while he was still a long way off, his father saw him coming. Filled with love and compassion, he ran to his son, embraced him, and kissed him. Luke 15:20, NLT.

One warm summer day my 5-year-old son announced that he was going to run away. I don't remember the reason, but he must have been unhappy with the family rules. Or perhaps he thought he had been treated unfairly. I don't remember. I told him I loved him and that I wished he would not leave, but it had to be his decision.

"I am leaving home," he repeated. I told him I would help him pack. We picked out some clothes, and he packed them into a small suitcase while I made a lunch for him.

At the front door I hugged him and told him goodbye. I told him again how much I loved him and that he was always welcome to come home. He said he loved me, too, and then he told me goodbye.

"Goodbye," he said in a matter-of-fact tone.

I peeked from behind the curtains of the big picture window as he went down the front sidewalk. I watched as he lugged his suitcase down the driveway. When he got to the end of the driveway he stopped, then set his suitcase down, and stood there for a minute. I watched as he finally sat down on top of the little suitcase, unpacked his lunch, and ate.

After he finished his lunch he sat there for quite a while before he stood up, turned around, and came back up the driveway. Once in the house, he went straight to his room and unpacked.

He was home. I am happy to tell you that he never ran away again.

Have you ever run away from God, maybe not literally but figuratively? Maybe you too have been unhappy with the family rules or maybe you feel like God has treated you unfairly. Why doesn't He do for you the good things He seems to do for everyone else? And so you are tempted to run away, even though you know you still love Him. He won't make you stay at home. It has to be your decision. But He is watching you and waiting for you to come back to His love.

The welcome mat is always out for you.

Ginny Allen

Snowstorm

For his anger lasts only a moment, but his favor lasts a lifetime; weeping may stay for the night, but rejoicing comes in the morning. Ps. 30:5, NIV.

One recent winter day my husband and I decided to visit our daughter, who was working in Indianapolis, Indiana. Realizing that the drive would take about 10 hours from Maryland, my husband suggested that we start from home in the middle of the afternoon so we could drive at least six hours of the trip.

About 3:00 in the afternoon we started off for Indianapolis. Three hours into the trip, we began to see snow falling. Thirty minutes later, when we took the exit to the next state we had to pass through, the snow increased so badly that it become impossible even to see where we were going. Driving became so dangerous that I asked my husband to find a rest area so we could pull off the road and just wait until the storm was over. My husband kept on driving, saying, "We do not want to be stranded at a rest area if this weather gets too bad. We need to find a town or hotel." At this point we were getting very worried, and we began praying that the storm would come to an end or just ease up for all the people that were on the road. However, there was no sign of the storm ending. Now we were worried about the roads becoming icy, as the temperatures were falling rapidly.

When we realized that the storm was not ending, we decided to look for a place we could stay for the night. As soon as we started seeing signs for hotels we were relieved, and finally we found a hotel and spent the night there. When morning came, my husband and I got back on the road.

We drove for just a short distance before we saw that if we had actually gone just a little bit farther from our hotel we would have found where the storm ended. The rest of our route we had little or no snow at all. It was so clear that, if we had endured only a little more, we would in fact have passed the storm and could have continued on our trip the night before.

As my husband and I drove, we learned two lessons: like the snowstorm we encountered, storms of life do not last forever, and if you endure just a little longer, trusting Him who has promised and never fails, the storms will pass, and with it joy will come with the morning.

Judith M. Mwansa

Above the Heavens

Your mercy, O Lord, is in the heavens; Your faithfulness reaches to the clouds. Ps. 36:5, NKJV.

On a plane, flying back home from Puerto Rico after a tour promoting my ministry, I was amazed by the magnificent view. There, above the heavens, I was in complete awe of God's handiwork. Needless to say, peace and gratitude overflowed my already-joyous soul.

I took mental notes of the blessings this trip had brought me, and how God had provided for my every need throughout my three-week tour. I'd seen His hand guiding each detail as I trusted and obeyed. Looking at the clouds below reminded me of how uncertain this life is and how much we depend on the loving care of our heavenly Father. What a blessing it is to know Him, my Creator and Savior!

Past experiences help strengthen our relationship with God and contribute to build our trust in Him. Today I'm facing challenges, but as I look at the pictures, I'm reminded of God's faithfulness. I can put all my troubles, challenges, and concerns in His hand and know that He holds the present and the future. I can sing as the psalmist did so many years ago and know that I will not be disappointed:

I have complete confidence, O God! I will sing and praise You! I will thank You, O Lord, among the nations. I will praise You among the peoples. Your constant love reaches above the heavens; Your faithfulness touches the skies (see Ps. 108:1, 3, 4).

I long to sing each day and praise the name of Jesus! But my greatest desire is to finish the journey to my eternal home where I will have the privilege of singing praises to His name, face to face, and be surrounded by God's people from every corner of the world. What a glorious day that will be!

What reminds you today of God's care? Are you prompted to sing a joyful song?

I pray that the faithfulness God has shown me in the past will hold me steadfast in the midst of today's trials, and we will continue to praise God. "Sing to the Lord a new song, and His praise in the assembly of saints. . . . Let the children of Zion be joyful in their King. . . . Let the saints be joyful in glory; let them sing aloud on their beds. Let the high praises of God be in their mouth" (Ps. 149:1-6, NKJV).

Rhodi Alers de López

The Fall

Now unto him that is able to keep you from falling, and to present you faultless before the presence of his glory with exceeding joy. Jude 24.

It happened one Saturday evening while I was at work in the emergency room at a local Adventist hospital. I was walking through the patient-care area with clipboard and pen in hand on my way to register an ambulance patient at bedside. Suddenly I began to lose my balance. After slipping, sliding, and skidding, my feet went out from under me, and I flew backward through the air. My back hit on the cold, hard tiles, my head snapped back, striking the floor; medical staff came running from every direction to help me.

"I'm fine," I said, jumping up dazed, slightly numb from the impact, and embarrassed beyond words. "I'm a bit bruised, I think, but otherwise . . ." My trembling voice trailed off as I saw the concerned look on my coworkers' faces. Moments later a nurse recounted what had caused the mishap: a drunken patient who had been fighting had been put at a sink to clean himself up and had sloshed water all over the floor.

"See a doctor, get X-rays, then go home and rest," someone suggested as I was whisked into a room to see the doctor. I was barely 30 then, vibrant, full of life, and ready to enjoy my time, raise my three children, and be an energetic worker in my church. Many hours and numerous X-rays later I finally went home—tired, achy, and unaware of the full impact of the fall.

The next morning every part of me hurt; this was the beginning of years of neck and back pain, migraines, and muscle spasms. One unfortunate, unforeseeable incident, and the course of my life changed to years of visits to doctors, physical therapists, and specialists. I was never the same. That fall had damaged me and greatly curtailed my full potential.

More than 34 years later I still wonder what could have been if my accident had never happened. Then I am reminded of another Fall, Adam and Eve's, which changed the course of history. Cast out of the Garden of Eden that fateful day, they were never the same. Nothing and no human could make things right again. The full potential God desired for them would never, ever be.

May we always be vigilant as we walk this Christian life, so we won't have a life changing fall, a fall from grace that will lead to eternal damnation.

Iris L. Kitching

Journeying Without Acceptance

Then the King will say to those on his right, "Come, you who
are blessed of My Father, inherit the kingdom prepared for you
from the foundation of the world." Matt. 25:34, NASB.

I had successfully completed my secondary schooling, but now I wanted higher education. I had received my acceptance letter and a scholarship to attend a local government university. Unfortunately, my father refused to allow me to attend this university because he thought I was too young. Dissatisfied with my father's refusal, I decided to explore various Seventh-day Adventist institutions in the Caribbean. I finally shared with my father that I had located a tertiary level institution called University of the Southern Caribbean in Trinidad; I could work on a diploma in English as a second language. After completing my diploma, I could continue to work on my Bachelor of Science. To my surprise, my father promptly agreed with my decision. Just imagine: the local university was just a two-hour drive away, while the university in Trinidad was six hours away by air with three stops on different islands.

The next day my parents scheduled my flight to Trinidad; my mother decided to accompany me. While I was gathering my documents for the university, the matter of my acceptance letter emerged—I had not even completed my application form. The next week I started my adventure into a new territory and a new language that I was still trying to grasp. However, I still had no acceptance letter. I was quite nervous going to Trinidad without the necessary documentation. I started to brainstorm a plan just in case anything went wrong. I planned to pretend that I fainted, or fake an illness, hoping that the immigration officers would allow me to enter into the country without one of the most crucial documents, my acceptance letter. My mother encouraged me to complete the applications forms on my way to Trinidad. I showed my completed application to the immigration officer, and he allowed me to enter Trinidad legally!

Within a few days of being in Trinidad my application was processed, and I was accepted. My dear friends, we too have an acceptance letter that we need for the university known as "heaven." There are only two possibilities: *Accepted*: "Come, ye blessed of my Father, inherit the kingdom prepared for you" or *Refused*: "Depart from me" (Matt. 25:41). Let us be certain to obtain our acceptance letter!

Nahomie Daubé

Count All Things Joy

Count it all joy. James 1:2.

Look for Jesus in everything. In everything you see you will find a blessing." The Bible says it this way: "Count it all joy." What an interesting quote, and one that I am finding true.

An employee told me that she and her husband had a reduction in their income. But she smiled because the reduction qualified them for a program that helped with their upside-down mortgage to the tune of $250 less a month that they would have to pay on their mortgage.

Another friend told me that he did a job for someone who refused to pay him. He asked me if he should fight the decision and talk more to the person about giving him the money for the cost of his gas and time. This would likely put a strain on their relationship and affect others he worked with. I encouraged him just to trust God and let Him work it out. That same day he was delighted to share that he had received a check from a TV commercial he had done more than 15 years before—double the amount he had expected from the job.

Another friend had a son who was a typical hardheaded young man who barely finished high school. He was irresponsible and unreliable, and had a child out of wedlock. After the birth the couple got married, and my friend loves and enjoys her grandson. As she raved about that grandchild, she commented that he was the best gift, though the circumstances were not right. I reminded her that the circumstances were absolutely perfect. Hadn't this new baby taught her son things that she couldn't for years: responsibility, grace, forgiveness, patience, and the awesomeness of love? Jesus was even in the timing, and it was such a blessing.

A patient was dying in the intensive-care unit. The chaplain was called, and the family said, "We just want prayer for us to unify. Although our mother had dementia, she never went one day without praying for us to be together. We are united in our decision to withdraw and want to do what she has always prayed for us to do, to care for each other." The worse thing again became a gift to their parent and to them.

Look for God in whatever your situation is today. In that difficulty may be a wonderful gift. "He knows us far better than we know ourselves, . . . and keeps us present before God. That's why we can be so sure that every detail in our lives of love for God is worked into something good" (Rom. 8:28, Message).

Wanda Grimes Davis

The Peacemaker

Blessed are the peacemakers, for they shall
be called sons of God. Matt. 5:9, NKJV.

O n a sunny Sunday I travel to the hospital to have lunch with my nurse friend, Annie, and her son, Jeremy, who is 7 years old. The hospital has a beautiful garden with benches, flowers, a small pond with fish, and tables for sharing a meal. Today I am responsible for bringing the sack lunches. I have sandwiches, nuts, fruit, apple juice, and cookies. As I reach the garden, Annie and Jeremy are waiting for me.

Jeremy tells me about art projects he's completed in school. Before we sit, Annie's pager interrupts our conversation. Emergency. I promise to take care of Jeremy.

I begin to arrange the sack lunches, and suddenly I hear two angry voices. I instinctively pull Jeremy closer to me. Two young men are arguing. I recognize the color of the scrubs they are wearing: surgical interns. I see hospital food trays on the floor. Their voices get louder. I am concerned. Nobody in the garden seems to care about breaking up the escalating fight. Nobody except Jeremy.

He wiggles free of my embrace, grabs two of the sack lunches, and runs toward the fight. As I run after him, I hear his voice calling out to the two interns.

"Hey, misters," he says. "Don't be upset about the food; I have lunch for you."

The two interns stop yelling. Jeremy calmly hands a sack lunch to each of them, helping them take out the items. He points at me, saying I make good sandwiches, and holds up the cookies in a ziplock bag and tells the interns this is the best part of the meal.

"Enjoy your lunch," says Jeremy as he runs back to me. I watch as the two interns sit, quietly, looking back at us. The fighting has stopped.

At our table there is one sack lunch left. Jeremy carefully opens it and says: "I think we can share this one." As he sorts out the food, one of the interns calls out to him: "Hey, kid, thanks for the lunch. You're a good kid." The intern gives Jeremy a "thumbs up," and Jeremy simply smiles as he hands me half a sandwich.

Dear heavenly Father, give me the wisdom and a brave, honest heart to be a peacemaker among both those who know of Your love and those who need to know of Your love.

Dixil Rodríguez

Holiday Holdup!

Do not be anxious about anything, but in every situation, by prayer and petition, with thanksgiving, present your requests to God. Phil. 4:6, 7, NIV.

Stop!" ordered one of two armed men who had stepped out of the thick forest onto the isolated road down which our crowded public transport vehicle was traveling. "We'll need everyone out as we conduct an inspection." Our family, en route to visit my parents over the holidays, huddled together in our seats. Shocked (as was everyone else at this sudden and dangerous turn of events), I nevertheless stared hard at one of the two men—he looked familiar to me.

Then I blurted out, "I think I know you from somewhere."

"Out!" he shouted. "And wait for us in the forest. We will deal with you!" When I refused to leave my seat, they rudely grabbed for me and shoved me off the vehicle. Of course, they suspected that if I did indeed know one of the gunmen, and if I remained alive, I would go to the police station and report them, resulting in a probable arrest. So they wanted me dead.

That's when I saw our frightened 10-year-old daughter bow her head in an attitude of silent prayer.

"Out! Out!" the two gunmen kept shouting at other passengers. "But take nothing with you!" They barked their commands while unceremoniously shoving more and more people out of the transport vehicle. I was grateful to observe they'd apparently forgotten about me as they now quickly rifled through passengers' luggage and personal belongings left aboard. My trembling little daughter, standing beside me now, continued her silent supplications. No one else spoke as the two bandits continued their plundering of our belongings inside the vehicle. Then, only eight minutes after they'd appeared on the road, the armed men disappeared into the forest. Reboarding the vehicle, the driver started up the engine. As we resumed our trip, terror turned to praise for the protection God had just manifested on our behalf. A number of people mentioned they thought they'd noticed our daughter had been praying—and thanked her.

My daughter confided to me that she'd promised God—if He spared us—that she would sing His praises wherever life took her. Today, years later, she continues to do just that.

How has God answered your prayers? How are you praising and thanking Him?

Debbie Maloba

A Christmas Present

He defends the cause of the fatherless and the widow, and loves the foreigner residing among you, giving them food and clothing. Deut. 10:18, NIV.

All the odds were against us. The sensible and realistic thing to do was to give up and accept it was not meant to be. Every possible office had been visited, letters written, and countless phone calls made—all to no avail.

My son was looking forward to starting university. Applications had been made, interviews attended, and a university place secured. The finance company had also been involved, and all appropriate documentation sent to them.

"Mom, just look at this letter," Kenny said in his soft-spoken voice. As I read the letter, I could not believe what I was reading! My son had been refused finances—they said he was not eligible. I couldn't fund his education myself. I looked at Kenny's face and saw the look of disappointment, disbelief, and confusion. "You are going to university, son," I said as I patted his back. We had been praying to God for the opportunity, and I did not see God letting us down.

The reasons sighted in the letter did not add up. As far as I was aware, my son met all the criteria to be eligible for funding. Thank God, I was out of employment at the time; had I been working it would have been extremely difficult to invest time and effort in making contacts to relevant authorities and to research the issue further. Hours were spent in prayer, searching relevant legislation, making phone calls, and visiting people such as the local member of Parliament. We prayed as a family—both in the United Kingdom and abroad; church friends buoyed us on with their prayers. While all this was going on, I was helping my son get ready for school.

The first day of the semester my son went to the university, and the authorities insisted he was not eligible for funding. I left Kenny, not sure what would become of the situation. He finished the first term, but there was still no progress with the issue of his funding.

I woke up one morning with tears streaming down my face, and prayed with a heavy heart that the Lord would guide and help me to accept His plan for Kenny's life.

Two days before Christmas I received a telephone call informing me that my son was indeed eligible to receive funding. Praise be to God, who is always concerned about our affairs.

Regina Ncube

The Accidental Spice

A gentle answer turns away wrath,
but a harsh word stirs up anger. Prov. 15:1, NIV.

I was happily dumping ingredients into the large aluminum roasting pan: oats, pecans, dried milk, allspice, and salt. Then I grabbed a large container from my spice shelf, dousing the mixture with a very large, unmeasured amount. I approximated.

There! That should be perfect, I thought. Cinnamon was, after all, one of the most important ingredients in my granola recipe. Not only does it give it that extra-special layer of flavor, but it makes everything smell so good when it is baking in the oven.

My husband had asked me to make granola he could hand out at work for Christmas. I couldn't wait to put the finished product in bags and tie them off with festive colors of green, red, and gold curled ribbon.

I took a big inhale to enjoy the waft of all of the yummy ingredients. But something was different! It didn't have its usual warm, sweet, spicy smell. It smelled, well, a different kind of spicy. *Oh, no!* Panicing, I grabbed the spice I had coated the dry ingredients with and looked at its label. Cumin! I had pulled the wrong spice off the shelf! And it was absolutely the *worst* possible choice for this recipe!

I did my best to scrape off all of the accidental spice, but some of it had gotten down in between the other dry ingredients, making it impossible to retrieve. I would just have to try to reapply the right spice—cinnamon—and hope for the best. I poured the boiling mixture of honey, brown sugar, and oil over the rest of the concoction, stirred, and put it in the oven. After it was done, I tasted it, but it didn't have its usual gentle and sweet flavor. Instead it had the bite, the kick, of salsa! This would be great in the context of chip dip, but my granola was ruined!

I thought about how I sometimes react too quickly in kind to harsh words. It takes only seconds, in the heat of the moment, for my flesh to rise up—it's like a computer-generated automatic "out of office" reply. Then escalation occurs.

Instead, I need to check the spice I have so quickly grabbed off the shelf before I make a total mess of my recipe. Taking care to intentionally choose my words, seasoning them with kindness and compassion and not with hurtful words, can change the conversation's outcome.

Kris Smith

Be Thankful

I depend on God alone; I put my hope in him. He alone protects and saves me; he is my defender, and I shall never be defeated. Ps. 62:5, 6, TEV.

A few days before Christmas I was visiting with my parents in Wynberg. I didn't feel like being at my house alone, so I decided to spend some quality time with the family. Many times I have left Wynberg late and usually arrived home safely. This particular evening Mom was very concerned and kept prodding me: "It's getting late; you must please go home."

"I'll go shortly; I'm busy with something." Eventually, with all the asking, I decided I better go home or else! Just before leaving, I received a text message from a friend—a beautiful and very sweet prayer. I just scanned through it very quickly. As I was about to leave, the landline phone rang; it was one of my aunts from Johannesburg. We chatted a bit, and then she told me, "Now do travel safely." I told her that when I got home I would let her know.

Part of my drive home included a notorious stretch of road known as Vanguard Drive. The first set of traffic lights were red, and all cars were waiting patiently for them to change. My small red bag was in the front on the floor, on the passenger side. All types of nuts were in there; no valuables, no cell, no wallet, nothing valuable—only various nuts.

A man walked in front of my car, came over to my passenger-side window, looked in, and was so close he was literally up against my window. It was very creepy, and I had a weird feeling. Suddenly I looked up and saw and heard the glass break—that pushed my adrenaline over the edge. I was already in first gear, waiting to pull away. I drove off like a bolt of lightning, and while trying to get away I ended up knocking into another car. The perpetrator never got an opportunity to take my bag or come back and attack me.

I was very shaken up after the incident, but I exchanged information with the other driver, then continued to drive home while glass pieces kept falling out and giving me a fright. While driving, I was also praying to God for His protection.

That night a lot worse could have happened to me; I could have been hijacked or killed. The angels and God were protecting me from harm and danger. God has a plan for my life—otherwise I wouldn't be alive right now. He has a plan for you, too—depend on Him alone.

Shelley Gordon

A Maple Leaf Set in Cement

*Inasmuch as you did it to one of the least of these
My brethren, you did it to Me. Matt. 25:40, NKJV.*

The sidewalk leading to the large hospital had been there for at least 30 years. Thousands of people had walked that way. Had anyone else noticed? I gazed curiously, if not admiringly, at the image of the maple leaves imprinted in the cement of the sidewalk. Not a lot, not overdone, just a few here and there. Someone, years ago, had taken the time to artistically imprint the leaves. Someone cared about the job he did. And someone noticed 30 or so years later, and it brought joy to her day.

I talked with a friend several days ago. She told me that when she was new to my office I took her out to lunch and made her feel welcome. "Your act of kindness has meant so much to me through the years," she told me. I had forgotten, but she had remembered.

I remember a Christmas Eve. Newly married, my family out of town, our house in the shambles of remodeling with boxes everywhere, I felt alone. I couldn't even provide a warm home for my new husband. As I sat on the floor and cried, the doorbell rang. It was a friend. "Merry Christmas," she said as she handed me a basket with a huge red ribbon. That evening my husband and I sat on the floor and shared homemade goodies from that basket. It made our Christmas Eve. She has forgotten, but I remember.

One morning I awoke feeling quite overwhelmed with all I had to do that day. Later that morning in the mail I received a letter from a friend. Enclosed was a little note that said, "When you feel like you're drowning in life, don't worry; your Lifeguard walks on water." That little note put my whole day in perspective.

My mother lived with me until she suddenly died of a heart attack. For weeks afterward my doorbell rang as children came to my door asking what had happened to the grandmother with the sweet smile who would sit on the porch and tell them stories. I never knew my mother was grandmother to the neighborhood children while I was at work all day. They will remember.

Like the maple leaves set in cement, as we go through life some of the kind things we do may be routine to us, but to someone they may mean the world. Inasmuch as you have done it to one of these, you have done it to Jesus.

Edna Maye Gallington

Christmas: Experience the Joy of Giving

Oh, give thanks to the Lord! Call upon His name; make known His deeds among the peoples! Sing to Him, sing psalms to Him; talk of all His wondrous works! Ps. 105:1, 2, NKJV.

It seems that weeks before Christmas many people anticipate the happiness of the season. People seem happier, kinder, and more forgiving. We try to think of persons who need a kind act, and then we try to give them something they would enjoy.

This year we made good bread for friends and neighbors. It would have been great to also share the fragrance of the freshly baked bread! They were grateful; then there were some surprising events that happened. Because we are 87 and 92 "years young" (and don't trust ourselves on ladders anymore), one neighbor decided to put up outdoor lights on our house for us. The colored lights did add to the holiday cheer.

Then one neighbor who was driving by stopped and said, "Hi, I'm James. I notice you have a little moss on your roof. Do you mind if I put some Moss-Off on it? I live behind you, and I will be working on my roof and then I will do yours—it will take only a few minutes."

"Fine, Santa, but what is the charge?"

He replied, "There isn't any charge; I notice that you help others."

We thanked him as he left with a big smile. In a few minutes we had the job done. I'm sure we (all three of us) had a warm feeling in our hearts because of this surprising act. So there is joy in giving and receiving.

The third surprise came after our family brunch and gift exchange on Christmas Day. Our daughter and her husband insisted on "picking up" the living room and washing all the dishes while we had a chance to enjoy our 2-year-old great-granddaughter.

Thank You, Lord, for Your many blessings—even when we are greatly surprised by them.

Of course it is Jesus who gives us the real joy in this season of the year, and it is in sharing Him that we are most blessed. The psalmist expressed it this way: "Then our mouth was filled with laughter, and our tongue with singing. Then they said among the nations, 'The Lord has done great things for them.' The Lord has done great things for us, and we are glad" (Ps. 126:2-4, NKJV).

Frieda Tanner

The Tonka Dump Truck

Bring ye all the tithes into the storehouse, that there may
be meat in mine house, and prove me now herewith, saith the Lord of hosts,
if I will not open you the windows of heaven, and pour you out a blessing,
that there shall not be room enough to receive it. Mal. 3:10.

My son, Drew, turned 4 the year I was seriously injured by a hit-and-run driver. Seven months after that event I was home from the hospital, but unable to work.

Drew was excited about the Christmas season. All he could talk about was the Tonka dump truck he was certain he would get for Christmas.

My mother and babysitter taught Drew, "Your mama is Santa Claus. It is Mama who works hard to put a roof over your head, food on your table, and gifts under the tree." However, this year she added, "But Mama can't work now, so there will be no Christmas presents under our tree this year."

Drew was unshaken. He told his grandmother, "Mama pays tithe. God says He will bless us if we pay tithe. He will see to it I get my Tonka dump truck."

My mother helplessly looked over his head to me. How does one deny such faith with ugly truths? I prayed, "Beloved heavenly Father, please do not let Drew be disillusioned by my inability to provide his heart's desire."

Drew continued to talk about his Tonka dump truck right up to 6:00 p.m. Christmas Eve when we put him to bed. An hour later there was a knock at the door, but no one was on the porch, in the yard, or on the street. Instead, there was a large box at the door, with a note: "Merry Christmas from your friends in the neighborhood." In the box were one gift each for Mama and me, and a dozen gaily wrapped gifts of every size and shape for Drew.

Drew wasn't a bit surprised to see the gifts under the Christmas tree, and the very last gift he opened was a Tonka dump truck. He smiled at his grandmother and said, "I told you Mama paid her tithe so God would give me my Tonka dump truck!"

Psalm 37:4 also says: "Delight yourself also in the Lord, and He shall give you the desires of your heart." He kept that promise as well. In this season we often see that it is the belief of children that teaches adults the true power of faith.

Darlenejoan McKibbin Rhine

The Golden Magnolia Leaves

*Dear children, let us not love with words or speech
but with actions and in truth. 1 John 3:18, NIV.*

At a recent church Christmas program the congregation was asked to share a special Christmas memory. Sitting in the warm sanctuary gazing at the cathedral ceilings, worshipping with music from the baby grand piano, being comfortable on the padded pews, and with carpet at my feet, I thought of our old church, built in 1938, which had been burned when our new church was built. We had all cried as its flames ascended, but even its windows no longer functioned. How we appreciate each stained-glass window now! The second coming of Jesus is my favorite window. It brings hope, especially when I think of my sister Bonnie.

Twenty years ago I held her hand as she whispered, "Trust Jesus," and died. She had devoted 30 years of her life to teaching, beginning her career while still in college and taking summer classes and correspondence to complete her degree.

Bonnie's first classroom was in our unfinished leaky church basement. Bonnie frequently spent evenings there, sweeping out water. As her eighth-grade students were near her age and size, she taught them, "Whatever your hand finds to do, do it diligently as unto the Lord."

Our family was very poor; so were others at our church, but we were rich in faith and joy, walking with Jesus. Bonnie was so generous in sympathy and service, so full of love! She did much for the people in her church and community. Emptied of self, Bonnie donated most of her earnings to support her siblings and anyone who needed help. There was nothing half-hearted about her mission; she believed in Christian education and enjoyed the precious time she spent with children in their formative years. Prayer was an important part of her ministry.

I remember one Christmas she and "her kids" made the Nativity scene come alive for the congregation. At the end of the program handcrafted gifts were presented to the families. One was a potted plant. Bonnie and her students had hiked in the snow to a nearby cemetery and had chosen leaves from the lower branches of a magnolia tree. They painted the magnificent leaves gold and placed them in red pots they had painted. A bow and a Christmas greeting card attached made the gifts look as good as from any flower shop.

In heaven I want to hike on cemeteryless land with Bonnie and all of "her kids," and maybe collect a few magnolia leaves. *Lord, could You please have some gold ones?*

Jane Wiggins Moore

The Wedding

Call to me and I will answer you. Jer. 33:3, NIV.

Weddings are just a lot of fun. But the older I get, the more I know that getting married can be risky business. I wonder what Bob, my husband of 45 years, would think of that statement. Well, it's true! We all come from different backgrounds and then have the odd idea that we can just say "I do" and everything will be normal.

When I think back to our wedding, I never gave a thought that we would do anything but live happily ever after. Ha! It was work. Bob grew up in a family that never asked where he was going or when he would be back. I grew up in a family that I practically had to tell my mom when I was headed to the bathroom. My father got off work in the afternoon at 4:00, and he was home by 4:30 on the dot. Can you imagine my shock when shortly after Bob and I were married my husband didn't show up until 7:00 p.m. and I expected him at 5:00? Through the years I've learned to go with the flow, and he has learned to come home on time—most of the time.

The wedding this weekend was in western Kansas, and it was held in a bar and grill. There was very little "frill" at the grill. The music was over a sound system, and the groom sang to the bride. The food was made by friends, and the wedding cake was yummy.

The interesting part was our family. As I sat looking at all of us, it brought tears to my eyes. We were a table of nondrinkers and smokers, not because we have never done it, but because most of us are recovering from something or other. Some have been heavy drinkers, smokers, and pot users. Some have been on meth, and you could tell it by the broken-down facial features, no teeth, and the blank look in the eyes. Having said this, my nephew was the first one to wish us "Happy Sabbath." I had forgotten it was Sabbath.

You may wonder, Why the tears? It's because my sister-in-law never gave up. She has prayed and pleaded with the Lord over her children, grandchildren, and siblings. As I sat there I saw the changed lives one after another, and I know it all had to do with her prayers.

So what about the parents who pray for their children, and they don't see the hand of the Lord? I asked this question of my daughter as I related the weekend to her. Her comment was "Their story is not finished yet." To those of you who are watching your loved ones make one bad decision after another, just keep on lifting them up. I have seen what God can do.

Nancy Buxton

Profile in Courage

"Behold, the virgin shall be with child, and bear a Son, and they shall call His name Immanuel," which is translated, "God with us." Matt. 1:23, NKJV.

Whenever the kitties were on the way to the vet, they knew it. From the carrying case in the back seat arose a mournful, hollow, despairing cry. With tears in my heart I longed to calm their terror. Speak their language. Be a cat with them.

I would be a super cat. Very smart, very articulate, and well able to calm their fears. I would be a human in the form of a cat. And, as soon as Herman and Martha had their shots, I would be me again. Abracadabra.

But what about actually becoming a *cat*? Becoming a tiny embryo, floating in a dark soup, growing and changing in a dreamless sleep? What about being squeezed into consciousness as a damp, blind, scraggly kitten? In due process I might learn to walk on four feet and win food and warmth by squeaking. I might develop the art of washing my face by rubbing it with just-licked paws. I would have to practice clawing my way up trees to escape bad dogs. All this would be infinitely harder if I became aware that I had unusual, human powers but had limited myself to being a *real* cat. Not a super cat.

How is it, I wonder, that before the foundation of the world God heard our hollow, despairing cries? And how did God make a deep, cell-level decision to intervene in our human tragedy? Not just learn to speak our language, not just to offer comfort. And wonderful as it is, not just to *be with* us.

With unfathomable courage God chose to become *one of us.*

Struggling to explain this mystery, Paul says that God stripped off power and privilege to become a mere human, a "nothing." John writes that the Word of God is the Creator and has existed since "the beginning." With great awe he points out that the Word chose to become "flesh and dwelt among us" (see Phil. 2:6, 7; John 1:1, 14).

"Unto us a Child is born," says Isaiah (9:6, NKJV). For the Incarnation is more than a brief intervention. It's a commitment. Though Godness is exerted to save us, God's humanness remains. Forever and ever. It is Christmas.

Kit Watts

So Many Questions—One Answer

This is how the birth of Jesus the Messiah came about: His mother Mary was pledged to be married to Joseph, but before they came together, she was found to be pregnant through the Holy Spirit. Matt. 1:18, NIV.

When I think of the Christmas story, and especially about the virgin Mary, I have so many questions. I wonder how old Mary was; Bible scholars tell us she was probably a teenager. So then my next question is Did she have a family, a mother and father? siblings? Why aren't they mentioned? We know how Joseph reacted to the announcement that Mary was pregnant by the Holy Spirit; at first he wanted to divorce her quietly, but changed his mind after a dream from the Lord. But what about her family—how did they react? After the visit by the angel announcing the coming baby, Mary immediately left to go visit her relative Elizabeth; it was a walking trip of about 60 miles (100 kilometers). It makes me think she didn't have another woman in her life to whom she could turn. How alone she must have felt! No one had ever before faced the challenges she did!

A few years ago my husband and I went to see a play about the Nativity. It depicted Mary's mother and father very much a part of the story, and very accepting of the situation. In one scene Mary's mother thinks about her daughter about to give birth to the Messiah, and she breaks into song with words something like "I'm going to be God's grandmother!" All very fanciful, but there is nothing in Scripture to tell us this.

Yes, I have a lot of questions, but fortunately there is one answer, the only answer to any question that really matters, and that is *Jesus*. The story does tell us, "She will give birth to a son, and you are to give him the name Jesus, because he will save his people from their sins" (Matt. 1:21, NIV). What a promise, what an answer to almost any question!

"Do not be afraid. I bring you good news that will cause great joy for all the people. Today in the town of David a Savior has been born to you; he is the Messiah, the Lord" (Luke 2:10, 11, NIV). Whatever you may face this Christmas Day, this year, Jesus is the answer to our questions, to our problems, to our future. Let's join with the shepherds and go to see this Savior: "Glory to God in the highest, and on earth peace, goodwill toward men!" (Luke 2:14, NKJV).

Ardis Dick Stenbakken

December 26

Chopped

Until the Ancient of Days came and pronounced judgment in favor of the holy people of the Most High. Dan. 7:22, NIV.

I enjoy watching a program on the Food Network called *Chopped*. It is a competition of experienced chefs battling to win a prize of $10,000. They begin with four chefs, and at the end of each round a chef gets "chopped" until there is one left. They begin by opening up a basket with random food items; in 30 minutes are expected to prepare a tasty, well-balanced, and beautiful-looking dish highlighting sometimes bizarre and uncomplementary ingredients. For example, they may open their basket in the appetizer round and find a chicken thigh, a jar of marshmallow crème, and turnips.

As the panel of three experts judge each one, I cannot help feeling sorry for the truly subjective nature of this competition. They begin by sharing what they liked in the dish and follow with what they personally disliked. Many times the judges disagree with each other as they assess the dishes. But, each round, they have to come to a consensus of whom to dismiss from the competition. As they start "chopping" those chefs that didn't cut the mustard, I think to myself, *The high standards they desire would all depend upon the taste of the judger. How could it really be an objective, fair win?*

Oddly enough, this show made me appreciate the judgment according to God's Holy Word. The judgment is not left up to a panel with differing opinions about our performance as human beings. God, Jesus, and the Holy Spirit are one in spirit and truth. There is nothing subjective about our salvation. And we can know that we will not be chopped! Because of Jesus' sacrifice on the cross, we can know the outcome of our salvation, because this is objective truth: "And this is the testimony: God has given us eternal life, and this life is in his Son. Whoever has the Son has life; whoever does not have the Son of God does not have life. I write these things to you who believe in the name of the Son of God so that you may know that you have eternal life" (1 John 5:11-13, NIV).

Let's praise and worship God for what He has done for us in Jesus! He has given us the blessed assurance of salvation.

Lee Lee Dart

The Bridge That Wasn't There

For he shall give his angels charge over thee,
to keep thee in all thy ways. Ps. 91:11.

My husband tells this story of the wonderful God we serve. Sixty years ago, as a very young boy, he remembers going on a holiday one summer, just after Christmas Day, to Maraetai Beach, about 50 miles from where they lived in Auckland.

There was the city to drive through, then some suburbs, and onto a gravel road, a road that went up and down some very steep hills; the road then went through a small settlement called Whitford. The road wound around several corners and over a very old, rather rickety bridge crossing an estuary. This bridge was narrow, allowing only one-way traffic at a time.

The local council had built a new straight piece of road, bypassing the village of Whitford. There was a new bridge to be built, a wider two-lane bridge—a bridge originally planned to be finished by Christmastime, but unforeseen delays meant that although the approach roads were complete, the new bridge had not yet been started.

As my husband's father, Jim, had pressing work commitments in Auckland, he stayed at home, and an uncle took the family down to Maraetai. So the family—cousins, other young friends, and my husband—traveled down to the beach with all the necessary things that would guarantee a great time for children: fishing lines, bikes, and swimming gear.

The weekdays passed, and everyone had a great time fishing off the wharf, swimming, and fishing some more. Late on Friday night Jim's dad arrived from Auckland. He was very tired after a busy week.

When the day came for packing up and heading home, nobody wanted to go. But on the way home, when reaching Whitford, my husband said his father did not go on the windy road, but instead drove up the new bypass road. Everyone instantly asked, "Why are you on this road? You can't come this way. It is not finished yet, because the new bridge hasn't even been started!"

"Well, this is the way I came on Friday night. I know this is the way I came."

"How could you? There is no bridge," countered someone.

"I distinctly remember coming this way," he affirmed.

Psalm 91:11 had indeed come true that Friday evening.

Leonie Donald

Icy Road

The Lord is good; he protects his people in times of trouble;
he takes care of those who turn to him. Nahum 1:7, TEV.

Coming back from humid, tropical weather with the temperature about 85°-104°F (30°-40°C), I landed in Frankfurt International Airport to be greeted with very cold air and snow everywhere. Indeed, it was beautiful. I asked my husband if he had changed the summer tires on my car to the winter tires; he hadn't. I was worried because I had to drive to work the following day, so I told him, "Let's switch cars," as his car was already equipped with winter tires.

The next morning it was really very icy, so I drove very slowly; the winter tires didn't help much. The car kept on sliding, and I did not have much control over it. When I reached the main road, the car began turning and dancing like an ice skater. I kept praying to the Lord to help me and keep me safe. Suddenly the car stopped in the middle of the road. I didn't do anything. I was scared to turn the wheel because it might start sliding again. Then the car slid to the side of the road, went through the ditch, then uphill. I was horrified to think the car might flip. This time I really prayed hard, begging the Lord to help me. The car slowly slipped backward again, went into the ditch, and stopped. It felt as though an unseen hand had controlled the car. It merely suffered dimples, the bumper fell off, and some scratches.

I was wondering why there was no oncoming traffic while I was there for more than 15 minutes. A woman passing by stopped, came over, and asked me if I was OK. I was still shaking. She said she would drive to the next gas station to ask for help. She came back with a big van and five strong men. They were construction workers from Poland. I was amazed as they lifted the Mercedes back onto the road. The car was just like a toy to them. I thanked the Lord (and I thanked each of them); then I continued driving without a bumper. When I almost reached the city, I saw a big accident, more than seven cars involved. I saw shoes scattered about, and an ambulance; unfortunately, it had slid off and had an accident. It looked awful. It then dawned on me why I had had the accident earlier. The Lord had kept me from being involved in the big accident. I remembered His promise in Psalm 121:8: "The Lord shall preserve your going out and your coming in from this time forth, and even forevermore" (NKJV). God is good, and He delivers us in mysterious ways.

Loida Gulaja Lehmann

Little Delights

It is more blessed to give than to receive. Acts 20:35.

Cyril used to have a family and a career, too. Well-educated, with a registered patent for an invention, he had never thought that one day he would find himself alone and advanced in age, ill, and poor. But these things do happen.

A woman with ADRA (Adventist Development and Relief Agency) added him to the new year's food help list. Cyril never imagined that he would receive more than a few packs of yogurt or a *banitsa* or bread. Cyril was stunned by the magnitude of the pack—more than little delights. He could not express his gratitude at the cardboard box with one whole turkey, pasta, cheese, yellow cheese ("I'd forgotten its taste"), sweets, lentils, rice, and dried fruit. But we were deeply impressed by the way he used the food. It's true that poor people help other poor people. The one who is hungry and does not have anything knows best what it is like to be hungry and poor.

A few days after the new year, when the same woman met him, Cyril thanked her on behalf of another family. "You created so much joy!" he said. "I know a family who is very poor; they have great difficulty in making ends meet, but when I visit them, they always try to give me cooked food, for they know I don't have electricity. Although the family lives in great destitution, they invited me to spend New Year's Day with them. They had planned a dinner with meatballs and two steaks: one for their son who is a university student, now unemployed, and the other to cut into pieces and eat together. The Lord forgive me, but I lied that someone else had invited me, because I didn't want to sponge off of them, since I didn't have anything to bring. But when I got the food pack, I looked at the turkey and realized I couldn't cook it on the gas plate I sometimes use for cooking. Besides, it's a sin to eat a whole turkey alone when such good people don't have a holiday meal. So I brought it to them together with half the cheese, and yellow cheese, and a very delicious sweet roll; they had given me two! Can you imagine their happiness? At first they didn't want to accept it. And then they eagerly insisted on my celebrating the holiday with them."

"It is more blessed to give than to receive" says today's text, so that the satisfaction of the giver is greater than that of the receiver! Little delights lead to a great gratitude to God, but also to the people whose hearts are open to the needs of those who cannot help themselves!

Emilia Stoykova

Jesus Is Sufficient

And my God will meet all your needs according
to the riches of his glory in Christ Jesus. Phil. 4:19, NIV.

I have been single for more than 20 years. After my divorce I was extremely anxious because I had no one to take care of me or my house, car, and so many other things. As time passed, I learned to pray about each problem, and God sent the help I needed. He led me to an honest car repairman and a reliable person to take care of things that needed to be fixed around the house. Even though I often felt I didn't have enough money for repairs, God always provided the funds.

Gradually I began to discover an important truth: Jesus is sufficient to meet all my needs. And He is sufficient for every woman's needs. I can say with confidence that He is a husband to single women (Isa. 54:5). When we are afraid, He will calm our fears. Isaiah 43:1, 2 is a constant encouragement to me: "Do not fear, for I have redeemed you; I have summoned you by name; you are mine." Precious promise!

Even before my divorce I discovered Jesus' all-sufficiency. When my husband became emotionally distant several years before the end of the marriage, God provided for my needs for emotional support by sending godly women to support me, even though I never confided the problems in my marriage. I experienced Jesus' care through their friendship and through my Bible study and prayer time.

God is sufficient to supply our physical needs. He who clothes the flowers of the field and is the Great Physician is faithful to provide for my needs, although not always my wants. However, He has helped me learn to distinguish between my wants and my needs, which helps keep me from being dissatisfied with my life.

I've learned that Jesus is sufficient for all those problems that seem beyond our control. He has answers for all of those problems that keep us from sleeping at night and that cause us anxiety. He does not always make the problems magically disappear, as we would like, but He does give us strength for each problem.

Most important, God is sufficient to save us. When we choose to trust Him, He is faithful to supply not only our temporal needs, but also our spiritual needs. When we stop trying to save ourselves and rely completely on His grace, He gives us peace that passes understanding.

Carla Baker

Then, Finally, I Can Be With My Jesus

And I heard a loud voice from heaven saying, "Behold, the tabernacle of God is with men, and He will dwell with them, and they shall be His people. God Himself will be with them and be their God. And God will wipe away every tear from their eyes; there shall be no more death, nor sorrow, nor crying. There shall be no more pain, for the former things have passed away." Rev. 21:3, 4, NKJV.

Sometime ago I heard weeping from my 5-year-old son Luca's room. I went to ask what was wrong. He looked at me sadly and said, "I want to die!" I was somewhat surprised and asked "Why?" He sobbed: "Then, finally, I can be with my Jesus, and He understands me!" I took him in my arms, but could not keep back smiling a little. We had spoken about what happens if a person dies. I had explained to Luca that every person who dies falls into a sort of sleep. He notes nothing more round him, and he also does not dream anymore. Then when Jesus comes again, all dead people will wake up from this "sleep," and the next one they see will be Jesus. From this time on, all believers can forever be with Him. He obviously had remembered all this.

Of course I explained to my son then that we must not want to die to be with Jesus sooner. Every day He is with us, and we can speak with Him anytime. Jesus is glad if we live well, and He is with us if we have hard times and wants to give us comfort and strength. However, this was not enough for Luca. He said, "But I want to see Him now!"

This event has touched me very much. My small son had understood that Jesus is the only one who understands him completely. He didn't want to wait any longer. He wanted Jesus to come now, immediately, to put His arms around him and to wipe away his tears.

Do you feel that way too? Do you feel this longing to be taken in His arms and have your tears wiped away by Him? I have good news. Jesus says: "In my Father's house are many mansions; if it were not so, I would have told you. I go to prepare a place for you. And if I go and prepare a place for you, I will come again and receive you to Myself" (John 14:2, 3, NKJV).

God alone knows when this day will be. However, as certain as this day will come, as certain it is also that Jesus accompanies us every day of our life, stands by us in all our worries, and would like to give us strength and joy. As we face a new year, let us walk with Him each day, even as He walks with us.

Caroline Naumann

2015 Biographies

Betty J. Adams is a retired teacher in California; she has been married 58 years, with five children, seven grandchildren, and three great-grandchildren. She has written for their church newsletter and *Guide*, and worked with their church community services. She enjoys gardening, scrapbooking, and her grandchildren. **Mar. 3.**

Priscilla A. Adonis writes from South Africa, where she is enjoying her new venture of gardening and her ministry of sending text messages to help and encourage sick, lonely, discouraged, and bereaved people. She also makes birthday, get-well, and thank-you cards. It's good to keep busy! **Apr. 3, Oct. 13.**

Sally j. Aken-Linke writes from Nebraska, where she enjoys her various positions at the Norfolk Seventh-day Adventist Church. She and her husband, John, enjoy flying to visit five adult children and nine grandchildren, as well as staying home with their garden and friends. Sally has been writing since she was 6 years old. **Jan. 13.**

Ginny Allen, a retired school nurse, lives with her pastor-husband (of almost 50 years), David Allen, in Vancouver, Washington. Ginny is best known for her interest in prayer. She founded Joy! Ministries, which encourages others to bring joy to the heavenly Father's heart while they listen for God's love song (also the title of Ginny's recent book). Ginny is a frequent speaker who is committed to living God's will for her life—"nothing more, nothing less, nothing else!" **Feb. 20, June 18, Dec. 8.**

Jussara Alves is a mother of four children, an educator, and a children's evangelist. She lives in Bahia, Brazil, and enjoys reading, walking, spending time doing crafts, and working with children. **Oct. 25.**

Georgia Lee Anderson has worked in Sabbath school classes for more than 30 years, and worked on the local church and conference women's ministries board for Washington State for several years before her move to Albuquerque, New Mexico. She had a children's book published in 2012 titled *Uncle Jesus*. She loves to write short stories and poetry, and to pray for others. **Jan. 24.**

Lydia D. Andrews is a certified nurse midwife, mother of three adult children, and grandmother of four delightful boys. She and her husband reside in Huntsville, Alabama, where she works as a labor and delivery clinical instructor. Her hobbies include reading, cooking, travel, music, and spending time with family. She is involved in prayer and women's ministries of her church. **Nov. 20.**

Raquel Queiroz da Costa Arrais is a minister's wife who developed her ministry as an educator for 20 years. She is an associate director of the General Conference Women's Ministries Department. She has two adult sons, two daughters-in-law, and one adored grandson, Benjamin. Her greatest pleasure is to be with people, singing, playing the piano, and traveling. **Jan. 12, May 3, July 21, Aug. 6.**

Yvita Antonette Villalona Bacchus has finished a master's degree in corporate communication. She is happily married to Roy Morillo and works as a freelance graphic designer and in the music department of her local church in the Dominican Republic. The devotional books have been a blessing to her, and she hopes to encourage other women to contribute. **Mar. 31.**

Taylor Bajic grew up in Chattanooga, Tennessee, staying there until she completed her first year of university; she then ventured to Newbold College in England, where she met her husband-to-be. She stayed in the United Kingdom for six more years. Her husband, Filip, is a pastor; they have recently moved back to Chattanooga, where they hope to continue their ministry. **Mar. 21.**

Carla Baker is women's ministries director of the North American Division of Seventh-day Adventists. As a native Texan, she thoroughly enjoys living in Maryland, with its abundance of flowers, trees, and lovely weather. She also likes flower gardening, walking in nature, traveling, and spending time with her grandchildren. **Mar. 16, Dec. 30.**

Jennifer M. Baldwin writes from Australia, where she works in risk management at Sydney Adventist Hospital. She enjoys church involvement, Scrabble, and crossword puzzles, and has been contributing to the devotional book series for more than 15 years. **Mar. 24.**

Grachienne L. Banuag writes from the Adventist University of the Philippines, where she is a student taking medical laboratory science. Her hobbies are reading books, listening to music, playing guitar, writing poems and other articles, and making scrapbooks. **Oct. 27.**

Mary Barrett lives in England and is married to a pastor; they have two grown-up daughters. She also works as a pastor and loves what she does! She has written several books and numerous articles. She likes to spend her spare time with family and friends and in her garden, attempting to grow produce for her family and her to eat! **Jan. 5.**

Filipinas Roda Bautista and her husband, Rodulfo Bautista, are busy in retirement in the Philippines. They have five children, two boys who are ministers (like their father) and two married daughters, both nurses (like their mother). Filipinas worked as a registered nurse in the Manila Sanitarium and Hospital (now Manila Adventist Medical Center). **June 20.**

Dana M. Bean is an educator from the beautiful island of Bermuda. Dana loves everything that is orange, the summer, lasagna, and writing. **Apr. 22.**

Dawna Beausoleil and her husband, John, live in a tiny town in rural northern Ontario, Canada. She is a retired teacher and enjoys reading, singing, painting and monitoring the antics of their two cats. She's had short articles and poems published in various magazines. **June 1.**

Vonda Beerman, over the years, has had the honor of sharing her music and testimony in person, by television, and through radio transmission to a wide variety of audiences throughout the world. The Lord has blessed Vonda with an "angelic" voice that she has dedicated back to Him. This exchange of gifts has provided her the privilege and rich blessing of a gospel music ministry. **Feb. 24, Oct. 17.**

Xoli Belgrave writes from North West London, England. She is married to her best friend, Antonio, and they are blessed with two lovely children, Jude and Fae. She spends her time balancing family life and a lay-preaching ministry (and all else she is asked to do at church), with a career as a project management training professional in the pharmaceutical industry. **Apr. 16.**

Ginger Bell is semiretired but still serves as women's ministries director for the Rocky Mountain Conference, which covers Colorado and Wyoming. She enjoys gardening, antiquing, decorating, and spending time with her family (five grandchildren) and friends. **June 7.**

Priscilla Matimba Ben loves women's ministries and loves to work with women. She is the wife of Pastor Strike Ben and the mother of one lovely daughter, Kagelelo. Her hobbies are gardening, traveling, reading, and homemaking. **Nov.16.**

Sylvia "Giles" Bennett lives in Suffolk, Virginia, with her husband, Richard. She is the mother of two adult children, David Mathew and Samantha Leigh, and two grandchildren, Kennedy and Derrius. Sylvia is the church clerk, the communications clerk, and the personal ministries leader of the Windsor Seventh-day Adventist Church. Her hobbies include reading and writing. **Apr. 30.**

Annie B. Best is a retired teacher in Washington, D.C., a widow, and mother of two adult children and three grandchildren. She enjoys reading and listening to music. Working as a leader in the cradle roll and kindergarten departments of her church years ago inspired her to compose a song published in *Let's Sing Sabbath Songs*. **June 21.**

Selena Blackburn writes from Nevada. She is a child of God who has been forgiven much and a fifth-generation Adventist with much to learn, she says. She is also a wife, mother, nurse, friend, woman: blessed. **Oct. 5.**

Julie Bocock-Bliss lives in Hawaii with her husband. She is an active member of the Honolulu Japanese Seventh-day Adventist Church in Manoa. She is the "mommy" of three cats and loves reading, traveling, and crafts. **May 16.**

Evelyn Greenwade Boltwood is the mother of two young adults and grandmother to two grand-sons. She is the western New York Adventurer area coordinator and Master Guide coordinator, as well as a member of Akoma, a women's community gospel choir that raises scholarship moneys for young women matriculating into college. She loves youth ministries and the Lord. **Feb. 6.**

Adriana Lúcia Bonatti is married with no children, living in Brazil. She was an export analyst for 14 years, though she is not working now. In church she participates in such social programs as Christmas in Action (Mutirão de Natal) and collecting food for needy families. She enjoys singing, traveling, and staying at home with her husband and her kittens, Pantufa and Pingado. **May 22.**

Tamar Boswell writes from Loma Linda, California. She is a registered nurse who loves to pray for others and leads out in prayer ministries at her church. She loves to read and travel, experiment with vegan recipes, and participate in community outreach programs. **June 24.**

Althea Y. Boxx is a Jamaican registered nurse perusing graduate studies. She is the author of a motivational devotional entitled *Fuel for the Journey.* She is also founder/president of the Flamingo Foundation for the advancement of health and educational scholarships. Althea enjoys writing, traveling, photography, and discussing politics. **Apr. 8.**

DeeAnn Bragaw counts it all joy to have the privilege of sharing with both adults and children a passion to experience God's Word in a fresh way! A speaker, author, and educator residing in Colorado, she loves to bike, hike, laugh, and learn. Her Web site is www.deeannbragaw.com. **Jan. 20.**

Ana Maria Nogueira Nascimento Brandão is a social worker and leads a prayer group. She likes to visit people in the community together with her husband. Her hobbies are being with her family, reading, cooking, and taking care of her house. Currently she lives with her husband in Artur Nogueira, São Paulo, Brazil. **Feb. 23.**

Janell Brauer recently moved to Arizona from the Bangladesh Adventist Union Mission, where she served as the children's and family ministries director. Her identity would primarily be as a child of God, and then an artist. In her spare time she paints, spends time with her wonderful husband or friends, walks, plays badminton, or works on some other creative project. **July 11.**

Sonia Brock lives in Palmer, Alaska, on almost 10 acres in a small cabin she built. Her dog is her faithful companion. She has had the privilege of driving a school bus for the past 23 years in the rugged but beautiful forty-ninth state. She is active in her local church, and it's a joy and privilege to serve—whether mowing the yard in the summer or greeting on Sabbath. **Aug. 12.**

Alison Brook resides in Berrien Springs, Michigan, and spends her time writing, performing, and recording songs for her music ministry. Her sophomore CD, *The Heart of the Matter,* was due out in 2014. **May 12.**

Vivian Brown is a retired educator living with her husband, Jimmie, in Madison, Alabama. She is the proud mother of three adult children and grandmother of six. She attends the Oakwood University church. Her pastime activities include photography, traveling, technology, reading, and teaching piano lessons and computer classes at a local senior center. **Mar. 28.**

Marielena Burdick, who writes from Colorado, wrote this while a high school junior. Mary looks at physical prowess versus spiritual strength: "When life throws me into turmoil, when someone I love dies, when friends betray me, I know that there is One who lets me soar on wings of eagles, who died *and* rose again, and who will never betray me, ever." **Aug. 31.**

Nancy Buxton is the women's ministries director for the Mid-America Union of Seventh-day Adventists in Lincoln, Nebraska. She has been married to Bob for more than 42 years; they have two married children and six grandchildren. She has a blog at nancyoutlook.wordpress.com, where you will find stories, women's ministries ideas, inspirational thoughts, and other fun things. **Dec. 23.**

Elizabeth Ida Cain works with a new motor vehicle dealer company in Jamaica as an administrative assistant and attends the St. John's Seventh-day Adventist Church, where she is a member of the women's ministries association. She loves the Lord, enjoys being a Christian, enjoys writing, and is a floral arranging art designer and instructor. **Oct. 4.**

Florence E. Callender is a published author, speaker, speech-language pathologist, and the president of DaySpring Life Options, a company that specializes in empowering people. She lives in New York with her teenage daughter and addresses many groups in seminars, workshops, and keynote speeches to help people be prepared and purposeful every day. **Ap. 25.**

Laura A. Canning was born in Kingston, Surrey, England in the 1950s and has three children; since they have grown, she has been involved with children's work and ministry in the local community. While working at Sandhurst School, she wrote a book, *Molly's Sweet Shop,* which was published in 2012. She lives in an area that was once Windsor Great Park in Berkshire. **Jan. 27.**

Eveythe Kennedy Cargill moved from Jamaica in 1974 and settled in Huntsville, Alabama. She teaches at Calhoun Community College. For 27 years she taught elementary or university students. Eveythe presently serves on the board of elders at the Oakwood University church. She has been married to Stafford for 42 years; they have two adult children and one grandchild. **Oct. 7.**

Esther A. Castle lives in Walla Walla, Washington, and has been widowed for 15 years. She has two adult children, four grandchildren, and two great-grandchildren. She worked with her husband for 13 years in Adventist boarding schools in Oregon and California, 12 years at Holbrook Indian School, and 15 years as a substitute teacher in the public school system. **June 30.**

Judy Gray Seeger Cherry is a retired paralegal/accountant living on Nebraska farm with husband, Earl. They have six children and seven grandchildren. She is a local church treasurer. She and her husband enjoy getting away to their cabin in the beautiful Nebraska sandhills. **July 14.**

Lyndelle Brower Chiomenti enjoys editing *CQ* Bible study guide for young adults, doing pet therapy with her keeshond, Timmer, and searching for agates along the shores of Lake Superior. She writes from Frederick, Maryland. **Feb. 1.**

Caroline Chola lives in Pretoria, South Africa. She is currently the women's and children's ministries director of the Southern Africa-Indian Ocean Division. She is married to Habson, and they have five adult boys and two grandchildren. She enjoys gardening. Her passion is to see women discover their potential and use it to the glory of God. **Dec. 7.**

Rosenita Christo has been an office secretary, college professor, head of the department, and magazine editor. She is now working at the Southern Asia Division in Tamil Nadu, India, as coordinator for Shepherdess, Adventist Volunteer Service, and secretarial management. She has two married children, and is the choir leader in her church, loves singing, enjoys gardening, and likes writing. **Apr. 17.**

Rosemarie Clardy writes from Candler, North Carolina, where she and her husband enjoy the blessings of country living while raising their three teenage sons, along with many family pets. They are volunteers at church and school. **Apr. 27.**

May-Ellen Netten Colon currently lives in Maryland and serves as assistant director of the General Conference Sabbath School and Personal Ministries Department, and director of Adventist Community Services International. For nine years she and her family served as missionaries in Africa and the former Soviet Union. **May 10, 11.**

Connie Cook lives in Creston, British Columbia, Canada, and is a full-time live-in caregiver. She has completed her training with New Tribes Mission and hopes someday to use her training on a cross-cultural mission field. **Mar. 17.**

Patricia Cove is a semiretired teacher, sailor, gardener, writer, and lover of nature in Ontario, Canada. Her husband, children, and their offspring are her greatest treasures. She is an active church elder who has completed a pastoral-care ministry course and plans to volunteer in local hospitals. Her favorite activity is sharing the good news of the gospel to all who will listen. **May 5.**

Faith Johnson Crumbly is a homemaker living in Hagerstown, Maryland, with her husband of 48 years, Edward Lawrence Crumbly, Jr. **Apr. 13.**

Celia Mejia Cruz is a pastor's wife, mother of five adult children, grandmother of seven wonderful grandchildren, church elder, and owner of Celi-Write, Inc. She edits manuscripts, psychological evaluations, and dissertations, and writes short stories from her home in the Tennessee Highlands. Her other interests are her family, her dogs, and helping with Pathfinders. **Jan. 9.**

Kezlynn Daisley-Harrow grew up and still lives in the beautiful twin islands of Trinidad and Tobago. She is a pastor in Trinidad and is married to a pastor. She is the first female minister in Trinidad; after her, two others were also hired. She is a budding writer, and this is her debut. She enjoys preaching, reading, and outdoor activities. **Aug. 17.**

Lee Lee Dart is a pastor at the Adventure Seventh-day Adventist Church in Windsor, Colorado. She is passionate on being a conduit of God's love to others and helping them know Christ more intimately. She is a wife and mother of two daughters. She enjoys traveling, art, and partnering with organizations that help widows and orphans all over the world. **Dec. 26.**

Nahomie Daubé is from the French West Indies island of Guadeloupe. She is currently studying theology at the University of the Southern Caribbean (USC) in the republic of Trinidad and Tobago. She is the eldest of a family of four children. **Dec. 12.**

Jean Dozier Davey and her husband, Steven, live in the beautiful mountains of North Carolina. She retired in 2003 from a career as a computer programmer. She enjoys spending time with family, cooking, reading, taking walks in Pisgah Forest, sewing, photography, and encouraging others. **Sept. 4.**

Avery Davis lives in England. She enjoys writing and recently completed a collection of conversations with Christian women. She considers it a privilege to be able to record and share their stories. **July 20.**

Rebecca Davis is currently the associate pastor at the Berean Adventist Church in Atlanta, Georgia. She is married to Justin Davis. They have one son, Justin Davis II, and a daughter on the way. Pastor Davis enjoys ministry and loves playing basketball when she is not pregnant. Rebecca praises God for the powerful things He continues to do through her and her ministry. He is faithful. **Nov. 6.**

Wanda Grimes Davis, at the time of this writing, was a chaplain at Florida Hospital East Orlando in Orlando, Florida. She enjoys teaching, speaking, dancing, and praising God. She is married with three adult children that bless her every day with stories of grace and blessing. **Dec. 13.**

Candace DeVore is editor of *Kids' Ministry Ideas* magazine. She lives in Maryland with her husband, Gary, his dog, and her two cats. She has two grown daughters and is grateful for all God's mercies. **Jan. 3.**

Sinikka Dixon is retired with her husband on Prince Edward Island, Canada,. She is an Adventist sociologist with a Ph.D. from the University of California, Riverside. She is multicultural and multilingual with publications in her professional field of social inequalities, aging, and community studies. She loves to read, travel, and participate in water and snow sports. **May 13.**

Leonie Donald thanks God every day for the beauty of Queen Charlotte Sound, New Zealand, where she lives. She enjoys long walks, "devours" books, and admits to spending more time in her garden than doing housework. Leonie and her husband of more than 45 years attend the Blenheim Seventh-day Adventist Church. **Dec. 27.**

Cheryl Doss is director of the General Conference Institute of World Mission. She holds a Ph.D. in Christian education and intercultural studies from Trinity Evangelical Divinity School. Cheryl and her husband, Gorden, spent 16 years as missionaries in Malawi and have two adult children who, with their families, are also missionaries serving in Egypt and the Philippines. **Mar. 29.**

Joan Dougherty-Mornan, writing from Ontario, Canada, enjoys discovering God between the pages of the Bible and through life's experiences. She has two daughters and a son. Her hobbies are reading, writing, crocheting, and keeping busy for Christ. **June 8.**

Louise Driver, now retired, lives in Idaho, where her three sons and four grandchildren also live. She works part-time as an elementary school librarian at two schools. Her hobbies are singing, music, reading, gardening, and traveling to historical places. **Nov. 27.**

Mary E. Dunkin is finding getting older interesting at this time. She has served in Pathfinders for more than 40 years and in many other areas of church leadership. Her greatest joys include her creating tons of fun stuff, being a history detective, making history fun, traveling throughout her home state of New Mexico with Al, her husband; she has one smaller dog named Colt Magnus. **Nov. 14.**

Ruby H. Enniss-Alleyne writes from Guyana, South America, where she is the assistant treasurer of Guyana Conference of Seventh-day Adventists. She is the family ministries leader and an elder in her local church; she loves the young people and hospital ministry. She is the mother of three adult children, and a few years back she lost her husband of 30 years. **Feb. 9.**

Doreen Evans-Yorke is a Jamaican-Canadian mother, educator, and certified child-life specialist who lives in Montreal, Canada. She spent 16 years working in three different countries in Africa: Cameroon, Kenya, and South Africa. Her hobbies include reading, writing, and playing various instruments. **Apr. 18.**

Ana Teorima Faigao lived in Maryland. She used to work at the General Conference of Seventh-day Adventists world headquarters and attended the Filipino Capitol Adventist Church. She was a wife and mother of two adult children. In 2013 Ana lost the battle she had been fighting against multiple myeloma since 2006. **Apr. 11.**

Gloria J. Stella Felder is an accountant who lives in Atlanta, Georgia, with her pastor-husband. They share a family of four adult children and five grandchildren. Gloria enjoys music, writing, speaking, playing Scrabble, and spending time with family, especially her grandchildren. She has written articles for magazines, and a book of poetry, *My Inspiration*, and is working on another. **Mar. 27.**

Mona Fellers, a longtime paramedic, has moved into the phlebotomy field; she also enjoys teaching emergency medicine part-time. She is women's ministries leader (she loves working with the women) and also heads the children's and homeless ministries at her church. She lives on top of a beautiful Colorado mountain; she is married with two daughters and one grandson. **Aug. 5.**

Adelaide Ferguson is a Sabbath school superintendent at Immanuel Seventh-day Adventist Church, Tema, in the Greater Accra region, Ghana. She is the West Africa and Tema municipal women's ministries director. She is the international baccalaureate diploma tutor and assistant examiner at Tema International School. She is the mother of one child. **Jan. 29.**

Vera Lúcia F. S. Ferrari lives in Pederneiras, in the state of São Paulo, Brazil. She is married to Luiz and has three children: Jonatan, Wilson, and Júlia. She likes to do crossword puzzles and to knit. She wants to be ready for Jesus' return, which is her greatest hope. **May 28.**

Carol Joy Fider, a retired educator, writes from Mandeville. Jamaica. She serves her church as an elder, family ministries director, and Sabbath school teacher. The yearning of her heart is to go with Jesus when He gathers the saints of all ages. She enjoys cooking, gardening, and mentoring young people. She and her husband, Ezra, have two adult daughters. **Jan. 22.**

Edith Fitch writes from Lacombe, Alberta, Canada. She retired in 1993 after 41 years of teaching. Since 1997 she has volunteered in the Canadian University College archives department. Her goal is to preserve all printed materials and photos in electronic format. **Jan. 1.**

Lana Fletcher lives in Chehalis, Washington, with her husband. They have one married daughter and two grandsons. Their younger daughter died in a car accident in 1993. Her favorite occupation was mothering and homeschooling. She is the church clerk, proofreads the bulletin, makes Creative Memories albums, and writes inspiring Christmas letters. **Jan. 16.**

Sherilyn R. Flowers is the author of the book *Personal Omens Expressing My Soul* (POEMS), released in 2013; it is a collection of inspiring testimonies, scriptures, and poetry. She was born in Belize, Central America, but now calls Los Angeles, California, home. She is very active in her home church and desires to lead the world to Christ. **July 24.**

Heide Ford is a licensed Adventist minister serving as a hospital chaplain. She feels blessed in the many opportunities God has given her over the years. Heide has served as a registered nurse, pastoral counselor, cofounder and associate editor of *Women of Spirit* magazine, and director of the Women's Resource Center. She loves dolphin and whale watching, walks with her husband, Zell, and nurturing friendships. **May 7.**

Gale Frampton, living in Ontario, Canada, is a freelance artist who enjoys spending time with God in the great outdoors. She loves working with young people and encourages them to follow the right path. **Aug. 10.**

Andrea Francis is a teacher at the Clement Howell High School in Providenciales, Turks and Caicos. She is actively involved in church life and works in the children's, Adventurers, Pathfinders, and young adult ministries of her church. She has a passion for young people and seeks to nurture them and build characters for eternity. **May 21.**

Forsythia Catane Galgao served as a missionary in Ethiopia for 18 years and in Madagascar for seven years. A quarter of a century spent in Africa! At present she is the English as a second language program coordinator at Asia-Pacific International University (formerly Mission College) in Thailand. **Sept. 25.**

Ardie Gallant is a calligrapher and graphic designer from Minnesota who moved to North Carolina to be near family. Her personal mission statement outlines who she is: Out of a lifetime of learning to rely on and praise my heavenly Father through shrouded valleys and awesome mountain peaks, I seek to cherish God's children as I am cherished by Him. **Mar. 5.**

Edna Maye Gallington is now retired from communication work for the Southeastern California Conference. She has published her first book, *Watching From the Shadows.* A member of Toastmasters International, she speaks at women's groups, church groups, retreats, and service clubs. Visit her blogs at www.ednagallington.com. **Dec. 19.**

Amanda N. Gaspard, M.P.H., is a certified health-care emergency professional who works as an emergency preparedness coordinator in New Hampshire. She served as a student missionary in India for sevem months. She is a Sabbath school teacher and pianist in her local church. Her hobbies include traveling, collecting coins and stamps, and reading. **Jan. 14.**

Marybeth Gessele is a hospice caregiver and a pastor's wife living in Gaston, Oregon. She has written two children's books endeavoring to help children understand death and relate to children with disabilities. Her hobbies include making quilts for foster babies and canning and freezing produce from their country property. **Sept. 28.**

Carol Wiggins Gigante is a former day-care provider and teacher at heart. She is an avid reader, photographer, and flower and bird lover, and works as a freelance proofreader. Carol resides in Beltsville, Maryland, with her husband, Joe; their dog, Buddy; and cat, Suzannah. They have two grown sons, Jeff and James. "Even so, come, Lord Jesus!" **Jan. 26.**

Ana Giovanella lives in Orlando, Florida. She is married to Pastor Francis Giovanella, and her biggest passions are children's ministry and helping others. **Mar. 19.**

Roxanne Girard and is a registered nurse residing in England. At present she is managing a nursing home and in her spare time loves reading inspirational books, chatting and motivating others. This is her first time writing. She hopes her devotional will provide inspiration to others as they read it. **Nov. 25.**

Evelyn Glass and her husband, Darrell, live in northern Minnesota on the farm where Darrell was born. They have three grown children and two grandchildren. Evelyn writes a weekly newspaper column and is active as a speaker and community volunteer; she belongs to a local writers' group and a quilting group. Evelyn recently authored "Women in the Bible and Me," a Bible study set. **Jan. 10, Oct. 28.**

Hannelore Gomez, from Panama, teaches Spanish in a high school in Virginia. Her hobbies are reading and traveling. Knowing the gospel since she was born has been her greatest blessing. **June 3.**

Ruth Middaugh Goodsite is a nurse in Michigan. She tries to do what she can for her church, and currently she is a treasurer. She enjoys reading, travel, crocheting, and walking her dog. She has two grown children. **Sept. 13.**

Teodora Goran is a nurse and has been working for five years for the health department and women's ministries of the Romanian Union. She does this part-time and works also as a literature evangelist. She really loves to work for the Lord, helping people around her to know Jesus. This is a great blessing for Teodora and her husband. She enjoys traveling as well. **Jan. 30.**

Shelley Gordon, a pastor's daughter, writes from South Africa. She is now separated after being married for seven years and is seeking work, as she resigned from her job of five years as an intermediate paramedic. Her hobbies include reading, writing stories, playing tennis, hiking and camping, listening to music, and watching her favorite Heritage Singers' DVD. **Dec. 18.**

Cecelia Grant is a Seventh day-Adventist medical doctor retired from the government service and living in Kingston, Jamaica. Her hobbies are traveling, gardening, and listening to good music. She has a passion for young people—to whom she is always giving advice. **Nov. 13.**

Mary Jane Graves lost her husband to cancer in 2009 after 58 years of a happy marriage. She is looking forward to the day when they can be together again. She lives in western North Carolina and is involved in her church. She enjoys gardening, reading, writing, family, and friends. **May 23.**

Marjorie Gray-Johnson resides in Port Saint Lucie, Florida. She is the mother of three adult children: a daughter, Michele, sons Daniel and Michael, and a devoted son-in-law, Mike. She has six delightful grandchildren and an energetic 85-year-old mother. She is a registered nurse actively pursuing graduate degrees. She is active in the health ministry and community service. **May 20.**

Thelda Van Lange Greaves was born in Guyana, South America, and grew up in Trinidad. She is a retired nurse and was married for 29 years to a very special man, Timothy S. Greaves, M.D., who has been resting in the Lord since May 8, 2010. Her hobbies include reading, traveling, gardening, piano playing, and contemplating God's love. **Oct. 24.**

Karen Birkett Green is a counselor and freelance writer who has contributed articles to many journals, including *Adventist Review, Adventist World, Insight,* and *Women of Spirit*. She resides in Charlotte, North Carolina. Karen and her husband, Xavier, are founders of ZavKay Family Services, an organization dedicated to strengthening families and churches through seminars. **Nov. 30.**

Carol J. Greene writes from central Florida. She is the matriarch of her family, which includes adult children, grandchildren, and a great-grandson. Praying for those in her sphere of influence is her major passion. **Aug. 23.**

Glenda-mae Greene, a retired university administrator, writes from her wheelchair in central Florida. Writing is her passion. Her devotional is based on a compilation of her diary entries. **Mar. 26.**

Gloria Gregory and her husband, Milton, a church administrator, have been involved in team ministry for more than 35 years; together they engage in presentations. She currently serves as the dean of the College of Education and Leadership at Northern Caribbean University in Jamaica. Their first granddaughter has brought additional joy to the family. **Jan. 7.**

Lillian R. Guild is a retired nurse, Bible instructor, foreign missionary, literature evangelist, and a secretary for the Voice of Prophecy Evangelism Association. She now lives in Loma Linda, California. **Apr. 14.**

Twinkle Guimaraes lives in Frederick, Maryland, and works for the business development division of a health-care organization based in the Washington, D.C., area. In her spare time she enjoys working with her husband on restoring vintage muscle cars, and supporting various foundations around the world for Christian missions, for curing cancer, and eliminating hunger. **Jan. 18.**

Helen Bocala Gulfan, who travels frequently, enjoys sharing God's amazing love and hope among people with whom He brings her in contact. It is her prayer that they will be ready to meet Jesus when He comes. She continues to serve as Shepherdess International coordinator and women's ministries director of the Southern Asia-Pacific Division in the Philippines. **Aug. 1.**

Bertha Hall is married to a pastor, Curtis Hall. They just moved to Tennessee from Florida. She is an educator who has received a position that is bringing about a change. Bertha enjoys working in the educational field, but mostly she loves working for the Lord by witnessing and seeing souls saved. Her goal is to see Jesus' precious face along with her family. **Dec. 4.**

Deborah M. Harris, longtime university professor and teacher of special-needs children, is president and CEO of Deborah Harris, Inc., a speaking and consulting business. Harris, known for her inspirational messages, has founded the powerful Praying for Our Children ministry (prayingforourchildren.org), which is going global. **Apr. 19.**

Peggy Curtice Harris is the board chair of WASH (Women and Men Against Sexual Harassment and Other Abuses: www.w-a-s-h.org.). Peggy's books include *Beginnings and Endings,* and *Deaconess Ministry* at www.adventsource.org; *Celestial Chronicles, Encounter With God, God Is Calling His Children Home, Indestructible Hope,* and *In God's Time* at www.authorhouse.com. **Dec. 1.**

Marian M. Hart Gay, a retired elementary teacher and nursing home administrator, works with her husband doing property management. A member of the Battle Creek Seventh-day Adventist Tabernacle for 35 years, she has served as a volunteer in many different capacities. Six grandchildren makes her a proud grandmother. Marian also enjoys spending winters in Florida. **Oct. 18.**

Beverly D. Hazzard, the daughter of medical missionaries, was born in England and grew up in Jamaica, Ohio, and British Columbia, Canada. A retired nurse administrator, she now lives in Kelowna, British Columbia. Mother of two adult children, grandma to five, she enjoys time with family, her dogs, travel, sailing, and mission trips. She is a church elder and school board chair. **May 19.**

Helen Heavirland is a writer from Oregon. She has enjoyed the privilege of serving while volunteering in Zambia, El Salvador, and Solomon Islands. The story of the man who showed Heavirland the lesson of the atlas (referenced in her contribution to this devotional collection) was originally told in one of her own books, *My Enemy, My Brother* (Pacific Press, 2007). **Mar. 2.**

Kathi Heise lives in the Black Forest of Germany, where she is active in the children's department of her local church. She is also part of the team for singles in the South German Union. She is creative, sings, reads, and laughs, and loves to be a grandmother. **Jan. 8.**

Nancy Heller lives in Gaithersburg, Maryland, with her husband, Irv. They have two married daughters, Denise and Jenny, and one grandson, Jonas. Nancy works at the Seventh-day Adventist world headquarters as an administrative assistant. Her hobbies include spending time with her friends, gardening flowers, piano, organ, and most of all, being a grandmother. **Aug. 27.**

Muriel Heppel is a retired teacher living in the lovely Robson Valley situated between the Rocky and Cariboo Mountains in British Columbia. She enjoys the church in McBride and participates as an assistant Sabbath school superintendent, assistant class teacher, and tutors in the church school. She loves the quietness of nature, bird-watching, reading, and traveling. **July 10, Nov. 12.**

Kathy-Ann C. Hernandez, Ph.D., is an associate professor for the Campolo College of Graduate and Professional Studies at Eastern University in Pennsylvania. She has authored journal articles and book chapters; her work has appeared in *Callaloo, Adventist Review,* and *PRISM*. She lives close to a natural park just outside Philadelphia with her husband and two daughters. **Oct. 2.**

Denise Dick Herr teaches English at Canadian University College in Alberta, Canada. She agrees with writer C. S. Lewis that "you can never get a cup of tea large enough or a book long enough to suit me." **Apr. 21, May 24.**

Rosemary Byrd Hickman, who lives in Florida with her husband, Ray, helped to begin Secret Sisters in their church 25 years ago. They have four adult children and 14 grandchildren. Until recently she worked at the Review and Herald Publishing in customer service. She enjoys reading, sewing, baking, sharing, and laughing with family and friends. **Nov. 17.**

Denise Hochstrasser lives in the wonderful mountains of Berner Oberland in Switzerland and is women's ministries director for the Inter-European Division. She has been involved in women's ministries for more than 25 years. She loves to travel but looks forward to return to her old farmhouse and little flower garden after each trip. She is married to Markus and has three adult daughters. **Feb. 4.**

Roxy Hoehn retired in Topeka, Kansas, after a lot of good years in charge of women's ministries for the Kansas-Nebraska Conference of Seventh-day Adventists. She's a happy nana to 11 grandchildren and six granddogs. **Mar. 12, Aug. 15.**

Karen Holford lives in Scotland, where her husband is the mission president and pastor of the Crieff church. She is a freelance writer and family therapist. She loves walking, upcycling junk into beautiful things, and having cozy dinners with her family. **May 17, Oct. 1.**

Tamyra Horst, wife and mom, serves as both the communication director and women's ministries director for the Pennsylvania Conference. A sought-after speaker, Tamyra has also written numerous books, including *Praying Like Crazy for Your Kids* and *Strengthening the Church Through Women's Ministries*. Her passion is to encourage, equip, and challenge women and girls in their adventure with God. **Jan. 15, Apr. 29, June 6.**

Jacqueline Hope HoShing-Clarke has been an educator since 1979 and has served as principal, assistant principal, and teacher. She serves the Northern Caribbean University in Jamaica as director for the Pre-College Department. She has a Masters of Arts degree and is currently reading for a Ph.D. She is married to a pastor, and they have two adult children. **Jan. 21.**

Kristen Hudson is a graduate of Oakwood University. She enjoys writing, reading, and listening to good music. She lives in Huntsville, Alabama, and likes to use the gift that God gave her to encourage others. One day she hopes to publish a book. **Feb. 7.**

Barbara Huff enjoys planning various programs for the Port Charlotte, Florida, Adventist Church, where she and her husband are members. She is thrilled to live in the same town as two of her three grandchildren. Barbara enjoys retirement so she can spend time growing orchids and feeding and watching the birds at her feeder. She says that her birds and flowers nurture her. **May 9.**

Cecilia Moreno de Iglesias is Ecuadorian by birth and Colombian by adoption. She is a pastor's wife and mother of two children, Jessie Alejandra and Pedro Andrés. She has a degree in social and political science and a master's in family therapy. She has worked for the Adventist Church for 30 years in various positions. She loves to work with families and women. She is now the director for women's ministries in the Inter-American Division. **Nov. 18.**

Shirley C. Iheanacho enjoyed more than 33 years of denominational service. Visiting and ministering to those who are sick and shut in, playing handbells, singing, encouraging others, writing, speaking at church events, and visiting her daughters and grandsons, Tim and Niko, are now among her favorite pastimes. She has been married for 44 years to her beloved husband, Morris. **July 2.**

Charlotte Ishkanian was until recently editor of the adult and children's quarterly mission magazine and "Inside Stories" (found in the Sabbath school Bible study lesson guides). She worked at the General Conference of Seventh-day Adventists her entire adult life, serving in several editorial positions. She has three adult children and one grandchild; she lives in Maryland. **July 6.**

Amanda Isles wrote this devotional when she was no longer at school in St. Lucia but back home in Dominica. She completed her bachelor's degree and is currently seeking employment, trusting that her God will provide her the right one. She was 22 years of age when she wrote her devotional. **Nov. 26.**

Joan D. L. Jaensch and her husband, Murray, live in South Australia. They have two married sons, two granddaughters, two grandsons, and one great-grandson and one great-granddaughter. Gardening and potted plants are her hobbies. **May 29 .**

Donette James-Samuel, who recently married, is a staff nurse living and working in the United Kingdom. She studied at what is now Northern Caribbean University. She is involved with Pathfinders, health and women's ministries, children's music, and singing on the choir. She enjoys working with the youth and elderly, traveling, reading, and listening to instrumental music. **Oct. 30.**

Tammy Jamieson, along with her husband, Jason, is raising three boys in Brooks, Alberta, Canada. Besides being a full-time mother, she teaches business and computer courses at the local college, and handles administrative duties for her church. During the summers Tammy enjoys outdoor and water activities, and travels with her family. **Sept. 7.**

Wilma C. Jardine attends Breath of Life Seventh-day Adventist Church in Maryland, where she sings in the sanctuary choir and serves as chaplain for the Buccaneers Pathfinder Club. She is a foster grandparent in the Prince George County public schools, has six children, seven grandchildren, and three great-grandchildren, whom she loves dearly. **July 17.**

Greta Michelle Joachim-Fox-Dyett is a wife, mother, artist, potter, writer and teacher. Most of all she is a child of the most high God. Greta, who is currently reading for her second degree in fine arts, lives in Trinidad and Tobago. **Nov. 11.**

Elaine J. Johnson retired after 30 years in day-care/preschool work. She has been married to her best friend of more than 45 years, and they have four children, 12 grandchildren, and three great-grandchildren. She enjoys country living in Verbena, Alabama, and is active in her small country church. **Mar. 10.**

Erna Johnson was born and raised in Iceland. She's the director for women's ministries in the South Pacific Division and is married to Eddy, a pastor; they've served the church around the world. She speaks Icelandic, English, and French; they have two adult children, and Erna loves being a grandmother. Her passion is helping women reach their potential in Jesus. **Apr. 20.**

Jeannette Busby Johnson lives in Maryland, which has many of the same letters as "Montana" (where she grew up) but none of the mountains. She has three adult children, six grandchildren, and a dignified coonhound named Ludwig (as in Beethoven). **Feb. 13.**

Karen J. Johnson is the president of the Rocky Mountain Adventist Healthcare Foundation, located in Greenwood Village, Colorado. She is married, with three children and eight grandchildren. She spent 34 years of her career in Adventist education before she began working for the Adventist Healthcare System. The major part of her career has been in fund-raising. **July 3.**

Sibilla Johnson is health director for Australia's Victorian Conference of the South Pacific Division, and national trainer and editor for the Community Health Education presenters' training course for the division. She has served in Papua New Guinea, Mongolia, Nepal, and New Zealand. **Aug. 22.**

Angie Joseph is a pastor's wife in Iowa, codirector of lay evangelism in the Iowa-Missouri Conference, and a speaker at women's retreats. **Mar. 14.**

Eileen M. Joseph resides in St. Croix in the United States Virgin Islands and attends the Central Adventist Church. She has served the church as women's ministries leader, Sabbath school secretary and superintendent, and assistant children's ministries leader. Eileen is the mother of five, grandmother of seven, and great-grandmother of three. She enjoys crocheting and reading. **Mar. 20.**

Nadine A. Joseph has been publishing devotional and inspirational writings geared toward inspiring university students to experience a deeper relationship with God and by living a life of "crazy" faith. She is working on her Ph.D. at Adventist International Institute of Advanced Studies in the Philippines. You can visit her Web site at www.nadinejoseph.com. **Mar. 7.**

Patricia Kay is a mother of three and grandmother of four, wife of a federal judge and longtime resident of Hawaii, where she is active on community boards and projects involving at-risk children and families. She attended the University of California at Berkeley and Westminster Theological Seminary, and is executive director and trustee of the Diane Patmont Foundation. **Sept. 30.**

Sonia Kennedy-Brown lives in Ontario, Canada. She recently retired from her nursing career and is in the process of writing her life story. She serves in several ministries of the church, including women's ministries and being an elder. Her greatest passion is to see others won to Christ. Her hobbies include reading, poetry, travel, and cooking. **Aug. 26.**

Iris L. Kitching eagerly looks forward to retirement to get more involved in creative endeavors and to publish eight or more of her children's books. She has worked at the General Conference world headquarters for 18 years, 10 in women's ministries and eight in presidential. She and her husband, Will, enjoy a simple life in Maryland and enjoy their children and grandchildren. **Oct. 11, Dec. 11.**

Mitzie Knight is a registered nurse residing in New York City. She became a baptized member of the Seventh-day Adventist Church while enrolled as a student at West Indies College (now known as Northern Caribbean University). She enjoys spending time at the ocean and hopes to learn to swim one day. **Sept. 29.**

Linda Mei Lin Koh is presently serving as director of children's ministries at the General Conference of Seventh-day Adventists. She enjoys working with children, especially with her five grandchildren. She also contributes articles to such denominational magazines as *Adventist Review, Adventist World,* and *Elders' Digest.* **June 12.**

Kênia Kopitar is from Brazil, but has lived in the United States in New York City since 2006. She feels grateful to God for her life, for the opportunity to meet wonderful people, and for the second chances that He gives us all every day. **June 10.**

Betty Kossick is the author of *Beyond the Locked Door* and *Heart Ballads* and part of about 40 books with other authors, including devotional books. She has 42 years as a newspaper/magazine journalist behind her. She and her husband, Johnny, settled in Calhoun, Georgia, on the campus of Georgia-Cumberland Academy in 2012. Her e-mail is: bkwrites4u@hotmail.com. **Oct. 8.**

Patricia Mulraney Kovalski is mother, grandmother, great-grandmother, and retired educator. She has served as church elder and Sabbath school superintendent and teacher. She continues to do English teas for neighbors and friends. She loves to travel, swim, knit, crochet, and read. **July 5.**

Kathleen Kiem Hoa Oey Kuntaraf, M.D., M.P.H., has been the associate health director for the Seventh-day Adventist Church worldwide since 1995. Prior, she worked in Asia as a physician, assistant ADRA director, and health director. She and her husband, Jonathan, have authored five books. They have a daughter, Andrea Kuntaraf-Crane, and a granddaughter, Chelsea. **Sept. 23.**

Mabel Kwei is a retired university/college lecturer who served in Africa as a missionary for many years with her pastor-husband and three children. She reads a lot, loves to paint, write, and give talks, and spends lots of time with very little children both in church and in the community. **Oct. 31.**

Sally Lam-Phoon serves the Northern Asia-Pacific Division of Seventh-day Adventists in Korea as children's, family, and women's ministries director, as well as coordinator for the communication and leadership advancement program. Married for 40 years to Chek-Yat, a gospel minister, she has two married daughters and two grandchildren. **Jan. 28, Mar. 4.**

Barbara Lankford is a child of God, a daughter, a wife, a mother, and a grandmother. She and her husband, Jerry, live in Burley, Idaho, and have been married for more than 46 years. They joined the Adventist Church following a Voice of Prophecy evangelistic seminar in 1973. She loves her family and her church family. She also enjoys making quilt tops, gardening, and knitting. **July 13.**

Iani Dias Lauer-Leite lives in Bahia, Brazil. She is a college professor. At church she likes to help in music and prayer ministries. **Nov. 8.**

Loida Gulaja Lehmann spent 10 years selling religious books in the Philippines before going to Germany and getting married. She and her husband are active members in the International Church in Darmstadt. Both are helping to plant churches in the Philippines and supporting lay ministries. Hobbies include traveling, nature walks, writing, and photography. **Dec. 28.**

Joan M. Leslie is a native of Jamaica, West Indies, and a teacher by profession. She takes great pleasure in reading and also loves to travel and crochet. Joan lives and works in New York. **May 27.**

Sharon (Brown) Long is originally from Trinidad but makes her home in Alberta, Canada. She has four adult children and two adult granddaughters. Sharon is a social worker who spent her 34-year career in child welfare. Sharon is married to Miguel Brown; they attend West Edmonton Adventist Church. Sharon has held various leadership roles in her church and loves cooking. **Jan. 25.**

Rhodi Alers de López writes from Massachusetts. Her ministry, ExpresSion Publishing Ministries, aims to inspire others to a closer relationship with Jesus. She's an author, singer, songwriter, and speaker, and leads a prayer ministry. Her bilingual Web site is: expressionpublishingministries.com. **Dec. 10.**

Rhona Grace Magpayo is a retired optician who enjoys helping people see better and has gone on mission trips to South and Central America and the Philippines. She lives in Maryland with her husband, Celestino Magpayo, Jr., who is retired from the U.S. Navy. She loves singing with the Sligo Friends Singers. **June 16.**

Debbie Maloba is the women's and children's ministries director for the East-Central Africa Division of the Seventh-day Adventist Church. She and her husband, Jim, have been blessed with five children, who have graciously adjusted to their new life in Nairobi, Kenya. Debbie loves to train women in leadership and to make ministry proposals. **Dec. 15.**

Carol Jean Marino has lived in Loveland, Colorado, since 2001. She calls herself "a Jackie of all trades," having worked at many different jobs, including: teaching English as a second language in South Korea two different times. She volunteers at her local library and local church, and has served as the custodian and church treasurer at the Palisade, Colorado, Adventist Church. **Sept. 3.**

Cassandra Marquez de Smith, age 10, writes from Ocala, Florida, where at the time of this writing she was in the fifth grade at Shady Hill Elementary. Cassandra loves to read, play board games, and sing whenever possible. She gave her heart to Jesus in April of 2012 and hopes that He will continue to lead her. **Feb. 15.**

Tamara Marquez de Smith writes from Ocala, Florida, where she lives with her husband, Steven, and their girls, Lillian and Cassandra. Tamara has taken a leave of absence from, an office in her local church to focus on her daughter Lillian's health. **June 25.**

Marion V. Clarke Martin writes from Panama; she was a physician, but now enjoys retirement and remains busy with her home, helping both a son who has health issues, and her granddaughter, and undertaking various church responsibilities, which include serving as a church elder and playing the organ and piano. **Jan. 31.**

Orpha Gumbo Maseko was born in Tsholotsho, Zimbabwe. Orpha holds B.B.A. and M.S.A. degrees in pastoral care and is a Ph.D. candidate in education leadership. She has held several positions in her church. She currently resides in South Bend, Indiana. **June 19.**

Premila Masih serves the Southern Asia Division as women's ministries director. She is married to Pastor Hidayat Masih. She has worked as a teacher for 26 years and served as a Shepherdess coordinator at the union level. She has two children, a married daughter, living in the United Kingdom, and a son who works for ADRA India. Her passions include home decorating, reading, and making friends. **Sept. 2.**

Gail Masondo is a wife, mother of two adult children (Shellie and Jonathan), women/children's advocate, chaplain, seasoned songwriter, Life in Recovery coach, author, and international speaker. In addition to philanthropic and creative endeavors (she was the co-executive producer of the acclaimed *Handel's Messiah: A Soulful Celebration* CD), Gail authored a memoir, *Now This Feels Like Home.* A New York native, Gail resides in Johannesburg, South Africa, with her husband, Sibusiso Victor Masondo. **Mar. 15.**

Rosalina Matheson was born in Bulgaria and raised in orphanages until she was adopted in 2000 by Les and Leona Matheson, and through the years she has learned about God. Rosalina graduated from Laurelbrook Academy and has attended Union College in Lincoln, Nebraska. She hopes to become an elementary teacher. **Jan. 19.**

Socorro Castro de Mattos is Brazilian, born in Paulino Neves, Maranhão. She is a retired teacher who enjoys swimming, poetry, reading the Bible, visiting discouraged people and praying with them, and singing in the choir. **June 13.**

Mary L. Maxson is a follower of Jesus Christ as an associate pastor of the Paradise Adventist Church, in Paradise, California. She is a lover of flower gardening; she plants as the deer eat the salad of flowers—month by month. Her passion is discipling persons as she watches the Holy Spirit transform their lives with the gospel of grace. **July 25.**

Gloria Joyce Crarey McCalla, Ph.D., is a retired educator who grew up in Jamaica but now lives in Miami, Florida. She and her late pastor-husband had four children who all have graduate degrees. One daughter is deceased. McCalla is one of the local elders at her church, the coordinator for prayer and shut-in ministries, and the leader of a Sabbath school class. **Feb. 21.**

Laurie McClanahan writes from Flatrock, North Carolina, where old age and retirement have taken over after years of selling religious books and being a Bible instructor, and chaplain, plus service for God in several other areas. **Oct. 6.**

Vidella McClellan is retired and lives in beautiful British Colombia, Canada. She is married and a mother of three and Grandmother of seven, and has one great-grandchild, as well as four step-children, seven step-grandchildren, and two great-grandchildren. She loves to work in her garden and among the flower beds, and has been active in the churches and community. **June 5.**

Gloria McDowall is a retired home economics teacher from St. Vincent and the Grenadines. She is the women's ministries leader at the Maranatha Adventist Church in Brooklyn New York. She enjoys reading, gardening, and helping those who are needy. **May 8.**

Nerida McKibben is an obstetrician-gynecologist with a strong interest in lifestyle medicine. Originally from New Zealand, she is now living in Silver Spring, Maryland, where she hosts a daily TV show, *Go Healthy . . . For Good,* for the Hope Channel. Her husband, Daniel, is a minister, and their joint passion is evangelism. **May 26.**

Judelia Medard-Santiesteban is an English teacher from the small island of St. Lucia. She is currently pursuing studies in the area of guidance and counseling. She has a passion for language arts, literature, and lifting the lives of others. She plans to merge these in ministry for Christ. **Nov. 2.**

Jane Rose Alves Medeiros writes from Macapá, Amapá, Brazil. Her husband, Eliel Medeiros, is a pastor in the central Macapá church, which is 59 years old; there are seven other churches in the city. She is a teacher who likes to paint and take part in women's ministries. They have two children, Erick and Anne Elise. **Apr. 23.**

Cassi Alise Meelhuysen was graduated from Union College in 2012 with a bachelor's degree in communications/journalism. Her life's vision is to bring water to the Masai in Kenya, Africa, through her project "Not Oh Well." **July 4.**

Gay Mentes lives in sunny Kelowna, British Columbia, Canada, with her husband, Alex, who is an artist. Together they enjoy reaching out to their community through the arts. They are parents to two grown children, A.J. and Sharlet. Gay enjoys being a grandma, doing her art, writing, photography, and working with flowers, (especially calla lilies). **June 23.**

Gertrude Mfune is a mother of four, two of whom are adopted, and a proud grandmother of one adorable 4-year-old granddaughter. She is a teacher with a degree in family consumer science and worked with ADRA for many years in Malawi, her home country. She resides in Laurel, Maryland. She has been married for 33 years to a pastor. **Mar. 18.**

Annette Walwyn Michael writes from St. Croix in the United States Virgin Islands. She is a retired English teacher and a published writer of Caribbean literature. Three adult daughters, three sons-in-law, and seven grandchildren are beautiful additions to her family. Her husband, Reginald, is a busy retired pastor. **Apr. 24.**

Brandi Mills, a fourth-year student at Canadian University College in Alberta, Canada, hopes to become a teacher who inspires others. She wants to share more of her experiences—filled with laughter and Christ—with her students. Brandi hopes to have more overseas adventures, as she plans to do missions again for a few years with her husband. **Apr. 28.**

Quilvie G. Mills is a retired community professor. She and her husband are members of the Port St. Lucie church in Florida, where she serves as a musician and Bible class teacher. She enjoys traveling, music, gardening, word games, reading, and teaching piano. **Mar. 13.**

Cheryol Mitchell, Ed.D., is the principal of the largest high school in Missouri. She has been an educator for 27 years in both the parochial and public school systems. She is an avid reader and enjoys spending time with friends and family. **Mar. 9.**

Eloisa da Silva Monken is an English, Portuguese, and Spanish teacher in Petrópolis, Rio de Janeiro, Brazil. She is the director of Adventist Serving in Action and associate in the ministry of deaconesses and women's ministries, in the central church of Petrópolis. **Sept. 5.**

Jane Wiggins Moore is a registered nurse, secretary, and teacher who has held many church offices, but her favorite is being a Dorcas leader. She was widowed after 36 wonderful years with her husband, John Moore. Their sons, daughters-in-law, and grandchildren keep her inspired to "be faithful unto death, and I will give you the crown of life" (Rev. 2:10, NKJV). **Dec. 22.**

Esperanza Aquino Mopera retired from nursing after an accident that disabled her right upper arm. She is a mother of four and a grandmother. Currently she is working with 20 volunteers in the island group of Polillo, Quezon, Philippines. **Feb. 18.**

Lourdes Morales-Gudmundsson is a professor of Spanish language and literature at La Sierra University. She is an ordained elder and director of women's ministries at the Campus Hill Seventh-day Adventist Church in Loma Linda, California. Her most recent book is entitled *I Forgive You, But . . .* She is also the current president of the Association of Adventist Women. **May 30, May 31, Nov. 3, Nov. 4.**

Lila Farrell Morgan is a widow with five adult children, five grandchildren, and one great-grandchild. She still attends church in North Carolina where she and her husband were charter members 50 years ago. She enjoys reading, walking, baking, table games, and keeping in touch with family and friends through e-mail and Facebook. **Aug. 14.**

Bonnie Moyers lives with her husband and two cats in Staunton, Virginia. She has two adult children and three granddaughters. She is a musician for a Methodist church and Presbyterian church on Sundays. She writes freelance, and her writings have been published in many magazines and books. She is a volunteer musician in her local church on Sabbaths. **Aug. 2.**

Joelcira F. Müller-Cavedon first met Adventists while living and working in Hong Kong, but was baptized when she returned home to Brazil. Her daughter and son-in-law are theology graduates working in ministry in Brazil. Jo has remarried and is now dividing her time between Germany and Brazil. The couple is helping to form an international church in the Stuttgart area. **Feb. 12.**

Judith M. Mwansa comes from Zambia but currently lives in Laurel, Maryland. She and her husband, Pardon, work at the General Conference of Seventh-day Adventists. They have adult children and one wonderful daughter-in-law. Judith enjoys reading, music, traveling, meeting other pastors' wives, and spending time with family and friends. **Dec. 9 .**

Caroline Naumann is married and has two children. She has studied theology at Seminar Schloss Bogenhofen and educational sciences at the University of Innsbruck. Her dissertation dealt with the subject of sexual abuse in childhood and the effects on a later partnership. She works in a crisis center with youngsters. **Dec. 31.**

Ingrid Naumann worked for more than 20 years as director of the women's ministries and the singles organization in the South German Union. Now retired, she was a pioneer of women's ministries in Europe, particularly in the German-speaking countries. She is an evangelist, mentor, and motivator. She has a pastor son in Austria, a daughter-in-law, and two grandchildren. **June 26.**

Regina Ncube was born in Zimbabwe but is now settled in the United Kingdom. She is a mother of two young adults and has served within the women ministries department. She is a qualified primary school teacher who has also worked within health and social care. She enjoys reading and writing, and working with vulnerable women and young girls. **Dec. 16.**

Bienvisa Ladion Nebres, who is from the Philippines, teaches in Thailand and continues to enjoy recalling the years and experiences she had working with her husband in Africa (Ethiopia, Cameroon, and Congo—formerly Zaire). She plays Scrabble when there is someone to play with and composes poetry when inspiration strikes. **Sept. 18.**

Anne Elaine Nelson is a retired teacher in Michigan who works with testing for schools. She has written the book *Puzzled Parents*. Her four children have blessed her with grandchildren and four great-grandchildren. Anne is a widow but stays active in her church. Her favorite activities are scrapbooking, music, photography, and creating memories with her grandchildren. **Feb. 2.**

Samantha Nelson, a pastor's wife, loves serving with her husband, Steve, and is vice president and CEO of The Hope of Survivors (http://thehopeofsurvivors.com), a nonprofit organization dedicated to assisting victims of clergy sexual abuse and providing educational seminars to clergy of all faiths. She and Steve love traveling and enjoying the beauty of God's creation. **Feb. 22.**

Stacey A. Nicely was born in Jamaica, West Indies, and grew up as an active Seventh-day Adventist Christian. She studied and worked at Northern Caribbean University, but now lives in Berrien Springs, Michigan. She graduated with a Master of Arts degree in community counseling and now is pursuing a Ph.D. She is a certified counselor in the state of Michigan. **June 2.**

Angele Rachel Nlo Nlo is a pastor's wife. She and her husband served for 20 years at the Seventh-day Adventist Church headquarters in Abidjan, Ivory Coast, for the West-Central Africa Division. She was the Shepherdess coordinator. She has degrees in family and public law. She is back in her home country, Cameroon, where she has started an evening school for young people. **July 31.**

Ruth Nyachuru-Muze lives with her retired husband in North Carolina, where she is a professor in nursing at a local university. She is very actively involved in teaching adult Sabbath school and health ministries at her church **Aug. 11.**

Elizabeth Versteegh Odiyar, of Kelowna, British Colombia, Canada, has managed the family chimney sweep business since 1985. She has twin sons, Royce and Ronald (married to Tiffany, grandson Jadon) and a daughter, Mai-Rhea. She enjoys mission and road trips, being creative, and homemaking, and hopes to become a writer and painter. **Jan. 11.**

Joyce O'Garro, a retired laboratory technologist of 20 years, took care of cancer patients. She is a qualified teacher who has taught from kindergarten to college, and a pianist who at 79 years of age still teaches piano. She has two grown daughters, one son-in-law, and three grandchildren. Her hobbies are reading, organizing, and planning programs. **Apr. 15.**

Elaine Oliver is a wife and mother, and disciple of Jesus Christ. A certified family-life educator, she also serves as associate director of the Department of Family Ministries for the General Conference of Seventh-day Adventists, and is a doctoral candidate in educational psychology. Her 30-year marriage to Willie Oliver and nurturing their two young adult children are her greatest joys. She loves orchids, bush tea, cupcakes, and long walks on the beach. **Nov. 9, Nov. 10.**

Jemima Dollosa Orillosa lives in Maryland with her husband, Danny. Jemima is a proud grandmother of a baby girl, Aryia Carrin. Jemima's passion is organizing mission trips. She also loves to travel, visit her daughters, and see places with the family and her "golden girls" friends. **Feb. 11.**

Sharon Oster and her pastor-husband have retired and live in Colorado, where they are enjoying the nearby mountains. After retiring from working with special education children and being diagnosed with multiple sclerosis, Sharon enjoys a quiet life reading, doing cross-stitch, and spending time with family: three children and seven grandchildren. **Feb. 5.**

Raisa Ostrovskaya writes from Russia, where she serves as the women's ministries director for Euro-Asia Division. Her husband is a pastor, and they have four sons. She likes poetry, cooking, and reading books. **Nov. 28 .**

Rose Otis initiated the first six women's devotional books of this series while serving as women's ministries director at the General Conference of Seventh-day Adventists. She is now retired in Maryland with her husband, Bud, and basks in more time with their two children and four grandchildren. They enjoy gardening and travel. **Apr. 2, Sept. 26, Nov. 15.**

Hannele Ottschofski lives in southern Germany. She has four daughters and five grandchildren. She is a speaker for the Hope Channel and is active in organizing women's ministries events. She has put together four devotional books for women. **June 4, Oct. 15.**

Heather E. Overstreet is a wife and the mother of three children. She is currently retired from the United States Air Force, holds a Master of Education degree in education and psychology, and is employed by the great state of Oklahoma. She is also the Oklahoma Pathfinder area coordinator for her conference. Her hobbies include reading, music, travel, and everything Pathfinders. **June 11.**

Sharon Michael Palmer, M.D., is married to Specialist Matthew Palmer, U.S. Army. They reside in Fort Benning, Georgia. **Feb. 3.**

Ziri Palu-Amala is married and blessed with two children in Zaria, Nigeria. She likes traveling, counseling, women's ministries, and reading. She holds a bachelor's and master's degrees in education and is the director of academic planning and deputy director general of the Federal Ministry of Science and Technology, Nigeria Institute of Leather and Science Technology. **Dec. 5.**

Revel Papaioannou works with her retired-but-working pastor husband of 57 years in the biblical town of Berea. They have four sons and 14 grandchildren. Over the years she has held almost every church position and is now Sabbath school superintendent, adult Bible class teach, church janitor, and tends the tiny garden. Free time includes Bible studies and mountain hiking. **Aug. 3.**

Erin Parfet is living in Kansas, though occasional sightings have been reported in London, Paris, Venice, and Geneva. She is a biochemist by training, with supplemental coursework in pharmacy and nutrition. Outside of work and the church, Erin blogs about environmental issues, advocates all things outdoors, and loves attempting new recipes. **Feb. 25.**

Barbara Parkins lives on a small farm in New South Wales, Australia, when she is not in Kenya living with the Masai and running her project; she has a school, a rescue center, and community center for the women. She has worked with women's ministries for 13 years and has traveled extensively, speaking in some of the most remote areas of the world. **Aug. 24.**

Carmem Virgínia dos Santos Paulo graduated with a degree in languages and literature and is a specialist in linguistics and teaching. She is a health and socioeducational agent. In her free time she likes to read, sing, and speak of God's love to others. At church she is the youth director and subdirector of music. She writes from Brazil. **Sept. 14.**

Jelena Pavlovic comes from Belgrade, Serbia. She was 22 years old and a student at the Belgrade Theological Seminary when she wrote the devotional, sharing her personal experience. She received a women's ministries scholarship and this is her first devotional submission. **Aug. 29.**

Céleste Perrino-Walker is a much-published author, editor, and textile artist. She lives on a farm in Vermont with her husband and two kids and is blessed with a great many animals. You can learn more about her adventures and her current work by following her blog at reindeerstationfarm. blogspot.com. **May 15, July 27, Nov. 7.**

Betty Glover Perry is a retired anesthetist of 38 years. Her husband, a pastor, is also retired; they are parents, grandparents, and great-grandparents. Her hobbies are playing piano/organ, research and writing, mentoring and counseling, and composing articles for the devotional book and a healthy living cookbook. She writes from North Carolina. **Aug. 20.**

Cheri Peters is the founder of True Step Ministries, a nonprofit organization that helps people break free from the damage of their past. She is the host of the popular TV program *Celebrating Life in Recovery*, broadcast by Three Angels Broadcasting Network. Cheri's book, *Miracle From the Streets*, tells the story of how God rescued her from a life of abuse and addiction. **July 16.**

Marilyn Petersen is a retired elementary teacher and church organist living in Silver Spring, Maryland. She loves animals and enjoys reading and writing. She has a daughter and two grand-daughters. **Sept. 6.**

Karen Phillips lives in Omaha, Nebraska. She is the single mother of four children and works as a human resource/safety manager. She actively leads a weekly women's Bible study called Treasure Seekers, sings in the church choir, and is a volunteer chaplain at a large medical center. Her time is spent with her children, prayer journaling, walking her two dogs, and traveling. **Dec. 6.**

Birdie Poddar is a retiree who comes from northeast India but has settled in south India. She has two adult children, a girl and a boy, and five grandchildren. She enjoys gardening, keeping house, cooking, baking, telling stories, writing articles, and composing poems. She does a handcrafted card ministry for those who need comfort and encouragement. **Feb. 19.**

Viola Ruth Poey writes from Laurel, Maryland. She currently works as a business manager for Washington Adventist University. **Nov. 5.**

Beverly Campbell Pottle has worked in Nairobi, Kenya; Beirut, Lebanon; and Nicosia, Cyprus, retiring in 2003 from working as an administrative assistant at Andrews University. She lives in Berrien Springs, Michigan, and enjoys writing, walking, genealogy, travel, and birding with her husband. She has had articles, a book on local history, genealogies, and poetry published. **Sept. 19.**

Cynthia J. Prime is an author and inspirational speaker who lives with her husband, Phillip, in Indianapolis, Indiana. She is CEO and cofounder of Saving Orphans Through Health-Care and Outreach (SOHO), a nonprofit organization serving orphans primarily in Swaziland and from child-headed households in HIV/AIDS-affected communities. **Oct. 20, Oct. 21.**

Shelley Quinn serves as speaker and codirector for Word Warrior Ministries, in addition to working as program development manager at Three Angels Broadcasting Network at their world headquarters. As a popular author and dynamic Bible teacher, Shelley is a sought-after speaker for revivals, seminars, retreats, and camp meetings. She writes from Thompsonville, Illinois. **Mar. 1, Oct. 14.**

Joyce Rapp is a retired lawyer who retreaded as a Bible worker; she has also been a third- and fourth-grade teacher, a music teacher, medical transcriptionist, and journalist. She is married to

Don, a wonderful Christian convert, and they have two daughters, one a lawyer and the other a freelance designer. **June 14** .

Katia Garcia Reinert is an advanced-practice nurse. Originally from Brazil, she lives in the United States in Maryland and serves as the health ministries director for the Seventh-day Adventist Church in North America. Katia enjoys spending time with her nephews and niece, and has fun biking, hiking, singing, and traveling the world on mission assignments. **June 17.**

Barbara J. Reinholtz is a former denominational employee who now enjoys retirement. She has served her church as a deaconess and in a variety of other capacities. Her favorite activities are spending time with her family, friends, and pets; crocheting; cooking; reading; and music. She looks forward to our heavenly home, where there will be no sorrow, pain, or death. **Nov. 22.**

Darlenejoan McKibbin Rhine, born in Nebraska, raised in California, schooled in Tennessee, now lives on Fidalgo Island, Washington, where she attends the Anacortes Adventist Fellowship. A widow with one son, she holds a bachelor's degree in journalism and is retired from the Los Angeles *Times*. **Dec. 21.**

Karen Richards, who writes from England, has been married for more than 26 years, and she and her husband have two grown-up daughters. She teaches in mainstream school, working in a reception class with children ages 4 and 5. She loves writing and believes that God wants her to share her experiences of Him in order to strengthen and encourage others. **Sept. 15.**

Jenny Rivera writes from Brisbane, Australia. She is a registered nurse currently undertaking postgraduate studies in stomal-therapy nursing. Jenny is an active member at the South Brisbane church, where she plays flute in the church orchestra, sings in the youth choir, and serves as a deaconess. She is also a proud aunty of six nieces and nephews. **Feb. 14.**

Taniesha Robertson-Brown is a teacher living in the Turks and Caicos Islands at the time of this writing. She enjoys reading, writing, and spending time with family and friends. Her ministry efforts are supported by her dear husband, Courtney. She is a previous contributor and also author of the book *Godly Families in an Ungodly World*. **Aug. 30.**

Andrea Rocha is from Brazil but has been living in New York City for more than 17 years. She is a registered pediatric nurse at Lenox Hill Hospital in Manhattan, taking care of kids who have had surgeries. She has a 17-year-old son named Joseph and has been married to Carlos for 18 years now. She is the director of the women's ministries department at the Luso Brazilian church. **Aug. 18.**

Avis Mae Rodney is a justice of the peace for the province of Ontario, Canada, where she resides with her husband, Leon. Avis is the mother of two young adults and continues to be awed by the blessings of her beautiful grandchildren. She enjoys early-morning walks, gardening, reading, and spending time with family and friends. **Oct. 9.**

Dixil L. Rodríguez is a university professor and volunteer chaplain who lives in Argyle, Texas. **Apr. 26, Dec. 14.**

Hazel Roole is retired and lives in central Florida, praising God for the extra years He has granted her. She is a deaconess at the South Brevard Seventh-day Adventist Church, feeds homeless individuals every third Sunday, and works with nursing home ministries. Singing hymns and gospel songs is one of her greatest passions. **Oct. 22.**

Jan Wall Rosen was born in Walla Walla, Washington, and moved to Denver, Colorado, when she was 12. She raised two daughters there while working full-time in her optical business. She has been semiretired for the past 10 years, and has traveled all over the world. She supports a variety of charitable organizations, and her favorite hobbies are gardening, skiing, and reading. **Sept. 11.**

Ella M. Rydzewski is a freelance writer living in Clarksville, Maryland. She previously worked for *Adventist Review* and *Ministry* magazines before retirement. **Feb. 27.**

Robin Sagel lives in Choctaw, Oklahoma, with her husband of more than 27 years, David. They have a daughter and a granddaughter. She works part-time at the Midwest City library and volunteers at the Parkview Adventist Academy library. She loves books! Her hobbies include reading, writing letters, e-mails, cards, and baking, and has had stories published in several publications. **July 18.**

Teresa Sales, a retired journalist/editor, lives in Colorado with her minister husband, Don, who is also a writer. Since retiring, she has taught creative writing to junior-high students, an age she enjoys. The couple has also served eight churches as interim pastor, and continues to be active in area churches. **Feb. 28.**

Leah A. Salloman is an elementary school teacher in the East Visayan Conference in the Philippines. She is a pastor's wife and a mother of two grown-up children studying in Adventist schools. She loves writing, teaching, and making programs in the church, with a great involvement in women's ministries. **July 9.**

Kollis Salmon-Fairweather is originally from Jamaica, West Indies, but now lives in Florida with her husband. She has served as an elder, Sabbath school superintendent, health and temperance leader, personal ministries leader, and chorister, and now coordinates a Bible class. She is retried from the practice of nursing but remains active. Hobbies include reading and singing. **Sept. 17.**

Clair Sanches-Schutte is the mother of two sons and is married to John, a pastor and psychologist. She has been working for the church for more than 30 years in different departments. At the moment she is the women's, children's, and family ministries director for the Trans-European Division in England. The Lord has been good to her, and she thanks Him every day for His love. **Sept. 27.**

Deborah Sanders lives in Alberta, Canada. She married her high school sweetheart, Ron. For Deborah every day is an "epiphany day," and she loves writing and sharing devotionals with others in the family of God. Ron is her helpmate in sharing God's love. They have two blessed children, Andrea and Sonny. She is looking forward to meeting you in Paradise. **Oct. 23.**

Jennifer Jill Schwirzer resides with her husband, Michael, in Philadelphia, where she conducts a private counseling practice and a speaking, writing, and music ministry. They have two daughters, Allison and Kimberly. Her latest book is *13 Weeks to Peace*, available through Pacific Press Publishing Association. **Jan. 6, Oct. 29, Dec. 2.**

Aimee Seheult has a love and passion to serve Jesus Christ in all aspects of her life, especially through her work with World Vision International. Aimee, an M.B.A. graduate from Southern Adventist University, is an accomplished opera singer and enjoys playing classical piano. However, what she longs for the most is to see Jesus one day. **Sept. 22.**

Jaimee Seis, of Germany, born in 1964, was already happy in her childhood days to know that Jesus is with her, and therefore would like others to experience God as a loving Father too. As a freelance writer she has written articles, sermons, and books in order make His abundant love known. **July 1.**

Omobonike Adeola Sessou is the women's and children's ministries director at the West-Central Africa Division, in Abidjan, Ivory Coast. She is married to Pastor Selom Sessou, and they are blessed with three children. Her hobbies include teaching, counseling, making new friends, and visiting with people. **Feb. 8, July 12.**

Donna Lee Sharp writes from Yuba City, California. A special joy is reaching out to her ever-expanding family scattered all over North America. She enjoys playing the piano and organ at a number of churches and at a care home, in addition to gardening, flower arranging, Sabbath afternoon storytelling, and bird-watching. **Mar. 23.**

Donna Sherrill lives in the country in Jefferson, Texas. She is retired and recently widowed after losing her husband to a lengthy illness. She takes care of an elderly woman and enjoys working in her garden and yard. **July 26.**

Bonita Joyner Shields is assistant director for discipleship in the General Conference Sabbath School/Personal Ministries Department. She lives in Brookeville, Maryland, with her husband, Roy.

She is author of the book *Living in a Man's World*, published by the Review and Herald Publishing Association. **Oct. 3.**

Alla Shumilo writes from Zelenodolsk, Ukraine, where she lives with her mother. She graduated from a teacher's training school and worked as an educator in a child-care center. She has two children: a daughter, Alionka (33 years old), and a son (20 years old). Her husband and she were baptized after an evangelistic campaign led by Begas Valera in 1998. **Nov. 19.**

Rose Neff Sikora and her husband, Norman, call the beautiful mountains of North Carolina their home. She retired recently from a 45-year career as a registered nurse. She enjoys walking, writing, and helping others. Rose has one adult daughter, Julie, and three lovely grandchildren: Tyler, Olivia, and Grant. **Aug. 25.**

Cheryl P. Simmons, M.Div., M.Ed., B.C.C., is a staff chaplain with AnMed Health Center in Anderson, South Carolina. She lives by the motto "Things could always be worse, but never with God." **Sept. 10.**

Ella Louise Smith Simmons is a vice president at the General Conference of Seventh-day Adventists in Silver Spring, Maryland, the first female to hold this position. An educator, she has served as provost, academic vice president, and professor in church and sector universities. She is married to Nord, and they have two children, three grandchildren, and one great-grandson. **Jan. 23, Mar. 6.**

Heather-Dawn Small is the director for Women's Ministries Department at the General Conference of Seventh-day Adventists. She has been the children's and women's ministries director for the Caribbean Union Conference, located in Trinidad and Tobago. She is the wife of Pastor Joseph Small and the mother of Dalonne and Jerard. She loves air travel, reading, and scrapbooking. **Feb. 17, Mar. 25, July 29, Nov. 1.**

Yvonne Curry Smallwood lives in southern Maryland, where she enjoys reading, crocheting for charity, and writing. She is a grandmother, and her articles and stories have appeared in several publications. **July 22.**

Kris Smith is happily married to a military chaplain and enjoys homeschooling their two ninth graders, Daniel and Alathea. She says, "One of my greatest joys is writing with the goal of encouraging others toward the Lord." She writes from Fairfax, Virginia. **Dec. 17.**

Maple Smith writes from Huntsville, Alabama, and is a nurse by profession; she was born in Guyana, South America. She enjoys spending time with Jesus and with family and friends, traveling, gardening, animals, and nature. In church she has held many leadership positions. She has been married for more than 29 years and is the mother of two adult children. **Feb. 16.**

Eileen Snell is a retired nurse living in Prescott Valley, Arizona. As a child she lived with her missionary parents in Kenya, East Africa, when the Mau-Mau uprising was active. As a teenager she lived with her family in the concrete jungles of New York City. Her interests include singing solos and in choirs, traveling, handwork, and spending time with her family and friends. **Oct. 10.**

Deborah P. Spooner was born in England but has made Barbados home. She holds degrees in business and theology. She served the church in various capacities, including lay evangelist, through which more than 100 souls were won to Jesus. She worked with the East Caribbean Conference for 13 years and presently serves there as the female ministerial intern. **Aug. 28.**

Pamela C. Stanford-Odle works as an English teacher at Midwood High School in Brooklyn, New York. She attends Maranatha Seventh-day Adventist Church, where she serves as assistant education director. She loves storytelling and writing. Her passion, however, is missionary work for the Lord. **Apr. 10.**

Sylvia Stark is an artist living in east Tennessee at the foot of a small mountain. Her artwork is displayed in several states and in South America. As a musician and singer she finds fulfillment in contributing to the worship experience at area churches. She also enjoys hiking, camping, backpacking, and working in her yard. She has been published in *Guide*. **Sept. 21.**

Eva M. Starner is an assistant professor in the Psychology Department at Oakwood University. She is a graduate of both Oakwood and Loma Linda universities. She currently has three adult daughters, two sons-in-law, and three wonderful grandchildren. She believes that God has called her to her current position, and she knows that when God opens doors, they stay open! **Aug. 19.**

Ardis Dick Stenbakken has edited this book from her home in Colorado; she has done this since she retired as director of the Women's Ministries Department at the General Conference of Seventh-day Adventists. She and her husband, Dick, love their two children and their spouses and four grandchildren. She is still hoping to find time to once again pursue some hobbies. **Mar. 11, May 18, Nov. 21, Dec. 25.**

Carol Stickle writes from Kelowna, British Columbia, Canada. She has enjoyed several different careers, but the ones she enjoyed the most are those interacting with people. She loves visiting family, including four adult grandchildren and one preteen granddaughter, Madeleine, who lives in Michigan. She also enjoys bird-watching. **Aug. 4.**

Emilia Stoykova has been women's ministries director in Bulgaria for the past eight years. She is working as an assistant pastor with her husband. They are blessed with three adult children, one son-in-law, and wonderful granddaughters. Emilia enjoys reading, walking in nature, and mentoring women, teenagers, and children. **Dec. 29.**

Naomi Striemer lives in Franklin, Tennessee, with her husband, Jordan, and dog, Bella. She is a best-selling author, a chart-topping Christian singer/songwriter, and a sought-after speaker who tours around the world singing and speaking. In her spare time she enjoys baking, board games, and the outdoors. **Jan. 17, Aug. 8.**

Carolyn Sutton writes from Alabama, where she lives with husband, Jim, their behavior-challenged farm dog, Bailey, and a number of assorted chickens. She and Jim are volunteer field representatives for Adventist World Radio. Their blended family includes two sons, their sweet wives, and three grandchildren. Carolyn enjoyed helping with this devotional book. **Feb. 26, Apr. 6, June 9, Aug. 7.**

Loraine F. Sweetland is a retired widow in Tennessee who lives with one little dog named Sugar, who is almost 14 years old. In June of 2011 Loraine learned that she has chronic kidney disease. She is learning all she can about the diet restrictions for this disease—which is a real challenge. She plans to help others with the information she is now learning. **Aug. 9.**

Frieda Tanner is a retired nurse who moved to Eugene, Oregon, more than 24 years ago to be near her daughter and family. She spends most of her time making nice Sabbath school items for children all over the world: 90 countries so far. Frieda is more than 95 years old. **Dec. 20.**

Aleksandra Tanurdzic was born in Bosnia. During the civil war in her country she went to Belgrade Theological Seminary in Serbia, where she met her future husband. She worked as a pastor, dean of woman, and assistent editor in the publishing house in Serbia. She now lives and works as a chaplain in the Chicago area with her beautiful teenage daughter and husband. **Mar. 30.**

Arlene R. Taylor is risk manager and corporate compliance officer for three Adventist Health hospitals in northern California. A brain-function specialist, she engages in research through her nonprofit corporation, Realizations, Inc., and the St. Helena Center for Health. Internationally known as a author and speaker, her electronic Brain Bulletin is free of charge: www.arlenetaylor.org **Feb. 10, Apr. 1, June 15, Oct. 16.**

Edna Thomas Taylor lives in Florida and is a conference women's ministries coordinator. She is the proud mother of two daughters and a son (Junia, Jamila, Jamaal), and three granddaughters. A musician, she enjoys reading, writing, and working with "Legacies," sharing God's love with young women. **Oct. 12.**

Geneva G. Taylor, often called GG by her friends, writes from central Florida. Now retired, she praises God for the strength to help others who worship with her at the Palm Bay church. **Apr. 12.**

Rose Joseph Thomas lives in Altamonte Springs, Florida, with her husband, Walden, and daughter, Crystal Rose. Her son, Samuel Joseph, is a student at Southern Adventist University. Rose is an educator, and she works at Forest Lake Education Center in Longwood, Florida. **May 2.**

Sharon M. Thomas is a retired public school teacher who lives in Lacombe, Louisiana. In addition to being an adjunct instructor at a community college, she enjoys quilting, reading, walking, biking, and traveling. She is grateful for the omniscient, omnipresent, and omnipotent God of love we serve. **July 7.**

Stella Thomas works in Maryland at the world headquarters office of Seventh-day Adventists in the Adventist Mission office. Her desire is to share God's love with the world! **Aug. 13.**

Teresa Thompson, living in Lincoln, Nebraska, is a caregiver for her husband, who has a brain injury from a tractor accident in 1999. She taught church school in several conferences and was librarian for College View Academy. She now does proofreading and editing, but mostly blogs at www.teresa-teresatalk.blogspot.com **Aug. 21.**

Ena Thorpe is a retired registered nurse living in Hamilton, Ontario, Canada. She loves to spend time with her three children, son-in-law, daughter-in-law, and four grandchildren. Ena also likes to play Scrabble, do Sudoku and puzzles. **Nov. 24.**

Rebecca Timon is an administrative assistant to Heather-Dawn Small, director of the General Conference Women's Ministries Department. She has one married son and a lovely daughter-in-law and a cat. She enjoys reading, writing, scrapbooking, and playing word or card games. She belongs to several small groups, and her mission in life is to encourage her friends to study the Bible deeply. **Apr. 4, Apr. 5.**

Tijana Tizic comes from Serbia and is a student at the Seventh-day Adventist Theological Seminary in Belgrade. She likes reading and writing; her short stories have been published in a few literary magazines, and she also writes for the Adventist magazine *Messenger* in her home country. She hopes that God will be celebrated trough her stories. **July 8.**

Joey Norwood Tolbert is the administrative assistant to the director of the Samaritan Center in Ooltewah, Tennessee, and teaches as an adjunct professor in the Humanities Department at Cleveland State Community College. Married to Matthew Tolbert for 12 years, they are the parents of two children, Lela and Charlie. Joey sings with Message of Mercy. **Apr. 9.**

Adel Arrabito Torres grew up in northern California, where she earned a nursing degree and met her husband. They and their two little boys currently live in Michigan, where her husband is attending seminary, but they dream of someday living in the mission field. Adel loves writing and is working on a book about her parents. **Aug. 16.**

Nancy Neuharth Troyer enjoys singing, line drawing, photography, and writing articles for His Voice men's chorus as their communications director. Nancy and Don and their daughter have traveled the world as a military chaplain family and military support center directors. Her first book, *The Other Side of the Boat,* chronicles the beautiful ways God has led in her life. **Dec. 3.**

Nancy L. Van Pelt was a certified family-life educator, best-selling author of 45 books and internationally known speaker. She traveled in 74 countries teaching families how to love each other. Her hobbies were traveling, getting organized, quilting, and having fun with friends. Nancy lived with her husband in California and felt blessed with their three grown children. Nancy passed away in November 2013. **Mar. 22, July 15.**

Marge Vande Hei is the mother of three and a grandmother of two. She has always lived in Green Bay, Wisconsin, and has been married for more than 34 years to her high school sweetheart. She enjoys reading, walking, and bicycling. Her friends say she is fun-loving; has a great sense of humor; always sees the glass half full, not half empty; is loving; and is ready to pray with friends. **Sept. 12.**

Heather VandenHoven writes from Angwin, California, where she lives with her husband of 20 years and her 12-year-old daughter. She's had devotions published in the *Adventist Review* and

Signs of the Times and is currently completing a book featuring her brother's walk through leukemia. Heather enjoys being a homemaker and is involved with her daughter's school. **Sept. 16.**

Agnes Vaughan lives in Charlotte, North Carolina, where she is a business and computer application instructor at a business college. She is the mother of two beautiful daughters and a proud grandmother. Agnes loves the Lord and is an active member of the Trinity Worship Center Seventh-day Adventist Church. **Nov. 29.**

Ruth Ann Hagen Wade has lived in Latin America since her marriage in 1963 to Loron Wade. She has been teaching in the Music Department of Montemorelos University in Mexico since 1985. The Wades have three children, David, Jonathan, and Lori Ann, and four grandchildren. **Apr. 7.**

Mary Wagoner-Angelin lives in Ooltewah, Tennessee, with her husband and their two daughters. Mary is a social worker at a psychiatric hospital and is pursuing her master's degree in social work. She is an active volunteer whose hobbies include humor therapy, exercise, laughing, and collecting vegan recipes/cookbooks. **May 1.**

Andrea Walker is a soldier on the battlefield for the Lord. She writes from Georgia, and this is her first submission to the women's ministries devotional book. **Sept. 9.**

Cora A. Walker is a retired nurse, editor, and freelance writer who lives in Fort Washington, Maryland. She is an active member of the church she attends in Charles County, Maryland. She enjoys reading, writing, swimming, classical music, singing, and traveling. She has one son, Andre V. Walker. **May 6.**

Dolores Klinsky Walker is discovering joy in "enhanced adulthood." Limited physical activity provides time to ponder God's ways, to write, and to pass God's love on to others. She is married, and they have three children. Dolores writes from Walla Walla, Washington. **Mar. 8.**

Nancy Wallack has been a pastor's wife for more than 20 years, a community health nurse, and leader of women's ministries in the Southern California Conference. Prayer became central in all women's ministries events, and multiple miracles were experienced as women took up the battle of prayer. Nancy and her husband, Jere, live in the mountains of Colorado. **July 28.**

Anna May Radke Waters and her husband, Herb, who have been married for 61 years, are enjoying retirement. They have five children, eight grandchildren, and five great-grandchildren, with another on the way. They enjoy traveling, playing games, praying for others, and sharing their faith. **May 4.**

Elizabeth Darby Watson, Ph.D., M.S.W., is an associate professor of social work with a wealth of experience in social work. She is a freelance author whose talents include creative writing, speaking, and children's ministry. Elizabeth is an intelligent, assertive, professional, and successful single parent, the mother of three adult children and five wonderful grandchildren. **Sept. 8.**

Kit Watts is a former assistant editor of the *Adventist Review* and founding director of the Women's Resource Center at La Sierra University. She lives on the dry side of Oregon. **Dec. 24.**

Lyn Welk-Sandy lives in Adelaide, South Australia. She works as a grief counselor. Lyn has spent many years as a pipe organist who loves church music, choir work, and playing the chimes. She enjoys nature, photography, and caravanning around outback Australia with her husband, Keith, serving where needed. Lyn is the mother of four and grandmother of nine. **Sept. 1.**

Shirnet Wellington, who now serves as an administrative assistant in the Inter-American Division office in Miami, Florida, is Jamaican by birth, a teacher by profession, and married to a pastor. They have two sons. Her hobbies include writing, reading, and gardening. **May 14.**

Penny Estes Wheeler, now retired, feels blessed that she had a career doing what she loved most—editing and writing. She enjoys scrapbooking and travel and recently added two European airports to her life list. She and her husband live in Maryland. Their five grandchildren are scattered across the U.S. and overseas. **June 22, Oct. 26.**

Sandra Widulle is married and has two children. She loves to express her thoughts in writing. In her local church she is engaged in the children's division and uses her creativity to decorate the church showcase. She lives in Germany. **May 25.**

Vera Wiebe has been a pastor's wife for 40 years and enjoys traveling with him; he is now a conference president in Alberta, Canada. She enjoys reading and music, especially helping organize musical programs occasionally. She has two adult sons and four delightful grandchildren for whom she loves to sew and knit. **July 23.**

Hyveth Williams is a minister of the gospel, teacher, and counselor whose ministry crosses racial and religious boundaries. Author of four books and an *Adventist Review* column, she serves as professor of homiletics and director of the homiletics program at the Seventh-day Adventist Theological Seminary at Andrews University. She also works to transform the lives of at risk youth and adults. **June 27, 28, 29.**

Kimasha Pauline Williams recently graduated from the University of the Southern Caribbean. The young Adventist resides in her home country, St. Maarten, and is communications officer at the St. Maarten Medical Center. Her poetry appears in the anthology *Where I See the Sun: Contemporary Poetry in St. Martin.* She enjoys reading, writing, and traveling. **Nov. 23.**

Robyn Williams resides in Charlotte, North Carolina, which she personally feels is a fantastic place to live. She works for Wells Fargo; within the past few years God inspired her to send out a weekly devotional e-mail to her family and friends; she started a blog, and TruthMedia published one of her devotionals. She was raised in an Adventist family and is quite involved with church. **Jan. 2.**

Sylvia Jackson Wilson, director of women's ministries for the South Atlantic Conference since 1997, is a retired teacher of 34 years; Sylvia received the North American Division Excellence in Teaching award. She is also noted for her students' dramatic speech choir performances. She is the owner of Prince of Peace Christian Academy in Greensboro, North Carolina. **Oct. 19.**

Nena A. Wirth, B.S.F.N., M.A.Sc., is a diet and nutrition consultant for the Eat to Live Learning Centre. She is also the author of several vegetarian cookbooks. She is a member of the Adventist church in Kitchener, Ontario, Canada. **Sept. 20.**

Bronwyn Worthington is a freelance writer living in the Inland Northwest, Washington State. Bronwyn's passion for writing began in first grade when her teacher selected her to attend a writing conference. She graduated from Whitworth University with a degree in education and an endorsement in English. Find more about Bronwyn at bronwynworthington.com. **July 19.**

Aileen L. Young enjoys family and friends and is happily married to Thomas Young. Her interests are music, art, writing, socials, and downsizing. Aileen lives in Honolulu, Hawaii. **July 30.**

Lianne Zilm (née Ritchie) grew up in Malaysia with a yearning to find meaning and truth. She came to know Jesus in her late teens and was baptized into the Adventist Church. Moving to Australia to study, she ended up getting married and settling down after university. She is now an active member at Birdwood Adventist Church in South Australia. **Sept. 24.**

Candy Zook is a writer, speaker, and former missionary who now lives in rural Minnesota. Along with writing devotionals, she is working on a book about India. She has three children and six grandchildren. **Jan. 4.**

Prayer Requests

_____

_____

_____

_____

_____

_____

_____

_____

_____

_____

_____

_____

_____

_____

_____

_____

_____

_____

_____

_____

So now I urge you, dear lady—not as if I were writing
you a new command, but one we have had from
the beginning—that we love one another.

—2 John 5, HCSB

Prayer Requests

_____

_____

_____

_____

_____

_____

_____

_____

_____

_____

_____

_____

_____

_____

_____

_____

_____

_____

By this all people will know that you are My disciples,
if you have love for one another.

—John 13:35, HCSB